THE PSYCHOLOGY OF THE SELF

A Casebook

Written with the collaboration of
Heinz Kohut, M.D.

Editor: Arnold Goldberg, M.D.

Contributing Editors: Michael Franz Basch, M.D.,
Meyer S. Gunther, M.D., David Marcus, M.D., Anna
Ornstein, M.D., Paul Ornstein, M.D., Marian Tolpin,
M.D., Paul Tolpin, M.D., Ernest Wolf, M.D.

INTERNATIONAL UNIVERSITIES PRESS, INC.

Madison   Connecticut

Third printing, 1984

Paperback Printing, 1992

Library of Congress Cataloging in Publication Data

Main entry under title:

The Psychology of the self.

  Bibliography: p.
  Includes index.
  1. Psychoanalysis—Cases, clinical reports,
statistics. 2. Self—Cases, clinical reports,
statistics. I. Kohut, Heinz. II. Goldberg,
Arnold, 1929- [DNLM: 1. Narcissism.
2. Psychoanalysis. LM460.5.E3 P9765]
RC506.P79   616.8'917   77-92188
ISBN 0-8236-5582-2

ISBN 0-8236-8262-5 (pbk.)

Manufactured in the United States of America

CONTENTS

CONTRIBUTORS

Michael Franz Basch, M.D. — Faculty, Training and Supervising Analyst, Chicago Institute for Psychoanalysis; Clinical Professor of Psychiatry, University of Chicago.

Arnold Goldberg, M.D. — Faculty, Training and Supervising Analyst, Chicago Institute for Psychoanalysis; Clinical Professor of Psychiatry, University of Chicago.

Meyer S. Gunther, M.D. — Faculty, Training and Supervising Analyst, Chicago Institute for Psychoanalysis; Associate Clinical Professor, Department of Psychiatry, Northwestern University.

Heinz Kohut, M.D. — Faculty, Training and Supervising Analyst, Chicago Institute for Psychoanalysis; Professorial Lecturer, Department of Psychiatry, University of Chicago.

David Marcus, M.D. — Faculty, Training and Supervising Analyst, Chicago Institute for Psychoanalysis; Clinical Associate Professor, University of Chicago.

Anna Ornstein, M.D. — Faculty, Cincinnati Psychoanalytic Institute; Professor of Child Psychiatry, University of Cincinnati, College of Medicine.

Paul Ornstein, M.D. — Faculty, Supervising and Training Analyst, Cincinnati Psychoanalytic Institute; Professor of Psychiatry, University of Cincinnati, College of Medicine.

Marian Tolpin, M.D. — Faculty, Training and Supervising Analyst, Chicago Institute for Psychoanalysis; Faculty, Child Therapy Program, Chicago Institute for Psychoanalysis.

Paul Tolpin, M.D. — Faculty, Training and Supervising Analyst, Chicago Institute for Psychoanalysis.

Ernest Wolf, M.D. — Faculty, Training and Supervising Analyst, Chicago Institute for Psychoanalysis; Assistant Professor of Psychiatry, Northwestern University School of Medicine.

ACKNOWLEDGMENTS

So much assistance has been given to us from diverse sources that we can only alphabetically list the people and institutions with the hope that each knows how personally significant each has been to us. We wish to thank:

Dr. Henry Betts, Director of the Rehabilitation Institute of Chicago and Chairman of the Department of Physical Medicine and Rehabilitation, Northwestern University Medical School

Center for Psycho-Social Studies

General Research Fund, Chicago Institute for Psychoanalysis

Dr. Stanley M. Kaplan, Acting Chairman of the Department of Psychiatry, University of Cincinnati College of Medicine

Heinz Kohut Research Fund, Chicago Institute for Psychoanalysis

Anne Pollock Lederer Research Fund, Chicago Institute for Psychoanalysis

vii

Dr. Daniel Offer, Director of the Psychosomatic and
Psychiatric Institute and Chairman of the Department of Psychiatry of Michael Reese Hospital

Dr. George Pollock, Director of the Chicago Institute for
Psychoanalysis

Dr. Harold Visotsky, Director of the Institute of Psychiatry and Chairman of the Department of Psychiatry, Northwestern University Medical School

We would like to express special thanks to Ms. Kathryn
Czajka and Ms. Eva Sandberg for their secretarial assistance.
Natalie Altman helped us immeasurably in the editing of the
book and has ended up a good friend as well.

We have been especially fortunate in securing the services
of our colleague Dr. Mark Gehrie, who prepared the index
for this work, and we are grateful to him for his help.

1

INTRODUCTION

This book is a response. It is a response to a persistent and clear request from a large number of clinicians who have read Heinz Kohut's *The Analysis of the Self*. Over and over we have heard about the need for more clinical data, more illustrative examples, more material that demonstrates one or another of the many issues and questions raised by that book. Operating within a science based on observation guided by clinical theory, our analytic colleagues have quite appropriately asked to see just what kinds of patients are to be considered suitable for analytic treatment in accordance with Kohut's recommendations. Further, they have wanted to know exactly how the analytic technique with these patients differed, if at all, from the usual procedure. And, as adherents of an *empirical* discipline, our colleagues have asked what the yield of these new and (to us) exciting ideas in depth psychology is in helping a larger group of patients. Most of all, our colleagues have asked to see just what we do, how we do it, and why we do it. This book is an answer to that request.

It takes a long time to learn psychoanalytic psychology and even longer to acquire its therapeutic skills. Our group

has learned a new psychoanalytic psychology and has also discovered that to assemble and present complete analytic cases is
a task laden with methodological pitfalls. Fortunately, some of
us have had the benefit of personal supervision by Kohut, and
all of us have benefited from his help and guidance. Here, essentially, is what we have done.

Primarily under the initiative of a local analyst, a group
of psychoanalysts who had gained experience with the analysis
of narcissistic personality disorders and were convinced of the
value of Kohut's theory of the psychology of the self decided to
gather completed analytic cases and discuss them in order to
decide how best to present them to a reading audience.

The group soon discovered the practical problems that
resulted from trying to produce a readable book when the
subject matter is clinical theory. We have used the format that
combines two essential ingredients: A description of what happened throughout the analysis; and comments explaining particular interactions of patient and analyst, the options open
to the analyst, and the responses he chose.

We made use of as many case histories as we could obtain
both within and outside of our working group. Students at the
Chicago Institute for Psychoanalysis and colleagues from
other localities made contributions which comprise a substantial percentage of the book. The geographic range of these
contributions has aided us in dealing with the problem of con-
fidentiality. The number of analyses performed in Chicago
constitutes only a fraction of the book. Any data identifying
the locale has been scrambled so that there is no way of determining whether it is disguised or original material. Therefore,
our debt to our colleagues is one that we must honor in silence
in order to preserve anonymity.

Our original plan was to publish a running commentary
alongside the cases which would emphasize or clarify or expand on various points in the analysis. This plan was aban-

doned when we met after having circulated summaries of our topical discussions: most of the significant ideas were now incorporated in the write-ups. That these were arrived at retrospectively is made clear in our text. Lest anyone think that our group was always of one mind, we freely admit to numerous differences of opinion. Our discussions of the circulated material were most fruitful and often brought us closer to a consensus, or at least to clarifying our differences. Although there were a few points of dispute familiar to any analyst (for example, "Was this patient *really* analyzed?"), these were not as a rule the predominant issues. There was, rather, a general impression that each of the patients had benefited enormously and that the classical clinical theory of psychoanalysis had little to offer in understanding these changes. Because these treatments had been conducted by analysts who were still in the process of learning Kohut's concepts, their case records displayed a striking lack of a clear conceptualization of the psychoanalytic process.

After we talked over each case, one of us was asked to rewrite it, using as many of the ideas offered as he or she felt were helpful. Each case was then disguised by a group member who knew nothing about the patient apart from the report. The disguised case was then returned to the original analyst to determine if any meaning had been significantly altered.

In the course of discussing the cases, we found ourselves reviewing the major ideas in *The Analysis of the Self*. Perhaps a brief overview of our lines of thinking will help to orient the reader and focus attention on what will be emphasized in the case reports that follow.

In the introductory chapter of *The Analysis of the Self* an attempt is made to delineate the category of patients Kohut had studied through the psychoanalytic method. The "Narcissistic Personality Disorders" showed certain clusters of

symptoms such as lack of enthusiasm and zest, perverse activities, and feelings of deadness; for many clinicians, however,
such a symptom complex was diagnostically insufficient.
Questions about the *diagnosis* fell into two categories: differentiation of narcissistic personality disorder from those in
which the main issues were narcissistic defenses against oedipal problems, and differentiation from those that were essentially borderline personality structures. To be sure, the category of disorders of narcissism is larger than that of narcissistic
personality disorders, but some clinicians have overlooked this
distinction and rashly equated any narcissistic manifestation
with the specific syndromes Kohut had in mind. Only a theoretical generalization, a step toward abstraction, can make the
issues distinct. One must use the concept of the cohesive self as
the guiding principle for the differential diagnosis. This crucial developmental step of a firm sense of wholeness (whatever
its precursors may be) is evidenced somewhere during the
second year of life, and its relative stability is a *sine qua non*
for future narcissistic maturation. The instability or propensity for regression of this enduring function or structure is the
most important diagnostic sign of a narcissistic personality disorder. Those individuals who have a basically disordered or
fragmented self or who spend their lives protecting themselves
against recurrent outbreaks of such a disorder are not part of
this diagnostic category. In other words, Kohut's clinical
theory essentially eliminates the catch-all term "borderline";
patients usually so designated are believed to possess a funda-
mentally psychotic make-up. In our nosology, then, psychotic
and "borderline" patients are not narcissistic personality disorders, though they indeed suffer from disorders of narcissism.
At the other end of the psychopathological continuum, char-
acterological defenses against the oedipal conflict often
present a diagnostic puzzle of a different sort. The stability of
the self is not a major issue in these cases, but an extreme sen-

sitivity to one's self-esteem is evident. No better diagnostic differentiation can be offered than the one Kohut gave in *The Analysis of the Self*: the crucial test is the patient's response to therapeutic efforts to interfere with these defenses. If one undermines the defensive narcissistic position in a classical "transference" neurosis, the nuclear oedipal conflict will emerge; the same intervention in a case in which the narcissistic phenomena are not defensive, but are manifestations of a narcissistic personality disorder sets in motion a regression and break-up of the cohesive self. To be sure, much of the content of the associative material in both categories of pathology is concerned with the oedipal drama, but persons with narcissistic personality disorders use these interactions to attain a feeling of life and vitality, and such conflict is thus a secondary matter in their pathology. In most instances, however, diagnostic considerations are not matters to be decided in a few interviews. It is the spontaneous unfolding of a typical set of transference configurations that is decisive. This brings us to the second area the casebook group focused on.

The most significant clinical contribution of Kohut's work has been the delineation, description, and elaboration of the *self-object transferences*. No one conversant with psychoanalytic literature can fail to recognize that many previous investigators have concentrated on similar narcissistic and/or preoedipal problems. Some have observed that the analysis of these patients regularly ran an atypical course, and others have emphasized one or another feature of a new approach. The wealth of material yielded by infant and childhood observation, for example, particularly in relation to the issue of separation-individuation (Mahler et al., 1975), has given rise to concepts in many ways akin to Kohut's work. But the major effort needed, and supplied only by *The Analysis of the Self*, and later *The Restoration of the Self*, was a comprehensive ex-

planation derived from and applicable to the analysis of
adults. In terms of the methodology of psychoanalysis, this
meant an explanation based on the typical unfolding of the
transference, on the basis of which it is possible to arrive at
valid genetic reconstructions. Kohut has described several new
transference configurations: the *mirror transferences* (which
are further subdivided into those called merger, alter ego or
twinship, and mirror transferences in the narrower sense); and
the *idealizing transferences*. The former relate to the therapeutic remobilization of the grandiose self and the latter to
that of the idealized parental imago. Each of these configurations has regressive as well as progressive or stable manifestations, and the analysis of a narcissistic personality disorder may consist of movement along one or the other of
these developmental axes, or it may involve shifts between
these two major forms of narcissistic transference. That a novel
cluster of observable reactions to the analysis can now be organized, understood, and followed along predictable routes is
of inestimable value in conducting analyses. As we shall see,
Kohut's achievement in developing these observations into a
theory that correlates them to early development allows us to
assume a truly analytic position. We can now avoid judg-
mental confrontations in which the psychopathology is reflected to the patients in the form of implicit reproaches for their
childish behavior. The analyst is no longer called upon to
work without a clinical theory. The cases in this book suffer
from the deficiencies of every similar effort to demonstrate the
unfolding of a transference; this is a process that is subtle, often vague; but no matter how difficult to capture in words, it
is relevant. The movements from one form of transference to
another give us our bearings in the psychoanalytic process and
lend support to our reconstruction of the childhood development of the patient.

As Kohut delineated the transference reactions in narcissistic personality disorders, so, too, he described and explained the problems of countertransference encountered in these analyses. For each of the transference configurations, one can commonly see typical countertransference phenomena, e.g., the fear of merger on the analyst's part during the merger transference, the resistance to being overstimulated by one's own grandiose exhibitionistic drives during an idealizing transference, and so forth. Such a comprehension of these countertransference reactions allows reasonable efforts at self-analysis of one's blind spots in doing this kind of analytic work. None of the cases to follow was recorded with an eye to such a total presentation, but efforts have been made to include as much as possible of the analysts' reactions to the patients' transferences.

It has been said that one way to view analysis is as an effort to appreciate not only the patient's childhood but also how the patient's parents experienced him or her as a child. Whatever our viewpoint, we attempt a genetic reconstruction of the patient's psychological development and childhood as they were experienced by the participants. From his work with these patients, Kohut formulated a series of developmental phases that correlate with the typical transference responses mentioned above. He carefully differentiated those he felt to be typical of normal development from those which seemed to be predominantly associated with adult pathological pictures. In every analytic treatment we attempt a broad recapitulation of the stages that the patient traversed as a child, and we try to pinpoint where such development went askew. An effort is made to trace the parental failings in providing what would be an environment optimal for such development. Over and over in the narcissistic personality disorders, we see the failings of these patients' parents in the arena of their inability to comprehend empathically the need of the child to have a reliable self-object to promote one or another form of structuralization. Various combinations of parental intrusiveness and parental neglect fail to provide the proper and fitting availability of the parent as part of the patient's narcissistic matrix. The spontaneously unfolding transferences of these patients will pinpoint their structural deficiencies and thus permit the analyst to infer the nature of the parental failure in the course of their development.

In *The Analysis of the Self* Kohut makes it clear that the essential aspect of the analysis of narcissistic personality disorders lies in the *working through* of the narcissistic transference. This is accompanied by the patient's gaining insight and is associated with the expansion of the reality ego. The working-through process consists of the ego's repeated reactions to temporary losses of the narcissistically experienced self-object. It results in the acquisition of new psychic structures and functions through the transformation and reinternalizations of the mobilized structures—what Kohut has called transmuting internalization. In order to achieve this, Kohut emphasizes equally the cognitive and affective components of interpretations by stressing that these must not be given mechanically but with correct sensitivity to the patient's feelings. Results of successful working-through are indicated by an accretion of drive-controlling and drive-channeling structures, by idealization of the superego through diminution of the idealizing transference, and by integration of the grandiose fantasies into reasonable ambitions and purposes.

We hope by the cases illustrated to demonstrate such working-through processes via the establishment of a stable narcissistic transference, the disruptions that inevitably follow, and the interpretations that allow understanding to fill the breach. A crucial dimension in this interplay is that of empathy, i.e., the proper feeling for and fitting together of the patient's needs and the analyst's response. It must be emphasized that a correct or ideal emotional position on the part of the analyst is insufficient by itself; interpretations must carry the brunt of the analytic process.

The activity of a psychoanalyst is *interpretation*. Analyses of narcissistic personality disorders are no different in this respect from those of the more familiar neurotic syndromes. Interpretive emphasis in these disorders is placed on the periodic unavailability of the self-object, which is what the analyst becomes in a self-object transference. It should be understood that what the patient experiences as the availability of the analyst is not a physical availability but an empathic one. The patient's reaction to interpretation is often one reflecting his narcissistic vulnerability. We frequently see a psychoeconomic imbalance resulting from an interpretation, i.e., the patient exhibits one or another form of overstimulation in response to it. So too, whenever the self-object function of the analyst is felt to be unavailable, there follows a period of imbalance and a picture of minor traumatic overstimulation. But correct interpretation will ameliorate such traumatic episodes and lead to the internalizing of structure, as noted in the discussion of working through. In the beginning phase of the analysis, interpretations are generally directed to continuity of the analytic process from one session to the next and to orienting the patient to the process of introspection. The middle of the analysis directs attention to the unfolding transference, especially to the role of the analyst as a self-object. The task of the analysis is to aid the patient, via interpretation, to understand his own vulnerabilities, their origins, and his specific methods of coping with them. Such interpretations are always in the service of reconstructions of total childhood situations, since a piecemeal grasp of the clinical situation must give way to a total comprehension of one's functioning, both in the present and during the formative years. Separations play a crucial role in these analyses because the physical absence of the needed self-object is always traumatic. As each and every disruption or separation or empathic failure of the analyst is experienced and understood, the patient gains internal structure until, at last, he is able to contemplate the final separation from the analyst.

The *termination* phase of analyses of narcissistic personality disorders is similar to that of the other analyses in terms of the recapitulation of the central pathology and subsequent work around this. There are, however, during the termination with narcissistic personality disorders some unique considerations relating to "transformations of narcissism." Kohut has written extensively on these transformations in terms of the maturation of the grandiose self and of the idealized parental imago into age-appropriate ambitions and ideals, as well as the potential development of creativity, empathy, wisdom, humor, and a sense of finiteness. These general considerations are given specific meaning in each of these cases as we note the patients pursuing and enjoying life in terms of their own performance and in the sense of having meaningful values and goals. The changes are marked, although the patients often give only subtle verbal expression to them. Some say that at last they can work on their own, others report that for the first time in their lives they feel genuine, or there may be some other manifestations of a firm sense of self. The alerting of analytic workers to this clear but quiet psychological configuration is a task made easier by studying detailed cases over a long period of time and noting how the self may attain a position of consolidation that was previously lacking.

Inevitably, not all of the cases presented cover all of the areas noted above. The first, "The Resolution of a Mirror Transference," is the longest; it is a vivid portrayal of an analysis from beginning to end, with special emphasis on how a mirror transference developed and was resolved. "Transformation of Archaic Narcissism," a somewhat shorter exposition, traces archaic narcissism as it assumes adult form. This is

followed by a lengthier report, "The Consolidation of a Cohesive Self," which offers the reader an opportunity of sharing
some of the analyst's problems as the case unfolds. The "Analysis of a Mirror Transference in a Case of Arrested Development" focuses on the therapeutic interaction and the working
through of the transference. "Commentary on the Analysis of
a Hysterical Personality" attempts to show how a case that
might classically be conceived of as one of hysteria may be
more fruitfully understood in the broader terms of a disorder
of the self. "A Case of Chronic Narcissistic Vulnerability"
presents an interesting diagnostic challenge and raises a
number of questions about the therapeutic procedure employed.

The anonymity of the contributors, of course, makes it
impossible for the reader to know whether the analyst was a
man or a woman. Assuming that, for one reason or another,
the reader finds this an obstacle, we can say that the cases described in Chapters 2, 5, and 6 were conducted by men, those
in Chapters 3, 4, and 7 were conducted by women.

In sum, then, this book is an answer to a call for more
clinical material to supplement Kohut's writings. But it is an
enthusiastic answer. Ours has been challenging but exciting
work, and to one degree or another we all believe that a major
conceptual shift has occurred in psychoanalysis. Such changes
in scientific enterprises may be revolutionary or evolutionary,
but there comes a moment when the participants are convinced that things are different. For many people this is painful, and for others it is joyous. The reader should be aware
that he is in the company of the latter. We feel that a new
orientation to certain clinical problems in psychoanalysis has
been offered by *The Analysis of the Self* and *The Restoration
of the Self*. We feel we can both understand and help patients
who previously were mysterious to us — or worse: whom we had
thought to have understood, but had unaccountably failed to

help. We are most optimistic about the future yield of these new ideas and believe that, so far, only the surface has been explored. We have little doubt that some day even better theories and methods will emerge, making obsolete many of the concepts that seem so novel now. But for the present we are in the midst of exploration, and we offer up our findings for your consideration.

A.G.

2

THE RESOLUTION OF A MIRROR TRANSFERENCE: CLINICAL EMPHASIS ON THE TERMINATION PHASE

The analysis of Mr. I. is presented to illustrate the vicissitudes of pathognomonic regression, the resulting emergence of a bipolar narcissistic transference, and its working through. The central intrapsychic events in this process of working through are the transmuting internalizations. These occur throughout the analysis, but are especially pronounced during the termination phase, which is therefore described in greater detail.

In the analysis of Mr. I., it was the idealizing transference that emerged first. It dominated the analytic process with a sharply delineated continuity, although frequently disrupted owing to regressive swings (to mirror and merger transferences) and fragmentations (Kohut, 1971, p. 97), from about the end of the first year to about the middle of the third year.

13

From then on through termination, the mirror transferences attained continuity and became the focus for the working-through process. The opening phase of the analysis showed a prolonged period of oscillations between the polarities of the patient's transference needs. Viewed in retrospect, a number of obstacles could be recognized as having retarded the therapeutic mobilization of the idealized parental imago. The patient's own inner resistances account for some of the "natural" obstacles. These intrinsic resistances alone would not, however, have prolonged the development of an idealizing transference to this extent had it not been that the analyst was uncertain about his initial diagnosis and, at the beginning, had no grasp of the new psychology of the self, which would have helped him to recognize the specific narcissistic transferences. Mr. I.'s disappointment that he could not be analyzed by the city's most prominent psychoanalyst (which he felt would have "realistically" fulfilled his need for an idealized father imago) further contributed to the delay in mobilizing the idealizing transference.

One significant element of the new psychology of the self which could only be introduced gradually into the analytic climate and serve as a guide for appropriate interpretive responses, had to do with the meaning the analyst attached to the early manifestations of narcissistic transferences. These should have been viewed, not as defenses against the unfolding of object-instinctual transferences, i.e., not as "defense-transferences," but as indications of the beginning mobilization of archaic narcissistic configurations, which had to be allowed to move into and occupy the center stage of analysis. Once this theoretical and technical obstacle was more or less overcome —the reader will see how persistently it recurred, especially during advances in the analytic process—and the analyst learned to perceive his own emotional position as a self-object in the transference, the more "spontaneous" unfolding and the sharper delineation of the idealizing transference became possible.

Successful working through of the idealizing transference and a further pathognomonic regression under the impact of the "threat of termination" in the middle of the third year of analysis mobilized the mirror transference proper.

The case report itself illustrates what has been outlined in this introduction. Whenever possible, the patient's own words are used. The analyst's interventions are quoted verbatim where available, or given as originally summarized in his process notes. (These summary statements are not in quotation marks.) The narrative of the analysis is interspersed with orienting (often theoretical) remarks about the analytic process, giving the reader samples of how the consultations with Kohut guided the analyst in his conduct of this analysis. These remarks are set off by being enclosed in brackets.

The Choice of Psychoanalysis for Mr. I.

Mr. I.,[1] a 25-year-old single industrial engineer, was referred for analysis after a diagnostic evaluation by a senior analyst. He was then seen four weeks later for his first appointment. Tall, handsome, carefully dressed, and soft-spoken, he was extremely anxious and spoke rapidly and in a somewhat rambling fashion in this single face-to-face session. He complained that he was unable to perform adequately on his new job; he was too preoccupied with his unhappiness with himself and the lack of direction in his life. On his job, he could not read or sit still long enough to finish his projects, and he could not do any work at home. He had to date almost continuously. He could not be alone "just with myself." If his date sat with him, he could do a little reading. He was always on the move

---

[1] Mr. I. also makes an appearance in Kohut (1971, 1977).

from one woman to another. He has had no enduring relationships—except one that lasted about six months, before
moving to his present job—none of the others had ever been
meaningful, and he experienced no real pleasure in any of
them. As he thought about this lately, he realized that he had
been miserable ever since his childhood.

Mr. I has a younger sister and two younger brothers. He
saw his father as distant, "not really a father to his children,"
and too preoccupied with himself and his own considerable
accomplishments as a businessman, sportsman, and community leader. Father constantly talked about his hobbies and
exhibited his work to everyone in a bragging fashion that still
disturbed the patient. The father had been well liked by
everyone, but according to the patient he was only superficially interested in other people.

On fairly frequent trips home from school, Mr. I. always
found his father preoccupied with his hobbies and could never
attract his attention. When he did, "it was only pseudointerest
for a brief moment." He once announced ahead of time that
he would be home on a particular weekend. His father left
him alone with his mother, for a day, to do something that
could easily have been postponed. When his father returned,
the patient resented his presence as an intrusion and felt as if
his father were a stranger to him. At this point he remembered
that someone had once called to his attention that he never
talked about his mother and he now realized that this was
happening again in this situation. He had always thought that
everything was okay in his relationship to his mother, but he
now realized that that was not true. He emphasized his
mother's blatant seductiveness.

In grade school he was painfully shy, afraid of sports and
injuries, especially to his eyes. He thought that he suffered
from castration anxiety: "I can say this, but don't really know
what it means."

His was a close-knit family. He had always written long letters to his parents, almost every night, from college. He had to tell his parents everything. Father used to tease the patient, saying that by the time he was 25, he knew every whore in the state where they lived. The patient then added, "I guess by now I have outdone him. I did everything there was to do. I hope to marry some day, but the way I am now I'd get nothing out of it." The girl he left behind when he moved to his present job wanted to marry him, but he was unable to commit himself, so she broke up with him. He knew that he was looking for the unobtainable girl. Recently, at his sister's wedding, he thought, "Now that she is married, I can never find the ideal woman." He added that this was a kind of incestuous thought.

Mr. I. was a very good student in high school and during the first two years at an Ivy League college, but later on he could never "live up to [his] potential." He had become more interested in his "sexual escapades" than anything else, and he was pursuing these rather compulsively.

He knew he wanted and needed analysis. The analyst concurred. All arrangements were quickly settled, and the analysis began the next day.

The analyst reflected upon his own diagnostic impressions and tentatively agreed with the referring analyst's diagnosis of a neurotic character disorder with phallic-narcissistic and obsessive-compulsive features. The patient's oedipal anxieties seemed all pervasive in the content of his first interview, just as in the preceding diagnostic interviews with the senior analyst: blatant competitiveness with father, fear of physical injury, especially to the eyes, and frequently intruding incestuous feelings and thoughts in relation to the mother and sister. The analysis was undertaken with the expectation that the patient would develop a classical transference neurosis.

The Opening Phase of the Analysis:
Toward the Pathognomonic Regression—
Oscillations Between Idealizing,
Mirroring, and Merger Needs

In his mind, Mr. I. "processed" his experiences during the last several months in terms of how he could recount them in his analysis, just as he had to recount all his experiences in those long detailed letters to the family.

The moment he started, he spoke rapidly, with great pressure, and remarkable openness. He soon felt that he would need eight to ten hours a day for a while to get the groundwork laid down, to say just the bare minimum about himself and his family. He seemed unable to leave out the slightest detail of his day-to-day experiences. He could not hold to his original plan of giving well-organized, orderly presentations of his life history, piece by piece: an hour about mother, an hour about school, etc., because current events pre-empted all of his time on the couch. He latched onto the analyst and the analysis with an addiction-like intensity. He said that the gain from just talking was already tremendous (session 3); he hoped it would not defeat the purpose. "Being here for an hour is helpful as an outlet." He sensed that he was already "dependent." He knew he could count on the analyst's being there at all times. He noticed that leaving the session the day before was very difficult, just like with the girl the night before. "When she says you better go now, I can't. *I* have to say that! I can't tolerate *her* saying it. I have to break them into the pattern." Here, he watched the clock, so he would know exactly when the session ended. When he left, he felt "my head was up at the ceiling and my body down on the floor. I felt disconnected." He could not talk to anyone for a while afterward. He said to himself, "Boy, this is what they talk about being psychotic for one hour. I have to pull myself together." He felt on top of the world, beaming all over, took a shower, cleansed himself, and felt relieved. He looked into the mirror and said to himself, "You look like you just swallowed your father's penis." Then he felt nauseated.

At first, he thought that he might not need a girl that night, but then warned himself that things could not change so radically overnight and it was unrealistic to hope that he could give up such a compulsion instantly.

Intercourse was "dull as hell — it doesn't do anything for you if you are a neurotic like I am," so he and the girl resorted to mutual masturbation. This used to be associated "with good fantasy life," but he did not even have that now. His fantasies "dried up." But at least when masturbating in the girl's presence, "I had an audience." He described his pleasures in eating and in spending a long time in the bathroom defecating. He liked all sorts of body feelings and sensations and looked into the mirror frequently. He loved music — never felt so intense as when he made music. Loved country music, hillbilly, Dixieland, and Bach. Played the trumpet and the piano. He has not been able to play music for some time, especially the trumpet (that was mother's instrument) because he held it in an awkward fashion; it accentuated the size and shape of his nose, and he felt then almost as before the plastic surgery. He would like to surprise his father and play the clarinet. He would give up anyting if he could play Dixieland on the piano the way his father does.

For him, the world was a bedroom, he said, populated with all those women whose phone numbers and addresses he carried around with him at all times so that he could call them and have them available at a moment's notice. "They serve as an outlet — drain energy better than masturbation. It is also a great athletic endeavor, adventuresome, it is also like having a cocktail, but I don't like to drink, so I have an orgasm instead."

One of his hobbies was taking pictures of nude girls. He had a large collection of them, and both parents said that they were "better than *Playboy*." His father, after having seen some of the pictures, finally admitted that the patient "screwed around more than father did."

As he continued with the various details of his frantic and often bizarre nightly sexual exploits with a growing number of women, he reflected on the kind of analyst he had asked to be referred to: "I needed somebody who was an all-around he-man because he would give me credit for this. Someone who would think it was wild, great, and who would really appreciate it."

It was in the climate of such expectations and wishes to be admired for his exploits that Mr. I. brought in a picture with an old man and his own father standing next to an automobile near a lake in front of their summer home. Uneasy about being inundated with pictures, the analyst fended him off by asking, "Why do you feel I ought to see it?" The patient responded that he would love to show off all his pictures, records, and poems.

Simultaneously with his other exploits, Mr. I. also began a more conventional, tentative dating relationship with one of his co-workers at his firm, Miss T. He was somewhat secretive about her and about the nature of their relationship at first, and remarked once that he could not trust the analyst with that yet. Soon, however, he began to drop some comments about Miss T. and expected the analyst to ask some further questions about her, which the analyst did not do. Once, just before a weekend break, he made another brief comment about Miss T., adding, "you'll have to wait for the next exciting episode until next week." After a brief silence, he continued, "I thought you'd ask me about her. It loses its punch because you don't ask me about it." Analyst: "I realize that you want to get me to be more actively curious." Patient: "When you say something like that, it seems like it is possible to think about it in a positive way. You mean to get attention?" He was aware of how much he wanted that—it was not unconscious, and that was what was so embarrassing about it. He wanted to be the best analysand there ever was. He hated to admit that he needed somebody else, he said. He had the thought that he could do his analysis himself and become famous. "Maybe I am on the verge of it now, and you are going to get credit for it. My case has to be the greatest!"

After the first direct expression of grandiose fantasies, Mr. I. talked at length about the things he has always been sensitive and embarrassed about. His awkwardness in social situations, in relation to people with status and money; his Jewishness, his big nose, for which he finally had a very successful plastic operation in Junior College, at father's insistence. He was a sickly child, with many colds, sore throats, coughs, and bronchitis. He could never breathe through his nose because of a septal deformity.

This sequence of the expression of hitherto not-so-well-concealed and conscious grandiose fantasies and simultaneous or subsequent self-contempt became familiar events in the analysis, but eventually disappeared.

Mr. I. and Miss T. parted company after a brief courtship, because she wanted to go steady, wanted someone she could depend on. She began dating another fellow. This usually made Mr. I. much more interested in a girl; he always needed a conquest. With Miss T., there were some moments of gentleness and caring, quite unusual for him, and an isolated phenomenon in his current life situation.

[Throughout this initial period, the analyst, while impressed with the intensity of the patient's constant overstimulation, poor impulse control, and frantic efforts to calm himself through a variety of sadistic sexual exploits, searched in his own mind for clues to the unconscious childhood fantasies that motivated the patient's behavior. He was initially im-

pressed with the frequent and scattered references to incestuous feelings in relations to the mother and sister; intense
competitiveness with his father (who had wanted to become an
industrial engineer and kept urging his son to take that path,
but who had remained "stuck in business"), his fear of sports,
fear of injury to his eyes, and the like. Yet, these were always
described with ease, without resistance. They were thus initially confusing the clinical picture for the analyst. He wondered whether these issues would become meaningfully engaged in the analysis once the transference neurosis developed
and would then be effectively interpretable. The analyst's
diagnostic considerations also included at this point the formulation that what he saw was not primarily a regression from
the oedipal conflict, but that severe pregenital fixations determined the patient's psychopathology and would complicate
the analysis. A particularly pronounced phallic narcissism
seemed evident.]

Relatively early in the analysis, the patient played out,
one weekend, the whole gamut of his usual sadistic and somewhat bizarre sexual exploits and reported them in great detail.
Several girls were involved in all of this. He could be cruelly
demanding of each one: showing up unannounced, leaving
abruptly in the middle of the night when expected to stay
over, and, on the way home suddenly deciding to spend the
rest of the night with another. "If you treat them badly, they'll
do everything you want them to do." With one of them, they
urinated upon each other and wallowed in the warmth of it.
He enjoyed that. He added, "The whole thing wasn't even
sexual this time; it helped me relax, and I went to sleep." The
analyst said that the patient seemed more frantic than usual
this past weekend, and it sounded as if he had to engage in all
of what he described under some pressure, even though he did
not want to do it. Mr. I. agreed and said that whenever he had

an erection, he *had* to do something with it. Perhaps later on he would have no erection and could not have intercourse. He had such constant "performance anxiety" that he had to test his abilities with each erection, practically. He was struggling with either being a lecherous, playboy type or searching for a decent relationship. At this point, neither was satisfying.

In response to the remark that he seemed so keyed-up and could not calm down, he said that was true, but sometimes he started on such activities when he was bored or could not be alone. The analyst's pointing to his being keyed-up reminded him of the fact that he had been thinking a lot about his sexually stimulating "seductive mother" these last few weeks.

The next day he was much calmer and expressed the hope that some night he might just be able to stay home, put his feet up on a chair, and read. He then added: "You commented yesterday that perhaps I had been so keyed-up for so long that I found it hard to slow down and relax. I must say that of all the comments anybody ever made to me yet, all have been what I have thought of myself, too, before, but this was different." He kept thinking about it and wondered if he could give up these frantic activities. He decided that he could not do it yet.

For three or four months Mr. I. seemed to be needing endless and continued stimulation, on the one hand, and a variety of efforts to calm and soothe himself, on the other. In the sessions he was still recounting every detail of the previous 24 hours or the weekend, wanting both to bask in the analyst's admiration of his sexual exploits and to keep his analytic experience completely under his control, in fear of overstimulation. He once expressed this by saying: "What would I do if I had an erection right here on the couch?" It began to disturb him that the analyst did not applaud the Don Juan in him, and he felt that his co-workers, to whom he bragged about his exploits, also disapproved of him or just remained indifferent.

This unsettled and confused him and may have been the last straw that precipitated his seeking analysis when he did.

His fear of stimulation in his regular contact with the analyst manifested itself from the very beginning. He could not glance at the analyst either upon arrival or upon leaving — especially the latter. Occasional chance encounters with the analyst outside the office stimulated him enormously, almost painfully, and he elaborated them in recurrent dreams with a highly incestuous flavor. These were "bedroom dreams" or "dining-room dreams," portraying what he experienced as inappropriate, highly stimulating intimacy. These dreams brought back a flood of childhood memories about exposure to the nudity of his parents, who believed in "being natural about it." On a recent trip home, he was shaving in the bathroom, naked, when mother barged in to ask him what he wanted for breakfast. He was "terribly embarrassed."

In reflecting upon his "overuse of" his penis, he said that on a deeper level he was "frigid" although he performed well. He was in love with his penis. When the girl was playing with it, he would often wonder: why should she have it? Too bad she doesn't have anything similar. Only through his penis could he let out all his tension.

During the first Christmas vacation, the first break in the analysis, the patient observed that he was "dating more desperately, in search for someone." It was only then that he realized retrospectively that he had already calmed down a bit in the analysis. He recognized that he was hyperexcited in anticipation of the analyst's return and recalled feeling very much the same when he was waiting for his first consultation with the analyst.

He remembered what he called a "brilliant dream" the night after the last session prior to Christmas vacation: "The setting was an old barn with many levels or floors; a Venetian building. I was there with two of my co-workers, there were three chairs, and we were having dinner. It all took place in your backyard. You came with a little boy in your hand. You were mean-looking and didn't pay any attention to me. You were yellow, Negroid, or Indian [he recalled that the analyst looked pale recently, very sinister and overtired]. You walked to another yard with your son. I was mad, or you were mad that we had chosen your backyard. You were truly cold."

Mr. I. was "overjoyed" about this dream, he said, because it brought some things together for him: his reaction to the analyst's leaving, his reaction to an accidental encounter in a nearby restaurant, and the fact that "it was like I was the little boy in the dream and I tried to suppress that feeling."

Along with feeling like a needy little boy, recognizing the feelings and the accompanying demands that he made on the analyst, he settled down to the point that he could now fill in some details of his past, since the urgency to report everything from the previous day abated. He would have liked a double hour, or for the analyst to take off one month and just listen to him. He took this as a sign that he was "addicted" to the analysis.

With the "addiction" there was also a lessening of frantic activities on the outside and the need for all details to be presented in the session—so long as he felt that he was "heard." Upheavals, both outside and inside the sessions, that triggered the resumption of the nightly escapades were more circumscribed and relatable to the patient's experiences in the transference. For example, once, in the context of needing double sessions or a whole month just for himself, the analyst dismissed him five minutes early "by mistake." (The analyst was unconsciously warding off Mr. I.'s neediness.) He then dreamed of incestuous closeness with his sister, reaching for her breast, and gobbling up a variety of pills. His associations were to periods of loneliness in childhood, often relieved by closeness with sister, to pills and tranquilizers to calm himself.

The analyst interpreted that Mr. I. felt deprived by the cutting off of five minutes before the end of the session, and in the dream, he made up for it in the manner in which he had always tried to do it, but never quite successfully.

It was now possible to deal with similar episodes by reconstructing what had led to frustrations in his transference expectations and expand that understanding with attempts at reconstructing some of the genetic experiences that led to his specific vulnerabilities. As a result, the capacity to observe and to describe his analytic experiences vividly and to express his needs and demands more directly increased. For example, when the analyst had to change the time of the session for a two-week period, the patient reacted strongly and said that he had a "transference to the time, too, the couch and the room." Since he now came early in the morning, there was "an empty quality to the rest of the day." "The constancy of the hours are very important to me. Just *any* hour degraded the sanctity of the analysis. When I left yesterday, I felt disappointed and unheard."

Episodes of mild to moderate disruptions, such as the one just mentioned, became more circumscribed, and the analyst progressively recognized more rapidly their precipitants in the transference. The "repair" of such disruptions by understanding what brought them about was also more rapidly achieved.

[Before turning to illustrative examples that indicate the nature of the developing transference, two additional themes, already clearly visible in the opening phase but not yet appropriately addressed by the analyst, should be described. The patient talked a lot about his lifelong pleasure in withholding his bowel movements, to accumulate a great deal of feces and then spend a half an hour or more on the toilet daily. "The pleasure is sometimes worth more than an orgasm." Withholding and slow, controlled letting-go had pervaded the opening phase of analysis as a means of managing his fear of excitement, namely, his (incestuous) overstimulation and the uncontrolled breakthrough of his intense grandiose-exhibitionistic wishes.

Initially, the patient wondered if the analyst would be strong enough to deal with all of his erupting emotions. There were some subtle and fleeting depreciative attitudes toward the analyst, he wondered if the analyst felt he had made a mistake by accepting him so quickly for analysis. A much stronger trend of needing, and having found, a perfect, most respected, prominent analyst, with superior powers of understanding, who would then appreciate and admire him and find him exciting and pleasurable to work with, later emerged against some resistance.]

The Middle Phase: Vicissitudes of the Transference and the Process of Working Through

Mr. I. noted with amazement that this was his first winter without repetitive colds and sore throats; he had missed no time from work. He attributed all of this to the power of the analysis. He was embarrassed that he began to see the analyst as powerful. The fact that he felt attached to the analyst bothered him considerably. He did not allow himself to think about it, but he noticed that outside of the analytic sessions, with his friends who knew that he was in analysis, he jokingly degraded both the analyst and the analysis. He saw the analyst as an El Greco Madonna-like figure with wide eyes, high forehead, and a waxlike appearance, then as a squatting Buddha, an oriental god made of gold. [Here was both the yearning for the idealized figure and also the averting of the anxious overexcitement by making him waxlike or gold. Miss T., whom the patient idealized and did not treat in the same manner as he treated other women, did have an El Greco Madonna-like face. She was also blond, in contrast to his very dark, sensuous-looking mother.]

In the sessions, he now more freely idealized the analyst's way of treating him. One day, he was quite satisfied with his own performance because he was not rambling, anxious and confused. He appreciated that the analyst merely listened and did not interrupt him; it meant that what he presented was completely accepted. The next day he said that that was a very good hour, even though the analyst said nothing. "Sometimes I need you to say something. Yesterday I didn't. If you had said something, you would have selected something to comment on. That would have insulted me, since you couldn't have commented on everything."

To him this meant that the analyst was now perfectly in tune with him, and it was in this context that Mr. I. first mentioned that he was almost ready to give up the women. He might even be able to come to his session without his wrist watch. He was secure enough not to fear being cut off: he could now picture that there would be a tomorrow, and he would not need to pack everything into one session as if this were his last chance. He wanted to be admired for all the changes he was reporting about and bemoaned the fact that he needed applause and recognition for every little accomplishment. And yet he just had one whole week for the first time without a date! But when the analyst later on inadvertently rebuffed an exhibitionistic demand, he badly mistreated a girl that night—the last cruelly sadistic attack on women observed during the analysis. The interpretation that he treated the girl the way he felt treated by the analyst that day "made me feel that the air has been cleared, and I feel repaired."

The patient repeatedly referred to his wish to make the analyst the repository of every detail of his total family and personal life history. But he could now say, "It's not your job to record my life history. You are not my biographer." (This also revealed his secret hope that the analyst would approach him as a biographer approaches his subjects, with total immersion and total identification.)

Mr. I. sensed that his homosexual fears, which began to creep up at this time, were somehow related to his fear of the prolonged summer vacation away from the analyst. He also began to ignore those girls at work whom he had been to bed with. This, he knew, hurt them very much, just as it would hurt him if the tables were turned. The analyst interpreted that the patient must have felt that in his leaving for a vacation, the analyst was indeed turning the tables on him. Mr. I. was surprised that "something like this could cause me to hurt the girls." Another way he was attempting to cope with the anticipated separation was in imitating the analyst's soothing, almost whisper-like [patient's description] voice with his co-workers. He began to be more quiet and silent. He said, " To use silence requires a very special talent." As the time of vacation approached, the relative calm of the sessions gave way to panicky and angry feelings. The analyst interpreted that the patient was most disturbed about the fact that he could not control the analyst's comings and goings and could not keep him in the city during the summer.

The patient recalled having been sent away to camp when he was only six years old—a very immature and sickly six-year-old at that—and he hated his mother for it. He still thought it was brutal to send kids of that age away from home. He knew he had problems with separations. He recalled that in college, after a lecture was over in the large auditorium and the student body began to leave, he would feel very much alone and have an erection. Only if he masturbated right then and there could he leave.

He also recalled an early memory: Saturday nights his

folks would go to the town's social club. His sister would get sick, run a fever, and scream for mother. He would become very anxious and beg the babysitter to call his parents. She would harshly send him back to bed without calling the parents; she didn't want to ruin their evening out. Once, when the parents were out of town for a weekend, the patient and his sister were separated, each with one set of grandparents. The sister got sick, and he was called to straighten things out. He took charge; only he could calm down his sister. The analyst remarked that the patient was trying to muster his old strength to deal with his own panicky feelings now, as he had done when a child, and was mobilizing this strength from the memories of having been able to cope when his grandparents were helpless.

Mr. I. recalled some persistent childhood fantasies: He fantasied possessing two girls and keeping them hidden and locked up in a hotel. He would be Superman and one of the girls would be Superwoman. They would be flying around all over. He never fantasied a sexual relationship with them. "They would be mine, always there and helpful. Consciously, this was a togetherness fantasy. That ties in with what we were talking about today." The analyst emphasized that in the fantasy the patient could enforce the togetherness, these girls could never leave him — how much he would like to have that kind of power over his analyst.

He wondered what he would try to say after return from vacation. Would he have to start from scratch? Would he be able to pick up where he had left off? Or would he have to talk about the feelings he had while the analyst was away? The analyst remarked that the patient seemed to fear that, during vacation, everything that had been gained might be lost. Mr. I. then talked about his nausea and headaches, which began just as the analyst was talking, and he linked this up with the feeling "as if I am telling you don't go away." In response to the question whether he ever had such physical reactions to being left before, the patient remembered that in college, once, when his folks were leaving after a visit, he was waving goodbye to them, he felt choked up and "right in here [pointing to his abdomen] I felt as if I wanted to vomit or masturbate or get some kind of release. I don't remember what I did then—maybe I took a cold shower or masturbated or just started something fresh to work it through symbolically." He further remembered that when he first went to camp [at age six], he was with his mother on the train all day long. It was a difficult train ride, but he remembered that on *that* day, during the train ride, they were "dependent on each other to get through." He was painfully anticipating that she would leave the next day and he would have to stay in camp.

A flurry of activity started again with the girls (without much of the overt sadism). He said that on a temporary basis these girls now served for him as a "comfort station," so that he could get through each day. Just like the little blue notebook he had in his pocket: whenever he was anxious he could take it out, look at it. He recognized that this flurry of activities started because he felt more of a need for comforting as a result of the analyst's leaving; he needed something to look forward to. He recalled the analyst's interpretation of the day before regarding an element in his fantasy which indicated that he needed a collection of girls, to hold on to them so that they could not leave him and therefore could not hurt him. By stripping them of their mobility in his fantasy, he had them permanently.

At camp, when he was alone at night, awake and frightened, he fantasied about S.L., a boy who lived next door and was three years older—tough, intellectual, and a leader—whom he hero-worshipped. He felt that S.L. was in his chest, in a secret compartment that he carved out. He was smaller and would fit in there; and whenever he ate, he would feed

S.L., too. "S.L. was someone who could not leave me, Superman. When I was picked on in camp, I would call upon him in fantasy for help. In our family, leaving was a tragic thing."

When he referred again the next day to the analyst's leaving as causing all this trouble, the patient was told that it was not the analyst's leaving, per se, that bothered him, that made him feel frightened and helpless, and mobilized his old anxieties, but the fact that he could not control it: just as when the girl said, "I'll go now," and he felt helpless and abandoned. That the analyst's leaving was, in a sense, inflicted on him; that he had no power to change it made it so traumatic and reawakened his feelings of abandonment and separation from childhood. He immediately responded with excitement: "Two hundred per cent agreement! You are damn right! [He got slightly hypomanic as he continued.] I'll go out there, mount a horse and charge and lead a battle, and I'll be in control. I'll grab for power—it sounds right to me: I have to be in control." When the analyst later included the patient's behavior with his dates as another example of needing to have everything under his control, the patient expanded on it by saying that after a few dates he usually began to feel that the girl expected something—and then the control would be slipping away from him. Then he felt the need to find a new situation in which he could establish or re-establish control.

With two more sessions left before interruption, Mr. I. calmed down considerably. He reported his most recent dream: "I was sitting at your desk for the therapy hour. It was a unique feeling. The desk was up against the wall. We aren't facing each other. I came in and started and went on for 30 minutes. Then I realized that I was supposed to be on the couch, and I became embarrassed. I didn't know where to continue. I anticipated getting up and lying down, but I could not do it. I had the same anxiety as when I first had anxiety lying down, or anxiety before leaving. These transitions are very uncomfortable. It's amazing how uncomfortable they are."

In his associations he focused on the fact that he remembered one previous discussion about control, and maybe he decided to be in control in the dream by sitting up. The analyst agreed. Mr. I. added: "There was an unrelated part to the dream about trumpet playing. I went away to a new school, a new band, took up trumpet playing, and I could do it well. Now I was less anxious and could play the trumpet better." He said he felt smug now, he felt he was good in his field and could be very good at so many other things. It was a different feeling for a change.

During the last session he was hesitant to get to any new topic. "I am closing the book or a chapter, I tighten up, I close up. You shut the windows when it is raining outside. You are not worse off, but you shut them. Time to tighten up the psyche and store everything away. It's not bad or a great loss, it just has to be done." Near the end of the session he reported a fantasy in which he was locked in with Miss T. on the moon. The analyst wondered if, in addition to having her there under his total control, this wouldn't also insure for him that he would not have to share her with anyone else. The patient without any hesitation said, "Yes, then I could keep you here; that part of you that is involved with me I wouldn't have to share with your family."

This preseparation period has been presented in some detail to show that around it the major themes, or *Anlagen* of the major themes, have now been introduced into the analytic process and have become meaningfully engaged. Viewed in retrospect, the beginning of this analysis does reveal the bipolar nature of the transference. Here, we already have glimpses of Mr. I.'s intense need for an idealized parent imago and a more persistent (perhaps, at this point, even more intense) need for mirroring, admiration, and approval. While such early breakthroughs of narcissistic transference manifestations do not indicate with certainty the ultimate nature of the transference that will emerge from the pathognomonic regression, they do hint strongly at the possibility of the development of an idealizing transference, a mirror transference, or both (cf. Kohut, 1971, pp. 138-139, 257). It will now be easier to follow the vicissitudes of the transference and their working through around the same themes up to the period of termination.

Mr. I. was quite excited about his first postvacation session. The last session had affected him "amazingly." He was impressed and stunned at having been told by the analyst: "Have a good vacation!" He magically kept this with himself throughout and thereby maintained his contact with the analyst. A few nights ago he noticed his "I-need-a-date" feeling emerging again, but he did not give in to it. He had his best vacation at home ever, got along well with everyone, even his father. When he left, mother kissed him on the lips, and this made him very uncomfortable.

He settled back into analysis quickly. He realized that he recontacted Miss T. during the vacation as a substitute for the analyst, but what he did not realize was that his behavior toward Miss T. was an expression of his gross identification with the analyst. He appeared to be gentle, understanding, undemanding, and supportive with her. He did not push her into a sexual relationship prematurely, but accorded her the nonsexualized "madonna-treatment."

He said he could not think of marriage to Miss T. yet, because he noticed that the analyst's response to him was still more important to him than anyone else's, including Miss T.'s. Also, he had already changed so much this past year that he could not yet predict where he would end up in terms of his aspirations for marriage. He linked the considerable decrease of masturbation, of sitting on the toilet long hours and the compulsion to date, to the fact that "we hit it off very well" upon return from vacation. He bemoaned only that, as a result of settling down and giving up the various frantic activities, he was now "nauseatingly average." He reported that during his vacation he "ceremoniously" burned his nude-photo collection — except for a few pictures.

He so much wanted the analyst to be as excited and stimulated by him and his analysis as he himself was, and he tried to attract the analyst's applause at every turn. The patient wanted more of an indication from the analyst as to how to behave, what was applause-deserving behavior (what would make me like *you?*), and when these were not forthcoming, he turned some of his fury against the analyst, but acted out some of it at work.

He could now use the analyst and the analysis as his safe anchor, however, and saw the analyst as very stable and in complete control of his own emotions, until one day he noticed an ad in the local newspaper endorsing a candidate for a political office. He saw the analyst's name among the signatures, and he was infuriated. This reminded him of his father who tolerated only one political opinion and shoved it down everyone's throat. It brought up a flood of affects and memories in relation to the father, but the most important aspect of this experience seemed to be that the patient was afraid that the analyst also acted impulsively. If the analyst was as unpredictable as the parents of his childhood, he could not be trusted. The patient accepted this interpretation and said some time later that it helped him refocus his understanding of his own childhood.

Mr. I.'s rage at the analyst for his "thoughtless political action" highlighted and brought more clearly to the fore how much he needed the analyst as a reliable external source of tension regulation. His fear that the analyst would leave him unprotected against rising exhibitionistic tension (because he himself could not control his own) had its roots in Mr. I.'s traumatic experiences with his parents.

Mr. I. felt that he did very well "on many fronts and on many levels" during the analyst's prolonged vacation. He now had an "enlarged ego" (in contrast to what he used to call his "thin ego"), but he wanted to withhold this from the analyst, saying: "If you were not here to see it develop, the hell with you!" He also wanted to retaliate by "taking a vacation independently (i.e., irrespective of what the analyst thought about it and even if he was to be charged for it). In the course of discussing this, he (accurately) detected some irritation in the analyst's tone of voice. He then felt that he had pushed the analyst to the "brink of [his] tolerance" and said that the stronger he himself felt, the more he expected the analyst to reject him. He was furious at his father in his fantasy as he took a prolonged shower the other morning, wishing his father would die: "How could he toss me around when I was little, hit the ceiling, humiliate me in front of the family?" He was sure that the analyst could not stand his rage, just as his father would keel over with a heart attack if he expressed to him how he felt.

The analyst failed to recognize, during this phase, that the patient's massive identification was an effort to stem the tide of diffuse anxiety, to increase impulse control, and to attempt to control tension relief through acting out.

The intensity of the transference near the end of the first year of analysis was expressed in a brief reverie on the couch: Referring to a thought he was having, Mr. I. said, "I want to convey this thought to you—you'll never know I had this thought—I'll never get to tell you about it—terrible!" Analyst: "Sounds as if you anticipate that you will always need me to—

what? — To witness every experience, to be part of your life that way?" Mr. I. responded that it was "rough thinking of it any other way. Getting invested and knowing you'd have to separate, quit, terminate — terrible! What's the sense of doing it? Not worth it. Reminiscent of my writing a letter home every day — nowadays I don't — I talk to *you* every day. When I can no longer talk to you every day, then what? That's where T. fits in. I am fond of her, but reluctant to let go of you because of this sharing, and then letting go scares the hell out of me."

While there was more direct expression of his archaic needs and wishes, these emerged against considerable resistance: "We are getting down to the *real me* now, and I don't like it. Too intense; I can't handle it! The thought of killing myself has gone through my mind. I am absolutely exasperated being *me*. I need you and hate the feeling — hate needing you!" He could not stand getting closer to Miss T. or to the analyst.

He always felt that he was either fantastic — the best — or nothing. He wondered about the origin of these "stuck-up feelings" side by side with feeling worthless: "*Me, in* the family always inferior and ashamed; me, as *part* of the family, to the rest of the world, I was best."

[In retrospect, it is easier to see the vicissitudes of the transference throughout the first year of analysis: Near the beginning of the second year, Mr. I. aptly characterized the nature of the transference when he said: "I want the analysis to be like a floor-show, but nothing ever happens in here." Both he and the analyst understood, by then, his extreme need for admiration and affirmation and the need for mutual stimulation (visual, tactile, and sexual). Without being able to evoke such responses on the outside or from his analyst, he could not maintain his self-cohesiveness either outside or within the analytic situation. This was especially true during the first half of the first year. During the second half, as the mirror transference developed some temporary stability, Mr. I. seemed better protected against the threat of fragmentation in his daily life, and his frantic, polymorphous perverse activities (to stem the tide of regression or to regain his self-cohesiveness) abated. Instead, the traumatic experiences that precipitated threats of fragmentation, now occurred mainly within the transference.]

The Establishment of an Idealizing Transference and Its Working Through

As we observed, the stabilizing function of the transference Mr. I. experienced heightened his sensitivity and vulnerability to the analyst's failure of empathy, to weekend interruptions, especially if the latter occurred after he attacked the analyst: "I am afraid that you won't be able to take it; you will collapse under my attack, and then you'll hit me where I am most vulnerable." He was constantly worried that the analyst would fall apart or have a heart attack in response to his fury. He was especially careful at the end of the week and could not tolerate leaving the analyst without re-establishing "good feelings" about him. Simultaneously, he described that he could now "take" some of Miss T.'s reasonable demands and even her periodic rejections much better and did not have to run away from them. But he added that it was still important "how much I get from you — when I feel I have gotten enough, then I have a lot to give to others — to T. that same evening — otherwise, it's like I have to save all I've gotten for myself."

For brief periods, in anticipation of the second Christmas vacation, Mr. I. said that he could now contemplate the end of the analysis. "I feel more autonomy—I can imagine doing without analysis. If you now said I had to choose between you and T., I would choose T.; six months ago, I couldn't have." When the analyst canceled his Christmas vacation, the patient greeted it as "good news," but the need to change the timing of a few sessions during that period exposed, once more, a pervasive vulnerability—his attachment to the particular hour of the day when his sessions were usually scheduled. "What infuriates me is that such a small thing—I shouldn't even notice it—gets me so upset. That you have such a power over me is unbearable." The analyst, now recognizing previous similar incidents whose deeper meaning was earlier less adequately understood, said, "What must make these changes so unbearable is that you feel them as arbitrarily inflicted on you, you are a puppet on a string, and I have the power to pull it." Mr. I. (with considerable excitement): "Yes, and I have no control over you! With these trips too, you can leave whenever you want to, and what *I* feel or *I* want doesn't count."

The experience of being a puppet on a string (see Kohut, 1972) then gave way to a prolonged feeling of overstimulation due to the analyst's presence during the Christmas holidays. He could now imagine that the analyst stayed at home to be with him, and he felt both stimulated and stimulating, as portrayed in the following dream: "It was an enjoyable dream. Bunch of people sitting around, playing some sex game: get an erection and see if you can get an orgasm! The music therapist came up to me and put her hand on my penis to see if it was getting hard. She did it under the guise of some official thing, but I knew she wanted to and enjoyed it. But it was kind of small, and I wondered if she'd enjoy it."

He added that he had a "pan-sex feeling" in the dream. Sort of teasing, pleasant; not "intercourse-sexual," but just "tingly-sexual." He became distant, appeared anxious, and then continued: He was fearful of telling the analyst about his dream because "maybe I was inviting you to some sort of a sex play between us." He recalled the possible precipitant of the dream. He wondered why his supervisor at the plant had never invited him to his home, especially around Christmas. Then he had the thought, and pushed it out of his mind, that he would go to the analyst's home and "get friendlier with you." His association to the music therapist's touching his penis also created some anxiety. He was afraid that the analyst would interpret the music therapist as his own disguised appearance in the dream. He then recalled that he ran into the music therapist (whom he knew) on his way to yesterday's analytic session. He rushed past her, and he saw her as "older, grey-haired, exotic, and exciting—funny, she reminds me more of my father than my mother." (The analyst was grey-haired, too.) The analyst then pointed to the mutual stimulation in the dream, the patient's erection, openly displayed and attracting the music-therapist-analyst, who responded by having to do it "officially"—as a way, perhaps, of coping with the overstimulation—and thereby saying, this is not exciting to me, I do it because I have to, but underneath, wanting it and enjoying it. Mr. I. said that he recognized how he could use that maneuver to avoid being overstimulated. When the analyst wondered what might have been so overstimulating to Mr. I. in the previous session, he said: "Too much conversation, and you said to something that I mentioned that it was a *good point*." Analyst: "So, if you got me to say something like that, you got me to touch your penis under the guise of analysis, when really I wanted to do it for my own enjoyment." Mr. I.: "Gee, that's too much, let me think—my mind got a bit jammed up." Brief silence, then: "I am a flirt, if you are not careful, I will trap you—seduce you into a wrong track. There are two levels, and you are addressing yourself to the symbolism of touching the penis. The literal meaning is still threatening. When you said that so openly, I was so threatened—*my penis itches now—I am uncomfortable*. This reminds me of my tendency to sex-ualize all kinds of needs—have not done it recently. Dealt with all my anxieties and all needs with sex; even when hungry in bed with a girl—more sex."

The analyst could now add that Mr. I.'s dream shed light on his recurrent fear that the analyst would say something, make a slip, or do something, meaning he could lose control, respond to Mr. I.'s seductiveness, and "touch his penis." Thus, in turn, the analyst would be seductive, to which Mr. I. would respond with an uncomfortable feeling of overstimulation—as the itching in his penis just now expressed.

The fear of incestuous overstimulation, the experience of what he called "bedroom feelings" in the analysis, along with his fear that the analyst would not be self-controlled enough, stable and strong enough, continued for quite some time. It was for these reasons, he said, that "I need a machine to analyze me because I hear too much [referring to the analyst's tone of voice, which might reveal his irritation or his occasion-al defensiveness when criticized] and it gets you into a mess. My being afraid that you will collapse is also a problem."

By the middle of the second year, Mr. I. calmed down considerably (both in and out of the analysis). His relationship with T. also "improved" (i.e., it became "more intense," "more real," and "much more important," but also more con-flictual and served as an additional "battle-ground" for working through his narcissistic transferences). He noticed that "if my relationship with T. or with you goes sour, I start to feel a kind of anxiety—a fear of becoming psychotic, totally out of control." This foreshadowed a deepening regression in the transference, contrary to the analyst's expectations, and the patient's own explicit fears that the relation with T. would "interfere and detract from my analysis." In fact, the vicissi-tudes of Mr. I.'s relation to T. were continually brought into the analysis, and the details illuminated the nature of the transference, aiding reconstruction and working through. He soon thought that he was in love with her, because he felt he wanted to spend the rest of his life with her, but could not tell her directly, "I love you," for fear that this was a final commitment, which he was not yet ready to make. Even this tentative appearance of what he began to feel as "love," immediately brought forth some doubts: "Am I good enough for her?" Later, "Is she good enough for me?" "Maybe she is perfect and much more than I can handle."

Mr. I.'s helplessness, powerlessness, and feelings of insignificance now moved into the center of his analytic experience. Once, he asked thoughtfully, with some despair in his voice, "Why do I have to have you acknowledge that I feel good before I *know* I feel good?" His own further reflections were of considerable significance: He felt that he was "a splat on the wall — when you throw hot rubber against the wall, it hardens and is like an octopus with suckers on it, clinging to the wall. Then nothing matters, only the clinging like a splat. It can't tolerate the rumbling of the wall. Any disconnection is a threat to the survival of the splat. That's how I am with T. and with you. I want you to be the wall — shut up and listen! If I would no longer have to be a splat on the wall, it would be a major accomplishment." He could feel strong, powerful, and important only in his attachment to the idealized analyst. Whatever disrupted this attachment — weekend separations, vacations, or even slight unempathic rebuffs — all felt like the "rumbling of the wall," endangering "the splat."

The analysis of the disruptions of this idealizing attachment invariably brought back some relevant early memories. In reflecting on his neediness now as it intensified when he felt that the analyst had less to give (he could become unexpectedly ill, he had a separate life, other interests), Mr. I. said, "You compromise your self-esteem when you are looking for something you want. You don't understand what it's like to be a kid—weak, can't stick up for himself; there is no justice when you are a kid. They used to bury me in the snow and beat me. Embarrassing for a kid to have his father bawl out the neighborhood kids."

A dream at about this time illustrates the wish to detach himself from the idealized powerful analyst and to attain his own greatness. "Parade, sort of a long country parade—not in the city with a band—people riding horses. I was going to ride a horse in the parade; couldn't get caught up. Should go ahead and join them, but I procrastinated to take care of my sister or something. I tried to get caught up, but couldn't. I was discouraged. If you missed five minutes, you couldn't [catch up with the parade]. My sister decided not to be in the parade and said I shoud go ahead. She was sitting in the lodge, given up her seat."

He was glad to have dreamed about his sister: "She was mine and I was hers. I always came to her defense and she always came to mine. In the dream, if she wouldn't have, I wouldn't have been able to ride in the parade." Her admiration always made him feel great and powerful, and he has desperately sought such admiration (for his "big penis," his "great mind") from sister-figures ever since his sister married.

[These initial attempts at detachment from the idealized analyst and the hoped-for feelings of strength from within, were short-lived and easily thwarted by the vicissitudes of the transference. It is clearest, at this juncture, in the transference to the idealized (mother-sister-girl friends-) analyst, that the two lines of archaic narcissistic configurations meet: Mr. I.'s grandiose self seeks admiration and affirmation, and his attachment to the idealized parental imago is to lend him extraordinary powers. These shifts in the transference, with long stretches of idealization alternating with clearly expressed needs and demands for mirroring and even regressive shifts to archaic merger, continued into the third year of analysis, when the mirror transference proper established itself with greater stability and continuity.]

At the time of the "parade on a horse" dream, disappointments in the idealized analyst led to renewed increase in masturbation and a preoccupation with what he called a "fetishistic drive to look at girls' legs that doesn't listen to reason, it is a hateful, mean, needful pursuit of women. I am chasing them because I feel unloved; I withdraw into myself; I masturbate because I am unloved, turning to myself as if I were my own mother."

The analyst's absences for scientific meetings, and the emotional withdrawal that may be occasioned by the advance preparation for them, provoked rage, revengeful death wishes — and then led to considerable insight. "I seem to care about you only as you affect me — because my life is dependent upon you. I need you without a blemish [i.e., as a better mother and father than he had], but it is such selfish stuff not to give a damn about you."

Disruptions of the transference were now experienced as "big rips" or "big cracks in the wall," endangering "the splat." But the analytic "repair" of the rips and cracks in the wall slowly transformed the splat from "an octopus with suckers on it" to one with "legs and feet, with a chance for separate existence." The transformation was slow, with frequent regressions, and with a parallel working through toward this separation in Mr. I.'s relation with Miss T.

He could now tentatively, against considerable fear of being laughed at, present some of his own idealized expectations of himself, of what he could *do* or what he could *be*. His thoughts about marriage also belong to this category of still protected "ambitions," which were slowly turning into realizable ideals. He even felt ready to take Miss T. home to meet his parents. The visit was a success.

While still at the level of needing to control the analyst with stubborn possessiveness, he said, in response to its interpretation by the analyst: "I can now separate the *you* I want you to be here, from the *you* who has an expansive life I have no control over and am not part of." He recalled that he could always talk with his mother, "so I know what women are like." It was different with his father. Father's answer to many questions was: "Nonsense, get it out of your system!" Father couldn't sit down to talk, he would say, "You keep talking while I go out to the kitchen and make some salad—you keep talking!" He wondered: "How much do you like me and how much are you just putting up with me?" Later he added, "I get the feeling you are more modern, fresher, on a higher hill—I need that."

As he could accept and feel more intensely, in a sustained fashion, his archaic needs for an idealized parental imago, Mr. I. discovered that he had exactly the same response to Miss T.'s absences or rebuffs as to the analyst's: "My worry is she'll disappear from my mind if I don't use her or need her as a 'therapist' and don't cling to her."

The clinging to and the need to control the analyst were still important: "I need to have the feeling of completion at the end of the hour—binding up the loose ends—especially on weekends. I have to know when and where the hour ends. I have to prepare the end gradually, by winding down and losing speed. Sometimes you seem to end the hour abruptly and you deprive me of ending it." Such incidents could create "a rip in the wall," which Mr. I. would want to repair quickly by somehow excusing the analyst's behavior so that he could retain the idealized image of him, to make himself feel good again. Another solution would be "to get rid of the wall and be my own man, but I can't do that *yet*."

Not only could he not do that yet, but when he planned a brief vacation he was enraged that the analyst did not insist that he stay home. "If you don't make me stay home, you don't love me." And he recalled again how much he suffered when he was sent away to summer camp at the age of six. "I had absolute, deep terror and panic over being left alone." Mr. I. could now reflect upon the stability of the analytic situation and its meaning to him, again in response to a change in the schedule—an unexpected cancellation of a session.

A dream pinpoints the nature of the transference: "You were driving a bus we were all on. I was in the back with T. You were in shirt sleeves. That doctor—amazing man: businessman and analyst! In his spare time he is even driving a bus; he is earthy and humble." In his associations, Mr. I. stressed that "there was a need or a wish to see you as more available and approachable, down to earth like the rest of us common citizens; friendly, driving a bus—but in an unusual position: responsible but not very important. A pilot equals God, but a bus driver is more of a flunky." Mr. I. had recently been talking about not having any ambitions other than "to have a happy life and sunbathe for the rest of [his] life." In further reflecting upon his dream, he said that the analyst was too hard-working, too busy, and too ambitious; he himself was not. "How can I identify with you if I want to take it easy?" The analyst interpreted the patient's effort to remain connected with the powerful analyst in his absence (in the big bus with the analyst) and at the same time, making him less important, less Godlike and more available (the driver in shirt sleeves).

Lessening the analyst's importance as part of working through the idealizing transference proceeded with frequent but brief and intensely experienced disruptions. There was a concomitant slow increase in Mr. I.'s own inner strength, fleetingly visible in some concrete ways. During one such moment, with considerable hesitation he braced himself to announce, "I'd like to get married! Not today or next morning, but I've done a lot of serious thinking and feeling; will need to do more. No doubt about it. T. is the girl I want to marry." The analyst, acknowledging the importance of such a resolute stance after prolonged hesitations and uncertainties (the patient had earlier mentioned his surprise at no longer feeling any ambivalence about his marriage plans and not feeling he had to rush into it), wondered why Mr. I. had to "protect" these plans from the analyst? "That is a good question," he said. "I don't know what I expected your response to be. Either I don't want a response—but I am not sure about that—or I don't need one, which, if it's true, I'd be glad about."

When he rediscovered his need for the idealized analyst and was again disappointed, he was enraged, thought of taking his shoes off and smashing the analyst's office. He described the aftereffects of a recent blow-up with T.: "I was infuriated, but I wasn't masturbating, didn't have headaches, and didn't call up other women; I just sat there and cried. That was a big difference. The splat system does not work. I have to get used to there being no wall to attach myself to—it is not a happy prospect."

A few weeks before the second summer vacation the anticipated separation brought forth both intense anxiety and evidence of his newly acquired strengths to deal with it. It was only after this second summer break that patient and analyst could understand the full impact of Mr. I.'s intense reaction to the analyst's absence. He was anxiously wondering how it would be to resume. He felt "flooded with all sorts of feelings" that would have to be talked about, but "it would take ten hours a week for several weeks." He was much more aware of the analyst's absence this summer, he said, than during the previous one. He was amazed to recognize "that I was dependent on you in a different sense than I always thought: for the pressure valve you supply—getting release and feeling better, the regularity and all that—but now it was something more elusive, at the bottom of my life, like a basement or foundation of the building—the same way I used my family before I started analysis." He recalled that in some of his dreams he had intercourse with his sister and in some others he had a homosexual relationship with the analyst. He knew that these were his ways of "achieving repair" [of regaining the lost self-object] and preventing further painful regression. He remembered very clearly the beginning of the analysis—what his life was like then. "It is all alien to me now—scarey; I can recall dialogues we had two years ago. Gosh, the content of these dialogues, my productions—so different . . . the stability I now have in my day-to-day living." When the analyst and Miss T. were both gone, he had a "burning feeling to call somebody, grab a girl; nothing else counted, no pride, no dignity. It was more than loneliness, worse than hunger, deeper than hunger. There are some base feelings associated with it, getting crude with some girls." [The difference was clear and might as well have been interpretively acknowledged. The patient did not actually have to retreat to his old anal-sadistic control of "little-sister figures" to bolster his sense of self-cohesiveness in response to the danger of regressive fragmentation during the absence of the idealized analyst—the cement of his self in the transference.]

In the context of talking about how he had improved in his work and in his relations to friends, Mr. I. began to talk, with a sense of urgency, about marrying Miss T. The analyst rushed in to prevent a "rash acting-out"—a premature marriage—by focusing upon the urgency. It should have been clear to the analyst that there was no real indication that the patient contemplated immediate action. There would have been ample opportunity to see whether the talk about marriage was an emotional shifting away from the analyst in response to the earlier rebuff, whether it represented a real improvement and readiness for marriage, or was a mixture of both. Raising these issues shortly afterward gave Mr. I. the chance to reflect on his still ambivalent feelings, but re-affirmed that he could see himself "getting there, bit by bit," and that he measured his own improvement by how he felt about the prospect of marrying Miss T.

In a dream that followed, he was nasty and derogatory to an old man. His father criticized him for it and reminded him that his grandfather used to know this man. Whereupon Mr. I. felt overwhelmed with kindly, warm feelings and wanted to go up to the old man and hug him. He couldn't hug him and then just wanted to be able to talk to him.

Mr. I.'s associations and the broader context in which this dream occurred, revealed his intense longing for the idealized father-analyst. It pained him, the analyst acknowledged, whenever his admiring and loving feelings were not accepted, but seen only (mistakenly) as "the other side of the ambiva-lence." He was tearful in response and, for the first time, said with emotion: "I am really ready to love the old man, but he couldn't take it, he'd brush it off!" The analyst was also able to clarify then that his earlier focusing upon the "urgency" in connection with Mr. I.'s marriage plans, rather than upon the urgency with which he presented it, must have been related "to the rift in here, to my not accepting your admiring and loving feelings. This must also have added to your anguished retreat and made you turn to T. for consolation." [Invariably, such interventions, whenever the analyst could appropriately introduce them, even if often somewhat belatedly, with specif-ic and concrete references to the events within the analytic ex-perience, quickly re-established the disrupted transference.]

A "minor event" soon followed and deepened both the patient's and the analyst's understanding of the father-son relationship, which was re-experienced in the transference. The patient saw someone he knew leave the analyst's office. He pictured this man as the analyst's "more important new patient" and he felt "shoved to the side." It was in this context, during the last session of the week, that the analyst started to dismiss the patient ten minutes before the end of the session. Mr. I. experienced this "mistake" as a withdrawal of narcissistic support from the omnipotent, powerful analyst. Mr. I. may well have correctly gauged this turning away from him since the analyst actually was preoccupied with something else.

The next Monday, Mr. I. arrived ten minutes late for his session. He reported that he made an appointment to see one of his supervisors at the firm for the hour of his usual analytic session. He realized his "mistake" as he walked toward the supervisor's office, canceled the meeting, and arrived at the analyst's office ten minutes late. He made no reference to the analyst's parapraxis, but as he talked about the weekend, it was clear that he felt "painfully left out." When the connection between his own and the analyst's parapraxis was called to his attention, Mr. I. realized that he had "completely forgotten it." This again, unfortunately, led the analyst to focus upon Mr. I.'s ambivalent feelings, rather than to recognize the meaning of the parapraxis separately and then to acknowledge the patient's need to retain the idealized image of the analyst in spite of everything that would tend to interfere with it.

[In response to the breaks in empathy just presented, Mr. I. tried to make the analyst less important for himself and turned to T. A dream, in which he drove away in his car, focused on his attempts to turn away from the analyst. The question arose, then, whether these were expressions of the working-through process with awareness that he was internally growing away from the idealizing transference, or whether these were attempts to turn the passively experienced traumata into active, self-protective measures, especially against the anticipated traumatic interruption of the analysis at the end of the third year of analysis. There were, by now, also some indications that these attempts were reverberations of the genetically significant turning away from the mother (in response to mother's new preoccupation?) at the birth of the three-year-younger sister.]

In the ensuing weeks and months, Mr. I. began to read journals, books, and novels on evenings and on weekends. He also felt that his relationship with Miss T., through the many struggles "of inner distancing and then a comfortable returning to her" with more reliable and less selfish love, was leading to a consolidation. "We are practically married to each other, without the final step of legal commitment." He was at times silent in his sessions and once said: "I am not anxious, I feel contained within myself. I don't even feel that I am here today, but I know I can't just withdraw into my private fantasies." The analyst now felt that Mr. I. was "locking him out" and interpreted it as, in part, still a protection against "being suddenly locked out or dropped" by the analyst, but also as a way to test himself out on his own. Mr. I. replied: "If I am closing you out to avert being more closed out from you, I am not aware of it, but there is more depth to it now on the other side: I remember telling you a few weeks ago, when I saw your new patient leave your office, that you were available to me only four hours a week, the rest of the time I was locked out and you were far away from me. That was the genesis of all I am going through now. But as much as I have a need to be close to you" (i.e., to admire and love the analyst and to borrow his strength), "I also have a need to be far away from you" (i.e., on his own, not needing the analyst's strength).

This "need to be far away" from the analyst, indeed contained his "wish to get beyond the splat on the wall business" and to protect himself against a possible termination six to eight months hence, should his work require his leaving the area.

A dream soon followed which ushered in a phase of intense working through of the anticipated separation and the issue of "growing ready to get married." "I was in a convertible, parked in front of a building; maybe T. just went away for a minute. A little dog wanted to play or get hugged — lonesome in the winter — got a blanket, bit it playfully, but it scared me. Scared, reached over and grabbed T. and I woke up." He recalled some friends' dog last summer; the dog became depressed when they left him at the veterinarian for two weeks and he also got a bladder infection. His associations contained numerous references to leaving people. He recalled the analyst's interpretation of "my anticipating having to leave here and beginning to withdraw, and work on separation — that's absolutely true!"

As Mr. I. continued "to think about separations" the rest of the day and remembered "our intellectual conversation about them," he began to feel "nauseated, sick, all worked-up; on edge, almost frightened. Hard to believe it can make you feel so sick, so quickly." He recalled that he spent a week in a children's hospital at the age of five, but had trouble when left alone even before that. Whenever his parents left town, if they split up Mr. I. and his sister, it didn't work. But when they placed them together at the grandparents, everything was fine. He could not recall prior separation experiences of his own, but mentioned that his parents used to let his brother cry in his crib for an hour and it made him hate his father, "because he lay down the law. What right does a father have to throw a kid around. I was always afraid of the old man, he had a bad temper."

During the ensuing sessions Mr. I. continued to complain of anxiety, headaches, and "unbearable nausea." He had to leave work one day, went home and desperately tried to cure himself with a very long, hot shower. He thought of masturbating, but didn't feel "sexed-up." He often had the fantasy before of wanting to taste his own semen, "which does sound erotic, but at the very instant of orgasm I lose that desire." But now, as he thought of it, he felt it would be a "magic potion — it would cure me." So he went as far as swallowing some of his sperms and "felt gratified by it." "Then poured hot water on myself as if I were anointing myself. Had goose pimples and felt real orgasm in all five senses. It was a complete experience." He felt that two years ago he experienced "this same thing as a homosexual conflict, but now it was an oral need. I needed something — I'd suck on anything. I needed to give to myself because I felt deprived, I could suck a girl's breast, a penis, a thumb, a popsickle — anthing! I was taking in what was meant for T., grabbing it for myself. [Silence] This is interesting to me, but now a bit embarrassing also." The analyst responded: "It is most important for us to recognize that you could supply something to yourself. You controlled it. Therefore you couldn't lose it." Mr. I. immediately replied: "That's how it felt, exactly!" [An interpretation that was thought of, but not given at the time, was that Mr. I. wished to suck on the analyst's penis, to obtain the strength he longed for, but then, regressively, he turned to his own penis.]

Upon hearing that he would not have to leave the city for another year, Mr. I. bounced back quickly. He was overjoyed, but let down because the analyst did not respond with warmth and enthusiasm to his news. Nor was Miss T. happy at the prospect of "sharing me with you for another year." At this point Mr. I. had a cold, felt irritable on the couch, and recalled that he was "stuffed up and couldn't breathe as a kid, during the day and at night he had bronchial spasms—he missed 56 days of school in the first grade. His cold, general malaise, and hypochondriacal preoccupations continued for the next few sessions. The analyst finally reconstructed the events leading to this episode of regression with the reference to his failure to respond to the patient's expectation that he share the excitement about the news of his extra year's stay in the city. Mr. I. interrupted to exclaim: "Why didn't I say that? Most obvious of all."

For a short while thereafter he complained bitterly that he no longer wanted to be in analysis; it was too costly anyway, and he wanted to plan on getting married. He said one day that he thought he should quit, rather than seeing analysis through to its conclusion; he always did quit when it came to the hard part, he said, whether it was in relation to playing the piano, the trumpet, school, or girls. "Also, I really feel good underneath, why should I keep coming?"

By this time the analyst realized that what he took as Mr. I.'s repeated "threats" of getting married and his newly expressed wish to break off the analysis could no longer be adequately understood as defensive evasions of the regressive transference affects, wishes, and fantasies. Rather, these were Mr. I.'s ways of working them through, of achieving his internal separation and growing away from his childhood self-objects and their current representative, the analyst, in the idealizing transference. Such interpretations had a remarkable impact. They invariably led, sooner or later, to Mr. I.'s ability to analyze for himself those elements of his behavior and experiences that still carried their archaic affects, wishes, and fantasies, i.e., those that represented a regressive pull, rather than a progressive, forward movement. This allowed the analyst to be more empathetically in tune with Mr. I.'s inner experiences and to translate their meaning to him more accurately. Yet, at times, Mr. I. felt traumatically overstimulated and became self-conscious, ashamed, and inhibited. For instance, on one occasion the analyst further elaborated a point Mr. I. himself had made. He was at first gratified that the point he made "was taken so seriously," but then felt frightened: "Did you go overboard? Did you get carried away? When I think you are friendly, it's threatening." One day he was so afraid of having an erection on the couch as his response to overstimulation that he masturbated ahead of time to make sure it would not happen.

The period around the third Christmas was most unsettling because of some external events. Their gravity overtaxed Mr. I.'s narcissistic balance and temporarily absorbed most of his "emotional energies," but also demonstrated the solidity of what he had already accomplished. Most significantly, he was pleased with the fact that he discovered "deep feelings" of love and concern for his father, whom he was able to aid most meaningfully during his suddenly discovered, potentially fatal illness. His death wishes toward his father, his childish rage that his Christmas was going to be ruined, could be placed in proper perspective. He realized that when he first talked about the malignancy to the analyst, "it was as if I was reading it in a newspaper," but then he was able to experience its full impact. "He never listened to me," he said about his father with less bitterness than before, "but now he does; something important is going on—a drama."

During a brief Christmas vacation amidst all this turmoil, he also proposed to Miss T. off-handedly, in a very ambiguous and tentative fashion, rather than with "the appropriate romantic trappings." She was equally tentative: "We'd have to see." Mr. I.'s tentativeness and caution about some important moves related to his fear of not being "appropriately responded to." He had always tried to protect himself against being suddenly traumatized by disappointments in relation to an expected and hoped-for reponse. He wondered if he had to "propose" while away from the analyst, so that he did not have to report it if he were not responded to.

He missed the analyst. He knew this because of his head-aches and nausea from time to time. He had done "a lot of feeling sorry for myself; was anxious a lot too, and crying for myself, but also felt well, amazingly." He was afraid at one point that the analyst would never come back, and he had an anxiety dream in which he was frantically searching for the analyst and woke from it sweating profusely.

Mr. I. had an easier time getting reconnected after this brief vacation. He enjoyed being "secretly engaged," and he seemed to "try it on for size, test out how it felt" and what re-actions it would bring to the surface. He experienced success-es in many areas: in his work, in his relation with T., and with his family. Yet, in response to his successes, he felt over-stimulated and endangered, which was dramatized in a dream: "I was fishing in this pond or lake. There were lots of fish. I could see them. Cast the jitterbug and was bringing them in. Maybe my Dad was there, I don't know. Decided to go after something better. Very big fish. Caught it. Thought P. could go for something even better, caught a big turtle. Got scared and ran to the shore." His associations included some pleasant, early memories at a pond and later at a lake. "Getting a strike on every cast had a personal pleasure con-nected with it." He would have wanted his father to be there, to witness it and admire it. He wondered why all of these ex-citing experiences, including the ones in the dream were sur-rounded by anxiety. He realized that he wanted the analyst's praise and approval, but he was afraid that the analyst might debunk his various activities to keep himself calm, or on an even keel. This concern over controlling the rise of "inner tension and overexcitement" became a central issue for a prolonged period of time.

After he returned from a visit home, he was somewhat frantic and hypochondriacal. In the next few sessions he spoke slowly and deliberately as if he had to keep everything under conscious control. When the analyst called this to his attention, he said, "I am aware of it. This may be a need to control you, too, to make sure you hear me, but I am also controlling your participation, guarding against too much from you." Mr. I. asked directly (for the first time) what the analyst thought of this interpretation. The analyst agreed with it, and added that apparently Mr. I needed and wanted to accomplish the "repair" at his own pace, in his own time, and dreaded the possibility of the analyst's nonempathic (sexually stimulating) intrusion. Patient and analyst readily extended this interpretation to a broad reconstruction of the past, unempathic parental intrusions (especially mother's) and father's inability to listen, but to treat the family with his anecdotes instead (i.e., indulge in his own exhibitionistic needs and rebuff the patient's). There was no attempt or ability on his parents' part (even now) to gauge what Mr. I. could comfortably cope with. He saw himself "stronger and more on the giving side now" with his parents. His current, somewhat fragmented state seemed to have occurred in reaction to his considerable improvement; a reaction to the fact that he had to face losing his unique position with the analyst sooner or later, as he once lost a similar position with his parents when his younger siblings came along. "One of my problems is separation—if I lose somebody, the anxiety I get is that I might as well be dead." Unresponsiveness, whether from T. or the analyst, "fitted into the same category." During the ensuing weekend Mr. I. was hoping to run into the analyst somewhere in the city: ". . . more important than usual, because I was half-dead Thursday. It would have been important for you to see me—that I was alive. Just for you to see me would have been an important communication."

[During the next few weeks Mr. I. succeeded in achieving greater mastery over his separation experiences from the ana-

lyst and he demonstrated his progressively increasing autonomy. From time to time he was still anxious and regressively
turned to sister-figures to replenish lost self-esteem. The
crucial difference was that initially these were acted out in
actual sadistic exploits with women; subsequently in conscious
fantasies, but at this stage of the analysis almost exclusively in
his dreams.]

The longings to have the analyst available on weekends
were expressed in erotic dreams involving his sister or his many
childhood sweethearts, with one or two of whom he had some
early, heavy necking and petting. By now he knew that these
dreams portrayed the reappearance of his old ways of coping
with emptiness and loneliness. It occurred, at this point, that
Mr. I. was away on a short trip and the analyst did not have a
chance to announce to him ahead of time that he would be
absent from the office on Washington's birthday. As he expressed his fury about the (to him) abrupt cancellation, he
warned the analyst to give him considerable advance notice
of termination when the time comes. He then announced that
this was the 400th session: "A special occasion, yet it gives me
an empty feeling." The analyst, referring to the "abrupt" cancellation, said that it must again have felt arbitrary to Mr. I.;
he must have felt at the mercy of the analyst, who could "cut
him off" anytime. "I don't want to be at your mercy," he responded angrily. "I associate it with being a damned fool. I
take it seriously [meaning his analytic experience] and somebody else doesn't [meaning his analyst]." Not being taken seriously was the most painful treatment anyone could accord
him. He recognized that in response he felt "depressed, lonely,
empty, and dead inside" on Washington's birthday. He
needed "some exciting sensations, some kicks, to get me out of
it." The hot shower was not enough and then he fell asleep,
exhausted. After a brief silence he added: "If I perceive you as

becoming uninterested, I lose my complete sense of whole-ness — then I need more stimulation to make up for it." For the next few days Mr. I.'s feelings of emptiness continued, further intensified by the fact that the analyst did not celebrate the 400th session. As the patient berated the analyst for this, he felt dizzy on the couch. "It must have seemed to you a very in-sensitive rejection," the analyst finally said, "that I did not share your mood to celebrate, or at least recognize your mood; you acknowledged the anniversary, I didn't, so it was all the more painful." "I almost cried when you recalled all the feelings for me. If I felt rejected here last Wednesday I must have felt it lots of times elsewhere. How much I must demand someone's 100 per cent constant attention!"

He reflected on the shifting of his concerns at some of the landmarks "around the 200th hour my own attempts of not spilling everything everywhere were in focus; around the 300th hour it was my finding new gratifications outside of here; and now, around the 400th hour, the focus is that nobody is coming up to me saying 'I am really pleased with your prog-ress.' What will it be at the 500th and 600th hours?"

His old sleep disturbance returned briefly. He described himself, in a reflective mood, as a globe with a defect on it like the Grand Canyon. "In analysis you try to work on it, excavate the surface of it so it can heal in. It's comforting that some-body, your analyst, knows how sick you are and he is not alarmed, not scared, not discouraged, but optimistic of what can be done about it." Then he became more anxious: "What if I suspect that even deeper defects are there and my analyst does not know they are there? I can't tell him because even he might get discouraged. But I don't want to conceal that."

[The struggle for autonomy, for greater independence and self-confidence as he moved away from the idealized-ana-lyst in a variety of ways became the focus of the working-through process. Mr. I. needed the analyst's empathic responses to this struggle, i.e., its interpretative recognition. He could now actively demand and express with great precision what he needed, whenever the analyst failed to understand him. The problem then arose that for a while the analyst was much more able to be empathic with Mr. I.'s need for merger and closeness and not yet empathic enough with his concurrent wish for autonomy, and more specifically, with Mr. I.'s oscillating struggle between archaic merger and separateness-independence. Mr. I. wanted to be sure that the analyst understood his needs that emanated from his "psychic defect." But he also wanted the analyst to understand he was beginning to enjoy his newly acquired independent functioning.

It became clear around these issues that in his childhood his many illnesses drew parental and grandparental attention to Mr. I.; but he was also "brutally" sent away to camp for whole summers between the ages of five or six to ten, which he resented. His mother's hold on Mr. I. was still evident in many ways. Strikingly anachronistic, for example, was that he had sent his dirty laundry home ever since he left for college and graduate school, and his mother regularly returned the clean laundry with a copy of Playboy magazine—as he had already mentioned in the diagnostic session. The analyst only recently learned that all this had stopped at about the beginning of the third year of the analysis.

Every attempt at moving further away from the analyst exposed to Mr. I. the insufficiency of his independent stimulus barriers and fostered the recognition that his idealizing transference served as a protective shield until he himself could develop and solidify his own. He could now again easily be traumatically overstimulated, confused, and hypochondriacally preoccupied, especially in response to sudden unexpected events involving his analyst.

Mr. I. had the increasing capacity to reflect upon the

precipitating events leading to his states of fragmentation, once he recovered his narcissistic balance. At such points, after some interpretive interaction, he would reach a new level of insight, and a more lasting capacity to maintain his own narcissistic equilibrium.]

Following the recognition of his "Grand Canyon-defect" Mr. I. said: "With this over- and understimulation we are down to something basic in me. When I first came in I complained of unexplained mood swings, now I know it's related to this. But I can keep it within a much narrower range now." He registered with satisfaction that "sex is not for relief now or for coping with my anxieties. It is an expression of an urge, which is a much nicer sensation. But when I am for weeks without it and then get the urge, it's hard to separate it from loneliness."

The analyst's unusually early intervention in one of the sessions that followed led to an unexpected psychoeconomic imbalance. It was quickly recognized, but the impact lasted until the beginning of the next session. Mr. I. was "sick, expecting a cold—which I know I won't get—the usual nausea and headaches, but milder." He recalled that the turning point was the premature interruption during the previous session. "I came in wanting to say that the cycle came full swing and I was going to get back to feeling in one piece again, some work was going to be done. I recuperated, was quite ambitious and not symptomatic. I elected just to say a few casual things first to feel at ease: feeling good, no urgency—and then you moved in. This overstimulation and understimulation is a major theme—a year ago I had an intense period being a splat on the wall. How are these two feelings related? When you are clinging so tightly, then you don't have to be over- or under-stimulated. You just hang on, let the wall worry about what's to worry about. But when you get free of the wall you have to deal with the currents directly. Are we just going around in a circle, without getting any further?"

Mr. I., in trying to understand why he reacted so intensely to the analyst's interruption of his slow, tentative, and deliberate easing into the session the other day, used some revealing metaphors: "When I am talking with a need to talk, there's got to be a listener. But the imagery is different this time, almost sexual: Two planes, one is refueling up in the air. In this contact—some sort of intercourse—they cannot be disturbed. It's not only necessary to refuel, but when this is going on, the aircraft is even more vulnerable to winds and currents. It is in great danger. When flying together in unity the radar could not detect them as two—the unity was there. In thinking of that, all of a sudden I remembered dreams I have had recurrently—always being interrupted; intercourse, interruptions." The analyst focused on the repetitively attempted mastery of the traumatically painful interruptions and on the need for undisturbed refueling in the merger transference. "Intercourse in these dreams was unity," Mr. I. said, "and interruption would mess it up—sexual not in a physical, but spiritual sense." At this point in the session, Mr. I. said he needed a "rest period." He felt it was a "great hour, good communication—really putting it together—makes me almost ecstatic and I begin to feel overstimulated. If we carry it further I'll ruin it. It fits so nicely. I don't want you to say something stupid now or me. Neither of us should ruin it."

The analyst recognized and interpreted the various ways in which the unity Mr. I. needed to experience had recently been disrupted. His response was lengthy: "True. To use a sexual analogy: Once you made the contact and had the experience you need to withdraw and recuperate and get back to earth. After intercourse, the couple in bed, smoking or reading—there is togetherness, but also a feeling of some sort of isolation. Regroup as individuals. After you have had intercourse, you can't keep having it, and it might even be unpleasant. I am sure this is right. Closeness and distance. Close, but not too close—in terms of verbal communication, not sex; once you feel understood and that need is gratified, for me it's a happy medium, a balance. Too much understood is as uncomfortable as not being understood."

The analyst could now say to Mr. I. that he wanted to maintain this unity (in the transference) when he felt he needed it; and that he wanted to move away and feel his separateness and independence too, whenever he felt he was able to. After confirming and expanding on this interpretation until the end of the session, Mr. I. found the transition from recumbent to upright position too rapid; he moved slowly and with special care. The analyst was much more quiet for a time, sensing that Mr. I. needed to consolidate his gains pretty much on his own.

[This delicate balance had to be carefully maintained, and the analyst was, on the whole, able to restrain himself from moving in unnecessarily or prematurely with his own interpretations. Mr. I. experienced his successes, including the insights he had independently gained, as frightening because they also increased the distance between himself and his analyst. Could his newly acquired inner strength and increased self-esteem be maintained once he left the analyst?]

He complained with some anxiety one day: "You are interfering with God's universe figuratively, by encouraging all of this to happen [i.e., his regressive transference]; you are allowing me to build a life—castle, dream world—that's built on ethereal foundations, that would leave me holding the bag. Like I am feeling very comfortable while I am coming here, but what would happen afterward? I only know what I felt like before, and if without you I'd be like that, I'd screw up everything again. What if my frustrations with you led me to latch on to T.?" This worried him for a while, especially the idea that it was his longing for the idealized analyst: "That may have been the genesis of my interest in T." He then thought of his indiscriminate relationship with women during the early phase of his analysis (and prior to that), and he was now, retrospectively, very much ashamed of it. He recalled that he could not enjoy sex then because he was so sick. The other day he thought: "If I could go back to three years ago, just for one day, it might be fun."

[In his dreams and fantasies Mr. I. was concerned that he was gaining strength by taking it away from the analyst. There was simultaneously a need to "debunk" the idealized analyst and to build up his own ideals and thus feel his own strength. He was afraid that the analyst would not be able "to take it."

There were some hints at the genetic precursors: Mr. I. may well have turned to his father during his mother's pregnancy (he recently dreamed of a tumor in the belly of a woman) without being able to evoke the necessary responses to maintain his narcissistic balance. There was some indication that father could not turn affectionately to the sickly child until his early teens, when Mr. I. was no longer chronically ill.]

As his successes continued, Mr. I. kept trying to understand why he needed to undermine his own accomplishments. "It is because of my fear of losing your approval, or the unity we talked about, or being the splat on the wall. If I am too aggressive, too much of a leader, it would cut me off the supply of empathy which I need. I obtain it better if I am at the bottom of the pack, rather than on top."

The analyst reminded Mr. I. of his fear that his gain would be at the analyst's expense. This elicited a striking, painful, not so early memory: "I always had a funny feeling around my father that if I was aggressive or forceful, he would not be the center of attention. At my college graduation festivities, father felt lost and quickly said 'Let's get out of here; you've had enough celebration.' He didn't rise to the occasion—his true color showed through." Mr. I. continued to see his father as childish and needy, competitive with his children for narcissistic sustenance. He recognized, with some resignation in his tone of voice: "My whole life needs an acknowledgment to know I exist; I always need a stamp of approval."

Mr. I. for the first time looked forward to his summer vacation—the third since he started his analysis—with pleasure. He and his fiancée were going to visit both sets of parents together and talk seriously about their marriage plans. This was the best vacation Mr. I. ever had. He was able to experience and enjoy every aspect of the trip; he felt more involved with everything and everyone. He woke up only one day "with my syndrome" (the headaches, general malaise, and hypochondriacal preoccupations). "When the family started to bug me, I became a bit overstimulated, started to control it, and did." He felt "whole," strong, secure, and did not need any confirming responses from his parents or other people, and just a little bit from T. Their sexual life was most satisfying, and they decided to get married late in the summer.

On the return trip, however, Mr. I. became aware of some homosexual fantasies. And although the first week of vacation was conflict-free, as it was time to think of returning, he became "slightly symptomatic: Must have had to do with feelings about coming back to see you. On the surface I was bragging to myself—no feelings about you, wonderful, got away for two weeks—but this was true only for the first week. The second week I had the urge to share everything with you—consciously laughable, but probably intense feelings about coming back to see you. That's how I explain these homosexual fantasies or longings." All this was accompanied by recurrent, frustrating dreams of failure in some endeavor. Mr. I. thought that these dreams seemed to undo his "sense of terrific success" during his two weeks away. Not only did he get along well with T.'s family, achieve "new heights in my sexual relationship with T.," but he was not too upset when mother gave a "wet blanket" response to his announcement of his marriage plans. His father was more positive, and he was surprised at that.

Upon return to his work he quickly settled in with a more creative and committed attitude. He was surprised that he did not need to be at the center of attention all the time. He now realized that he was conflicted about coming back to the analysis "and getting reinvolved." He reported a dream about his father. "The old man said he'd break my back, and I stood up to him. I'd take him on any time, beat him up. He told me he didn't think I could. I told him to put his arm out and I crushed it. Better not mess around with me, I'll beat you up — and he let up."

After talking some time about his father's illness, his own successes, he felt the dream indicated: "I am strong now, on my own, and you can't push me around."

In discussing his marriage plans, he was cautious at first, for fear that the analyst would be disappointed and would also give him a "wet blanket" response, but then he continued to look at his plans in a strong, self-assertive manner and also remained quite open to analyzing them.

There was no anticipatory "cracking of the wall, threatening the splat" as the analyst's vacation was about to begin. During the last few sessions, Mr. I. was somewhat disengaged, low-key, and calmer than he had ever been approaching a long separation. He was clearly aware of the difference. "I am not happy being so involved now, because our sessions are coming to a screeching halt. I am probably working through termination again, like I did last fall before I knew I could stay another year. When I get back in the fall I will know it's the last chapter. This summer is my last rehearsal for the big finish." He soon wondered: "When would be the best time to finish analysis? I am not ready for a definite answer on it yet. If I have to leave town early summer, perhaps I should terminate in March. I will have 120 sessions left then when I come back in the fall, enough for one chapter—maybe not. Well, anyhow, I am the healthiest I have ever been on this couch before. Thinking recently of you more as a human being, almost just a human being."

Unexpectedly, however, during the last few sessions, the familiar reactions to separation appeared. The last session was quite intense. He was "wound up, excited; everything suddenly went to pot—hard to believe." His hemorrhoids began bleeding, he had diarrhea, nausea, headaches. He thought he would not make it through the day at work: "I am disorganized and in a fog." Tension mounted, until he translated what it all meant: "I'll miss you! Couldn't say it directly, got to say it with symptoms." "To avoid embarrassment and shame," the analyst added. "I feel like crying now—I could cry outside of here at a time like this, but not in here. 'I'll miss you' is too real, too familiar, too personal. I'd never say that to anybody! Would I say that to my father? No, I'd say, 'Don't forget your wallet, your keys—write when you get there.' I might say I *will* miss you. Would I say that to my mother? I might. . . . I hate leaving the last session. I should say then I'll miss you and have a good time! I probably wish your plane would crash, but I shouldn't say that. Maybe you are superstitious. If you are my analyst, how can you be gone—what kind of analyst is that?"

In the fall, the analysis resumed as scheduled, and Mr. I. reported that everything went well, even better than expected:

"I missed you, but I was glad you were not there!" He came back reluctantly, he said, and felt strong resistance against "getting involved again." The analyst's silence was now screaming at him, "Get down on your knees, Buddy, and beg in the mud, and admit you need me and want to get involved." To continue in analysis felt degrading. The interruption underlined the fact that the analyst was a stranger to him.

[It took only a short time for Mr. I. to settle back into the analysis and to resume his struggle for greater independence from the idealized analyst and for the autonomy of this self-esteem regulation. There was further working through of the fear that if he became too autonomous, he would not be able to merge again with the idealized parent imago.]

He knew there was more to be accomplished. He said (for the first time in these words) that he was "feeling *idealistic* about new horizons in work, the new car, new books, and more learning; to accomplish and to do means more to me than ever. These used to be empty slogans."

He soon realized, through an encounter in the waiting room, that another engineer he knew fairly well had started in analysis. He was visibly upset and said it was a "degradation of this couch, a blasphemy on analysis, like a profanization of the church; a sacrilege, makes a mockery of analysis." Just at the time when he wondered what kind of feelings the analyst might have had about him, there came this blow. "I am pissed off, not moving over on this couch for another God-damned sibling; don't need another younger brother in this outfit. I am beginning to appreciate the power of the unconscious." The next dream pointed to the earlier suspected genetic significance of his mother's pregnancy (tumor-in-the-belly dream): "A nightmarish dream: Teaching some students. Then they were no longer students but pregnant women. Teaching them exercises they didn't want to do. Then only a few remained. I am being taught how to dribble basketball by a coach: slowly, and grab it with your hand." He may have dreamed this or something like this more than once last night. It was frustrating, over and over again. "The plot of the dream: I am confident at the start, I begin teaching. Lose my pupils and end up being a pupil myself — gradual descent. One of my defenses against not being confident is humility — a defense against lack of confidence. Last few weeks I had a success problem especially in relation to you, trying to beat you and get free. All these mysteries about secret stuff, seeing you naked, secret things you do." Analyst: "Any connection between the dream and your feelings about Mr. L.?" Mr. I.: "I just got some tears in my eyes when you asked that question. A feeling of being a star, and losing it, ending up at the bottom of the barrel; in a passive role, in a frustrated position, having gotten nowhere. Learning and being a pupil is frustrating. I got a fear about Mr. L. that he'll be a better patient, taller, more masculine, aggressive, smarter, more settled. He is nowhere as regressed as I was. I am not the center of the world, I have learned that here, and it's helpful. Takes some of the pressures off. But I have stupid fantasies. You started with a new patient for my benefit, because I am at that stage that it could be helpful to face competition." After some further fantasies, all designed to retain him at the center of attention, he returned to the dream. The analyst wondered whether "the many pupils leaving the teacher" wasn't our frequently recognized reversal. It was one teacher (analyst), who turned away from him and started with another patient as it had become definite that Mr. I. would leave by next summer. He was quiet for a while, then said, "What would you do with the pregnant women, then?" Analyst: "What would you do?" Mr. I. immediately thought of his mother's pregnancy with his younger sister; the next sibling, a brother, was born when he was ten

years old. "Both experiences meant something to me, the
latter more conscious, the former not. Girls do get more attention. Two of my early memories have to do with the birth of
my brother and sister." After describing and reflecting on
both memories, he wondered: "How could I have felt de-
throned?" During the next hour Mr. I. returned to the dream:
"After yesterday's session a new association hit me: You have
the pregnant woman in the dream, who is going to have a
baby; whose love will have to be shared by two kids. Instead of
being an analyst, I was a teacher. I reversed you also, and you
were a pupil, so you are the pregnant woman." The analyst
used Mr. I.'s reaction to Mr. L., and his transference interpretation of the dream, to reconstruct how Mr. I. must have
felt when his siblings were born. How painful it must have
been when he had to "move over" and make room for his sister,
then for his brother (and somewhat later for his second
brother) and thus lose being the center of his mother's attention. There was a very long silence. When he spoke again, he
said that he had some flashbacks to his childhood, like a
movie: "How they (parents) used not to understand; go, say
hello to so and so; go, say such and such in social situations. I
remember always trying to get attention. Lying in bed one
time, banished to the babies' room — it was a demotion, I was
displaced [ages four and five]; I could not sleep there. I was
playing with a wrist watch. . . . Then I hit my sister with a
ping-pong ball gun. Father broke the gun on his knee and
screamed; mother tried to protect me."

Within a short time Mr. I. reported increasing rapport
with his co-workers, saying: "Peers no longer bother me as
they used to; I feel more comfortable with them." At the same
time, he was also frightened at the prospect of being traumatized if he too rapidly "debunked" the idealized analyst. He
said: "An anchor is good, when you are insecure, but I am
ready to move. So this gives the whole relationship a new

quality." He reacted with depression and lassitude over the next few days to his wanting to be so rapidly and totally independent. The analyst's somewhat lengthier attempts at reconstruction he experienced as overstimulating and disruptive. He began his recent sessions with brief silences, "to control you, to make sure you will shut up, and don't ask any questions. If you do, my motor gets wound up and runs; then thousands of associations crowd into my head."

[It became abundantly clear that Mr. I., faced concretely with the final separation in about one year, was making every effort to become the regulator of his own narcissistic tensions. It took some time to realize that it must have seemed to him as if the analyst was trying to retain his formerly central position as a regulator of Mr. I.'s self-esteem in the transference.]

As Mr. I. insisted on attaining full control, he was puzzled by a memory from age six. "I was at camp and did the dumbest things. On arrival they took away all our stuff; they asked us to turn in all our money. I had two pennies and didn't want to turn those in. I had to have them; they gave me the greatest comfort. But I was also afraid to keep them. Told the counselor I had two pennies. He laughed and didn't understand the value of those pennies."

"We could understand it now," the analyst said, "as your wanting to go it alone, hold onto something comforting, something that is entirely your own; almost as if saying: 'I will soon have to do it for myself, and I am preparing to take over. Don't interfere with that, be quiet!' Holding on to those pennies must have given you some stability. But just as then, now, too, you are afraid of being ridiculed for insisting on being so self-reliant." Mr. I. agreed and commented that it felt much better to him when the analyst talked at the end of the hour, as he did just now.

Fear of overstimulation was another dominant current concern, especially in the sessions, but during the preceding weekend at home, too. He had put his hi-fi equipment at its loudest to escape his own mind, to drown out some of his fantasies. "One fantasy ties it up—some day people will find out how really great I am. Analysis meant to me, long before I started, that somebody else had to know all of this." He recalled that early in analysis he wanted the analyst to look upon him as "some special member of your family—an unusual endeavor—a great patient, you were honored to take him on; or so sick that you with your special talent were asked to take on."

In this context it was easier to appreciate Mr. I.'s need to "celebrate" his 500th analytic hour (since a similar need at the 400th hour was unempathically overlooked). Mr. I. now wondered whether we would make it to hour 600. Then, "Why don't we just make it arbitrarily six hundred. Five hundred and ninety-nine would kill me, 600 has more sparkle." He knew that he would be terribly embarrassed if this anniversary were really celebrated by the analyst. Celebrating it would be wrong, and overlooking it would be wrong.

He talked about bringing in his diaries of age eight and reading from them to the analyst. His old, grandiose self-concepts emerged related to intense and pervasive childhood loneliness and lack of response to him, which both analyst and patient could now meaningfully tie to a variety of compulsive early sexual activities (from age eleven or twelve on). "My life's history has been an almost continuous search for something sexual. I was morbidly interested in parties, kissing games, hiding behind the bushes with girls and fondling them. A desire you can fulfill, but a greed you never can! Why does a guy in the fifth grade have to be so preoccupied with sex, thinking more of it than most people? Was I running after something I wasn't getting from my parents?"

[The archaic grandiose fantasies served the same function as did his diaries, to confirm him to himself. His ability to relinquish this old grandiosity and replace it with realistic self-esteem was now hinted at, with his wish to share the diaries. This sharing was in effect their relinquishment. The isolated preciousness of the early grandeur seems to diminish or fade considerably when it is shared in an adult setting.]

Shift to a Mirror Transference and Progress toward Termination

As the analyst succeeded in being less intrusive, Mr. I. first welcomed it, but then became restless and complained about the analyst's withdrawal. He attributed his depression, disinterest in his work, and his general apathy to his having to face the fact of termination. Then he reported "another idea, on a fantasy level. "I was feeling empty; heartburn, stomach trouble. I had the fantasy that somehow if I could—fasten your seatbelt, it's such a deep fantasy that it loses something when I put it into words—if I could swallow a big penis, half erected, that kind of texture—if I could keep it suspended between my brain and my stomach, it would make me feel better. [See p. 19 for an earlier statement which then seemed to be abrupt and "out of context."] Weird. Somehow, if you were to pull your penis out of me, I would fall apart. I would be a hollow shell. I am shaped like one of those tiles up there with an indentation. That indentation has to be filled up continuously, with you or with penises. That is part of how I feel when I am depressed; it goes along with separation and termination" (cf. Kohut, 1971, p. 72, n4.).

Mr. I. finally did bring in his diaries a few days later and read some passages to the analyst. They chronicled in great detail the events of the day, apparently omitting none, and were reminiscent of the way he presented himself in the analy-

sis initially, and of the nightly letters he talked about which he
sent home from college for years. The analyst noticed an interesting element. There were repeated references to anniver-
saries. For example: "Three years ago today I had my third
tooth pulled," as if to account for and to maintain the continuity and cohesiveness of his fragmentation-prone self.

Mr. I. offered these samples "as background for showing
you more later. I can feel the me in them, almost as if it were
today." He also felt that it was silly to bring them in and to
focus upon the silly details of years ago. He made some reference to his early experience in the analysis, when he brought
in a picture and, later on, a picture album.

The analyst reinterpreted that experience now by saying
that he did not understand then what Mr. I. was trying to express with what he brought in, and he responded to it inadequately by not wanting to see it. He no longer thought that
was appropriate and the task would have been to understand it.

There was a very long silence. "I am lying here, experiencing all these feelings in response to your response. Lying
here quietly and observing time. Happiness, tearfulness,
respect for you to say you were wrong—that's big to do that—a
feeling of being reunited again with the neurotic but nice kid I
was then, because you said it was O.K. That kid was just let
out of jail." It was difficult for him to hear from the analyst
that he was wrong, because that was not what his father would
have said. He also felt now that it was not a major mistake,
only a minor one. He recalled that he needed to bring everything about his life to the analyst's attention then, "As if that
were the main task and I would have been tempted to read
them all, even if that would have taken a whole year." The
analyst could now respond by saying that it was indeed the
task then to bring into the analysis what Mr. I. experienced as
a child, and to understand it. His diaries seemed to have

served an important purpose, which could finally be understood.

A few days later Mr. I. brought another sample of his diaries and again read some selections. He felt, in response to a question by the analyst "that it is the same person writing and recounting the events, who is in the analysis, who has to comment on everything; ritualistic, compulsive, to cement down each day and then dismiss it. It must have been a security blanket, a way of assuring meaningfulness." As the analyst was searching for an answer to why now, Mr. I. interrupted him: "The most important thing is, I was very reluctant to bring these in and yet also felt a strong need to do it. That's where we can start." The analyst agreed.

[However, he failed Mr. I., in one important respect at this moment. He became somewhat intrusive with his interest in the content of the diaries and in what they revealed about Mr. I.'s childhood. He was interested in the contemporary document. Thus, he did not recognize the importance to Mr. I. of sharing the diaries with his analyst as a great step in parting from old, isolated, secret, grandiose aspects of himself.]

The next morning Mr. I. reported a two-part dream (cf. Kohut, 1971, pp. 159-160). Part 1: "On a dock fishing, caught a big fish still on the pole, carried it into the cottage to show it to Dad, and probably to Mom too. Expected him to say, 'Good fish.' He said you can clean it! I didn't want to; just wanted to show it. The fish then shriveled up a bit as a result of the conversation." Part 2: "The Government has crucified one of my friends, G.C., for some very un-American behavior. I saw him on the cross, hugging a statue of Jesus. Then it was Jesus on the cross; he was so big, splendid, great, the downfall of this man on the cross added to the splendor of the occasion. He was suddenly slumping, the muscles suddenly relaxing, and he was dying." Mr. I. woke up and immediately interpreted the first part of the dream: "I brought the diaries to you, and instead of you saying, 'It's very interesting,' you asked all those questions. I thought, no sense in bringing them in, you didn't admire them." He wondered whom he was crucifying in the second part of the dream. Since G.C. often reminded him of the analyst, it would follow that he crucified the analyst, but since he himself often identified with G.C., it could be that he crucified himself. He then focused on the arbitrariness with which the Government can do such a thing, if they did it to G.C. The analyst (using Mr. I.'s associations) focused on the fact that perhaps the destruction of the archaic greatness, both his own and that of the idealized analyst, was depicted in the dream.

[It became clear only subsequently that in expecting approval or praise, but having been rebuffed instead, the patient retreated from a high-level mirror transference to an archaic merger fantasy. The interpretation should have centered around this regression, including the precipitant experience.]

The next day Mr. I. again contemplated the end of the analysis. "What if I think of something to say and can't the next day, because there is no next day? Or a weekend that would last forever? What if I have a sequel to that dream? Would I call you? I don't know what to expect." He surveyed his experiences in analysis, offered a kind of summary, as if he were writing it in his diary. The analyst wondered what put Mr. I. into the mood of the survey and the anticipation of the end. "The way you responded to my dream. It put me in a good mood. I didn't know how to deal with all that crap from the weekend. I needed a little feedback, and you responded, you took it all seriously, so I felt good. The survey? The end?

We are about half-way point in the year, termination is almost upon us. I am now looking beyond. I throw out ropes to future mountains, to avoid muds and creeks; winding things up in six months is not a long time."

[This pretermination phase, during which Mr. I.'s idealizing transference continued to occupy center stage in interpretive focus for a while, saw a decided shift in the nature of the transference. First, in brief episodes and then, more consistently and with greater continuity and cohesiveness, a high-level mirror transference (the mirror transference proper, cf. Kohut, 1971,) was mobilized, variously manifested in its higher and lower forms, and worked through in the termination phase of the analysis.

The patient's pride in his independence and his feeling of greater equality with the analyst in many respects (after considerable working through of the idealizing transference) seemed to go hand and hand with the increasing manifestation of the archaic grandiose self in the mirror transference proper, with regressions to more archaic twinship and merger transferences in response to unempathic responses from the analyst. However, these were mostly within therapeutic bounds now, in the sense that even with temporary regressions and fragmentations they led to further insights and to transmuting internalizations.]

Each session was "a little show, a little production," and Mr. I. felt again that the analyst's entrance into it might mess it up. But there was a further nuance: "When you enter as part of the production, you mess it up; but when you don't enter as an appreciative audience, then you mess it up too." An example occurred when Mr. I. handed over a check to the analyst personally, for the first time, and the analyst said: "OK," rather than "Thank you." Mr. I. commented on it early in the same session, and the rest of the hour indicated that he wanted the approval and admiration of the proud father (or mother) for his earning more money and handing over the check proudly. The analyst was an "unappreciative audience" in the mirror transference. The mild consequences appeared in the next few sessions, and the analyst was able to point out to Mr. I. that he was disappointed when the analyst did not respond with more positive acknowledgment to his giving him the check personally. (The analyst was momentarily taken aback, since Mr. I. had had difficulty in talking about money for a long time, let alone handing over the check personally.) Mr. I. responded calmly at first, but then became hypomanically overstimulated, talkative, and tried to prevent the analyst from talking. He clearly sexualized his tensions by talking about being a "leg man" (interested in girls' legs) "as a fetish almost, maybe a phallic symbol, really a penis, disguised because they are girls' legs." He had some afterthoughts about the incident with the check: "Maybe you are so rich that my check does not matter to you. I can't make an impression." He also added that the upcoming fourth Christmas vacation, "the last Christmas in this analysis," with the background of the "termination in the air" caused him this "minor turmoil."

This led to the question: "When should we finish up? Would I get more out of termination if I didn't leave my job and this city at the same time?" He wanted his choice to be most therapeutic and most comfortable and least upsetting and overwhelming. "I want to experience it in a dose that's therapeutic." The analyst responded that what would be most productive and least disruptive would have to be discovered by the two of them jointly. Mr. I. remained thoughtful and silent for a while and then said: "Likely connection between termination and what's been going on deep in my mind is fear of death, death of my father, the death of my omnipotence, which could protect me." This session ended with his comtemplative, somber mood, and ushered in the termination phase (including the brief, intense, but fruitful anticipation of the impending final Christmas).

The Working Through of the Mirror Transference in the Termination Phase

The termination phase brought forth an intensification of the kind of sensitivity that had been present throughout, but most recently in relation to the events surrounding the first direct handing over of the check to the analyst. Mr. I. realized that he felt so wound up that he could barely stand anything. He wished he could lie down in a room full of cotton, where he would be protected against overstimulation and its consequences of falling apart. "I haven't been as neurotic as I am now in more than a year. It's the rug-being-pulled-out-of-under-me feeling. Oh, my God, all this stuff we haven't analyzed. I need another ten years. Must be a termination phenomenon . . . seems like everything is related to separation." There followed a lengthy dream with a colorful ceremony in a synagogue, including ballet dancers and a circus. The principal ballerina dying in her dressing room, won't be able to finish the ceremony: "I perceive you as loss of a father during the next vacation [within a week or ten days], but I don't feel as sick today as I anticipated. I could cry, end of the week, end of the year, end of the analysis. You never said when we would finish. My parents never had all the goodies, now I found these things in you—not all the time, but sometimes. I will never have it again. I am suddenly supposed to go through adolescence in six months. How am I going to graduate—be Bar-mitzvah—the synagogue ceremony in the dream—I can't go that fast. Never be able to have this again. It's corny to say, but it's a sad state of affairs. Is that why I have these homosexual dreams which turn into incestuous dreams with my mother or sister or old girl friends? Sexualized—I just remembered the first year of analysis. You went away for Christmas and I called B., my old girl friend. You said at the next session I was lonesome. That was the first good interpretation that made sense. The legs were in focus then—the phallic-fetish substitutes."

The day before the beginning of the Christmas vacation, he said "My whole problem right now is related to separating from you for Christmas and then forever. If I need you and don't want to admit it, then I get the headaches. If you talk, then that further humiliates me because I realize how much I need you. Then I get worse and worse." He was rather kind and understanding in relation to his wife's pre-Christmas problems, her crabbiness and nagging, "by reacting to her anxiety beneath it all and not to the surface." As he elaborated on some of the details, the analyst remarked that Mr. I. was behaving toward his wife as he expected the analyst to behave toward him. Thus, his frequent emergency solution appeared (identification with the analyst, but now with the more positive aspects) in response to the vacation separation and the impending termination.

"Gee, I knew what you were going to say—you said it last June, too, and it clicked with me. I could have told it all to you." He then pulled a sheet of paper from his pocket and said, "I might as well read this to you—it's not unlike what we are talking about—I put it in here several days ago. It has to do with what I should be, my ego ideal."

The notes he read were started in college and continued in graduate school. "I was searching for where I was going, what to be, what to do; searching for a meaningful and worthwhile life, filled with creativity, music, and social conscience—never could achieve it, but my grandiosity never permitted me to think that I couldn't accomplish it." He felt that he now had another chance, a more realistic chance. He also wondered why he had to write it all down and add to it from time to time for five years—but not since he had been in analysis. "There is a lot of security in putting it all down."

Mr. I. had anticipated with a great deal of excitement the reunion with the analyst after the vacation. The vacation days (other than those he and his wife spent at home with his parents) had been "drab and colorless." He recalled that the night of his last session he had his most severe hemorrhoidal bleeding, and he was terribly scared. Only later did he realize that the day before had been the anniversary of his father's bowel operation. He was now trying to find a proctologist and go through a careful examination. "I am a little panicky about that." He reported a remarkable change in himself in relation to his father while he was at home—a peaceful relationship, with some affection. "But my mother drives me nuts; she makes me cringe, vomit, feel screwed up. She is brazen, clueless, selfish, crude, unthoughtful, depressed and makes me feel guilty." He was frequently upset by his mother's "crudeness" and recalled an early childhood incident of feeling painfully ashamed when she exhibited his brother's penis to a neighbor woman.

Mr. I. found the analyst quieter than usual. This was strange to him after just returning from home where everyone talked incessantly. "When you say nothing, I don't know how to react. I am out of practice. It's weird. I have this sensation in my foot again—you can put it down as a 'footnote'—the best pun of the year—neat!"

[Mr. I. had a frequent momentary, or somewhat longer-lasting sensation in his foot, the inner aspect around his ankles, in states of overstimulation or at moments of intense longing for the analyst (-mother-sister). The meaning of this often quite isolated, abruptly appearing, then disappearing sensation remained unexplained. So did the fact that Mr. I. was most uncomfortable and disturbed whenever it appeared.

After a recent dream with a sexual scene with his sister, the analyst suggested that childhood sexual games with his sister, perhaps lying next to her and touching her with his legs, might be the (genetic) origin of this transference-symptom (a symptom that had appeared during the analysis). The analyst suggested later on that some sexually exciting experiences with mother might have determined this isolated symptom. There were no convincing specific memories to substantiate it, although the over-all feeling, especially based on the timing of the appearance of the symptom in the analysis made its current meaning plausible to Mr. I.]

The "footnote" on this occasion referred to the fact, Mr. I. said, that "we are not yet reconnected since your return." He had a dream about flying a kite. At first he thought the kite was himself — off into space as with the rocket prior to vacation. Then he thought of the kite as the analyst, and Mr. I. was holding on to him. The issue of being connected, disconnected, and reconnected was his major preoccupation. The idea of flying off into space, separating from the analyst, was both painful and exhilarating — more exhilarating than painful, perhaps, these days, as the analyst was beginning to sense — but the re-entry was giving him trouble. "Never had as much trouble with your vacations, actually, as I have with the two weeks or so after you get back — that's certainly true now. While you were gone I was able to be myself without having to depend on you." The analyst commented that Mr. I.'s complaints of "the drabness and sameness of the days of vacation" must have had another positive aspect to it, namely, his ability to have kept himself calm and composed inside, although he may ultimately have felt that he overshot the mark and then began to feel the emptiness and monotony. Mr. I.'s response was, "I feel like crying — so hard to think — funny, I am going through it again and again — funny to see myself so foolish; I have no problems, except in here now. I feel, gee, it's all such good stuff, like in college. I want to get into it, work on it, but instead I want to go home and sleep. I feel drowsy now. I can't handle it today—maybe tomorrow." The analyst added that being understood after not having been understood for a while was too much, overstimulating, and the sleepiness and drowsiness was a way he tried to tone it down. There was silence, and the analyst noted that Mr. I. was on the verge of tears. Then: "How much can a guy like me take? You are absolutely right, but can't you wait until tomorrow and then you can make the very same point?" This went on for a while without the analyst finding the proper dosage and timing for his interventions, although he was able to interpret the consequences or wait for Mr. I.'s own interpretations.

The idea that being understood could also be so disturbing to Mr. I. reverberated in him for some time. He wondered whether termination was also difficult for the analyst. Perhaps that was why the analyst was talking so much, "so active in theorizing and explaining the past" as *his* reaction to the anticipated termination. "Or is it a problem of overstimulation in you," he continued, "and you talk more against your will? I haven't analyzed that yet!" He had the thought the other day that he would tell the analyst: "Cut it out, don't expose me to that!" Later he added that he no longer reacted with falling apart, that he could immediately recognize what the analyst said or did and that it was "amazing to me how confident I feel about you, that I can trust you. The world has changed since I have been in analysis." This referred to his increasing sense that "there was a you #1 and a you #2; the real you and the you I have created in my mind. If I met the real you, that wouldn't trigger much, but I could get choked up about the other."

He reported a dream over the weekend that followed: "At a filling station by myself. I go ahead and fill it up (as I

actually do), but the damned thing does not shut off when
full, and I can't get it shut off, spills all over. Then I shut it
off, but it slipped and it started back at zero, and there I was,
inside the store, either working there or trying to buy something. Maybe something homosexual was going on." In his
associations, Mr. I. thought at first that the overflowing gaso-
line had a sexual meaning, but then wondered if the dream
was "some sort of a response to what had gone on here lately."
The analyst focused on the latter issue, upon Mr. I.'s need to
fill up the tank by himself and his fear of the overflow, which
he could not control. The dream reflected Mr. I.'s sensitivity
to the analyst's interventions—was the analyst overreacting,
overanxious and overstimulated? Mr. I.: "It's that damn termination. I see why you ask for more specifics. I have trouble
with flying off into space because of the re-entry. What if you
discover that your equipment is not in order? You will have a
disastrous splash down." The analyst, remaining within the
metaphor, added that, whenever Mr. I. felt that his landing
instruments were defective or the analyst's radar didn't function perfectly well, he lost contact with ground control and became frightened. Mr. I. responded: "I now believe that despite these troubles I can make it on my own." He was reflective and continued: "What concerns me about these rocket
ships is their coming back to the earth's atmosphere. Do I have
the right equipment? I know it is faulty in some ways, but is it
reparable? I'll land somehow—repairs have been made for
three and a half years now, but will it be enough?" He wondered whether he would have to accept the deficit as something to put up with and put in the perspective: "This is me."
He was overstimulated by his own analogy: "That space capsule moves so fast it can't change its direction. My old images
are helpful. The splat on the wall is my dependency, and the
rocket ship or space capsule, my independence with all its
perils." He did not know whether the analyst really talked too

much, but it reminded him of his childhood when all members of his family sat around the dinner table. Everybody talked or wanted to talk, but no one listened. He used to talk to his sister a lot, when his parents were gone, almost the same way as he now talked to his wife to calm himself down.

It turned out that in spite of the overstimulating effects of the analyst's interventions, which then could be brought into analytic focus, another important element emerged. A senior partner of his firm gave a "pep talk" to the junior executives. As Mr. I. reported about it, he recognized that he was elated by the implication it all had for him: "Father and son should work together." When the analyst inquired about the meaning of this reaction, Mr. I. said: "I feel we have worked together here. I have felt abused from time to time in here these last few weeks because you were insensitive and talked too much, or as you footnoted, too sensitive, and it was intolerable for me. There is a dramatic change in me since yesterday's session, so I must have felt that you were sensitive in the right amount as to what my problem was. Believe it or not, you are still with me—you won't let me crash land. But it's funny— came as a surprise—you are still analyzing, figuring stuff out. Don't know why it should be a surprise. You are not just going to give up when this job is almost over. Ground control and radar are still functioning. This must be very important to me. I am not faking it, when I am so sick as I was yesterday. Something psychological causes it and something psychological stops it. That's pretty amazing. Must be that kind of stuff that does it [i.e., the well-dosed understanding]. Had the appreciation the last few weeks—sounds kind of primitive and over-simplified—but a feeling which is well integrated that when I get cut off, I feel hopeless. I need a point of reference, a base of operations, a relationship to give meaning to all my activities. I don't need as much as I used to from somebody else. But if I don't get it I feel let down, sick, and futile." The analyst

agreed and refrained from attempting a genetic reconstruction. He felt it would be more useful to postpone it. Mr.
I., as he struggled with the same issues in the next few sessions,
was frequently silent, and so was the analyst. Mr. I. finally
said: "Silences are accomplishments. It took me more than
three years to get some silence—chalk one up for me!"

Mr. I. commented on a replay he saw of Fellini's movie
"8½," about which he had spoken during the first week of his
analysis. He was then strongly identified with the provocative,
arrogant director of the movie who collected all past important figures around himself and controlled and manipulated
them; he was in complete charge. Now, as he saw the movie,
he recognized the flashing back and forth between reality and
fantasy, present and past. "I could not understand it some
years ago." He was still identified with the movie director.
"Now I see it as the eventual death of infantile sexuality in a
man—omnipotence, grandiosity, thousands of girls with no
real relationship to them, narcissistically having the center
stage, conducting. It's all neurotic, infantile, oedipal, Catholic
church versus the whores. Shooting himself is giving up all
that stuff—that's what analysis had been for me. It's difficult
to give up all these infantile things." He was wondering how it
all happened in the analysis that he could give up so much.
"One reason—I tell you—one reason you are a good analyst;
you have always consistently maintained your confidence in
me. Your confidence in the potential of my health. Whatever
I said—even when I argued with you about the twenty dollars
extra charge when I missed a session—even when I said I was
psychotic, you reacted as if I were capable of responding in a
healthy way. Having gone through this time with you, it was a
real therapeutic experience for me. If you had ever given me
back the twenty dollars, deciding you were wrong, I would
have resented it for the rest of my life; it was so solid, you
would have destroyed it by undoing."

Whatever pain he had during the analysis, from the analysis or the analyst, he now ascribed to the fact that: "You can't operate on the gall bladder without opening the abdomen, and you can't operate on the childhood neurosis without regression." The implication was that in regression there was more chance to get hurt, and therefore there was more pain. So he could not blame the analyst. He said with considerable affect: "I'll take this unit, you and me, put it in a capsule, and bury it somewhere deep inside me — it will always be there and give me self-confidence and consistency."

[The question of what Mr. I. was going to be able "to take away" upon leaving became the focal issue. The problem of separation from the self-object indeed entailed the question of whether his own independent psychic structure would now be strong and stable enough. Mr. I. also seemed concerned whether he would ultimately be able to incorporate the analyst's approving, optimistic, and confident interest in him. All this led to hypochondriacal bowel preoccupations, along with the exacerbation of bowel and rectal symptoms of more than ten-years duration. His attempts at self-regulation of his separation experiences were thus still partially sexualized in the hyperstimulation of his bowels, and his imagery depicting the process of structure formation through his internalizations was still in crude oral or anal terms: he put the analyst-patient relationship into a dark, deep spot in himself.]

Mr. I. finally consulted a proctologist. He had no hemorrhoids, but a spastic anal sphincter and some chronic dermatitis and edema around his anus. He was hyper-sensitive to any stimulation in his entire GI tract and was advised to consult an internist. Mr. I. considered it a triumph that he could quickly arrange to see the internist after having been unable to have a complete physical examination for years. He made his own diagnosis in advance: "Maybe I am physically hypersensitive to the world the same way I am emotionally hypersensitive. When I was a kid I knew I was destined to have something physically wrong. I 'knew' I wasn't going to live past the age of twenty—I now have the fantasy that finally somebody is going to put it all together." He recognized a paradox: "Getting all these physical things taken care of comes with the feeling of well-being, which is now more solid underneath."

In this same session (hour 545) Mr. I. raised the question of the specific date for termination. The analyst indicated that the two of them should talk about it and Mr. I. should express his thoughts and feelings about it. The idea that the setting of the date was to be a joint decision jarred Mr. I. for a moment. "That implies you have no divine plans and that we'll finish because I am leaving and not because I am finished. What is 'finishing,' anyway?" He wanted a "clean finish." The suggestion that he should set the termination date was "quite threatening," and he avoided it for a short while, but then, early in February, he began "the process of setting it." He counted out the days on a calendar and, after weighing the pro's and con's of an early termination in a month or two, he decided that the 600th hour would be the most desirable. "I would hate to end with 582 or 590—I'd never remember that—but 600 I'd remember for the rest of my life. Ridiculous." Without yet enunciating that he wanted to stop on May 29th, he returned to his preoccupation with his bowel symptoms. He thought he saw a bottle of "Mylanta" on the analyst's desk and pictured him having the same GI symptoms. Then he announced that "a real deep idea just ran through my mind, some kind of a confusion or blending of the boundaries between you and me—like a concern that you and I are connected in some bizarre fashion . . . not clear who is influencing whom . . . you might have intestinal trouble like me." The analyst reminded Mr. I. of an earlier statement: "You said that you put me and you into a dark deep spot in yourself, to keep me there and take me along. You want to swallow me up whole, to carry me away when you leave because you are afraid that you won't be able to maintain all that you have accomplished." "I have a strong urge to vomit," was Mr. I.'s immediate response. "I would expel you—just had a funny idea—sorry for the stupid intrusion—what if they find you in there on the X rays?", he joked, partially achieving mastery. But then he experienced the interpretation traumatically, and reacted to it with nausea. He ended the session by recalling that he just started doing Canadian Army exercises the night before: "I expect a lot of new freedom after finishing analysis. I'll be my own man after four years on this train ride with you; I'll stop the train and get my feet on the ground. My intention is to keep at it [the exercises]. The regularity builds something up, just as analysis does.

While waiting for the diagnostic session with his internist to discuss the preliminary X-ray findings, Mr. I. experienced "a major shift" in his bowel habits: "I have successfully gotten myself off the toilet. Don't need to sit there for long periods any more, I can do other things. . . ." In musing about his lifelong bowel habits, he recognized with some amusement that "I must have often regressed to verbal diarrhea in here—especially in the beginning." He then remembered that in addition to beds and couches in his dreams there were many toilets. "It all fits now, I used every means to get pleasure and excitement." Just before his diagnostic session he dreamed over and over again one night that "the diagnosis could not be made until the X rays were seen."

[This sounded like a "traumatic dream," which may well have been the expression of the incompleteness of the identification and the internalization process at this point.]

He felt sick again during the weekend, an episode of mild fragmentation, which brought back the memory when both he and his sister were still "real little," he may have been five and his sister two; parents were on vacation for a whole week (the analyst was shortly to be away for two weeks). "They made the mistake of separating us, me with one set of grandparents, her with the other. Both of us got sick, and we had to get back together again. It's a nightmare, getting sick without your mother there—that's one early memory that fits with panic and sickness. (It will be recalled that, in another early memory, reported earlier in analysis, Mr. I. had to console his sister and put her to bed at the grandparents' home because they could not calm her down.)

After a long weekend, the analyst returned on Mr. I.'s birthday (session 554). He was in a somber, reflective, and nostalgic mood. The analyst sensed the return of earlier, similar moods, the wish to be celebrated, and said (in part quoting from Mr. I.'s frequently used expressions throughout the analysis): "No fanfare in here, no cake; the bands are not playing and there is not a God-damned bird singing." "There never are enough people to celebrate it with me," he replied. "It is never as special a day as when you were a child. Sad, that you won't be able to wish me a happy birthday [next year]." He continued in the same emotional tone, reminiscing about the childhood birthdays and his mother's affectionate (perhaps at times intrusively affectionate) caring. He talked about aging, and also about wanting to be done with the past. He was not the "big-town-man" and not the "little village boy," and he should not be wanting the same things he wanted then. Yet, it was not easy to give up the past.

He reported a vivid dream: "I was riding this horse in a race. I figured I'd relax and let the horse do the running. I'd be so relaxed that I'd come in first. L. said to go to the horse first and make friends, to be in good communication with it.

It all turned into a race of engines." He felt the dream must have had something to do with termination, with his birthday, and his concern about his mother's recent hospitalization for an as yet undiagnosed ailment. After some detour about current affairs, he returned to the dream: "If in conflict, just ride the waves, the crest of the waves, pick a winning wave if you can; don't even drive it, just relax and let it ride you to victory. If I have a struggle over the next two weeks [the analyst's vacation] I should just relax and let it work out. You'll pick it right. You usually do the right thing except for four or five instances I can recall [he mentioned them]. Otherwise, you do the right thing."

[There was no opportunity to examine this dream in detail at the time. The horse was possibly the childhood self, with another rider — the alter-ego analyst next to him. The horse changed into an engine, which, in contrast to the horse, was mechanical rather than alive. Could this be a reference to Mr. I.'s current analytic dilemma in relation to his self, its future and ambitions? Could the self survive the anticipated loss of the self-object mother-analyst and be maintained independently? These were indeed the central issues of this termination phase.]

Prior to leaving for vacation, Mr. I. heard that there were no pathological findings on his X rays. The internist found a very hyperactive GI tract, stomach filled with gastric secretions, a hyperactive duodenum, but no ulcers or other deformities.

Upon resumption of the analysis, Mr. I. reported a very good two-week period.

[Mr. I. was now ready to commit himself to a specific date. His termination problems were strongly engaged. He reacted to the loss of the self-object-analyst in two opposing ways. On the one hand, with further regression, even to the point of temporary fragmentation and loss of reality (he repeatedly thought he saw the analyst's car follow him; the hypochondriacal preoccupations); and on the other hand, with an increasing degree of freedom, initiative, and creativity which he had not known before. He was planning to take a three-month trip to Europe for the first time; to spend his summer there before assuming his new position in the fall. This was the result of a struggle between clinging to the analyst until the last moment or daring to break loose and go on a trip he had previously only dreamed about.]

The commitment to a specific date was not, however, a simple matter. Mr. I. oscillated between wanting an earliest and a latest day, and these oscillations always provided an opportunity for further analysis. Every session seemed to matter. Mr. I. finally commented as he reflected on his "greediness": "After tons of food we ate in our lifetime, today's lunch still mattered." This preoccupation with the exact date seemed more like an elaborate preparation for landing, since Mr. I. made a commitment to end with session 600. Thus, even without the specific date, he announced that it was "fasten-your-seat-belt time" before landing suddenly. He recalled an incident that poignantly depicted how he felt just at this moment: "I was twelve, my folks put me on the train to N. It was a long ride, rolling through forests and hills. I was wandering all over the train. Arrived in a big terminal and waited and waited. Felt lost and lonely. They told me to stay put, not to budge. Then my uncle arrived. You probably sit there wondering how this is related to termination. Well, there is a touch of underlying emptiness, only a touch of it now, kind of blah. In two days maybe it will be in full bloom. Part of me values these sessions, part of me makes mockery of them now." He had the fantasy that if he did not mention that it was the end of the week the analyst would think that weekend separations no longer bothered him. Mondays and Thursdays had special importance in the past because the analyst could see the progress especially clearly on those days, and Mr. I. was hopeful that he would "get a few gold stars, and maybe the analyst would, too, but now, week after week, there are no more great floor shows, no big earthquakes. Everything is too quiet."

Near the end of the week Mr. I. reported a dream depicting his neediness and his ability to give to himself: "A little kid walking around on the street with seizures, epilepsy, but if someone hugged him, related to him, he didn't have any. I walked up to him, hugged him; he liked it. Went into this store, deformed kid, something was wrong with him, but I was going to adopt him. The little boy in the dream had a big head. Makes me think of me, deformed, injured, but needing a hug to help me get through." The analyst merely sharpened the meaning Mr. I. himself attached to the dream by underlining that the one who needed the hug (the expression of affection and comfort, the soothing that would prevent the seizure) and the one who gave it (who expressed the affection and protectiveness, "the adoption") were both Mr. I. himself. "It is meaningful to see both as me."

As Mr. I. went through his, by now, almost routine of oscillation between ending early (i.e., one month from now) or later (two months from now), the analyst commented that Mr. I.'s central concern seemed to be how to avoid excessive frustration on the one hand and overstimulation on the other, and how to make sure he had his own independent means of regulating his tension as he prepared himself to do without the analyst-self-object.

Mr. and Mrs. I. gave their first big party for friends and colleagues. Mr. I. was aware of not wanting to draw much attention to himself, wanted to be in the background. He actually felt a bit uncomfortable when he did get some attention. He remembered how desperately he wanted to get attention three or four years ago, even at the expense of making a fool of himself. The analyst said that Mr. I. was experimenting with trying to be very different at the party, but could not carry it off comfortably. "It is related to what you said before about my avoiding to set the date to control over- or understimulation, it was the same problem at the party. It was almost predictable."

In further reflecting on his attainments, Mr. I. said: "The first year of analysis might have been sufficient for me; the second year would have been very worthwhile. What I gained since then I never expected." For the first time in a long time he felt he was floating at the couch and it was tipping backward—"like so often in my childhood, but instead of being frightened now, I enjoy it as an old familiar feeling." The analyst, drawing on some earlier exchanges, remarked that this was how some old, frightening feelings had become "detoxified," and when they intruded they signaled that whatever had been revived from the past was no longer dangerous, but may even bring a warm glow, as just happened. Mr. I. agreed and then thoughtfully wondered: "Can you ever redo the 'basic fault,' the primary problem, or do you work with secondary growth?" He himself was not sure, but he thought that in his case both were true. The analyst agreed and remarked that Mr. I. discovered the answer from his own experiences. When he was dizzy and lightheaded on the couch the next day, he saw it as a reaction to the "compliment" in the previous session.

It did seem that Mr. I. was now further along in being able to contemplate a separate independent existence. He was still building up his inner security, but without devouring the analyst. He admitted the change movingly and with gratitude for the understanding he received in a climate of commitment to "the me" in him. He was struck by the self-acceptance he achieved, including the archaic, hitherto warded-off parts of himself, which resulted from his analytic experience.

In session 574 Mr. I. finally determined the date, exactly two months hence, that would indeed end with his 600th hour — if neither analyst nor patient had to cancel a session. Now it was the date that counted, and Mr. I. became depressed, gloomy, and irritable. He was also scared that his feelings about termination would be "too much for my circuitry." He was fearful that he would "blow a fuse and develop nausea and the rest of it."

The analyst picked up the "fuse" analogy and summarized for Mr. I. what they jointly understood thus far about his difficulty in tension regulation. He also elaborated on the nausea which Mr. I. disparagingly related to his own primitive incorporation of the analyst *in toto*. The analyst focused on the developmental aspects of this internalization and pointed to their last-minute, emergency aspects, when they occurred so grossly, so abruptly, and resulted in his nausea.

He realized that "there was no longer anything I needed to talk about or need help with — just that I have this reaction — dreaded it for years — this final separation. Analysis was the only thing that gave me some stability. Will I have it on my own?" Mr. I. was again highly sensitive to any unnecessary interventions by the analyst. To safeguard the remaining sessions and with reference to a recent comment by the analyst that he may not have been in perfect tune with a subtle feeling Mr. I. was expressing, he said: "I need you to listen again; you said too much last time. I don't want you to say you didn't have good empathy at that moment. The other day you stepped down as God when you said something like that. This is an emotional experience and not a discussion." He felt that he could say anything now, he felt more equal — with his wife too. Before his marriage he worried whether he really needed a woman who was below him in many respects, not his equal, to look up to him and make him feel good all the time. "That's one way of feeling good, but I didn't want that. I thought I had to have it. Marrying someone like T. is very different. Got its difficulties and rewards. Depends how much of a blow to your narcissism you can take or how much gratification you need for her looking up to you. We are more equal; I can take that now."

Mr. I. felt that "the space ship was coming in for a landing—re-entry—can't sit there and savor it. You are coming in fast. Too late, you got to go ahead and bring it in. You can fool around out there, in outer space, but there may be more danger in that now." He realized that the deeper issues were his feelings about ending, he could not put them into words, as yet, he felt. "Maybe some months from now I'd get upset and would want to call you. I can call myself! Despite some of what you said lately that I will be able to take much of it [i.e., his gains] with me—horseshit!—I'll take *all* of it, 110 per cent of it! You may not know it—you can't know it. Bundles of stuff I am taking with me—I couldn't even list them all."

It was in his dreams that Mr. I. now experienced his most archaic affects and reactions to the final separation. He reported two dreams (in two consecutive sessions). The first one consisted of two parts: "In the first part I am hitched to an aluminum-bar frame, and I lie on my belly in analysis. You paint the frame all different colors. I can't look, I have to sense all the different colors. It's weird." In the second part of the dream: "A mouse intrudes under the cover, but a cat rescues me by chasing the mouse away. I felt relieved and liberated." Mr. I. felt that this was a sexual dream—"painting, stroking, fooling around with me." He felt shamed in the dream by the analyst because of his passivity, just lying on the frame. This seemed so real, he attributed the feeling to the fact that the analyst did not help him with choosing the date, let him sweat it out alone. He thought he was naked when lying on the frame, exposed, aggressively exposed, so he could be seen; sensuous, erotic, with just a belt and shoes—his analytic experience—the analyst doing the painting of the frame. The analyst remarked that the patient needed the frame to accomplish his task, the frame as the analyst, and now Mr. I.'s own internal structure. "Yes, I can add to it now, it's the dismantling of the couch, piece by piece—why am I still lying on it? I am flying away now."

[Mr. I. did not work on the second part of the dream, where passivity seemed to turn into activity. The issue of gaining independence, which still had its hazards, was continually engaged in the work toward finding a reliable solution. The dream (and the association of dismantling the couch piece by piece) did seem to depict the process of internalization. Under the pressure of the separation-termination, these processes were intensified, and when the pressure was experienced as traumatic, the sexualization of these internalization processes assumed their old, archaic forms—oral and anal incorporation and passive homosexuality—but now in his dreams only. (See pp. 19 and 75 for earlier examples and p. 102 for later ones.)]

The second dream was reported in the next session. "I was in the office with X and told him something clever which impressed him. He called Y over to tell him. The scene changed, I was in this dark room with the phone off the hook. Somebody saying, 'Hey, open the window.' I am beginning to be poisoned. There are fumes in the air; I was groping to open the window." Mr. I. was impressed with the two opposing feelings in his dream, his cleverness (i.e., his health and successes) and his feeling endangered and poisoned. The analyst remarked that Mr. I. seemed to experience the open showing

off of his cleverness as a dangerous poison. [Here, the loss of
the self-object analyst led to the dangerous resurgence of archaic grandiosity. This led to an exaggerated independence
(with the phone off the hook), which cut him off, isolated him,
and led to a temporary crumbling of his reality testing: he experienced the danger of being poisoned by this archaic grandiosity. At the same time, outside the analytic situation he was
only minimally affected by occasional brief regressions. Termination was due in a month, and he continued to plan his
extensive travels before settling into his new position.]

During the remaining eight weeks, the termination issues
gained further in their intensity and in their centrality in every
session. Mr. I. worked on "termination," by which he meant
letting go of, or growing away from the self-object-analyst
and taking over the functions assigned to him in the transference. The piecemeal takeover, the internalization of these
functions was a continuous process, especially throughout the
second half of the analysis. But now, in the termination phase,
and more particularly during these last weeks, the occurrence
of these internalizations was quite pronounced on many levels
and in many situations. The processes of this takeover, the
"transmuting internalizations" (Kohut, 1971) that result in the
formation of psychic structures, were dramatically recon-
cretized in many of Mr. I.'s activities and especially in his
dreams.

Mr. I. also seems to have needed to "debunk" the analyst
repeatedly to accomplish an increasingly more realistic perception of him. This had gone on throughout the analysis, but
became intensified during the termination process.

Mr. I. reflected upon some of his expectations early in the
analysis. When he wanted to bring his diaries and photos to
the analyst, "I felt someday, somebody would read my diary,
see my photos. Somebody will finally look and understand and
know me, acknowledge it all, make it real so that I could go

on. I had that notion as a child when I wrote in the diary. Somebody had to hear it all! Why?" Analyst: "You said it yourself, so you could become real." "I didn't want any interpretations. I just wanted somebody to hear it all. You have heard it all. You really know me. Seems like now I don't have to wait for that any longer. If I would only have been understood, that would have been enough! But understood and accepted, that would have been enough! But interpretations on top of that — really enough!"

A colleague's sudden death and the many dying people in his current dreams gave Mr. I. a chance to contemplate the impermanence of the self and of relationships. He realized that "this morbid preoccupation with death" expressed some of his feelings about ending his analysis. The analyst focused on another aspect that seemed to him strikingly different in the way Mr. I. reacted to his colleague's death. On previous occasions such events always made him focus upon himself and how he was affected. On this occasion he was very sensitive to how others at the firm, even the boss, reacted selfishly and could not really focus their emotions upon the dead colleague, but only upon themselves and the firm. Mr. I. was appalled how quickly everyone wanted to return to "business as usual."

In session 581 Mr. I. reported the following dream: "Trumpet or clarinet. This guy swallowed the clarinet, and he managed to breathe so that it played, with his mouth open. The clarinet sounds were coming out." Mr. I. recalled his repeated fantasy of having swallowed the analyst's penis, with which he now associated the swallowing of the clarinet. He realized that he was swallowing it whole, taking it with him and making it part of himself. He thought that analysts retain their patients too, when they write about them, and he thought that someday the analyst would write a paper about him and incorporate him into a new idea; he would thus be remembered. The analyst emphasized that Mr. I. swallowed him "whole"; he would need to digest and to assimilate what he "swallowed," but it was significant that the music came from the inside, from Mr. I. himself.

[The clarinet, the analyst's penis, his voice — the source of his influence and strength in the analytic situation — was now inside of him. Mr. I. once described the clarinet as his mother's instrument, but that aspect of the clarinet was not recalled by either patient or analyst at this time. Not only was there the wish that the patient incorporate the analyst, but there was also the opposite wish, that the patient remain with the analyst, inside of him, through being incorporated into the analyst's scientific writings.]

In session 582 a two-part dream brought some aspects of Mr. I.'s "termination feelings" into focus. "We are comedians, on stage, performing. I am at the edge of the stage, he is with the audience. Slapstick, corny performance. He'll chase me off stage, and that will be the end." The second part: "To a concert. A friend is directing the band. Clapping to make him feel good." Mr. I. felt that "we are nearing the last act of this performance. Here we are going to end it all. Are you going to chase me off the stage? Slapstick, corny. I said the other day that everything I thought of telling you at the end sounded corny. Don't know how to give a compliment." Regarding the last part of the dream: "Directing a band is pure narcissism when you are up there. . . . [Silence] It's a jarring process going on, getting unlinked from analysis. My dreams are working at it before I do."

[The analyst might well have reflected to Mr. I. elements of the mirror transference in this two-part dream, since the patient often used "the stage" as the metaphor for the analysis, with the audience as his analyst. He was clapping to make his friend feel good — a friend who was often Mr. I.'s stand-in in dreams and associations during earlier phases of the analysis. The analyst could also have included the recognition that this dream was less crudely exhibitionistic.]

Mr. I. used every opportunity to sort out the nature of his accomplishments in analysis. In session 583 he suddenly recognized that he had seventeen sessions to go: "I can't picture what I need them for — except to grasp the existence of them, not the end of them. You got to be sure you registered it, acknowledged it. It isn't mostly insight, but ego-capacities, different functioning. Every minute of the day I am different from what I used to be. The underlying force was to the stability of this relationship. Once it got me stabilized then I was able to develop a stable relationship with others — with myself too! Now I can leave with more stability and transfer my ties to others."

He mused that he would soon be free of this analysis, and the privacy of his dreams would no longer be invaded by the analyst. He was calm now, he said, but he anticipated some panic near the very end. He might not be able to say some things then, so he should say them now. "Many things changed, but I did not have a chance to report about them." He was eager not to leave the analyst with some misconception about himself. Analyst: "This concern is still a remnant of something that pervaded this whole experience here — that unless I think you are whole and perfect, you are not." "Yes," he replied, unless you think anything about me — any reality is not a reality unless you know about it. But we can't establish reality once and for all!" He felt that what the analyst said was a tangential interpretation. Mr. I. was more concerned about — no, actually feared — that after analysis was over he might suddenly find out something about the analyst that he did not know. "Like how many kids you have, or how great they are. That would have made me say different things here, experience something differently. I would want to come back to say these things." The analyst replied: "You are right, nothing can be made so stable and complete that it would be taken care of once and for all. You value the stability you achieved and now would want to have it absolute—guaranteed, so you should never feel that something should have been experienced and understood differently."

In session 584 Mr. I. was outraged at himself. In the process of winding up a joint project with a woman co-worker, he made a pass at her, and he was distraught about it. "It made no sense, it was the old pattern—bad news—I will not tolerate that kind of behavior in myself—not me! I won't be that kind of person; I despise myself when I do that." He finally analyzed the experience as a "return to my emergency behavior—I am scared of finishing." The analyst said that under the stress of termination the newly acquired capacities can be temporarily lost, and Mr. I. sounded concerned that he would not take along with him all of his new acquisitions. Mr. I. said that all this made him have increased respect for the seriousness of the termination experience. He was relieved to hear that the new strengths are more vulnerable.

By session 586 Mr. I. was "more philosophical" about the experience, helped by a dream in which he had a "romantic exchange with another woman at work." In his associations he was exceptionally hard on himself at first; he called it "malignant yearning and greed," but then said, "Now that it is related to the ending of my analysis I have two ideas about it: One, knowing that you and I will be parting and you will be withdrawing from my everyday life—the need for some sort of something to fill in the basic fault, to patch it up, soothe it—this need for something is there. The other: this need could be perceived by me as a sexual one because of its urgency, giving rise to lots of sexual impulses. Well, in a general sense, sexual."

Mr. I. was not yet satisfied with the understanding of the episode and its broader implications. He thought that termination must have triggered feelings of rage, which he could not fully experience in response to the analyst's withdrawal, could not express toward him and was now taking out on himself. The analyst underlined that Mr. I. did sexualize the need that arose out of the threat of losing his (self-object) analyst, because of the temporary loss of his newly acquired self-soothing capacity. This was also an opportunity to make a broad reconstruction of what had gone on earlier in the analysis and refer to the genetic precursors that emerged in bits throughout the analysis. The analyst completed his somewhat lengthy "summary" by referring to the fact that Mr. I. hoped to take along 110 per cent of what he gained, and therefore every current relapse was even more frightening. Mr. I. was thoughtful and quiet for a while, and then responded reflectively (without feeling overstimulated): He would accept feeling the way he did during the last two years for the rest of his life—especially compared to the ten years prior to that. He knew that part of the 100 per cent—he laughingly said, it could really not be 110 per cent—was already inside of him—he had no doubt about that. He felt that he would be able to acquire more in other relationships now, "in relationships that won't be one-way, or for my benefit only; but that's a matter of percentages. The marriage is a two-way relationship for me now—a bit of out of whack during this time of my termination, but I am not always regressed there. The marriage is readily available as a source for providing what I will lose here, even if I can't use it just now." After a brief silence, he continued: "It's the process of acquiring the unavailable that has been life-saving. It isn't a hug that gives me what I need, but the process of making it available when it's not available — the conquest, rather than the treasure, which is seemingly so necessary for me."

In session 587 Mr. I. spoke about the analyst's anticipated twelve-day absence and reported a dream from the previous night: "I dreamed about a grain elevator — it was completely filled up with grain. The first thing that comes to mind is a pun: I switched from 'take stock' to 'stock up' — this grain elevator had all the supplies." Mr. I. was angry that the analyst insisted that he could not take 100 per cent along with him. "You let me feel good, but you don't let me take it along with me. My impulse problem with sex subsided in 24 hours." He felt analysts were not perfect.

He remarked that the vacation seemed of no significance, unless it was part of what triggered the grain dream because his eyes and emotions were already focused on the very end. He was glad that his last dream told him that he was "stocking up."

[The analyst recognized somewhat later that his emphasis on what Mr. I. could not take along, even referring back to his need to take along 110 per cent, which was hardly possible, was an attempt to analyze — perhaps here again, somewhat intrusively — Mr. I.'s exaggerated expectations. It was as if the analyst's own pride in his own accomplishments had to be perfect and complete, or as if he had to show Mr. I. that he needed the analyst to the very last moment (the latter undoubtedly an intrusion of a countertransference attitude). Yet, Mr. I. did not react traumatically and continued his own "taking over" and the consolidation of what was transmutedly internalized. It was an important "lesson" for the analyst, when he realized that the mere recognition and acceptance of Mr. I.'s successful attempt at taking over the functions previously assigned to him were regularly followed by Mr. I.'s own spontaneous analysis and recognition of those "exaggerations." There was no need to direct attention to them or to work on them directly.]

Session 588, in the middle of the week, occurred the day before the analyst's vacation, leaving only twelve more sessions until termination. Mr. I. had a dream the night before: "I was going to a new school, brand new—not only starting a new school, but moving from class to class. Wondered what day it was, but could not tell from the schedule. Natural, I thought, it's a new school, so I couldn't tell. Walking through a modern central place, lobby, nice plants. Then another scene: gym class. I was late, changing to my gym pants. Wrong one on. Somebody said it didn't matter. Everyone was late, getting used to the new schedule. Some thought: Gee, all I have all day long are physical education classes—no academic subjects. New school must be my new start in life. Those pants, silly yellow ones with black dots on them. Yellow has something to do with you [there had been many references to yellow in the analysis that clearly related to the analyst]. Wearing your pants or my pants? Won't make a hell of a big difference."

He still wanted to know about the chance for a face-to-face ending: "How do you end? With a review? A diploma? Will I get a badge?" The analyst responded that he understood the importance of that moment to Mr. I., "that he would not like to end it the way all other sessions ended and that he must have thought that his wish for a 'grand finale' could be more planned and controlled if he sat up." "Yes. What range of celebration can there be lying down?! The usual session comes and goes quickly. The last session should be—you commented a week ago that I had trouble expressing openly my warm feelings. That won't change magically in three or four weeks, yet I want to express it—a deep basic gratitude—if we could structure it, so it's built into it. To mark it in a special way could take the burden off me." He wondered if the analyst understood his predicament. The answer was yes. Then he said, "I can't be free associating until the last minute—it wouldn't make good sense." The analyst could have interpreted this as Mr. I.'s wish to take over his own internal tension control, to be in charge of his own thought and prepare for a nontraumatic, safe landing, but before he could do that, Mr. I. continued, recalling that he started out in analysis wanting to structure the first few sessions, to tell his story in a chronological, orderly manner. "It turned out I had a problem with that for about a year."

[The dream about the new school also concretized the structural changes Mr. I. achieved and still expected. The wearing of the analyst's pants, or pants that could not be distinguished from those of the analyst, reflects a less archaic identification, perhaps, or one not completely internalized, but no longer perceived as traumatically disturbing—it was not an oral or anal incorporation with nausea as its consequence. As Mr. I. put it: "It won't make a hell of a difference whose pants they are." Is this transmuting internalization in *statu nascendi*?]

Upon resuming analysis with session 589, Mr. I. described that he had a great week, he and his wife also took a vacation. He picked up where the previous session ended—how to finish analysis. The ups and downs that still occurred in this period were well under his own control. The fears that accompanied his termination experiences until the very last session (parallel to his acquired strength) were expressed in a dream he reported from the night before the resumption of the analysis for the remaining twelve sessions.

The dream was about some experimentally used children—like little dolls, practice kids. They died at the end of the treatment. His wife was handling some of these kids. Mr.

I. pulled himself up to a ledge and was able to hold himself there in safety. His associations immediately brought him back to his analytic experiences. "Analysis stirred up feelings and there was a chance to work on them. Nothing magic, no completely new me. Hurdles conquered, thanks to analysis; more self-understanding, but no magic—just what I am." Perhaps as another attempt to "debunk" the analyst and his role in the transference: "You get plugged into whatever outlet there is in the room. Analysis is a pathological state of getting to be too preoccupied with yourself—not an end in itself by any means." As he calmly reached the end of this session, Mr. I. commented that, "In a few days I'll be more stirred up, even symptomatic—now I am less involved."

Session 590 began with anxiety that was expressed in the choice of the first few words: "Well, Sir, for I don't even know who you are, we are winding up. Only ten more sessions to go. Is there nothing else we need to do? I don't feel anything is resolved. I am just as squeamish about you as I always was, maybe a little less. You are not a real person to me. In two weeks or even two months, you won't become one. I am asking myself to integrate this experience into the rest of my experiences: The most positive experience I ever had—but hard to integrate it because it was with an unreal person. Well, that's not true either; you are real, but I couldn't see you. [Silence] Seems as if I should withdraw, but you shouldn't; you should stay here till the finish! I should stop telling you what happens day by day—because that will have to stop in a few days. [Silence] I tell you, Sir, I strongly suspect I am covering up things on purpose, because I don't feel too inclined to place myself at your mercy now—got to do it on my own. Down deep, still stuff going on. I am inclined to look at it, but not inclined to share it. Want to have a clear state of mind until the end." Then he added, in a very different, more relaxed and matter-of-fact tone of voice: "I mean, now that I've said

all that, I can mention these things." The most significant was
the recurrence of his fantasies about the woman co-worker,
with whom he was still working on finishing the joint project.
These fantasies suddenly stopped after the weekend was over
"and my heartburn started—some sort of a yearning I guess."
The analyst responded (regretfully) that it was understandable
that Mr. I. wanted to squelch these fantasies and feelings and
did not want to express what was stirred up in him.

[The analyst failed to recognize here the essence of Mr.
I.'s attempts to take back the control of his regulatory functions, which he had assigned to the analyst during the analysis.
Instead, the analyst believed that the final resistance had to be
overcome before termination, that is, the nonanalyzed areas
should still be analyzed. The analysis was not derailed, and
Mr. I. continued to move toward termination with the idea
that he would regulate his own reactions through his own efforts. The analyst planned to correct these errors, summarize
what had happened, and then let the patient regulate his final
good-bye.]

Mr. I.'s response to the interpretation of the "final resistance" was to comment about "the end of an era—ceremonial
meetings now, rather than actual work meetings—confusing.
It's a pile of baloney. I just don't want to bother with the last
ten meetings. I do and don't want to avoid them."
Mr. I. weathered one more two-day depression, apathy,
and no energy to do anything. "I didn't want to feel better. I
felt better for feeling bad. I wanted to feel even worse—
numb." The analyst interpreted this episode as related to Mr.
I.'s feeling that the analyst did not yet respond to his wish to
end the analysis in a more formal, prescribed manner. "Damn
right! If I lie down I have to end it by myself. If I could sit up I
would end it with you, the way we started. I got on this couch

as part of one hour, why can't I get off it the same way and not at the end of the hour. Then it would take initiative on my part to linger around longer and talk to you, whereas if I get up in the hour, I could to that without embarrassment, because it would be built in."

The analyst simply said that Mr. I. so much wanted and needed to regulate his own responses and that this was appropriate. He could decide how he wanted the analysis to end.

Session 593 ushered in the last two weeks of the analysis on a Monday. The beginning of this session was reminiscent of the early periods in analysis when Mr. I. had to report every detail of the preceding weekend. Now too, Thursday through Sunday "was pretty miserable. I had my old syndrome — nausea and headaches. I didn't know how I was going to make it through each day." He went into the details and then reported "a great dream of success" from Sunday night! "T. and I were out fishing and I saw this muskellunge — it came right up. Took my bait, and I said to T., 'You got to net this fish; you got to bring your line in, shut the motor, and bring your net in.' She didn't listen. Some guy on the shore was yelling 'Take a picture of it; hey, do this; hey, do that!' In exasperation, I reached over with one hand, got the net, and I got him — that easy! Big fish. I was tickled to death; in my family that's a great thing. We went to shore, walked along a promenade lit up with bright colored lights at night, and we've got the muskie with us."

Mr. I. was pleased with his dream and was going to write home about it. "If you can't catch one, the next best thing is to dream about it." He was lucky, and he wondered if he was trying to fulfill his father's expectation of him in the dream. Or the analyst's? Or his own? Did he want to show off the giant catch to the analyst-father for approval and admiration — the approval and admiration he never had from his father? He thought the analyst was ashore, yelling to him what to do, but he said to himself, "Quit listening to him and net your own fish!" Mr. I. sensed that the dream was also a gift to the analyst. While throwing out some old papers during the weekend, he came upon a typewritten copy of his lengthy first dream. "I could give you an autographed copy of it," he said. He laughingly told his wife about it over the weekend. He also felt that he now had to start interpreting his dreams all by himself. The analyst merely added: "Without that guy from the shore yelling to you how to do it." Mr. I. agreed enthusiastically.

The next few days his co-workers commented to Mr. I. that he appeared depressed and less vigorous than usual; he himself was aware of it, but he felt good in spite of being depressed, almost as if he enjoyed having strong feelings about the termination experiences, in contrast to not having been able to feel anything in depth for years. As he talked, he felt tears welling up in his eyes. "I don't think I am crying; this is just some sort of a reaction to leaving." Whatever might be going on underneath, consciously he was pleased about feeling well and was calmly preparing to leave. He was just "gently looking around to pick up a piece here and there, tie up loose ends." He didn't want any more great discoveries. He heard others talk about grief reaction, anger; he didn't experience that, but only "a falling-apart kind of reaction, worries about my health and my old syndrome. Then, when I experienced my syndrome, I experienced depression too." He wondered how the analyst experienced termination: "When I left yesterday I thought—what's happening to him? You haven't said much these last few sessions, just let me know that you were there, but not getting into new big areas. I don't know what your reaction to termination is: routine? dramatic? Something that would cause you to withdraw?" The analyst wondered whether Mr. I.'s own necessary slow withdrawal made him doubt whether the analyst would be with him all the way. He recalled for Mr. I. his earlier statement that he himself ought to be able to withdraw, to stop free associating, but the analyst should be there with his total presence to the very end. He sensed that Mr. I. still wanted him to witness from the shore (without yelling to him what to do) how successfully and with how much ease he caught his huge fish.

The week ended with Mr. I.'s anticipation that the following week would be horrible. The finality of the good-bye was scary. He had looked at his diaries again lately and noticed that every June, before his separation from his parents to go to camp, all his symptoms were there. He was amazed at how regularly they recurred in analysis. What would happen to that now? "My psyche is underneath ten times more powerful—that's what counts." He felt himself getting panicked, all churned up, frantic, waiting for a final, great, gigantic dream, to get out of the analysis with a bang. Yet he also said to himself that "most everything was said. Just survive the splash down!" The analyst took this opportunity to respond more explicitly to Mr. I.'s recent efforts to take over many of the functions he had assigned to the analyst throughout the analysis: his wish that he be his own "diary" now, rather than needing to share his thoughts and feelings; that he interpret his own dreams and that he should be able to celebrate them or arrange for their celebration himself, just as he did at the end of the dream when he caught the huge muskie. Mr. I. interrupted the analyst gently: "I always had a certain tendency not to experience everything to its completion by myself. How do you take over that? You can't practice it too much, it's like parachute jumping. That's how I feel—scared. I know I am as ready as I will ever be; packed, practiced, but scared. Might just end up freer than I ever was—from parents and from you. This is my second chance to get free. Will I need a third chance? I will never be in as bad of shape as I was a few years ago." Suddenly Mr. I. looked at his watch—the session was almost over. He talked about "getting permission to sit up at the end." The analyst reiterated what he said before, that there was no prescription for how to end. He indicated that rather than telling Mr. I. to sit up or not to sit up, they could look at Mr. I.'s hesitancy in taking over this last function. He responded with relief: "That's good, you imply there is no need to change the rules unless necessary. Part of it is gaining control, taking over, and the transition. I am afraid—it's peculiar, I am afraid in here but not out there. I thought I needed to bring this experience on the couch into reality, by sitting there on the chair and just looking at it. But even this idea, when I am out there, is not important. In here it is."

On the morning of session 599 he felt sick and frightened for a moment; he thought he might have to miss the hour, but then it passed. Tried to think of the other side, how much fun it might be to get it over with. He could not feel that yet, maybe later, now he could only think it. He did build up quite a reserve of good feelings. "These will now be mine because I won't be with somebody I'd have to part with." He was both excited about this and also dreaded it. He felt, now, overstimulated almost to the point of feeling "silly, numb, like drunk; everything is churned up. But me, I am off in space somewhere and laughing at it all." He recalled that T. sent her compliments to the analyst. She apologized for having been mean about it all from time to time. She thought it was better to be angry at the analyst than at her husband. "She said to tell you that you did a real nice job. I thought I'd pass it along." The analyst expressed his thanks. Mr. I. reacted intensely: "Gee, when you said, thank you, I wanted to cry. Suddenly everything changed. I quit being my neurotic self—this was reality. What I say is real, getting right down to the line. I don't want it to get too real. When I said real, it cleared my nose. I don't want it. I'd rather be under the weather and in a fog in time of this crisis for a few more days."

The final session began with Mr. I. paying his last bill (which he had not yet even received). For him it was "part of the completion." He said he was shaky, embarrassed, and scared. He wanted to have "a great dream, a three-part dream, at the end. It doesn't matter, I guess." Instead, he could only recall a few fragments. "One was vague, some of your kids were in it. They were going somewhere. I was changing my mind about restaurants. . . ." In the other dream "I was parachuting. One might well crash at the bottom, but it didn't matter, the jumping off was important — which is how I feel now." His wife gave him a card and a present for "graduation." She was cute about it, and he cried. She congratulated him for getting his sheepskin — that would lead to fame and riches. The card was signed: "Congratulations from the one who loves you." This made him cry too. The present was a bubble-blowing kit to blow some bubbles when he no longer had his analyst to whom he could free associate.

"What will happen to my relationship to you? The analysis will be over but you will remain. What if I run into you and I am still inhibited? What if something happens next week? What if I recall something important I should have told you about? Well, it will all be mine, it's all over. You have to accept that too, that things will continue to happen. I won't end this all right here." He tried to put all of this in clearer perspective and said: "In high school the work is toward a goal, grades, position; for that day of glory, the final report card will be all A's. You put it into a scrapbook and never see it again. Getting there is half the fun. It isn't that one day that it's all about. The real stuff went on before the graduation ceremony." [Silence] The analyst added: "Nevertheless, the graduation was important for you then. You recalled many times how impatient your father was, and that he could not celebrate it with you, so it must be important to you now too.

You did anticipate a kind of grand closure." "No matter what kind, it won't be enough, because that's the system in here, like when I got married. This just couldn't be the place to record or to celebrate it." He continued to reflect on what he expected in analysis and finally said: "It's not a way of life, but it's a means to a way of life. It was for me."

Then he felt dizzy and dissociated, "flying a thousand miles an hour through space. [Silence] The spacecraft has come down, landed, oh — in the ocean. Lots of things need to be taken care of — excitement, tension — the astronaut can come out and go home — 600, a lot of sessions, wow! Almost four years. Not a long time for college — for me it was an awfully long time because I was so different — so it's more distant — four years — for either of us — one patient, one analyst, one endeavor. [Laughingly] If you ever took a train trip as a kid to visit an aunt, all excited, frantic, it was a good thing that the engineer was calm and had his steady hand on the controls — something to be learned here about that. Fantastic, just fantastic." He looked at his watch, took his pulse, and said "It's 104 but feels more like 200. [Silence] I don't have any thoughts [laughs], only feelings." The time was up. He got off the couch, turned around, smiled, and said "Thank you very much. I appreciate it." He shook hands with a firm handshake. The analyst smiled too and wished him good luck. Mr. I. turned around and left quickly.

Conclusion

These concluding remarks will supply the broad outlines of a reconstruction of Mr. I.'s psychopathology, based on the vicissitudes of the transference, to illuminate the central curative process and the nature of the termination of this analysis.

Mr. I.'s psychopathology quickly unfolded in the analysis.

It manifested in his inability to modulate inner tension: too much of it (a feeling of overstimulation) required immediate, frantic, and uncontrollable discharge; too little of it (a feeling of emptiness) required immediate and frantic self-stimulation of various kinds. To put it differently, Mr. I. had serious difficulty in maintaining his narcissistic equilibrium and, on his own, was unable to regulate his self-esteem. He was talented in many areas, but he could not pursue his professional ambitions or extracurricular activities (especially music) without serious inhibitions.

Mr. I. attached himself to the analyst (self-object) immediately, with an intense, addiction-like quality, but he continued, both in and out of the analytic situation, to re-enact his habitual, lifelong modes of attempting to deal with over-stimulation and understimulation.

As mentioned in the introduction, an idealizing transference might well have developed with dramatic rapidity, had the meaning of the early "addiction" to the analyst been correctly assessed and analytically responded to. The validity of this assumption — recognizing that the analyst's responses do affect the emerging transferences — is buttressed by subsequent events in this analysis and has also been confirmed from other analyses.

The oscillations within the bipolar transference would, of course, have emerged anyhow, in keeping with a more "natural" sequential unfolding of the pathogenic experiences, starting with the chronologically more recent traumatic experiences and eventually reactivating (if necessary and possible) more archaic pathogenic events.

In the case of Mr. I., the genetically more recent experiences had to do with his disappointment in his father. After he had been traumatically disappointed by his mother's "abandonment" of him in favor of his newborn sister (at the age of three) and subsequently in favor of his younger brothers, it was clearly his attempt to regain lost self-esteem, power, and perfection that made him turn (with intense attachment) to his idealized father—only to be severely disappointed again. It was this effort to derive omnipotent power and perfection from the idealized father that was revived in the sustained idealizing transference. It would be an unwarranted oversimplification to view this particular idealizing transference exclusively as a "father transference," since the original idealizations subsequently also involved efforts to invest (secondarily) his mother, and later on, his sister (and then any available self-object) with the desired power and perfection. The endless search for an idealized parental imago must have been necessitated by the traumatic disappointments Mr. I. experienced in his father. These, then, interfered with the phase-appropriate transmuting internalizations of Mr. I.'s narcissistic investments, his archaic affects and fantasies.

Disruptions of the idealizing transference repeatedly exposed the underlying weakness and fragility of the self—"the splat on the wall"—revealing also the nature of the genetic traumata that must have led to the arrest in the development of the idealized parental imago. During these disruptions the transient appearance of archaic grandiosity and exhibitionism, in the form of a mirror or merger transference, brought to light the pre-existing and/or parallel pathology in the grandiose-exhibitionistic self, which was subsequently revived in a secondary mirror transference.

The analytic process shows that with the progressive working through of the idealizing transference, and overlapping with it, a further pathognomonic regression revived the grandiose-exhibitionistic self. Thus, a secondary mirror transference established itself with clearly discernible continuity, which then dominated the analysis from about the middle of the third year through its termination.

The vicissitudes of the mirror transference (largely, but

not exclusively, a "mother-transference") revived the traumatic absence of adequate mirroring, confirming, and admiring responses from the mother, and showed a turning to the father and still later to the sister (and still later on to any available self-object) to obtain what was unavailable or not reliably and predictably available in his relation to his mother. Mother's turning away from Mr. I. upon the birth of his sister was just one circumscribed, massive trauma amidst frequent painful separations from a sickly child with multiple psychosomatic symptoms. In addition, the inadequate shielding from excessive (incestuous) overstimulation in relation to open parental nudity; the parents' intense preoccupation with themselves, with each other and their own narcissistic needs; the mother's frequent depressive withdrawal (in relation to the birth of her children?); and Mr. I.'s attempts to cope with these as a child, all were revived in the mirror transference, shedding light on the genesis of his narcissistic psychopathology. A brief description of this psychopathology in metapsychologic language will enhance our grasp of the central role of transmuting internalizations in this analysis.

Mr. I. exemplified an arrest in the development of the narcissistic sector of his personality, involving both lines of development — hence his bipolar transference. The arrest in the "idealized parental imago" (its maturation and concomitant transformations) resulted in the absence of those psychic structures — especially the idealization of the superego — which are the end-results of this line of development of narcissism. The arrest of the "grandiose-exhibitionistic self" (its maturation and transformations) resulted in the absence of psychic structures — especially those of self-esteem, the capacity to enjoy activities and goal-directed ambitions and purposes — which are the end-results of this line of development of narcissism.

Throughout his life Mr. I. attempted to compensate for

his "missing psychic structures" (Kohut, 1971) by "using" others as self-objects to fulfill the functions he could not fulfill for himself. Prominent in the manner in which he "used" his self-objects were the specific ways in which he experienced them as part of himself or he experienced himself as part of them. His early memories and childhood fantasies depict, in concretized fashion, his unsuccessful attempts at internalizations and structure building—i.e., the lack of phase-appropriate transmuting internalizations (e.g., memories of his close attachment to his sister, the fantasy of keeping two girls captive in a hotel as Superman, the fantasy of a miniaturized version of his friend, S.L., placed in a carved-out spot inside his chest). They illustrate his needs in particular contexts (e.g., traumatized separations from mother) and the attempts to attach himself to those who could fulfill them permanently. In addition, the history of Mr. I.'s preanalytic life was replete with gross identifications with idealized father figures in the persons of friends and teachers—without adequate transmuting internalizations. There was also evidence of continued (and disturbing) archaic attempts to acquire psychic structure through regressive, oral, and anal incorporative fantasies. These were expressed in his many frantic efforts at "sexualized repair" of fragmentations, but could never lead to the acquisition of missing psychic structures.

The reader can follow these efforts, as they reoccur in the analytic situation. One particular line of development of a hitherto unsuccessful mode of internalization illustrates the fate of these attempts in the analysis remarkably well. Mr. I. reported very early in the analysis (p. 19), what was then an isolated, abruptly expressed fantasy. He stood in front of a mirror, looked at himself, and said: "You look like you just swallowed your father's penis." This was just one archaic mode of internalization among many others (some were further advanced and less sexualized), with which he aimed to acquire aspects of his father. The transformation from early sexualized modes to those of higher levels and forms can be traced in dreams and fantasies throughout the analysis. These do not develop in a straight, progressive line, but oscillate with the transference, showing forward movements and regressions and leaving behind traces of transmuting internalizations. The results of these are only visible at first in the over-all improvement of the capacity to modulate tension and to regulate self-esteem, but show the acquisition of more discretely discernible functions as the analysis progresses. The penis turns into the trumpet, the clarinet, the analyst's voice; and the interpretive grasp of their meaning, along with the minute, tolerable failures in the analyst's empathy aid their bit-by-bit transmutations into psychic structures.

The termination phase shows a massive recurrence (especially in dreams) of archaic efforts at internalization, as last-minute emergency measures. There is a reworking of archaic modes and forms of structure building to more mature forms. The context of their occurrence reveals the nature of the original traumata that prevented phase-appropriate successful transmuting internalizations as well as those aspects of the analytic process that permit or enhance their current successful transformations into psychic structures. A good example of the latter is Mr. I.'s dream in which he swallowed the clarinet. Significantly, the clarinet continued to play music from within him. Although this was again a gross identification via oral incorporation, the digestion and assimilation of the analyst's symbolic strength were aided by interpretive working through of this and similar efforts (see pp. 99-100, also cf. Kohut, 1971, p. 168).

These transmuting internalizations have been described as central to the curative process in this analysis and in the analysis of narcissistic personality disorders in general (Kohut, 1971). The termination phase of this analysis demonstrates, in addition, that analytic method and insight were also acquired by Mr. I. in the form of a self-analytic capacity. Its rather stable presence during the termination phase was taken as an indication by both patient and analyst that, in spite of the many questions raised about its timing, this was a satisfactorily terminated psychoanalytic process.

3

TRANSFORMATION OF
ARCHAIC NARCISSISM

In summarizing a completed analysis, not all aspects of the analytic process can be equally emphasized without making the reading of the material cumbersome. The focus in this report has been placed on the description of the transformation of archaic narcissism into its adult forms. In order to keep that focus relatively clear, all other aspects of the analysis have been dealt with in summary fashion. The patient's past history is summarized under a separate heading, which does not, of course, mean that Mr. M. shared his memories and the significant events of his past all at once. Some of these were revealed in the initial diagnostic study; the greater part emerged in the course of the analysis. Because it was in the middle phase of the analysis that the beginning transformatio₂ ₌ of archaic narcissism into its adult forms could be recognized, this phase is reported in greater detail.

How does transformation of archaic narcissism come about? The transformation occurs through the mobilization of the archaic narcissistic positions in the transference and the working through of these transferences in the course of the

analysis. The archaic forms of narcissism—the grandiose self
and the idealized parent imago—are infantile configurations, which because of repression (or disavowal) had not participated in the progressive development of the psyche. Such
failures in development are due to the traumatic childhood
experiences in the narcissistic realm of the personality (Kohut,
1971). The dynamic presence of the repressed narcissistic configurations in the unconscious has to be conceptualized in a
manner similar to the conceptualization of fixation points that
occur in response to traumatic frustrations of infantile libidinal and aggressive impulses, namely, that they give rise to
symptoms, inhibitions and, in the analytic experience, to
specific forms of transferences. If the original trauma occurred primarily in relation to infantile narcissism (its grandiosity, exhibitionism, and its need to endow the caretaking
other with power and perfection through idealization), the
transference that develops expresses these narcissistic features
rather than the derivatives of the arrested or poorly resolved
oedipal conflict.

   In this case sample, no effort will be made to trace the vicissitudes of the narcissistic transferences, though their nature
will be indicated at various junctures in the summary. Rather,
the emphasis will be on the specific manner in which these
transferences have been worked through. Working through of
the narcissistic transferences—which is the process whereby
their transformation from archaic to mature form takes
place—does not differ from the working-through process
related to instinctual fixation points. Fenichel's description of
what constitutes the aim of analysis is equally applicable in
cases of narcissistic personality disorders; the aim of psychoanalysis is the "reconnection" of repressed infantile impulses
with the rest of the personality. In the process of working
through, the reconnection occurs gradually with the help of
well-timed and empathic interpretations. "If the energy which

was bound up in the defense struggle is joined again to the personality, it fits itself in with it and with the genital primacy arrived at by it" (Fenichel, 1941, p. 21). The result of working through the narcissistic transferences, however, is not the achievement of genital primacy, but rather an increase in the basic drive-controlling and drive-channeling structures of the ego and a strengthening and an increased narcissistic cathexis of the values and standards of the superego. The superego can then function as a source of approval and help maintain the patient's previously tenuous narcissistic homeostasis.

In this clinical sample, the transformation was primarily related to the infantile grandiosity and exhibitionism as these were mobilized first in a twinship and, later in the analysis, in a mirror transference proper. The patient, who had a gift for writing, could not sustain himself at his work because his visual images, in which his ideas first appeared, created too much excitement for him. The images were associated with infantile exhibitionistic fantasies which created the excitement. The fantasies exhausted him; they did not provide him with the steady flow of energy he needed in order to be able to work. The containment of the excitement and its channeling into creative writing constituted the transformation of archaic narcissism into its adult form.

The patient engaged in certain activities in the course of the analysis that indicated the gradual taming and channeling of his originally overstimulating grandiose fantasies. These activities served as "way stations" in the process of working through and eventually provided him with the full control of his visual images in the service of his work as a writer. The gradual increment in the basic ego matrix resulted in his increasing ability to freely abandon himself to his fantasies without fear of overstimulation. To conceptualize such activities as "way stations" indicates that they are recognized as extra-analytic experiences which the patient utilizes in the course of analysis to complete specific (in this case narcissistic) aspects of his development. Such a concept fruitfully links the meaning of extra-analytic experiences with the events of the analytic process itself.

The Clinical Example

This 30-year-old man, Mr. M.,[1] sought psychoanalysis following his wife's leaving him after six years of marriage. He wanted to know how he may have contributed to the estrangement and separation. He was also dissatisfied with his current job, which was financially and in terms of its status value very desirable but which left him unfulfilled. Prior to this interview, the patient had two diagnostic interviews with another analyst, whose report emphasized Mr. M.'s good school and work records and the stability of his ego and superego functions. He did not find the patient depressed, but rather hurt and puzzled by the fact that his wife had left him.

Mr. M. was of medium height and build. He dressed casually but was always well groomed. He worked for a local TV station as a writer. The job was dependable, but he felt it to be very limiting. He hoped the analysis would make him independent of employment by helping him overcome what he experienced as a block in his ability to be a creative writer. He had trouble sustaining his energy when he worked; he had trouble getting up in the morning and was irregular in his work habits. His apathy and lack of initiative made him feel only "half alive."

The diagnostic interview took place in June. If analysis was to be the choice of treatment, he was to begin treatment in September. The patient appeared comfortable in the inter-

---

[1] Mr. M. is described by Kohut (1977), especially in Chapter One.

view, but his concerns in relation to analysis found expression in his first questions to the analyst. He wanted to know: What happens to her patients when she goes on vacations? Will there be another analyst to take care of him? What if the analyst dies in the course of his analysis? Does she have arrangements for him to continue so that the time and money he has invested in her will not be wasted? He obviously wanted to have some evidence of her commitment before he could commit himself to the analysis.

Past History

The patient was adopted at the age of three months (once during the analysis, he became panicky at the thought that nobody might have taken care of him in the first three months of his life). His older brother and younger sister were also adopted. The children were about two years apart in age. His adoptive mother could not have children because of a severe heart condition. He remembers her only as a sick woman. The adoptive parents were immigrants from Europe with a strong family and church orientation. The father was a toolmaker; he disappointed the patient by his inability to give leadership to their family life. He was a "soft-skinned," soft-spoken man, who impressed the patient as passive and in some ways effeminate.

Mr. M. was eleven years old when his mother died, but the loss was still very acute in his mind. His father remarried two years after his mother's death "because of the children." The patient could not think of this woman as his mother. He felt the marriage meant the loss of his father too, who now became totally devoted to his new wife and to her family. After father remarried no references were made to his mother; her memory was not kept alive—symbolically expressed by the fact that the father failed to erect a tombstone for her. The patient's anger about this was not conscious to him until he was deeply engaged in working through his feelings in relation to his mother's death and his father's remarriage.

The patient had recently learned about his brother's homosexuality. This disturbed but did not surprise him. In the course of this analysis, the brother married an older woman who took care of him.

Mr. M. himself had frequent sexual dreams about young boys, and he had occasionally felt that older men, including his father, were sexually attracted to him. He did not think of himself, however, as someone who had reason to worry about homosexuality. Rather he was worried about his wife experiencing his love-making as sadistic, while he thought of it as "play fights." It worried him that this may have been her reason for leaving him. In connection with her claim that he was sadistic when sexually aroused, he wanted to understand the reason for his engaging in sexual fantasies that contained some form of playful torture, such as one or the other of the sexual partners being tied down. These fantasies could either soothe and comfort him or entertain him when he felt lonely. There were never any beatings involved. A similar fantasy, which emerged in the course of the analysis, was of renting a big comfortable house where he would keep some women who took care of several children. The women would be on welfare, dependent on him and controlled by him.

The patient also described vague somatic experiences: a strange sensation in his nose upon inhaling, and frequent cramps in his legs — symptoms that worried him but for which he was afraid to seek explanation. He was preoccupied with his body and its functions, but was most erratic in caring for himself. Days of virtual starving would be followed by indulging himself, eating in restaurants too expensive for him.

Though Mr. M. did not state this explicitly, what he expected from his analysis emerged relatively early. He expected that it would clarify the nature of his sexual behavior for him. (Was he "sick" sexually, as his wife implied? Were his quasi-sadistic fantasies affecting his sexual relationships with women?) He hoped that analysis would help him become a creative person, so that he could become a free-lance writer and, with this, an independent man. He also expected that the analysis would correct what he perceived as a defect in his thinking, namely, his inability to understand logic. The patient had very much wanted to earn a postgraduate scholarship to study history while he was in college. Only his failure to master a course in logic prevented him from getting the scholarship. During the analysis, he checked out changes in himself by going back to the philosophy books he had used in college to see if he could now better comprehend them.

Analyzability

The question of analyzability was primarily related to the possibility that Mr. M. was suffering from an acute form of depression, the consequence of his wife having left him. He came for analysis soon after that, and he had a history of parent loss and adoption. The possibility of an anaclitic depression was suggested by his concern at being left by the analyst, his inability to get up in the morning, and by his apathy and the lack of initiative.

But the manner in which the patient responded to the two-month delay between diagnostic interviews in June and the beginning of the analysis in September was not in keeping with the diagnosis of an acute episode of depression: He expressed his annoyance about the delay and dealt with this and related issues in a businesslike, somewhat arrogant manner; he was neither anxious nor pleading. The diagnosis of depression could be fairly safely excluded on the basis of this affective state and the way in which he related to the analyst.

The nature of his past object relations (parents, siblings, wife) appeared ambivalent, with much repressed anger. But most importantly, the patient had a sense of "unreality" about his feelings toward these important people in his life. He was concerned about his wife's perception of his "play fights," since he could not be sure that these were not indeed expressions of his wish to hurt her. It was in connection with these issues that the analyst considered the possibility of a borderline condition. But his good work history, in spite of his subjectively experienced difficulties, indicated the reliability of his ego and superego functioning, and there were no clinical symptoms to support the possibility of a borderline condition.

At the time of the initial diagnostic interview, it could not be decided whether the apathy, lack of initiative, and the lack of a sense of fulfillment in his work and in his relationships were due to narcissistic psychopathology or whether these were expressions of a psychoneurosis, that is, of oedipal psychopathology. The differential diagnosis could only be established by the nature of the developing transference, namely, whether the analyst would be experienced as part of the patient's self or as a separate and autonomous object.

The Early Phase and the
Emergence of Specific Narcissistic Transferences

During the first couch hour, Mr. M. reflected on his antagonism toward the analyst in their first meeting. He explained this in terms of his reaction to her small but highly visible physical defect. He spoke of his fascination with people who are damaged in any way. At the same time, he also felt that her defect was an imposition on him. He would now have to watch out for her, not even in his thoughts could he be angry at her. The defect was a sign of weakness, similar to his mother's chronic illness. His mother had to be protected from the children's ordinary rowdiness and exuberance; his father had frequently warned the children that they had to be quiet because their mother was very ill and might die. The patient imagined that the analyst's defect resulted from some kind of torture she had been made to endure. This was what fascinated him. Speaking about this in the first hour appeared to be Mr. M.'s attempt to deal with the analyst's defect head-on, in a counterphobic way.

Also in the first hour, he spoke of an affair he began during the summer "till I get to see you again." He had several rather passionate affairs with women throughout his analysis.

In the fifth hour, the patient asked if he could tape-record his sessions. The analyst suggested that they first understand the meaning of his request. The patient decided not to bring the tape recorder, but, instead, he began to make nightly notes on his typewriter. He was probably never going to look at these notes, he said, but by having made them, his "analysis can't get lost." The various meanings of this evolved only in the course of analysis: He wanted to be in physical possession of the material, e.g., to be able to "replay" it, to be in control of what was said. He needed to control his regression, his own affective responses as well as those of the analyst. He had to "play it safe"; the surprise of an unexpected comment created intense narcissistic tensions in him. Then too, the notes and note-taking served the function of reducing the possibility of overstimulation; words had special significance to Mr. M. because they were highly valued by his articulate father. Similar to his interest in history and in his own origins, the notes served the purpose of establishing a sense of continuity about himself.

Whereas the patient appeared to associate freely relatively early in his analysis, his fear of the analyst's reaction to what he said remained of considerable concern to him. He thought this had to do with his alertness to changes in his mother's moods and how responsible he felt for these. He had always searched her face for clues as to how she might feel about him. His earliest memories related to such experiences: "I was sitting in the bathtub, mother was giving me vaseline, I was pulling back the skin on my penis. I was watching her expression, sensing that she thought she could not do this, only I could." The memory expressed the little boy's pride in himself, which, however, was mixed with concern whether he created pleasure or possibly discomfort in the onlooker. He was particularly sensitive to the response of his "audience" when he thought he was showing off. Mr. M. was afraid that worrying about the analyst's reaction to him indicated that he might become enslaved to her in a similar way; that he could not express himself freely without being concerned whether or not he had pleased her.

From the beginning, Mr. M. was concerned about his ability to control his emotions in the analysis; he needed to know how well he could regulate his affects on the couch. Too much affect would make him vulnerable to the analyst. In order to see whether or not he could safely regress, he conducted "an experiment" with himself. His friends told him that when they were on LSD they were able to imagine themselves in their mother's womb. This had something to do with the way LSD affected one's sense of time. He wanted to see if he could go into himself and come back safely. He did not take LSD, but he lay down quietly in a dark room and allowed himself to relax totally. This proved to be a frightening experience: As he felt his extremities becoming numb, he became sick to his stomach. "I had to keep contact with my body, massaging my cheeks, so I won't die, go away. . . ."

The self-induced regression apparently resulted in a sudden psychoeconomic imbalance, threatening him with loss of self boundaries. By stimulating his nonfeeling body parts, he regained the sense of self-cohesiveness. The patient compared this experience to the ones he frequently had when he worked on his writing; he could not safely abandon himself to his writing, he was afraid he might become dizzy, have a sense of floating away as if he were "spinning off into orbit." He could not pay attention to the content of his work as he became preoccupied with his mode of producing it. He had to take certain precautions before he could sit down to write. In order to have some form of release, he would either masturbate or produce sexual fantasies. After such precautions, it still took him some time to get into the work. Even then, he would have to break off frequently. As he explained: "I am afraid of staying and floating away. In so much of the writing, I am not in control."

The difficulty in initiating and sustaining his energy for productive work appeared to be related to regulating the level of excitement when he was overstimulated by grandiose (exhibitionistic) fantasies. The states of overstimulation alternated with mental states when such fantasies were repressed and he had to struggle to maintain a sense of aliveness in himself and in his activities. His body, too, was subject to this sense of deadness. He would rub the surface of his body or stimulate himself in some other way (by running, for instance) to produce the sense of aliveness. During his adolescence, he had the habit of pulling his hair which had a similar effect on him.

From early in the analysis, Mr. M. had strong affective reactions to the analyst's comments: "When you talk, I rise in ecstasy, I don't take it in; the ecstasy is that you are talking about *me* and when you are right, such elation!" The patient reported the first dream directly related to the analyst in the eighteenth analytic hour: He was with Jacqueline Onassis "who is sophisticated and soft-spoken, like you. I felt happy in the dream to be associated with her."

Soon after this first dream, transference affects were mobilized which had nothing to do with soft-spoken ladies, but expressed his fear that his feelings would be disregarded by the analyst; he felt the threat of being intruded upon. This, too, found first expression in a dream, which he reported in the 31st hour: A middle-aged woman moved into his apartment, and she was redecorating it. This annoyed him. Everything was deep avocado and very ornate. "I was annoyed by the intrusion—I didn't realize she would redo the apartment—I was just sitting there watching it all."

In his associations, he described the woman more fully: She wore sensible shoes, "was built like my mother, sort of." Mr. M. did not associate the middle-aged woman with the analyst, but when she drew his attention to that possibility, he said, "Yes, she was a schoolteacher-kind. I was afraid of you yesterday for the first time." The analyst focused on his annoyance in the dream, which she thought indicated his fear that she will "re-do" him while he is sitting passively by. This was true, he said, and since he was afraid of her responses, it was good he didn't see her face: "You may be cold and not mother me the way I want you to—I don't like to think about that." (With the deepening of the analytic regression, the patient felt frustrated because he could not see the analyst's face and thus judge her mood and reaction to him.)

The patient reflected further on the woman in the dream and decided that, indeed, she represented the analyst: "I saw her from the back [the patient usually followed the analyst into her office] in a suit, dowdy looking, a no-no character." To see her as a dowdy, schoolteacher type was to lessen the possibility of sexual stimulation, which he would have experienced as a form of intrusion. The distortion of her appearance served the defensive function of controlling the level of excitement. Later in the analysis, the patient had a dream in which the analyst wore "basic black" after he had seen her in a colorful print dress. The black dress remained the symbolic expression of his wish that the analyst remain in the background, that her personality should not in any way intrude on *his* analysis.

In view of Mr. M.'s initial concern over separations, the first lengthy separation (two weeks during the Christmas holidays) went without difficulty. But when the analyst returned, Mr. M. spoke of his anger and announced that now his typewriter was getting all his affects. It was after this first vacation that the patient began to speak of his weekends having become oppressive to him. He had taken to the reading of Victorian novels during the weekends and felt "consumed by fantasies of violence." He became irritable with the analyst. Brief delays in starting the hour caused him to be sullen and withdrawn. He was angry at the thought that — against his best intentions — he had become enslaved to her: "I am on a conveyor belt — I am not moving, I am being moved." It was particularly painful to him that, while he felt that the analyst's control over him had increased, he didn't feel he had any power over her.

Was this fear of being controlled a resistance against a developing merger transference? Or had the sense of helplessness related to separations over the weekends and during the Christmas holidays reactivated a pregenital conflict? Mr. M. had spent the first three months of his life in an orphanage. His reactions to separations could well have represented a fear of being abandoned. Further analysis of his reactions to separations, however, proved to have the same meaning as other of his transference reactions, such as his irritability with the analyst and the feeling that he was on a conveyor belt. They all exposed a specific form of narcissistic vulnerability, namely, that the analyst will disregard his feelings, whatever they might be, that what he thought and felt would not matter to her. The disruption of his analysis during weekends and holidays represented such a disregard for his feelings; the analytic hours were suspended no matter how he felt. Being on a conveyor belt expressed this feeling as well; he felt himself becoming passive as his needs for the analyst and the analytic experience increased. This made him vulnerable. He was afraid that the more dependent he became on the analysis, the more vulnerable he would become in relation to the analyst.

Such concerns at first appeared nonspecific, related to the regression in the analysis. Mr. M.'s fear that he might be controlled and emotionally exploited, however, had transference significance. He feared control and emotional exploitation in all his intimate relationships.

Mr. M. experienced the emotional exploitation as a form of humiliation. He expressed this complex set of affects in the form of a "picture," which he described in detail. Since this picture — or image, as he referred to it — appeared to be a visual representation of his childhood perception of himself and of his emotional environment, it will be used in this summary as a representative image into which innumerable childhood experiences have been condensed and telescoped. The image was that of a twelve-year-old boy standing naked in the middle of an empty room. His hands were on his hips, he had an impish smile on his face, as if aware of some power he had over the people who were watching him. Someone was taking a picture of the boy. He appeared lonely but arrogant with a sense of grandeur about him. His loneliness and isolation were intensified by the fact that his body was illuminated by the stark light of a single light bulb. The boy was in a foster home or may have been adopted. The "image" disturbed Mr. M.: "In a certain sense, I am afraid that I might have been too attractive to my own father. . . ."

Associating to the "image," Mr. M. focused on the father taking pictures of the boy and being unaware of the boy's discomfort as he stood there naked. Standing naked in the middle of an empty room concretized for him the lack of warmth and the unprotected exposure of his childhood. There was something painfully overstimulating in being stared at and photographed as if he were on display. The impish smile, the arrogant posture were a direct response to his environment's interest in him. The arrogance remained characteristic for the patient in situations when he felt that he was on "display." The arrogance had something to do with his feeling that he had a special power over his parents. Neither of his siblings had that. His brother was a trouble maker, probably related to his jealousy of the patient. His sister was meek and remained in the background. But he was the star in the family. He was considered the smartest among the siblings, and he was the one who was sent to an expensive Eastern college. Later in life, he resented the frequent references his father made to this, feeling that he will forever have to remain indebted to them.

The idea that his father may have been sexually attracted to him intrigued Mr. M., since in reality he had no reason to believe this was so. Rather, for him, this expressed symbolically a feeling that he was emotionally exploited by his father; that he possibly may have been adopted to meet some special (possibly sexual) needs of his father's. He thought of emotional exploitation in sexual terms since now, as an adult, it was in the context of sexual fantasies or in actual sexual encounters that he could most clearly see how one person may use his power and exploit and thereby humiliate the other. In his sexual fantasies, in which one partner tied down the other, and in his "play fights" with his wife he dominated the others, he was the powerful one. The emphasis in these fantasies was on humiliation rather than on the need to inflict pain or cause physical harm. It was not clear to the analyst whether the fantasies served the purpose of turning passively endured childhood experiences into a sense of active mastery or whether the memory related to the father was the expression of his latent homosexuality. The answer to this question was difficult because the analyst did not know what was important here — the content of the fantasies, which was sexual, or the experience of having been humiliated as a child. The sexual content makes one think of the negative Oedipus complex which could have been responsible for his latent homosexuality, while the passively endured humiliation was a narcissistic injury which the patient was now actively dealing with partly in fantasy and partly in reality.

The analyst interpreted Mr. M.'s first references to the possibility that his father may have been sexually attracted to him as a child's wish for closeness with the father. She understood this as a simple projection, an expression of the negative Oedipus complex. While such a possibility could not be excluded, the patient's associations were not dealing with issues of latent homosexuality as much as with the importance the experiences of humiliation had in his sexual fantasies and some in his actual sexual practices. The experience of humiliation appeared to be sexualized in these fantasies. Kohut (1971) makes the point that in childhood and adult perversions a painful affect becomes sexualized in an effort to "stem the tide of regression" at times of severe frustrations. In childhood, as well as in later life, perverse fantasies and activities appear to serve the defensive function of turning a painful affect that was passively endured in childhood through erotization into a sense of active mastery. While the sexual context affords the sense of mastery over the painful affect, it also provides a discharge channel for narcissistic tensions whether these were aroused from frustration or from overstimulation.

In the analysis, too, certain events indicated that Mr. M. used the erotization of painful affects as a way of mastering them. The reading of Victorian novels over weekends and holidays could be understood in this manner. These novels had a content similar to his fantasies; they dealt with quasi-sadistic sexual encounters. Identifying with the dominant, exploitative figures in the novels, he mastered the sense of helpless rage he experienced at times of separation and at times of humiliation.

An incident indicating that he turned a potentially humiliating experience into active mastery in his fantasies occurred when the patient began the hour saying that as he walked into the office behind the analyst, he had the wish to push her down, to see her "helplessly sprawled on the floor." At first, it appeared as if his wish was to hurt the analyst physically. After some time, however, it became obvious that the patient's intent here was not to cause her physical harm but rather to cause psychic pain, to inflict humiliation. While the fantasies of humiliating others served the primary purpose of turning passive childhood experiences into active ones, they also recreated a sense of omnipotence and arrogance in the patient. But these were hollow experiences; they gave him temporary comfort when he feared that those who had become important to him might emotionally exploit and humiliate him. (The appearance of omnipotence and empty arrogance in the transference, as well as Mr. M.'s reactions to relatively small breaches in the analyst's empathy, confirmed the diagnosis of narcissistic personality disorder. The appearance of childhood solutions, such as arrogance or haughty withdrawal, to childhood narcissistic traumata in the transference is analogous to the appearance of the infantile neurosis of an unresolved Oedipus complex when this is recreated in the transference neurosis.)

As Mr. M. began to recognize certain salient features in himself as repetitions from his past in the present (primarily the manner in which he protected himself from feeling humiliated by appearing arrogant and haughty), he experienced a sense of relief. He felt relieved because much of what he felt about himself could now be put into a better perspective and this gave him a sense of mastery. But the insight also disappointed him: it made him feel very "childish."

As the genetic precursors of his transference feelings began to unfold, the patient became curious about the analyst.
He wanted to know if her experiences in the analysis were
similar to his. Did she go through the ups and down he was
going through? His questions appeared to be attempts to
break down all barriers between himself and the analyst. He
told of a fantasy that when people talked to each other, the sex
of one changed to that of the other. This way they could understand each other better and achieve a greater degree of
harmony. He also had a dream about Siamese twins: "It was a
side view of Siamese twins, they were tied together. There was
a sense, too, as if my shadow was along. The girl was leading,
the other was behind, very harmonious. . . ."

The narcissistic transference, which now appeared to be
well established as a twinship transference, provided the patient with a relative sense of calm and harmony. This was
shattered, however, when the analyst, in one of her interpretations, referred to Mr. M.'s grandmother as if she were still a-
live. The patient was very much attached to his grandmother;
she was the only person he felt was truly invested in him. He
and his family had lived in the grandmother's home for two
years after his mother's death and before his father remarried.
This was a very important period in Mr. M.'s life. That the
analyst did not remember that the grandmother was dead was
unforgivable. In the past, whenever the analyst recalled a particular detail of his past, Mr. M. felt "held" by her. Now he
felt as if she had dropped him. The experience created a disruption in the self-object transference which resulted in a
sense of confusion rather than in the patient's withdrawal into
a haughty silence. He was constantly anticipating the repetition of this particular trauma; he dreaded re-experiencing
the feeling that what was important to him could simply be ignored or forgotten by others. Primarily, he worried that in
some way he caused the analyst to forget about the importance

his grandmother had for him; that her failure to be empathic with him was ultimately his fault. This was a familiar feeling; he always felt responsible for his parents' reaction to him, and he spent a lifetime assuring that it be a positive one. The analyst offered her interpretation in the form of questions: "You must wonder, have I dropped you because you weren't good enough to be held? Or have you been in some way at fault for being dropped so carelessly? These are questions every child asks of himself when hurt or openly rejected."

Such disruptions in an analysis are unavoidable. They appear to serve the same function in the analysis as failures of parental empathy do developmentally. In the course of development, optimal failures in parental empathy lead to structure building as long as such failures are nontraumatic and occur in a generally accepting and positively mirroring environment. In the analysis, disruptions in the self-object transference constitute "optimal frustrations" as long as the analyst understands and accepts the patient's transference needs.

The self-object transference here was re-established (and an aspect of working through occurred) when the analyst interpreted the meaning which her forgetting the grandmother's death had for Mr. M. She said that forgetting something important to him was as if she had forgotten him or not cared about him. He felt carelessly dropped, similar to experiences he had as a youngster when he enthusiastically described something to his father, who either did not respond or changed the subject.

The Middle Phase and the
Transformation of Narcissistic Structures

Many genetic and transference threads had converged in the analysis at this point. As described earlier, Mr. M.'s transference affects focused on a particular issue, namely, that the analyst might disregard his feelings and thoughts; that as the analyst became increasingly more important to him, she would use her "power" over him by controlling or manipulating him. Genetically, the focus was on his having felt emotionally exploited because he was not responded to in terms of who he was, but in terms of what he could do for his parents.

The patient repeatedly approached the question of his adoption. His siblings spoke about this often; he himself considered it irrelevant. Now he wondered, could this have explained his insecurity? Maybe this was why he tried so hard to please his parents? There was a difference between his mother and his father in this respect. His mother was genuinely responsive to him and appreciative of him but her illness put a barrier between her and the rest of the family. He regretted how hazy his memory had become over the years in relation to his mother. What stood out in his mind was his concern over her health and how he always wanted to do something for her. It was hard for him to think that he may have felt she let him down by being ill and by her early death. In contrast, he felt his anger and disappointment in his father acutely. At the time the father remarried and failed to "reassemble" the family, Mr. M. became fully aware of his father's inability to recognize the feelings that important events (such as his mother's death and his father's remarriage) had for him and for his siblings. For example, the mother's name was not mentioned after she died, and the children were not taken to visit her grave. Nor was there any discussion regarding the father's remarriage and how the children felt about their new mother.

Mr. M. came to feel that his marriage might have failed because he expected from his wife what his parents could not do for him: to appreciate him for who he was rather than what he could do for her. His wife was a young aspiring artist in need of his encouragement and support; she was in no position to recognize and to be responsive to his need for optimal mirroring.

At the time Mr. M. entered analysis, he felt that he had to get out of his job because it wasn't his. The job was everything his parents would want for him — primarily status — but he experienced it as an empty shell; some kind of front which brought him recognition but no fulfillment. At this time in his life, he wanted to write: writing would be "his thing"; he was determined to make himself not only financially but primarily emotionally independent by achieving this goal. The patient vividly described his difficulty with creative writing. His ideas occurred to him in visual images. Though he was exceptionally articulate verbally, the written words could never quite express what he perceived visually. When he attempted to write, his thoughts raced in his head, making him feel dizzy, light-headed. Such overexcitement would be followed by a period in which he felt drained of energy. He then had to stop, take a rest, or do something else.

What was the relationship between this state of mind and his feelings that — contrary to appearances — he did not feel adequately mirrored in the essential features of his self, by either of his parents? It was this question to which the notion of infantile grandiosity and exhibitionism provided the answer and which guided the analyst's interpretations. In Kohut's view, the child's exhibitionism and grandiosity becomes gradually tamed and structuralized into the developing psyche in response to parental mirroring of the child's realistic assets and achievements. Mr. M.'s childhood self-perception that he was arrogant, a "show-off," indicated that his infantile grandiosity and exhibitionism did not undergo normal developmental changes. The image of the twelve-year-old boy carelessly exposed while others viewed him, and his father photographed him, expressed his childhood self-perception in a condensed way: He was "on stage" all his life, "performing" and in full knowledge of his effect on his environment. But this was at the expense of feeling genuinely mirrored (if mirrored in his "image," he would have experienced a warm glow instead of the coldness of the bare room). He appeared self-assured and arrogant, but felt empty. He took his clues from the responses he evoked rather than from how he himself felt. His arrogance did not protect him from being vulnerable and in need of external bolstering all the time. Schematically, this state of affairs could be expressed with a vertical split in the psyche; his "surface" attitude and behavior appeared confident and relatively effective, but the deeper layers of the psyche were not participating meaningfully in his activities; his activities remained mere "performances." He was frequently praised, but this made little difference in his self-perception in "depth." For Mr. M., the consequence of the disturbance in the transformation of archaic narcissism into its mature form was most distressing in the way it interfered with his ability to write creatively. In order to write he needed the resources of his nuclear self. In writing, he could not and did not want to pretend.

As the first summer approached, the patient had to deal more directly not only with the interruption of his analysis but also with the upcoming divorce procedures. He still had not told all his friends that his wife had left him; the whole idea remained distasteful and painful to him. He had violent fantasies about taking revenge on his wife: He would throw her down the steps and drag her by her hair or take her for a ride and push her out of the car. In spite of his plans of giving his wife a hard time with the divorce (which he did not do) and having an altogether miserable summer, this first lengthy vacation (six weeks) was not as difficult as he expected it to be. When the analyst returned, the patient told her that in her absence, he had imagined her in her bathing suit on a beach. This picture helped him think of the setting in which she was thinking *of him* while she was away—a confirmation of the narcissistic nature of his attachment to her.

During the summer break, Mr. M. read some books on sex offenders. He was distressed that these were people who as children were left alone and whose parents were emotionally aloof. Was he susceptible to something like this, he wondered. To exemplify his own parents' lack of emotional responsiveness, he related how much they disliked it when he cried or made any kind of a "scene." He had an aunt who was a different kind of person; he remembered her as having been warm and giving, someone who—contrary to the customs in those days—nursed her baby in public. This memory served as a stimulus for a "vision" the patient had on the couch: He saw a big breast filled with milk. The significance of the vision for him was not seeing the breast or its size, but his frustration that while the breast was clearly in sight, he could not see the face of the woman: "I am not nursing. I am desperate to see the woman's face. I get as far as the neck, but I can't see her face." His inability to see and "read" the analyst's face became a source of considerable frustration to the patient. He had always taken his clues from his mother's face; has he pleased her, has he not?

Now, in the analysis, he felt as if he were left in the dark, could not tell if the analyst's face expressed delight or disapproval. His need for mirroring in the transference became acute. The interpretation focused on his strain to see the woman's face behind the readily available breast. His childhood frustrations were not related to food or bodily care, but to his constant search for a mirroring response. The analyst asked Mr. M. whether the wish to see her face was a repetition of an almost compulsive need to search his mother's face to see if he had succeeded in pleasing her, or was he hoping for a response the aunt was more likely to give, an unconditional response in which he felt affirmed?

This interpretation, put in the form of a question, elated Mr. M. because of its great importance to him and the question led to a profitable period in the analysis. He re-examined the nature of his relationship with his wife and could recognize that there too he had repeated the patterns of his childhood in many ways; he had tried to elicit his wife's responses to his "performances," to actions he did not experience as part of himself. In the analysis, he began to dread the repetition of this particular childhood pattern. He did not want to be responded to because he was "charming" and "clever." But he wondered whether the analyst could tell the difference between his need to be bolstered because of his narcissistic vulnerability and his expectations that she recognize and appreciate his realistic assets. This was a period in which the analyst's empathic capacity was most severely tested; a period which led to the firming up of many tentative insights already described.

The self-object transference at this time appeared fairly securely established. This may have accounted for Mr. M.'s activities in community affairs, activities he thoroughly enjoyed. He gave several speeches, and, analyzing his (primarily exhibitionistic) anxieties in relation to these performances, he learned a great deal about himself. His increased activities, however, had a tenuous quality. He described himself as still feeling "exhilarated" and "heady" when he spoke in front of groups.

Being as busy as he was, he continued to have trouble getting up in the morning and continued to be very erratic in his writing habits. His writing remained perfunctory and gave him no pleasure. He felt that delivering a speech was easier than writing because "the audience keeps you in balance," whereas writing is solitary. If there is no audience, there is no structure—then too much depends on him, in terms of maintaining his narcissistic balance. After giving a successful speech, he worried about his temptation to brag to the analyst. He now felt "filled up with himself" and embarrassed at how much he needed the analyst's recognition for his accomplishments. He could not accept his wish for praise and continued to condemn himself for his "excessive need" to be responded to for his every accomplishment.

During this period, Mr. M. dreamed excessively; most of his dreams had to do with reunions, travels, and remodeling of old homes. In one of these dreams, he was in a bus looking out the window. He was traveling to a reunion and feeling comfortable. The dream made him feel secure. Though he was not in charge, since he was not the one driving the bus, he did not feel that he was being passively carried along; he was looking out the window, and could see what was happening. Traveling, he thought, referred to his analysis. He takes "trips into himself" and discovers new things. The dream seemed to have expressed a change in him. A change from having felt powerlessly controlled by the analyst to now feeling more as an active participant in the analysis. Even though he was not driving the bus, he felt secure with the driver. He trusted her. His associations to the dream included one which was related to his wish to tape-record his analytic hours when he first began his analysis. To have tape-recorded his analysis would have been still another way in which he wanted to establish a sense of continuity about himself; "I need to know where I come from and where I am going because of my hazy origins and no particular destination." Another reunion dream brought an association of his brother who was thinking of some day having a reunion with his real parents. This turned out to be his own wish, similar in meaning to his desire to write a historical novel, both expressing the wish "to bring to light what was."

Mr. M. imagined that the breakthrough of his creative energies would occur in a sudden burst. He compared the feelings he wished to have to sustain his efforts at writing to the feelings he now had when he ran. His running generated energy rather than consumed it. The running, the writing, his wish to get immersed into the researching and writing of a historical novel were all interrelated: "When I hook all these things together, I will surge to the moon." He laughed as he said this, indicating an increasing acceptance of his grandiose fantasies as the source of his creative activities. This acceptance constituted an important aspect of the working-through process. So did the dreams about reunions and travels: these had a common theme indicating that his sense of continuity was being established in the course of his analysis by discovering and connecting himself with parts of his past.

The patient's relation with women could be more readily recognized as being related to transference experiences than any other of his activities outside of the analysis. He had rather intense, sexually active relationships, though in none of these was he truly invested in his partner. The analyst's interpretations focused on the function the affairs had in his emotional life at the particular time in the analysis in which they occurred. She dealt with two aspects of his sexual relationships: one that they reflected his wish to control and possess the analyst the way he "possessed" his women, and the other that they appeared to function as "way-stations" in the process of internalizing some of the analyst's functions which he experienced as being primarily mirroring and echoing of his self and which needed to be confirmed in order to be experienced as real. (The interpretation of the mirroring and echoing needs and their genetic reconstruction in the analysis has to be differentiated from gratifying such needs. When interpreted, the narcissistic need remains mobilized without being gratified in the analytic situation. The patient then gradually builds ego structures, which handle these needs endopsychically by self-approval [Kohut, 1971].)

An outstanding example of an experience that occurred outside of the analysis but had a special significance for the process of analysis was related to the patient's having become friendly with the fourteen-year-old son of a good friend. He had known this family for some time. There were four children in the family, two of them were boys; a sixteen- and a fourteen-year-old. Mr. M. was particularly aware of the subtle but important ways in which the father expressed his respect and love for the two boys. He admired the younger of the two boys for his self-assured independent attitude which grew out of self-confidence rather than out of rebellion. He compared himself to this boy, saying: "I never tried to be independent, only to be good and successful." The patient took the youngster out several times. They attended and enjoyed rock concerts together and went to ball games. The boy was open in his admiration for the patient, and he in turn was conscious of enjoying his importance to the boy. At first, Mr. M. was disturbed by the importance this relationship had for him, but he was relieved that his love for the boy was devoid of sensual or erotic affects. ("I love John, but I don't want to make love to him; I would rather do that with my girl friends.") The meaning of this relationship was highlighted by a small incident: The two of them attended a ball game when Mr. M. noticed his girl friend in the ball park. He was hesitant to greet the girl in fear that he would rob the boy "of my complete attention." When he decided to greet the girl after all and sensed that the boy was not jealous, Mr. M. experienced an extraordinary degree of elation. He became almost dizzy and felt that something very important had happened to him at that moment. He had to go home and figure it all out. ·

The working through of the meaning of this relationship constituted a relatively brief but very important part of his analysis: The relationship was a form of restitution which occurred essentially on two levels: The patient admired the young man's independence, his separateness and sense of completeness, which were still incomplete achievements for him. His identification with the boy was indicated by his expectation that the boy would be jealous when they met his girl friend, since he, himself, had suffered jealousy when his father remarried. At the same time he was also the admiring, responsive father to the boy he wished he had had at the age when he had turned to his father after his mother's death. He wanted to protect the boy from the narcissistic trauma of feeling suddenly excluded, as he wished to have been protected by his father at the time his father remarried. The patient idealized in the youngster those assets which he failed to acquire in his own development; the boy's autonomy and his apparent lack of vulnerability, which was coupled with a great deal of sensitivity. The idealization of these assets hastened their internalization. Through the restitutive functions of the relationship, Mr. M. gave himself "another chance." As the boy's "father," he admired and encouraged the youngster's emotional independence and healthy self-esteem, and in his identification with him, he firmed up these very qualities in himself.

It may be questioned whether it is correct to call such an extra-analytic experience working through; some may consider it a form of acting out. But inasmuch as the friendship itself, with admiration for the boy's independence, helped the patient firm up his own increasing sense of separateness, I consider it part of working through.

As the second Christmas vacation of the analysis was approaching, the patient felt that this time the break in his analysis would create a new type of frustration. He experienced a strong forward movement in the analysis and resented that he had to wait at this time. Just before the actual break, the patient became very irritable with the analyst. He felt violent, wanted to pick a fight: "Nothing I can do could ever satisfy me

—the anger of being dependent on analysis. . . ." The analyst acknowledged that the timing of this interruption was indeed unfortunate, but he interrupted her: "Such clarifications don't bring solutions, these are words." Instead, he said, he would look for a girl to fall in love with. When the analyst said that this would prove that he is truly independent of her, he only became angrier: "You are tying me down by saying this." His dependence on the analysis, particularly his feelings toward the analyst made him contemptuous of himself: "This is childish. It is a problem enough to see my anxiety related to your leaving; when you talk about it, it just becomes more disgusting." He decided to grow a beard in the analyst's absence to startle and impress her upon her return.

Mr. M. was particularly distressed when he couldn't put the meaning of the analyst's leaving into perspective: "Some of the anxiety is connected with the lack of vision of what is going on here—I can't give it perspective. This does not surprise me, but I have a sense of dying or perishing, this is what shakes me. I expect this energy to be drawn out of me, it is impossible to generate it. This, in spite of the fact that my life with people is gratifying—when I am alone, I eat up myself. Even the fantasies now [the quasi-sadistic fantasies which used to arouse him sexually and then comfort him], I flip through them like filing cards, just to show how unsatisfying they are. Not surprisingly, it comes down to you: Why doesn't this relationship sustain me?" The analyst responded with references to his childhood experience: her leaving having reawakened feelings of helplessness when the grownups in his childhood did what they pleased, unconcerned with his feelings and wishes. She recalled what the patient had earlier told her about his mother's death; how he laughed to deny his pain and anger, that, after all his efforts to be her good little boy, she had irrevocably left him. The analyst also said that Mr. M. seemed to be afraid that she would mock him for his need to possess and control her. (The fear, which was so overriding in the early part of this analysis, that the analyst would exploit him emotionally and that because of her position she would humiliate him, became reactivated at times of separation, at times of stress.) He replied: "More than anything, I was afraid you would reassure me—that you would say with a forward look that everything would be all right." Insofar as the analyst had not reassured him in the past, this statement was an indication that the patient was aware that his experiences related to separations were essential aspects of his analysis. The understanding and interpretation of these experiences constituted a crucial part of his total analytic experience.

Mr. M.'s increasing ability to analyze his experiences became most obvious in relation to the following event: Earlier in his analysis, he began to write commentaries on his analysis. After several attempts at shaping this into a story by displacing his affects into fictitious characters, he wrote a very expressive short story. He told the analyst what he wrote and how he developed his ideas, and he openly expressed the wish that she praise him for his work. She did not praise him, but interpreted the reason for his wish to be praised. Essentially, her comments were related to the frustrated childhood wish that his assets be recognized by his parents as his and not be used by them to enhance their own self-esteem. He now needed affirmation of his assets and abilities in order to feel their reality, especially as these pertained to writing. The patient left the hour disappointed and angry.

The analyst had the distinct feeling that something of significance had occurred which she failed to appreciate and respond to with full understanding. So she was surprised when the patient came in the following Monday and reported a very pleasant weekend. He felt the weekend had been good because of the work he had accomplished in his analysis the week before. He saw the essence of this work in his clear realization and verbalization of the wish that the analyst praise him for the story. Though at first he was disappointed that she did not do so, later he realized that it wasn't her praise that really mattered. What mattered to him was that he recognized the importance the praise had for him and that he was able to verbalize his wish for it. This insight, which was independent of the analyst's interpretations, brought the patient considerable relief. He could now more fully appreciate how analysis worked; not by the analyst's praising, soothing, or comforting him, but by his own acceptance of his wishes after these had been recognized and accepted by her. The insight gave him a sense of mastery and affirmed his increasing independence and sense of separateness in the analysis.

The story he wrote indeed had special significance. While it was part of him, it was a story in which he had successfully taken distance from his affects without either overdrawing or paling the features of the characters he portrayed. One could consider this an instance in which liberation of the narcissistic energies took place, where what he created was experienced as real and genuinely part of himself, even though the confirmation by an admiring other was still necessary for the final affirmation of the product and with it, of himself. Although the analyst did not respond to Mr. M.'s mirroring needs, he did not turn away from her in anger, but retreated to a level of insight he could consider his own, independent of her. His self-approval did not relate to the story he wrote, but to his insight concerning the importance the analyst's praise had for him. This had re-established his narcissistic equilibrium and made the analyst's praise no longer important to him.

The winter of the second year of the analysis found Mr. M. very busy socially. Now that his friends knew of his divorce, he saw them more often. He cleaned up his apartment, removed some old draperies which obstructed his view of the city, and gave some successful parties. He was also very active in church and civic programs. Two of these activities served as outstanding examples of the manner in which the narcissistic energies bound up in the repressed and disavowed grandiose self were gradually deployed and were being transformed into their mature form. For some time, the patient had entertained the idea of establishing a writing school, but for one reason or another, he repeatedly discarded the idea. Now, he woke from his sleep one night with the idea "reborn." The idea of a writing school excited him, and he was worried that this would again be a quick flash which he would not be able to put into action. Perhaps to protect himself from this possibility, but also because it was more realistic, he went into partnership with a young man who took care of the business aspects of the undertaking. Mr. M. was not yet ready to do free-lance writing, but became enthusiastic about helping other people discover that they could write. The analyst considered this a very direct expression of his identification with her, one which was in some aspects too crude to be lasting, but which afforded him an excellent opportunity to consolidate the gains he made in analysis. He read a great deal of the related literature and told the analyst with excitement about the lectures he prepared for his nightly classes. She was a "good audience" as she listened to him describe how one has to learn "to break down one's ideas into manageable portions" and how he was helping people "increase their receptivity to word imagery."

At first, Mr. M. experienced some hypomanic states in connection with the ideas he had about the writing school: "I am going from one exhilarating thing to the other. I feel like a giant balloon. I am exhausted from having all this oxygen." As the project progressed, however, he experienced a "steady flow of energy" instead of the bursts of hypomania which had always been disorganizing to him in the past. In his own work, he began to use a technique he first developed in the teaching of his students. There were two parts to this technique of

writing which he used in his teaching. The first part was to encourage his students to use visual and tactile imagery in describing their ideas; he encouraged them not to be afraid to
"feel their thoughts." The second part consisted of translating
the imagery into words by "breaking them down into manageable portions." To the patient, the most difficult aspect of the
work was to allow his own images to emerge without their becoming overstimulating and thereby disrupting to him.
Working with his students on this project step by step was an
exercise that confirmed his own increasing capacity to contain
his images and to channel them into words. The words and the
way in which the story unfolded vividly retained the feelings he
had intended to express.

Another of Mr. M.'s activities having a special significance for the transformation of archaic narcissism was related
to his ability to learn to play a musical instrument. He considered his ability to learn to play a musical instrument an
important criterion for his progress in analysis. Just as being
able to play a good game of tennis with a woman signified a
degree of mental health to him, he thought his inability to
learn to play an instrument was an expression of his neurosis, no different from his writing block. Here, too, he felt his
biggest handicap was that he would become overstimulated
and therefore unable to execute the music; instead of creating
rhythm, he would become exhausted. The experience of
learning to play the instrument was very much the same as
his attempts to write. At first, performing on the instrument
was too important to him, and he could not practice. He a-
voided his teacher in fear of making mistakes in front of him.
When he once practiced for a prolonged period, imagining
that his neighbors were listening attentively, he felt victorious
at being able to continue after making several mistakes. However, the importance of learning to play the instrument lay not
in overcoming the fear of failure. Rather, he feared that not

being able to experience the rhythm of the music, he could not provide himself with the means of channeling and harnessing the excitement generated by his exhibitionistic fantasies whenever he imagined a large audience before whom he would perform. He imagined that to play a musical instrument well, that is, to feel the rhythm, would provide him with the same sense of cohesiveness that running did. The exhibitionistic wish to be listened to by an excited audience had to be correlated with an ability to master the overstimulation "bodily," by experiencing the rhythm and communicating through it with his audience. He told of a particular musician in a concert whom he admired because of the perfection with which this man achieved harmony with his audience by inducing his rhythm in them. This sounded like a much desired and highly sublimated form of merger between the player and his audience.

To reflect again on the nature of the narcissistic transference within which these developments in the analysis had taken place, it is best to describe one of Mr. M.'s dreams which indicated that this was a period in which the mirror transference in the narrower sense prevailed. The dream occurred when he was particularly pleased with the progress of the analysis: "It was a surrealistic scene, a piazza of a sort, there were several children around. I moved on as if to get to my instrument, but it turned out to be a column against which I had to push rhythmically. You were on a balcony with another woman. One of you wore a black dress, the other a colorful gown. You were telling the other woman how I could do this rhythm exercise. When I knew you were looking, I fell apart —I woke up, and I literally started losing parts of me, they were falling off, like my arms. I had the feeling of embarrassment for not having done the rhythm exercise." He gave some further details about the columns on the piazza and the liveliness and colorfulness of the whole scene.

The analyst's first impression was that this was a highly erotic transference dream and that the patient became anxious because of his sexual excitement and that he experienced the consequences of this in the form of a severe castration anxiety with his body parts falling off. In his associations, Mr. M. attributed great significance to the change in his mood in the dream; from a confident one to being scared when he realized that he was being watched by the analyst. The change in his mood occurred "when the importance of being watched was greater than the performance. . . ." The rhythm test was to test coordination, like running or playing tennis. The whole scene was like one at the Olympics, the people wore sport suits—like they do at the Olympics. The emphasis was on the importance of being watched and being approved of. He thought that the dream expressed his continued anxiety about exhibitionism and that in the dream this was related specifically to the analyst. His next associations focused on the women on the balcony. He thought that both women, the one in the dark dress and the other in a colorful gown, represented the analyst. The patient then recalled the dream in which the analyst wore "basic black" as a way of making her less intrusive and sexually exciting to him. Why was he seeing her now in both the black dress and the colorful gown as well? He still needed her nonintrusive, calming presence, in which her own self did not play a part (the black dress), but he could also perceive and tolerate more of her personality represented by the colorful print dress. The vivid colors of the columns on the piazza, too, indicated his increasing ability to contain his excitement. The sight was pleasant rather than disorganizing.

During the same period, toward the end of the second year of the analysis, Mr. M. had another transference dream indicating that he had now more consistently experienced the analyst's empathy without the fear of being controlled or exploited by her. In this dream he associated the analyst with his aunt, who was always available to him emotionally without intruding on him, without making demands on him. She was just there, in the "background." "I knew she was there, I didn't talk to her much, but she was around." The analyst reflected on the importance it had for the patient throughout the analysis to put the analyst a "comfortable distance" from himself; she should be there, available, but not intrude with her presence so that he would feel obliged to consider her and to please her. He compared this to the function of a coach: "You are the coach, but I want to keep you on the bench. I am not a sportsman, but this image helps. I must keep you on the bench, otherwise the team [that is, himself] will disintegrate." He again spoke of his parents who, in their need for him, could not stay in the "background" and allow him to feel who he was and what he wanted for himself. He wondered whether the success of his analysis may in some way be a feather in the analyst's hat? Was she motivated to do it so that she could gain recognition for herself: The question represented a recurrence of the fear of the original trauma: Was he "adopted" in his analysis because of the analyst's narcissistic needs and purposes, or was the analysis for his own growth and development? At the end of the termination period, there was little doubt in the analyst's mind that Mr. M. not only accepted her satisfaction in the success of the analysis, but that he experienced this as a complement to his own pleasure in a work well done.

Termination and Follow-Up

Several months before Mr. M. began to speak of termination, he spent considerable time talking about his parents and his current conflicts with them. He had the fantasy of telling his father: "Why didn't you love me all these years? Give me one good reason!" The fantasied answer from the father would be that the patient ought to be grateful for many things he received from them, such as having been sent to a very good college. His angry outbursts began to be mixed with the consideration that nobody had really done him in out of maliciousness. As he developed increasing empathy toward his parents, he berated himself for not having been empathic with his wife. She was an aspiring artist, and he could never give her the encouragement she needed. He was too needy himself, he thought, to have known what she needed from him in their marriage.

During this period, Mr. M. had several dreams in which either his parents left him or he left them. He felt that he was "gently" pulling away from them. One of his dreams had particular significance because it indicated that the analysis was not only a new beginning for the patient, but that his new experiences now could become connected to satisfying experiences in the past. The dream was about a new house which was built on the place of the old one he used to live in. Everything around the house was familiar to him. The road he used to walk on now led to a group of new apartment buildings. "They were pleasing too, lit brighter than the old houses." The dream expressed a sense of continuity about himself: the new buildings were built on the old lot with the familiar surroundings.

His increased empathy toward his parents and his acceptance of their limitations was poignantly expressed in the following memory: He was eight or nine years old and was receiving boy scout badges, maybe three of them. His mother was in the back of the auditorium. He couldn't see her, but he sensed her pride. His mother's image in the background was extremely hazy, as if she had just rushed into the auditorium with her apron still on. Her image was so hazy that he couldn't be sure whether she was really there or not. He wondered about the apron. Certainly, in reality, his mother would not have worn that in an auditorium. As Mr. M. thought about this detail, he realized that it was less important to him now whether his mother was really there, but rather that he could now feel intensely the wish that she should have shared that moment of pride with him. He also appreciated the fact that his mother may have wanted to be there, but because of her failing health she could not participate in many of his activities. Father's emotional absence was harder to forgive.

The gentle pulling away internally was occurring in relation not only to his parents but to the analyst as well. The patient felt good, more energetic on his job. The writing school, which was independent of his employment, continued to provide him with a great deal of satisfaction. He felt genuine pleasure with the school, a little bit like being in love with it: "I have to laugh how infatuated I am with my accomplishments!" The feeling was a pleasant sense of elation, exhilarating rather than disrupting, in contrast to what it had been in the past, when intolerable narcissistic tensions under similar circumstances had disorganized him.

As mentioned earlier, Mr. M. had been "measuring" the progress of his analysis in terms of his contentment and pleasure in his work related to the writing school, the nature of his fantasy life, and in the way he was able to learn to play a musical instrument. Shortly before the date of the termination was set, the patient told the analyst that he had bought an expensive new instrument just at the time he decided that he no longer wanted to play music. The analyst offered the interpretation that Mr. M. bought the instrument to concretize the end of a phase in his life. The musical instrument served a special purpose which he no longer needed; it was to test his ability to freely abandon himself to the rhythm of the music without becoming overstimulated. He now had something better to express his images with, something that represented him more genuinely than music did, such as his increasing ability to express his images in writing.

As his life outside of the analysis became more gratifying and the internal changes could be traced through his dreams and associations, Mr. M. began to contemplate termination. When he then developed a rash on both of his elbows, he was strangely proud of it. He remembered that his wife had a rash when she went through a separation experience. The rash, in the patient's mind, was his body's signal that he was ready to terminate. There was, however, anxiety related to the final separation, which he expressed in a fantasy about his own funeral: he wanted the analyst to be at his funeral because "aside from you, nobody knows the parts I am put together with."

The analytic process moved toward termination, but the date of the actual termination was not yet set. Mr. M. spoke about termination and dreamed about it. The dream he considered his most specific termination dream had to do with someone's graduation: It was a ball with many Jewish people present. "You were there crying, unhappy about my leaving." He associated to the analyst's Jewishness, which he had not referred to before. The analyst asked why it was she who was crying. (Her question was related to the possibility that the patient was projecting his own sadness or that Mr. M. wanted her to share his feeling of sadness with him.) Mr. M. recalled that in the course of analysis he had many times wished the analyst's feelings to be identical to his own. Now, too, he hoped she shared his sadness, for that would assure perfect understanding.

In keeping with his wish to link himself up emotionally with his past, to establish a sense of continuity about himself, the patient, at this time, traced his past in terms of physical localities. He made a trip along the river where he grew up. He had never visited his mother's burial place, and was now determined to find it. He had once looked for it, but since it had no tombstone, he couldn't find it. He was now successful in locating it. She was buried next to her parents, which comforted him.

In the final phase, Mr. M. made a few wrapping-up remarks about his analysis. He was glad he decided to terminate at this time. He considered this optimal timing when he compared it to the analyses of his friends, which were "almost permanent arrangements." He was pleased "how little we did in pressing images into elementary Freudian molds. . . ." This surprised him. "One of your successes was to keep the images on levels where they were working. If you hadn't done this, I would have resisted that very much." He thought that the infrequency with which he referred to his mother was a true expression of the haziness of her image in his mind. He now seemed to have a much clearer picture of her; a reflection of a clearer perception of his own self.

Prior to termination, the patient gave up his regular employment and began to travel in order to gather material for free-lance writing. His articles sold well, and he considered this a successful beginning of his career as a free-lance writer.

The analyst met Mr. M. two years after termination at a large gathering. He greeted her with obvious pleasure and wanted to talk to her before introducing her to his young bride. The patient looked well. He had continued to write since the termination, not historical novels which he eventually hoped to do, but articles in which he had to use his own resources and writing skills to a much greater extent than in his previous job. His interests remained related to visually aesthetic subjects. He wrote about the evaluations of color and texture schemes and their application by architects. He considered himself a critic of contemporary tastes. He enjoyed the independence of free-lancing, and since leaving his job he had made many new contacts.

About his analysis, he said that he had continued to pay close attention to his dreams for about a year after termination. He didn't dream nearly as much as he had during the analysis, but his dreams continued to be not only an important source of insight but also an inspiration to him. He made a special point of mentioning that the analyst's understanding of the meaning of his friendship with the fourteen-year-old boy was a crucual experience of his analysis. It was then that he most appreciated her nonjudgmental and empathic attitude.

Conclusion

Among the many questions that could be raised in relation to this analysis, one appears to be of particular importance: Was this analysis conducted with too narrow a theoretical point of view? Was it therefore too restricted in its scope? Psychoanalysis, the most thorough of psychological forms of treatment, aims at the reworking of the "total personality." In this report, however, the analysis appears to have been conducted in relation to a specific segment of the personality, namely, in relation to the working through of the narcissistic transferences, which in turn enabled the transformation of infantile narcissistic configurations into their adult forms. This leaves us with the question how the analysis had affected this young man's love life. This is of special importance since his quasi-sadistic fantasies had apparently intruded on his actual sexual behavior. Following his separation and divorce, he had had many short-lived relationships with women. He had also felt vulnerable to homosexual seductions.

Kohut, in his discussion of the therapeutic transformations in the narcissistic personality disorders (1971), distinguishes between specific and nonspecific changes that can be observed in the analysis of these patients. The nonspecific changes relate to the patient's increased capacity for object love. The specific changes occur in relation to transferences which become established in relation to either the idealized parent imago or to the archaic grandiose self. In this case, the narcissistic transferences were established in relation to the grandiose self. The working through of these transferences permitted the gradual transformation of infantile exhibitionism and grandiosity into drive-channeling structures so that, instead of the disorganizing effect that these infantile configurations had on his personality, he could now productively engage in his creative activities.

The nonspecific changes relative to the patient's increasing ability for object love should now be traced briefly: from a disturbed and ungratifying marriage, the patient moved to a series of affairs. In none of these relationships was he truly invested. The actual relationship with women, his sexual fantasies, and the manner in which he responded to homosexual "seductions" were attempts to turn his passive childhood experiences into active ones. He became an exploiter. He could feel "powerful" by recreating a sense of infantile omnipotence in their relationships. Such experiences, however, had left him without fulfillment and satisfaction.

The turning point in the nature of the patient's object relations both with men and women could best be observed when he befriended the fourteen-year-old boy. He was relieved that he felt affection rather than sexual attraction for the boy. It was during this friendship that he had established an enduring relationship with a young woman. The patient's increased capacity for object love that was less and less burdened with archaic erotization appeared to be related to the fact that he became secure in his own acceptability and could therefore, "self-confidently and effectively offer his love (i.e., extend his object libidinal cathexis) without undue fear of rejection and humiliation" (Kohut, 1971, p. 298). In this case, we would have to add: and without the fear of exploitation.

Viewing the fate of the object-libidinal cathexis in this manner, its development appears closely tied to developments in the narcissistic sector of the personality. Changes in object cathexis in the course of an analysis are manifested in the varied appearances of object love and object hate. The conflicts and ambivalences related to these drive derivatives create transference symptoms which affect the content but not the essential aspect of the narcissistic transferences.

4

THE CONSOLIDATION
OF A
COHESIVE SELF

This report is based on a retrospective review of a four-year analysis which began before the publication of Kohut's work on disorders of the self. The patient appeared to be well suited for analysis of an oedipal problem complicated by a significant preoedipal regression. As the treatment got underway, however, a variety of intense extra-analytic transferences seemed to proliferate at the expense of a transference neurosis. Furthermore, interpretations designed to clarify the deflection of feelings and thoughts away from the analyst were of no avail. In fact, these interpretations frequently elicited explosive rage reactions and passionate protests. I began to feel puzzled because the storms of rage and protest often subsided as quickly as they had arisen and the work of the treatment seemed to progress in the interims.

At the end of the second year, while I was still trying to understand the basis for the patient's rage reactions, she became seriously depressed. The depression was accompanied by open outrage at the disappointing analyst, an outrage which replaced her earlier railings against her mother and the others who frustrated what she considered her legitimate desires for love and acceptance. This "transference neurosis" seemed to be inaccessible to analytic insight and resolution. Her endlessly repetitive accusations that the analyst should not have permitted her to get into such a depressed state tempted me to conclude, with Freud (1915), that she belonged to that class of women "of elemental passionateness who tolerate no surrogates. They are children of nature who refuse to accept the psychical in place of the material, who, in the poet's words, are accessible only to 'the logic of soup, with dumplings for arguments'. With such people one has the choice between returning their love or else bringing down upon oneself the full enmity of a woman scorned. In neither case can one safeguard the interests of the treatment. One has to withdraw, unsuccessful; and all one can do is to turn the problem over in one's mind of how it is that a capacity for neurosis is joined with such an intractable need for love" [pp. 116-167].

Freud was referring specifically to intractable demands for erotic love from the analyst and to the impossibility of preserving the transference for the purposes of analytic work. However, the most general significance of his remarks might well apply to the transferences of the patient I shall describe, and to the transferences of a group of patients whose disorder is joined to a seeming intractable need for love and recognition.

My patient attributed her intractable needs to her childhood experiences with her mother. She stubbornly maintained that instead of loving her and warmly accepting her body and bodily needs, and her growing individuality, her mother "destructively undermined" and "fragmented" her. Furthermore, she maintained that instead of giving her the praise and approval she considered her due, her mother "reflected off" her—i.e., she took over her accomplishments and assets for her own enhancement and thereby robbed her of what pleasure she could derive from herself. She was equally adamant in her insistence that her father had enjoyed her throughout her childhood and young adulthood until his sudden death deprived her of this source of pleasure in herself.

In spite of the chronic sense of injury and the passionate claims for acceptance and love, the patient could not adequately be characterized as infantile, anaclitic, pregenital, or borderline in her over-all personality organization. She herself recognized that she was suffering from a deficiency in the ability to approve of herself, and she regarded the acquisition of this missing "self-approval" capacity to be the psychological task par excellence of the analysis.

While I agreed with her regarding her deficit, I was first inclined to the view that the feelings of deficiency originated in a repressed oedipal and preoedipal conflict. With these conflicts in mind, I thought some of her accusations against her mother screened jealous, competitive, and destructive impulses toward an ambivalently loved-hated and looked-up-to childhood rival for the father she loved so much; and it seemed to me that other accusations were aimed at the preoedipal mother who spurned her love and deprived her of the equipment she had bestowed on her favored brother. Although from the very beginning I also heard a ring of genuine truth in her complaints about her mother, the explicit work of interpretation failed to take the mother's personality disorder sufficiently into account. As a consequence, the patient began to behave with the full enmity of a woman scorned and misunderstood.

In the light of Kohut's descriptions of the mirror transference, the impasse in the treatment and the patient's transference took on a very different appearance. Her complaints and her clamor for love and confirmation did arise, as she insisted, from a deficit in her inner psychological structure. Her mother, suffering from a severe distortion of her own body image and from a chronic need to bolster her own image, was unable to provide the mirroring confirmation essential for the child's healthy self-regard and enjoyment of herself. When this insight was appropriately conveyed to the patient, her inability to accept the psychical in place of the material proved to be more apparent than real. Interpretations of her rage, depression, and hopelessness as a transference reaction to the analyst as the unresponsive mirroring self-object, when coupled with genetic reconstructions of the intrapsychic impact of the mother's self-absorption, had a twofold effect. First, these traditional psychoanalytic tools (interpretation and reconstruction) sufficed to appease the psychological hunger for acceptance which was the direct manifestation of the structural deficit; and second, these tools sufficed to set in motion a gradual process of transmuting internalization which led to structural accretion in the relatively circumscribed area of maximum vulnerability which had such profound effects on the patient's feelings about herself, her mood, and her overall functioning.

As the "self-approval" structure was consolidated, the unrelinquished and seemingly unrelinquishable childhood wishes "passed" as though of their own accord. Because I was finally able to listen analytically and to hear the clamor as a legitimate and comprehensible cry arising from the depths of a chronic childhood insufficiency, the patient concluded the analysis with the capacity she sought. With it she was able to maintain on her own a total body-mind-self that she experienced as harmoniously put together and suffused with the inner glow of pleasure that she had repetitiously demanded from the self-object as long as her cry was not understood.

The Opening Phase

Diagnostic Interviews

Mrs. Jeanne Apple was a pert, attractive, pleasant-mannered woman of 31 who came for consultation with her mind made up that she needed an analysis. She was tastefully and neatly dressed in tailored, informal clothes, and she wore her striking red hair in a short, casual style which suited her over-all appearance very well. In spite of her main complaint of depression, Mrs. Apple seemed to be lively, energetic, and vigorous—eager to describe herself and her emotional difficulties. For some months she had attempted to overcome her depression by "self analysis." Failing to relieve herself, she decided to seek treatment.

Mrs. Apple had been happily married for ten years and was the mother of two sons, ages seven and five. She associated the onset of her depression with the sudden recurrence of an intestinal disorder which she thought had been permanently cured six years earlier. With the reappearance of loose stools, mucous, and gas, she began to feel tense and depressed. However, she did not return to her internist. Instead she instituted his previous medical regimen (Lomotil and Librium) for herself. Because her symptoms continued unabated, she reluctantly sought his advice. She resented the fact that she was told that a strict, bland diet and additional medication were indicated. She announced with satisfaction that her symptoms were currently "under control" on a "Jeanie Apple diet." (By this she meant that she knew what she could and could not eat and it was unnecessary for her to be told to diet.)

Although Mrs. Apple was obviously intelligent and well informed, she was very vague about the original onset and details of the disease which she had been told was ulcerative colitis. [Since the patient was under the care of a reputable internist, I did not question the diagnosis. Much later I learned that the original diagnosis was never established by proctoscopy, nor was the patient proctoscoped at the time of the recurrence.] She thought the symptoms "came out of the blue" some time during her second pregnancy and that she was ill with diarrhea, slight bleeding, weight loss, and fatigue for six to nine months. She improved with conservative medical management during the pregnancy, and her progress continued following delivery. Although her father died suddenly before her full recovery, she did not experience an exacerbation in spite of the fact that his death was a "staggering emotional blow." Mrs. Apple recalled that her internist "gently implied" that there was an emotional basis for her disease and suggested psychiatric treatment. When she remained asymptomatic, she felt no need to pursue his recommendation. Neither her mourning the loss of her father, the rigors of caring for a difficult baby, nor a strenuous move to another part of the country affected her physical status.

Mrs. Apple spoke of her husband Shelly with affectionate warmth and admiration, although her face momentarily clouded over with apprehension as she described their gratifying relationship. The move just mentioned was undertaken five years earlier when Shelly decided to leave a well-paying position as an industrial chemist in order to pursue a less remunerative but more rewarding academic career in chemistry. His faculty position at an excellent university brought him great satisfaction. Both of them enjoyed the academic community in which they lived and in which together they took an active part.

She described five-year-old Tommy as a great source of concern and distress to her. His aggressive, hyperactive behavior in nursery school made her fear that he would fail to make a school adjustment. Although she sought treatment for him when he was four, she was told by an experienced and competent child psychiatrist that he did not need treatment and that he was simply the kind of child whom she would have to learn to manage. The anticipated failure to adjust in kindergarten did not materialize; however, she is constantly enraged with Tommy. She feels that she has a marked problem with him because he is exactly like her brother Jack, who is three years older than she. Tommy and Jack are the only people to whom she has ever raised her voice. With his red hair and green eyes, Tommy looks just like Jack. [She did not mention the obvious fact that Tommy's coloring was also identical to hers.] Her fears about Tommy are based on the fact that Jack never did well in school and his teens were marked by violent rages and conflicts with her parents. Her father, a successful physician, was ambitious for his son to follow in his footsteps. Although Jack completed college and started medical school, he dropped out after a year and drifted from job to job. His marriage to a woman from a different social class aroused further parental disapproval. Although no longer "totally irresponsible he's never really made ends meet. He's wasted all his potential—he must have been bright like everyone else in the family."

Jack's moods used to set the day for the family; if he got up angry, the day was ruined by fights. Tommy's moods now have the same effect. He is "rebellious, defiant, and provocative. Johnny, aged seven, is the opposite. I've totally suppressed him. He's intellectually gifted, but he's too inhibited. When he was a toddler, if I told him not to put a foot over the kitchen threshold he'd finish his cookie before he moved. He complied. I thought I was doing great. Tommy has never complied. From his birth on, I've never been able to satisfy him. I didn't know it until he was two months old, but he wasn't getting enough to eat." Furthermore, she thinks Tommy has "depressions" every March. For the past three years he wakes up with night terrors and has fears of death. Then, during the day he seems tired, "more regressed," refuses to dress himself, tie his shoes, etc. She suppresses her anger over his shirt tails' being out, over the mud he tracks into the house, and over his general unruliness "until it all bursts out and then I am astonished at what I hear myself saying to him."

Mrs. Apple characterized herself as a "compulsive" person. Unless everything is neat, clean, and in its place she feels she will fall apart, lose control, and never catch up. She makes lists to be sure she can check off everything she has to do. "There's something inappropriate about these fears. I'm a very competent person and I always have been. I have a mother problem too." She was not aware of the "mother problem" until her father's sudden death from a massive pulmonary hemorrhage at the age of 64. Although her mother still lives in the distant West Coast city where she grew up, even her infrequent visits are a terrible ordeal. "My mother is domineering and wants things her way. So am I! I manage to be polite to her the first few days. Then I become exasperated." Mrs. Apple recounted typical examples of the behavior which incensed her, "My mother insists on closing the living room drapes. I like them open so I can look out of the window. She comes in and rearranges the furniture." She tries to cope with the visits by entertaining her mother, who likes to be busy. Although she herself hates to shop, she goes with her mother who loves shopping. Her mother will be arriving soon and, "I know I will finally say to her, 'Mother, if you want to move the couch you may, but when you leave Shelly will move it back.' And I know finally I will go over and open the drapes after she has closed them, and so it will go."

Mrs. Apple reflected, "I never had a problem with my mother in high school because I was so popular and successful academically and socially. Looking back, I don't think I should have been allowed to hold so many offices. There were other deserving people too, but I always got everything. There were not many Jewish families in the area. I was the first Jewish girl to be elected to a class office and to be on the school paper; I was president of my clubs, etc." As she continued the account of her achievements, she mentioned that she got into the university of her choice (a university noted for academic excellence) where she was a premedical student and obtained a B.S. degree in microbiology. This information led her to volunteer, "I have another problem. I wanted to be a boy. I wanted to be a doctor like my father, but I hated pre-med courses, and I realized that I couldn't be a doctor just to be like him." She was contemplating changing to another curriculum in her junior year when she met and fell in love with Shelly. Their plans to marry when he finished his Ph.D. made her decide to continue with a major in microbiology and to finish school in three and a half years instead of four. In retrospect she thought she should have been in another field. She is far more interested in political science and history than she is in the sciences. She worked in microbiology until her first child was born and expects to return to work when her children are older. However, she is not yet sure about what she wants to do.

Until this point in the diagnostic interview Mrs. Apple communicated quite spontaneously. When I asked her to go on, she said she thought she had told me everything of importance. Encouraged to see what else occurred to her, she immediately launched into a further description of the disturbing details of her current relationship with her mother. She carefully selects gifts with her mother's taste in mind, however her mother never simply accepts a gift. She always sends them back with a letter, "the gloves are the wrong size, the purse is the wrong color, will you exchange them? etc." And she finds herself not accepting her mother's gifts. She is particularly incensed when her mother sends a check. She was unable to explain what was wrong, but somehow she feels that her mother gives gifts as a routine without thought of her. Her mother does not go out and buy her something, whereas her father did. Nor does she arrive with presents for her grandsons. "Instead she expects me to take her shopping and to select something for them. On the other hand," she added bitterly, "the first thing she does when she gets here is to rush to shop for gifts for Jack's children and his wife."

Trying to cooperate further with the earlier suggestion to simply tell what occurred to her, she mentioned that she is terrified of heights. Shelly loves to hike in mountainous areas. Once while vacationing in the High Sierras, she managed to climb to the top of a mountain with him and then stood there and cried in terror at the prospect of the steep descent. Shelly helped her down. With an engaging smile, she added, "I continued to climb on the rest of the trip because I didn't want to be left behind." In the same context she recalled a recurrent childhood dream: "I was running in panic from someone who was chasing me. I'd wake up in a panic when I was falling into a well or off a cliff." To my inquiry about other early memories, she said she remembered herself in kindergarten playing the triangle. It was a pleasant memory.

When I told Mrs. Apple that I concurred with her feeling that analysis was indicated, she immediately responded by describing her goals: "I want to understand myself so that I can manage better especially with my mother and Tommy." Equally emphatic, she said that she wanted to deal with "the psychological cause of the ulcerative colitis." I expressed caution regarding the latter goal, while accepting the former. I said that in my opinion the psychological etiology of the disorder was not so clear-cut. She did not take up my caveat [the ultimate meaning of this expectation and its working through will be discussed later]. Instead, she responded obliquely, "I don't expect to be a new person. I don't think anything can do that. For example, I don't expect the analysis to make an author out of me. If I had talent and worked at it I might become one."[1]

In the fourth hour we met to discuss specific arrangements for the analysis. Mrs. Apple walked in with, "You're lucky you're in this nice cheerful house. It's so depressing outside." [Ostensibly, she was referring to the gray, rainy day. Numerous dreams of houses and preoccupations with her house recurred throughout the analysis.] She informed me that her mother had arrived and she found herself being sarcastic, or seeming to deliberately bait or provoke her. She was puzzled to find herself saying, "How would you feel if your grandsons aren't Bar Mitzvah? You'd better start thinking about it!" She knows how her mother would feel about it — 'it's a disgrace,' etc., and she wonders if she is deliberately provoking her mother into a tirade. On the other hand, she observed, she anticipates certain things her mother does that annoy her very much, and she tries to avert these. For example, she will say, "Mother, please don't say anything about my sister-in-law's house in front of the children." She explains to me, "My mother has come away from a visit to see a friend's new addition to her house with, 'Jeanie, did you see that crack in the ceiling?'" Or, she will caution her mother in advance, "The temple will not be as nice as ours at home; the lunch won't be as good, etc.' My mother is always making comparisons, finding fault with others, and saying, 'Ours is better.'" At the end of the hour, she left her purse at the foot of her chair opposite me. I noticed it and called to her. She accepted the purse with a slightly anxious, self-conscious laugh as if she were embarrassed by a *faux pas* or parapraxis.

---

[1] Kohut discusses the possibility that the analyst's premature realism interfered with the full remobilization of the exhibitionistic display and core infantile ambitions of a potentially creative, productive "anal self" (1977, pp. 264-265).

The Major Themes

The treatment began in September with a planned interruption in February. The major themes of the treatment were sounded in the first six months. From the first hour, the patient's voice became shrill and loud, and she was frequently on the verge of tears of rage and exasperation as she took up the burning issues that inflamed her: Tommy, her mother, her sister-in-law and in-laws, the possibility of building a new house, her "irritated" colon and its management, her husband's passion for climbing. A first hearing might create the impression for some that the patient was like a spoiled child who was preoccupied with trifles and petty affronts. [She reviewed this issue herself during the termination.]

Her troubles with her younger son were uppermost. Voice shrill and quavering, she documented his misdemeanors and soon asked, "Can you give me direction?" She accepted my encouragement to go on so we could gain understanding of the problem. She said she reasons, talks, and explains to him until finally she becomes "hostile." Then she imposes a variety of punishments — sometimes she imposes so many restrictions she no longer can remember what they are for! Anyway, they are all ineffective. While comparing him with her brother, she added that he lies just like Jack, "and I have a fetish about honesty." Since it sounded to me as though she could not distinguish lying and dishonesty from the tall tales and exaggerations of a five-year-old, I wondered why, as she put it, she has such a fetish about honesty. She replied that her father had instilled honesty into her as the highest moral ideal. She wants Tommy to be honest, to take initiative, to have ambitions, and to be self-directed. [Clearly the patient valued the attributes of a cohesive self; she failed, however, to see that her demands for a five-year-old were at best premature and at worst disruptive for his age-adequate performance.] She was always very obedient to her parents, whereas Jack was unruly and disobedient; he stole from her, from her mother's purse, from her mother's friends' purses when they came to play cards, etc. She went on to think about "the honesty thing." She realizes she feels the way Johnny feels when Tommy takes his candy. Johnny saves his candy and then when he goes to find it, it's gone. She never had privacy from Jack. He was always going through her things, he picked the lock on her diary, and her parents never did anything about it. When I simply underscored that she realizes she feels the same with Tommy as she felt with Jack during her childhood, she recalled "something else I thought of after the last hour. My mother always shopped for bargains for me and always bought my clothes on sale. I can remember only one dress purchased at the regular price. I always had to run downtown on the spur of the moment to try something on she found on sale." [Moved by her tone of voice, I recorded the observation in my notes that she seemed to experience her mother's bargain-hunting as cheating her and as evidence that her mother did not value her enough. I did not, however, verbalize this "diagnostic interpretation" to the patient. Instead, I believe that I filtered my empathic closure through a classical theory regarding the girl's defensive distortion of the mother's behavior based on the female castration complex. In retrospect, it seems to me that the observation that she felt cheated of being valued enough comes closer to understanding the core of the psychological disorder and of the patient's psychological state vis-à-vis her mother. It also seems to me that a theoretical bias led to a significant blind spot — I ignored my own capacity for empathic closure because it did not fit together with firmly established conceptions of oedipal and preoedipal development. In this light, many of the patient's stormy reactions during the analysis can be seen as replicas of the rage and hopelessness she experienced during her childhood when she felt emotionally cheated.]

While elaborating on the theme of her mother's excessive economies on her clothes Mrs. Apple recalled that her mother's sisters always said that her mother was selfish and self-centered. In fact, she never knew that her parents were well-to-do. After her father's death she was sure she would have to support her mother. Only then did she learn that her father had left a large enough estate for her mother to live very comfortably. It distresses her to see traits in herself which she dislikes in her mother. Like her mother, she too can be frugal, negative, and hypercritical, and she makes a great effort to be different from her mother. [The theme of wanting to be different from both parents is illuminated in the working through. The material suggests that the wish to be different can be in the service of normal growth and development, and that in instances of narcissistic pathology in the parents the wish is in the service of the struggle of the self to survive. I am emphasizing that "the importance of being different" from the parents is not necessarily an outgrowth of conflicts concerning oedipal development.]

Leaving her thoughts about her mother for the time-being, Mrs. Apple began to talk about her screaming at the children. She feels guilty because she frequently screams even when she regards their needs and demands as quite legitimate. Nevertheless, their demands conflict with her essential need for time to herself, particularly to read. I was struck again by her account of her sweet reasoning with the children and her full-scale explosion when reasoning failed. I wondered why she tried so hard to reason with them and found it so necessary to explain her expectations. In the following hour she returned to this question, "I thought about what you said about my explaining so much. I think it was because I never conversed with my parents. With my father there were intellectual discussions; he talked about an interesting case or various public health issues; something between my father and me led me to want to become a doctor, but I was smart enough to know pre-med courses didn't interest me. [Mrs. Apple's father combined a pediatric practice with an active involvement in preventive medicine.] I didn't talk with my mother at all after she refused to answer when I asked where babies come from. When I was thirteen—no, twelve, ten, maybe nine, she refused to answer, 'because you may tell the other girls in the neighborhood, and I don't want it said that it came from Mrs. L——.' *That's what she thought about me!!* [The patient sounded very agitated.] I never went to my mother again with a question. My girl friends confided in me, but I didn't confide. I wrote in my diary or I wrote poems and stories." [Later in the treatment, memories of a childhood girl friend whom she did trust and feel close to emerged during a "girl-friend-twinship" transference.]

I heard the patient's cry, "That's what she thought about me," as a continuation of her feelings about her mother pursuing bargains. Her intense indignation, vehemence, and bitterness sounded identical in both instances. Nevertheless, because of my theoretical orientation at that time, I did not tell the patient what I heard. Instead, I wondered if this bitter memory of mother's refusal to enlighten her screened an internal oedipal prohibition, and I waited for further developments in the transference to clarify this issue. At that time I did not yet appreciate the fact that the development of the transference and of a viable working alliance go hand in hand. In this case, in order to promote both developments, it was essential for the patient to know that the analyst understood the nature of the specific narcissistic injury she experienced at her mother's hands. An approximation of a correct response would be, "You seem to feel that your mother was more in-

terested in the bargains than in your feelings about wearing
them; and you seem to feel that, instead of being able to listen
to you and your questions about growing up, she worried
about what people were going to think about her."

It was misleading to think of these memories as either derivatives of, or as screens for, repressed conflicts with the
oedipal and preoedipal mother. These memories condensed
and telescoped an essential aspect of the patient's actual emotional experience with her mother during all of the developmental phases. If she could have put into words what she tried
to tell me over and over again in the form of the memories and
the experiences she recounted in such detail, she might have
said, "My mother always accented herself and her concerns.
Instead of thinking about me, she was always thinking about
herself." In point of fact, however, it is the analyst's function
to find words for the patient's early experiences. By not understanding Mrs. Apple's endless accounts of narcissistic injuries I
was unwittingly inflicting the same injuries. So long as the
frustrated and greatly intensified developmental needs for appropriate mirroring were not grasped, her accounts continued
to be filled with minutiae and "trivia." I have deliberately included examples of these accounts in this report, for, far from
being trivial, obsessive, or defensive, these details were the
vehicles or carriers of the subtle form of emotional deprivation
which was being experienced again. Without explicit understanding of this new edition (transference), the patient's reactivated childhood demands to be seen and heard on her own
terms instead of her mother's were continually being stimulated and frustrated and rebuffed. It was this situation which
ultimately resulted in the traumatic state that disrupted her
cohesion and hope.

The recollection of her mother's refusal to answer her
questions made Mrs. Apple vehement in her expressions of
contempt. "My mother's opinions and values were incredible!"

She recalled that before her marriage, her mother offered the unsolicited opinion, " 'I'm sure Shelly will be considerate.' She meant in sexual relations. And even worse, she told me not to walk around naked in front of my husband! 'When you're young it's great, but when you're older he'll be comparing.' " She interrupted her recollections with disgust: "I don't want to hear my mother's ideals and values!" This led to another memory, "I'm annoyed every Christmas. My mother gives me robes. The robe is a reminder of the fact that she objected to me and my brother walking around in our underwear and she always insisted on robes. That brings me to my hang-up about clothes! My mother was always dressed. She never left her room without being fully clothed. But she wore terrible old clothes to clean house, torn stockings, etc. Then the rest of the time she was attractively dressed. I will never wear old jeans, torn sneakers, sweatshirts. Tommy loves them." [Much later I recognized that the foregoing material also telescoped early experiences which the patient could not formulate in words. The memories of her mother's insistence on concealing the body and her "disgusting" garb for the cleaning conveyed the intensity of her feelings about the lack of intimate, soothing, playful physical contact with a mother whom she felt was unresponsive to her body and was involved instead with "things" —her furniture, draperies, knick-knacks, etc.]

She continued, "Recently Shelly told me I'm crazy because I don't allow Tommy to go shopping with me if he's wearing jeans. I insist he change his clothes. It's a battle. Shelly says, 'He looks like a five-year-old,' and that I should discuss it with you." The remark came at the end of the hour, and she did not pursue it. Instead, she continued to elaborate on variations on the theme of mother's not answering her question about babies, mother's accusing behavior when she once told her she kissed her date good night. Once again she reiterated, "I never told her anything again." Then she asked

me hesitantly and apologetically, "What is your psychoanalytic philosophy? I realize I could have asked you that
when I first saw you." I commented that asking must be important to her, since she had told me so much about her anger
and disappointment when she asked her mother a question.
She was very impressed, "The idea that the two are connected
would never have occurred to me. Maybe there is a connection." I asked what she wanted to know. Hesitantly, she asked
about my training. I responded directly. Then I told her it was
understandable that she wanted to know. She was probably
feeling anxious about entrusting herself and revealing herself
to me, inasmuch as she had schooled herself in not confiding.
The next hour she said she had left denying to herself that she
was anxious. "Then I decided if I were honest I realize I am.
It's one thing to have taken the step from my intellectual conviction about analysis and another thing to have sold myself,
to be accepted in treatment."

At this time Mrs. Apple became very anxious and preoccupied with the possibility that she and Shelly would design
and build their own house. "I always wanted it, and now it's a
possibility I'm doing exactly what my mother did—bringing
up all the negatives. My mother never found a house to her
liking. She was always looking. I don't want to spoil Shelly's
enthusiasm, but I have all these lists of pros and cons." I wondered if she had a problem getting what she always wanted.
Once again she responded with the admiring, impressed, surprised reaction that was becoming characteristic. She
repeated several times, "How interesting!" She associated to
the fact that now, as during high school, she is always asked to
be the president of every organization she belongs to. "It
doesn't seem fair since there are other people." [The patient's
considerable organizational skills were very much in demand.
During the analysis she originated a number of innovative and
successful community and school programs. It took me a long

while to understand that she was not downplaying herself as a defense against competitiveness, guilt over her successes as compared to mother, brother, etc. Quite the opposite proved to be the case: getting what she wanted—recognition, approval, admiration for her actual capacities—left her still without the *sense of pleasure in herself and her own activities that had been missing in the formative stages.* Now, lacking an internalized sense of pleasure in herself, she felt vaguely miserable and unsuccessful because she had all the ingredients for a happiness she felt forever eluded her.]

Soon afterward she returned to her feelings of helpless anger with Tommy. "I can't stand the dirt he brings in; I shouldn't have had children; I think I wanted to be a boy. I don't like feminine tasks, clothes. I originally chose a man's field, and I'd rather be out in a man's world anytime." She reiterated her resentment over the fact that her mother is never pleased with her gifts. Mother rejected father's gifts and now is behaving the same way with her. "After my father died I realized there was a change. I had always been the child looking up to my parents. Now I see that my mother wants me to be more materialistic and to be head of every organization so she can tell her mah jong ladies a list of her daughter's accomplishments."

Thus, once again, the same theme emerged: her mother did not respond to her and her accomplishments and achievements with spontaneous recognition, admiration, and shared pleasure. Instead, she boasted about her daughter in order to enhance herself. In doing so, she perpetuated her own narcissistic disorder by depriving her child of the phase-appropriate mirroring experiences that promote normal self-esteem. In the absence of the phase-appropriate analytic explanations regarding her rage and loss of a sense of well-being when her mother took over her accomplishments, the "extra-analytic transferences" referred to in the introduction began to intensify. She became shrill as she described her feelings of rejection by her husband's family in spite of all her efforts to establish close, meaningful family relationships. Half wailing and half enraged, she denounced Shelly's younger sister, "She's so self-centered. She's interested only in her possessions, her children, her house." She explained that the loss of her positive relationship with her father makes her turn toward Shelly's family, and she is always beside herself at their indifference. Together with what seemed like a monotonous insistence that her in-laws neglected her, Mrs. Apple reviewed her religious orientation. Throughout childhood, adolescence, and young adulthood she had always complied unquestioningly with her parents' adherence to Orthodox Judaism. Through her compliance she won their acclaim and approval. Following her father's death she lost her religious feeling. Although she went through the Orthodox mourning observances because her father would have wanted her to do so, these rituals no longer had meaning. She recalled that during her brother's early adolescence he became a religious fanatic. Then, just as fanatically, he turned against the religion her parents valued so much.

The patient's traumatic state vis-à-vis unresponding mirroring self-objects mounted, and in this state she refocused on the behavior of her son Tommy. Again it became apparent that she was comparing Tommy from early on with the disturbed behavior her brother manifested as a teenager. Tommy disrupts games or removes himself if he can't win, and he always blames someone else for his failures. As a younger child he used to endanger himself physically by dangerous climbing exploits, and his hitting and biting were uncontrollable. She is terrified that he is just like Jack who in high school had violent and uncontrollable rages. During these frightening rages he ran around the house brandishing a butcher knife, threatening anyone who came near him. Although he never inflicted the physical harm he threatened, he was extremely destructive. He would finally run into his room where he would break doors, furniture, windows. She was trying not to repeat her parents' mistakes when she sought psychiatric treatment for Tommy. She knew, even when she was just a young child, that Jack needed treatment. During her early adolescence, she too became very involved in the observation of various Orthodox prohibitions with the belief that if she were good enough she would somehow make Jack better. It appeared as though the patient was describing an elaborate system of reaction formations against aggressive wishes regarding her brother. Consequently, I suggested to her that her early precocity regarding Jack's disturbance and her intensified efforts to be the good child were undertaken in order to protect herself and him from the frightening and guilt-inducing feelings which she was experiencing again with Tommy. She was impatient in her rejection of this interpretation, and she was adamant in her insistence that, unlike her parents, she had realistically recognized Jack's need for treatment. When she asked for direct advice in managing Tommy, I said it would take time to understand the problem she was having with him. In this context I wondered if she had been dreaming and reminded her that her dreams might provide access to some of the psychological reactions which otherwise could not be understood. She was prompt in her reply, "I never dream. It's all conscious with me." She did not appear for the next hour. When she returned, she said she was depressed because she felt so dumb when she realized she forgot the hour.

An interpretation of her fear of her own inner workings and of the possibility that these were not always part of conscious, rational control, led, several weeks later, to the first reported dream of the analysis. "I'm awakening, but it's in my childhood bedroom. I also visualized my brother's bedroom."

She associated spontaneously. "The bedroom in the dream was the one in the second house I lived in from age ten on. I never liked my bedroom. My brother had the one I wanted. It had a porch you could climb onto. He had all of the new furniture, custom-made drapes and spread, etc. I had all of the old furniture and everything about doing my room was a hassle with my mother. I had tailored taste and my mother liked pink and ruffles for girls. I couldn't stand my mother's taste." In a tone of disgust she recalled mother's overly elaborate decor. "My mother objected to my wanting plaid wallpaper because it wasn't feminine! I conquered with a compromise: I found pink plaid." As she continued to associate, her voice began to rise and quaver when she was reminded of how she felt when her mother-in-law recently gave her an "inappropriate gift." Her mother-in-law should know by now that she has tailored tastes and not give her glamorous lounging apparel. She was also shrill as she talked about the most recent snub she felt when her mother-in-law was obviously more involved with Shelly's sister than with her. Finally, as though following on her own associations, she concluded, "The dream must mean that I was jealous of my brother. That makes me think of two interesting things." She went on to say that since starting treatment she has come to the realization that she fights with Tommy "on his own level." Now she sees that if, for example, she does not argue with him, he is a different, cooperative child.

This material suggested that the patient could try to comply with the basic rule and that an actively observing ego was entering into an alliance with the analyst. Soon afterward, she recalled a recurrent childhood dream. "My brother went into the army and was killed." Her first associations seemed to involve a negation and an intellectualization: "I'm not aware of feeling rivalry with him, but I think the dream must mean that I wanted him out of the way." Then she reviewed the differences in her feelings toward her two sons. She enjoys Johnny and wants to help him overcome his social inhibitions. On the other hand, Tommy is just like Jack whom everyone "oogled and aagled" because he was so handsome. ("Oogled and aagled" sounded like a condensation of "oohing and aahing," and going "ga ga" and "ogling" in admiration.) Tommy is also athletic like Jack, who played on all the school teams. "I was never athletic till I got married." These comparisons led to new recollections. Jack was not toilet trained until after he was five. Her mother tells her she was toilet trained at nine months. She concludes that she must have been very compliant, and I added that her mother must have valued her precocity. Her thoughts about toilet training reminded her that two weeks ago, when she forgot the appointment and was depressed for being so dumb, she had bloody stools for the first time in years. She announced that the blood had already disappeared and that the colitis was "under control." [This was the beginning of a typical pattern. She avoided all mention of an exacerbation of the bowel symptoms until they were brought "under control." I began to feel somewhat uneasy. It seemed as though the patient were trying to conduct the analysis by herself, much as she conducted her own medical management. And yet, as shown in the following material during the fourth month of treatment, there was abundant evidence that a transference, albeit a warded-off one, was already established.]

Mrs. Apple reported that she had an absolute drive to read psychoanalysis and that her reading had given rise to a dream. "I was in a public place with a stack of books. I'd read six or seven in one afternoon. A man passed by who noticed how much I'd read. Then it was as though I were single again and I was longing for Shelly to call to ask me out." She associated to her "fantastically happy" marriage and to the fact that, for no cause at all, she used to worry during her courtship that Shelly would never marry her. "So the second part of the dream is an 'I've had this before' kind of dream." She was extremely upset and negative when I attempted to link the affects of the dream and associations with her current longings and fears concerning the analytic relationship, which was going to be interrupted for the first time one month hence. This was the first of the injured reactions to interpretations that were to become a challenge to understanding. With the working alliance in mind, I responded to her bristling manner by clarifying that an understanding of what happens in the analytic relationship is a means to understanding herself. She became excited and enthusiastic at the prospect of a relationship, "not just a cold analyst," and with the idea that the relationship would repeat what she had previously done with others. She stressed that she wanted it to be like one with a peer. She did not want a negative relationship like the one with her mother.

The patient's shift from bristling injury to enthusiasm was the beginning of the rapid swings that also were difficult to understand until I realized that they came about as a consequence of a disruption and reinstatement of the mirror transference. In retrospect, it appears to me that the patient heard the proffered transference interpretation as though the analyst-mother (or father) were stressing her own importance at a time when the patient was already deeply involved in presenting the reactivated childhood exhibitionistic self for approval and admiration and the reactivated fears of being overlooked. Failing to elicit the responsive echo to her display, she bristled and raged. The clarification intended to encourage the patient to enter into a cooperative alliance was heard as an encouraging response to her display by the mirroring mother-analyst who took a "warm" (not cold) interest in her.

The same invigorating enthusiasm appeared shortly afterward in an unrecognized twinship-alter-ego dream. "I'm playing tennis with a woman I've been told is a good player. I'd never played with her. It seemed real. It was a very pleasant match." [It will be recalled that when her wish for a response to her display of how much she was able to read in the analyst's field was disappointed, she expressed the wish for a peer relationship. Now it seems as though the patient turned to the analyst as the "good player" with whom she enjoyed a meaningful back and forth in a serious-playful exchange which she enjoyed.] The lack of explicit response to these developments in the transference and my silence in response to a reported dream which I did not understand were taken as a rebuff. She said coldly, "I guess you don't care to comment," and she launched into a tirade about her mother sending her a check instead of a personally selected gift. She feels spiteful and thinks about sending mother a check instead of a present with a "buy yourself something" note like mother's to her. Shortly, however, her enthusiasm for the analysis returned. In the two weeks remaining before the five-week interruption, she elaborated on new discoveries she was making about "what I think must have been jealousy of my brother." [I took the "intellectualization" and "doubting" to be a manifestation of compulsive defenses which were still necessary protections against the intensity of her jealousy of her brother.] She realized that her view of her brother as a failure was only partially accurate: even during his stormy teen years he was a very successful school athlete and therefore a "Big Man on Campus." Both parents rejected his athletic accomplishments as unworthy and as bringing him into too much contact with non-Jews. Moreover, she recalled earlier memories: he excelled in everything over her — more than can be accounted for by the three-year age difference, she thinks. He was physically more attractive than she, and more talented musically and artistically. Mother displayed his things, not hers. Mother told stories about children's photographers wanting his picture in their windows. She added that she now takes various adult education courses with Shelly. She enjoys doing this with him, and she's not jealous even though she realizes he is brighter than she. She persists even though she'll never be the world's greatest intellect. Immediately after this, she wondered why she gets so angry at Shelly when he says, "Let's go hiking," when she'd planned to barbeque, or when he calls from the lab and says he'll be home late for dinner. Her anger is just like her mother's toward her father when he was late. Her next associations were about her mother's annoyance with her. She gave up thumb-sucking because her mother objected. Instead, she sucked her tongue. She guesses her mother never noticed that. She also rolled a piece of her clothing between her fingers and at the same time rubbed the fabric behind her ear. She still sucks her tongue in her sleep and awakens rubbing behind her ear. Just before the interruption of the analysis, her basement flooded in a heavy rain and she was extremely upset. It reminded her of her childhood "horror" and rage that her parents' basement flooded recurrently. She and they were always bailing it out and cleaning up sewage, and they never did anything to remedy the cause. [Eventually I understood and interpreted the patient's traumatic states, and eventually, when she dreamed anxiously of water rising, she referred to it as her "symbol" and learned to begin to calm herself down. However, the genesis of both the traumatic states and the erotized self-stimulation in a chronically faulty self— self-object unit were not clear until much later.]

When treatment resumed, she said everything went so well she was beginning to think she didn't need treatment, until the last week when her mother-in-law slighted her and she became enraged. Her voice rose again and she began what was to be a prolonged period of agonizing doubt and indecision as to whether she wanted to build a simple new house or buy a "big, ostentatious house in the hills like Shelly's sister's." She was horrified to discover that she was in such a conflict and that she could want to be so "materialistic." She recalled her mother's visit during part of the recent interruption and the conclusion she came to, "There's no possibility of having a relationship with this person." She felt that her mother tore her and her brother (in absentia) apart with criticisms. For example, she started to let her hair grow longer (shortly after the treatment began), and when her mother saw her, she said, "Don't you think it makes your nose look bigger?" Mother never let her wear her hair long when she was a child because she said long hair made her nose look bigger. [Later the patient came to view her nose and hair as "symbols" of what she dubbed her "fragmenting relationship" with her mother.] While her mother stayed with her she had nightmares. In one of these she was at a summer camp and screamed for her mother to wait for her. Mother was driving a car, and she just laughed and drove away. She became so enraged in the dream she began hurling rocks.

While agonizing over the plans to build the house and while considering the finances involved, she recalled that, either shortly before or after her birth, her father spent three months in a TB sanitarium on the suspicion that there was a reactivation of an old tubercular lesion. Thereafter, her mother always fussed over his health, and, moreover, acted as though there were financial pressures. "When I needed a new pair of shoes she invariably asked, "Do you really need a new pair of shoes?" Nevertheless, Jack was always sent to expensive camps, and he was given a car "because he was a boy and needed one more." She, on the other hand, was given choices. "Do you want the expensive camp or the cheaper one?" She was always reasonable and chose the cheap camps. Besides, she liked the camps she attended. In the midst of these preoccupations she learned that Shelly's sister was going to have plastic surgery on her nose. She could hardly put words to her tearful rage, "She's already beautiful anyway! It's ostentatious like her house. She wants to be perfect! I always wanted to have surgery on my nose. My parents always laughed it off." I commented that apparently they didn't realize how important her feelings about her nose were to her. In what she called "a sudden flash," she recalled that all her life she'd heard how gorgeous her brother was, how people stopped on the street to admire him, and so forth. "That's why I wanted to have my nose done!" She calmed down when I said that her mother's absorption with Jack was a source of intense distress to her from childhood on.

During the mounting tension and rage since the resumption of treatment, colitis symptoms recurred. When she told me about the symptoms and I inquired regarding her medical care, she became furious. *She* would manage this herself; it was psychological, and consequently she was going to control it by understanding herself in analysis. I simply acknowledged how angry she felt at my bringing up the necessity for medical management and her anger because I thought it was necessary. Once again she calmed down and continued her recollections. For the first time, she talked about the unaccountable alternations in her sex life. She alternates between feelings of intense mutual satisfaction and feelings of revulsion or dissatisfaction with Shelly's love-making. She recalled her affectionate relationship with her father and remembered that he played tickling games with her, held her in his lap, and things like that. Her memories of her mother were only of having to do housework she hated, her mother's fanatical cleaning, including weekly turning and vacuuming of mattresses, and her mother's not letting her drink black coffee. I wondered, in connection with the latter, whether her mother was worried about such things because she was concerned about her health. She answered that her mother drank coffee with milk and sugar. Then she recalled a story mother told about her: supposedly at one year of age she had a feeding problem. She regurgitated food which she had held in her stomach for two to three days, [cf. later material. It sounded as though the patient was describing a mild form of Merycism[2]]. Her baby pictures certainly don't look as though she had a feeding problem. On the other hand, Jack was markedly overweight. She continued, "I resented the fact that when I was in eighth grade I had to get up with him in the morning and manage his moods. My mother was avoiding him. I wonder why I never complained and never told her that was her job."

While the intensity of her reactions to current uncaring and self-centered mother figures continued, she began talking about what she called her "imperfect" or "ugly self." She realized that she'd carried this image of herself with a big nose for years. She insists, then, that objectively she is correct. She does have a big nose, and she's not a Miss America. On the other hand, she realizes there's something about her emotional reaction to the fact of the big nose she has to understand. I concurred. She said she can never receive compliments. If they don't coincide with her "objective judgment" about herself, she feels they are not genuine or that she is being teased. "If I say to myself, 'You look good,' I always qualify with, 'You look good for *you*; you look as good as *you*

---

[2] Merycism or rumination is a well-defined syndrome occurring mainly in infancy. Food is regurgitated from the stomach, vomited, and/or re-swallowed. This functional disorder is regularly associated with a grossly disturbed mother-infant relationship (personal communication from Dr. Julius Richmond; also cf. Kanner, 1937). Although rare, Merycism has also been reported in older children and adults. I treated a six-year-old boy who regularly regurgitated, rechewed, and reswallowed stomach contents. It is entirely within the realm of possibility that during her infancy Mrs. Apple selectively retained the disliked carrots and regurgitated them several days later.

can look.'" That is why she is so insistent about Tommy being properly dressed, and that is the origin of her perfectionistic housekeeping even though she hates and resents it. She wonders how she became so opposite in taste to her mother. "Does it involve rivalry, or is it defensive because I felt rejected?" Mother bought her a shower gift when she was getting married, saying, "I bought this Swedish modern for you. I knew you'd like it because I hate it." Mother wanted her to buy an elaborate wedding dress, although she wanted a plainer gown. She complied with mother's choice and then became overwhelmingly depressed. With tremendous apprehension she begged her mother to be allowed to exchange it. "I think *I* wanted to be seen as beautiful—not the dress! This story is very relieving—revealing." As with previous (frequent) slips of the tongue, the patient took no notice of this one. Although until now I had not called any of them to her attention, I commented that it must have been relieving to her when her mother recognized it was important to her to have the wedding dress she wanted. She agreed it was relieving. Then she went on to say that the slip was very surprising to her. How interesting! She'd meant to say *revealing* and it would never have occurred to her that it was also *relieving*. Shelly calls her Mrs. Malaprop because she always uses the wrong word. She thinks she has developed the defense of humor about it and laughs with Shelly and her friends, but really she feels hurt and criticized. I suggested that her, "how interesting," was also an attempt to master feeling hurt now, along with the fact that she was genuinely interested in the emergence of feelings of which she had been unaware. She began to talk about her perfectionism again. She wants to use big words to sound very intelligent; when she does a good report she's surprised she can; she strives to do perfect programs in her volunteer work, etc.

A more complex interpretation of the slip would have

assisted the patient further. The remark that it must have been relieving to her when her mother recognized her need to choose could have been followed by a tentative genetic reconstruction of the psychological situation that fostered her tension states and depression. In addition, however, the other aspect of the slip should be addressed by agreeing that the story was revealing and by explaining that she wanted her mother to see her as beautiful and not put so much emphasis on the dress; and by explaining that she must have been chronically and painfully disappointed by her mother's lack of response to her normal childhood wishes and needs to display herself and to be enjoyed and admired for herself. From here, the full mobilization of the childhood exhibitionistic wishes in a mirror transference that could be interpreted would have been a short step. Instead, there was a lengthy detour during which time the themes already stated recurred over and over again.

Often enough, my spontaneous responses were fairly attuned to the patient and to her sensitivities. However, many interpretations proper aggravated the still unrecognized narcissistic disorder both because they were inexact and because they did not take the traumatic tension states into consideration. Thus the ground was laid for the paradox mentioned earlier. On the one hand, the patient continued to be cooperative, she was frequently immersed in the work of the treatment, and she obviously regarded the analyst as an ally who understood why she was chronically enraged with her mother and yet wanted to persist in improving the relationship: she contemplated many of my interpretations seriously, and in particular she began to recognize that her frequent dreams of explosions were manifestations of her own tension and rage. On the other hand, she was incredulous and indignant when I made certain transference interpretations. Many of her dreams indicated that almost any interruption made her feel snubbed, neglected, ignored, or deserted. She dreamed that she was with her husband and some friends in a bar during a weekend. When she returned from the ladies' room they were all gone; while she was alone she heard explosions outside. She had no money to return home and could not understand why Shelly had left her alone. Her associations included the remark to me, "This is no time to leave me when my mother's here." However, the explicit interpretation that she was reacting to interruptions with feelings of abandonment and rage evoked irritated protests. She insisted loudly that I was trying to make it seem as though she were reacting to me as she reacted to her mother, and she insisted that was definitely not the case. When I did not push the matter, there were other dreams indicating that she felt protected from danger situations by the presence of a calm, supportive woman who was assisting her to cope with the danger. At these times she went on with what appeared to be the self-analysis she started on her own.

She began to recall more about her brother's early disturbance: he was never bowel trained and he developed megacolon from withholding stools. When he finally had a stool it was huge and hard, and whoever followed him in the bathroom had the misfortune of having to break it up with a hanger kept in the bathroom for that purpose. Mother made a big deal about the fact that she was left-handed and that it was so hard to teach her to knit or do needlepoint, because she did it in the "wrong direction." Jack knitted better than she did, and he made clothes for her doll! She wondered about the relationship between her mother and Jack. He became obese because he ate everything she fed him, whereas she resisted. Jack never did well in school, and he began to suffer from her many successes. How could she be jealous of him when she was so much more successful than he was? She began to complain that her mother always "fragmented" her by remarks about her nose, her rear end, her voice, her friends. She has never gotten over her father's death — he loved her and he was positive with her. She began to feel she was making progress. She was more relaxed and supportive with Tommy, and he was more manageable. She could stand back and observe her mother and not get so angry.

During these positive swings in the cycle she began to feel more confident, hopeful, and positively assertive. The negative swings were triggered by interpretations she found, "ridiculous, absurd fabrications!" She accused me of "insulting the whole analytic process!" Since I did not understand these accusations at the time, she was left feeling unprotected in the midst of a traumatic state; then she turned more coercively and demandingly to her husband and in-laws, and was even more volatile when she did not find the response she was looking for. Then she became depressed, anxious, and began to feel she was losing the one relationship she had which was of value, namely, that with her husband. She became obsessed with thoughts and fears of losing him and of his dying, and she felt more helpless in relation to her child's disturbing demands, and further traumatized him. And she complained endlessly about the fact that she was driven to give and do for everyone and received no gratification for herself.

In essence, these swings were repetitions in the unrecognized mirror transference: just as she had turned to her mother, she turned hopefully and expectantly to the analyst for the mirroring responses which would support her vigor and self-assurance. When the response was not forthcoming, she felt "fragmented," desolate, and on her own again; enraged and hopeless, she redoubled her efforts to use her own capacities without feeling that they were up to doing what she needed to do for herself — to feel pleasure in herself and what she was doing; driven and overburdened, she responded gratefully to nonspecific efforts to be helpful to her and turned once again toward the mirroring self-object — only to be disappointed again.

A summary of the major trends in the first half of the second year follows: obsessional preoccupations with building the new house filled the hours. She inspected the most minute details of the construction. If the details were not "perfect," she became excited and enraged at the contractor, workmen, and at her husband, who left everything to her. When I grasped the inspection process sufficiently to enlighten her about its origins in her feelings about herself and her image, she began to realize she insisted that the house had to be totally perfect, and concurrently she began to resign herself to the fact that her demands for perfection were impossible. Then she became obsessed with the idea that her mother would come, would see the house as imperfect, and would not respond to it with, "I like it." She said tearfully, "I could like it even if there are flaws. But my mother will come and take away my pleasure." She was furious that the contractors told her she was too demanding; and she protested against interpretations suggesting that an externalization of her inner conflict about getting what she wanted made her mother into the spoiler of her pleasure in her house. She reported a dream which she thought was stimulated by her preoccupation with the building problem and the moldings that did not match.

"We were moving some place. Someone was trying to sell us a house. I didn't like it. It was very old, stucco, painted flowers on the walls. We were going to put all this modern furniture in it. People were trying to convince me how charming it was. My reaction was it's not for me. Someone was trying to stuff something down my throat I didn't like, and I couldn't get through to Shelly that it wasn't for our family. I felt total frustration."

She associated, "I'm not able to get through now to Shelly. The contractor is trying to stuff down my throat molding that doesn't match." I refrained from interpreting this dream as a possible protest against being stuffed with interpretations she did not like, for I was becoming aware that such interventions were not productive and simply increased the patient's agitation.

A positive cycle was initiated soon afterward when Mrs. Apple was complaining bitterly about the fact that her mother-in-law was always giving her advice on how to raise her children. I commented that her mother-in-law evidently gave so much advice because she was guilty and defensive about her own failures at mothering. (Mr. Apple's older brother, like her brother, was a "psychological failure" and an outcast.) To the remark about her mother-in-law, she responded eagerly, "That rang a bell." She realized then how terrible she feels when a child is rejected by his or her parents. Shelly's brother was "the apple of his mother's eye" until he was seven or eight and behaving in a way that no longer pleased her. His father turned away from him at the same time, and now both parents are embarrassed by their inadequate son and do not even want to be seen with him. She vowed again that she would not repeat with Tommy what her parents did with Jack and what her in-laws did with their son. She won't isolate Tommy from the rest of the family (as they did their son) even when he is impossible. She can identify with a child who has been rejected even though her problems are not as severe as either her brother's or brother-in-law's. To my comment that her in-laws must be very vulnerable and insecure to be so embarrassed about being seen with their son, she said, "It's like my mother with the drapes. She has to close them so that everybody will know they're there!" To my observation that her mother has the same vulnerability as her in-laws, she said, "I've always

been independent and done what I wanted to do, but I've
never gotten the approval I wanted. I wanted someone to
say, 'I approve of what you're doing as long as it makes *you*
happy.'" I commented that she would have to understand
what she was missing in herself, and she said, "If I understand what I need, it's my own self-approval." I agreed, then
I pointed out that she seemed to feel as though her mother
treated her as an extension of herself. She vigorously confirmed this observation with, "Yes! She says, 'my child is
toilet trained, my child is taking violin lessons, my child is
the president of her sorority, my child is building a house.' I
was an extension of her! No one said, 'I like you because
you're you.' That's the desire I have. As soon as my mother
closes the draperies she's telling me my way is wrong." [An
interpretation of the relevant genetic and transference issues
regarding the deficit in self-approving structure would be indicated here. For example, I would tell the patient: The disrupting rage you feel toward your mother erupts because you
are still trying to get her to acknowledge you as you. Instead,
she treats your draperies as though they are her own — i.e.,
she continues to treat you as though you are she. When my
explanations to you are not on your track, you feel the same
kind of rages toward me; when I grasp that you want to feel
approved, confirmed, enjoyed, and recognized as you, your
tension states and rage subside. Then you feel that you are
you, not an extension of me and not as though I am
trying, like your mother, to take you over as an extension of
myself.]

[My interpretation that she felt treated like an extension
of her mother was "incomplete" (Glover, 1931). It nevertheless had a significant impact. Despite the fact that I was not
yet thinking in terms of the formation and firming of the self
by way of the appropriate mirroring experiences that con-
tribute to the child's feeling that he is a person in his own

right, and did not yet understand the demands and the rage that are a consequence of frustrated and intensified developmental needs for precisely this form of mirroring (M. Tolpin, 1977), the patient felt adequately supported by the unrecognized self-object transference.] Mrs. Apple herself began to examine her uncompromising demands for perfection. She realized that she was behaving toward the house and its construction as her mother had behaved toward her when she was a child. "Wanting things to be perfect is a personality trait I don't like in myself, and at the same time I go on wanting the house to be perfect." Shortly afterward, however, she announced, "I've come to the realization that the door in the kitchen has to open the wrong way because of the plumbing." She began to laugh, "My mother is the only person in the whole world who will notice!" I said quietly, "Besides you," and she laughed again adding, "I start to laugh every time I begin to think about it! It's the epitome of what's been going on in my life."

I suggested that her laughter and her more accepting view of the house as a manifestation of herself came about as she was suddenly relieved from the burden of unconscious guilt which prompted her identification with her mother's criticisms. Her beginning humorous self-acceptance was short-lived. She evidently heard this interpretation concerning unconscious guilt as a criticism akin to her mother's criticisms. She insisted, "I liked my straight hair even though my mother made all these comparisons — 'isn't it too bad you have straight hair and Jack has curly hair?' I didn't think I was defective because I didn't have curly hair like hers and Jack's. *She* was saying it's a defect, 'you're not as good as Jack and me.' I understand my rage about my mother being so critical, but I still don't see how I can cope with it." Then she added, "My mother says she doesn't criticize me. That's true! *I* make the inference that her remark means that the house is imperfect. She didn't criticize directly. She'd just say, 'Your brother has curly hair, and you have straight hair.'"

It would appear that the patient is once again in the throes of crucial psychological problems which are considered to be ubiquitous in the girl's development. However, it seems to me that this material throws new light on these developmental problems. What is habitually referred to (cf. Erikson's [1950] remarks concerning orality and anality) as the female castration complex, penis envy, rage toward the phallic mother who deprives the girl of a penis, and so forth, is not simply an artifact arising from residual castration anxiety and a consequent inability to see women except through men's eyes. These well-known configurations e-merged in Mrs. Apple's analysis as the manifest content or as the tip of an iceberg. The base of this particular iceberg seems to lie in the faulty empathic merger between mother and daughter in which the self has its origins. I believe that the patient expressed her feelings of emotional deprivation and tried to explain these feelings through her impassioned accounts of not getting the special room with the porch (penis) she wanted, of hating ruffles (her own genitalia), or of her mother's comparisons to her brother in which she was found sadly wanting. [These manifest complaints are usually understood as reflections of the deeper problem of the woman's personality organization. Her feeling that her brother's room was "better" because it had a porch on which to play could be taken as a displaced expression of penis envy and of feelings of inadequacy and inferiority due to the lack of an adequate "executive organ" (Nagera, 1975). In fact, however, the patient was not jealous and enraged because her brother had a penis and she did not. She was enraged because her mother needed her, as well as her brother, to be an extension of herself. She was dimly aware that her brother had suffered more than she had as a consequence of being the "mother's phallus" (another semantic bad habit) and that his ultimate attempts to extricate himself from this position, without assistance, had doomed him to psychological failure. Nor was the primary goal to get the penis-baby from her father: she wanted him to save her from the narcissistic entanglement with her mother, and she also wanted him to save her brother.]

Continuing, the patient declared, "My childhood desire was to please her, not to be found fault with, not to be fragmented by her talking about my nose, my tush, my hair. My only desire is she'll say the house is gratifying. There was nothing I did where she'd say, 'That's terrific!' So the fantasy still exists. I don't want her to come and see the house piecemeal. I want her to see it in all its glory and like it or not like it." [It should be particularly noted that Kohut's contributions on the feeling of fragmentation associated with the breakup of the cohesiveness of the self had not yet been published. It should also be noted that, like most analysts, I was unable to "hear" the significance of what the patient was saying until I had the conceptual assistance of a new analytic discovery. My experience with this patient's use of the "language of the self" and its disorders is not unique. Many other patients used this language. The difference is simply that my capacity for analytic listening now has a wider range.]

The intensity of the revived childhood need to be seen and affirmed in order to feel all of a piece and not fragmented reached a crescendo. Failing to get the specific analytic understanding of her need to be told, 'you're terrific' in response to her revived exhibitionism, the patient's narcissistic need was erotized; however, this emergency mechanism (erotization of the deficit in cohesion-maintaining structure) failed to prevent the mounting anxiety of an impending "crack-up." The emergency erotization and the failure of this mechanism are illustrated in the following dream. "Shelly and I were driving in the car, but we were making love. He was touching my breasts and kissing them. We decided we should stop to have intercourse—he was driving the car bent down and couldn't see where he was going. It was too dangerous to keep driving. I was aroused, and my fear was that he couldn't do this and drive without cracking up." She added that a rational part of her mind was operating even in the dream, so she knew it was unreal.

In the next hour she announced, "I was very surprised by the intensity of my feelings yesterday. Rationally I don't feel so torn apart and hurt by my mother; on the other hand, I can't deny the feelings I have. They're real. I walk out of here and think, 'I don't really feel so ugly and defective. I don't understand what you're saying, and I can't accept it.'" I agreed that her rational appraisal of herself was not the problem. She viewed herself positively and did not think of herself as defective. The problem lay in the fact that her rational attitude did not protect her when she felt re-exposed to persisting childhood feelings of rage toward her mother.

This interpretation intensified the patient's hopelessness. "So this superrational self of mine doesn't function in a rational way. That's typical of me. So the whole thing is a big fraud. This front of functioning independently and perfectly is breaking down in these sessions. I'm not able to say anymore to the painter, 'Paint the wall again, it's not right'; and I'm not able to say, 'All right, it's not perfect, so we'll paint it again in two years.' So I want someone else to take over to settle the whole thing."

From this time on, Mrs. Apple's insistence that she was "fragmented" by her mother intensified. "I got a letter from my mother today. She writes, 'Are you letting your hair grow? I have long hair now, I'm not sure if I like it.' I can't be the one to grow long hair, now she is. That's exemplatory [3] of what goes on with my mother and me. Is it then that it's taken away from me? Now it's not mine anymore, or is it mine compared to hers? Is she letting hers grow because I am? Is she trying to compete?" She was too overwrought to wait for answers to these questions, and I had not yet conceptualized her overwrought state as a reaction to the chronic exposure to a mother whose narcissistic disequilibrium drove her to try to merge with her daughter.

She began to try to restore an internal sense of order by exerting compulsive control over external disorder. She returned to making lists and to being "superorganized" amidst the impossible mess of the new house. She worked at the disorder late into the night and further depleted her energies. "It's like everything's falling apart! So I gathered all the loose ends together in my house—I worked till 1:00 A.M. That's why I feel better today. So I've superorganized again and everything is going smoothly. Yesterday it was like the end of the world. Something rational has happened today, so it's not the end of the world!" The next day, however, she was saying, "There's something wrong with my involvement with the new house. Why shouldn't I be excited? It's always there's something that isn't right, and the truth is there is really nothing wrong with it. I don't have a bubbly feeling. I thought I'd be in my glory to be able to do this! And I have this uptight feeling again—I feel anxious about something I want to be happy about."

Shortly afterward she became frightened that she was cracking up. Shelly accused her of getting satisfaction from

[3] "Exemplatory" was probably a condensation of the words exemplify and explanatory. She must have meant that her mother's saying, "I have long hair now," exemplifies, and is explanatory of, their relationship. This kind of malapropism-parapraxis-neologism typically occurred during the patient's traumatic states when she vehemently tried to insist on her right to be a separate person with her own style and struggled to resist what she experienced as her mother's need to take over her unique characteristics.

needling his sister and said, "You are exactly like your mother." "I got furious at him. I said, 'Don't *ever* compare me to my mother. All my life I've been compared to my mother!' If you don't like what I do, judge *me*! Don't compare me to my mother. I blew my stack. It's a frightening thing. When I left here, I thought *you* felt, 'She has inner strength, she'll go forward.' I was walking a thin line. Now I feel I could have a nervous breakdown. What Shelly said hit off something that doesn't have anything to do with him and what he said. I felt I was being fragmented again. I felt like everything was slipping away." Eventually she felt able to pull herself together and function again. "The house is back in my control now."

She was disturbed by a dream in which someone was picking her house apart. She asked, "Why am I so furious? I want to be able to say to my mother, 'You may not like it, but I like it.' I woke up with blood in my stool for the first time in six months." I commented that the state represented in the dream suggested that she was experiencing the analytic work as picking her apart. She was exasperated: "Here I go again. I don't feel that. Rationally I know that individual things are going to be looked at here. I can look back and say I was angry my mother tore me into pieces. She never said, 'Despite the fact that you have a long nose, you are a pretty person.'" I ventured the opinion that she needed someone to come and see her house and say, "I like the whole thing." To this she rejoined, "It's occurred to me, 'Who am I doing this house for?' It's for myself. I'm not interested in showing a show piece. Yet, when Marge [a close friend] comes and likes it, I'm pleased." [It would have been helpful for the patient to conceptualize the notion that her echoing, approving friend performed an affirming function that she could not yet carry out with her own endopsychic structure.]

The work of the next hour led to a significant insight. "I

was dying to come. I had the most incredible phone conversation with my mother, and I'm trying to analyze it." Mrs. Apple recounted the "incredible conversation" and the fight with her mother that ensued. Her mother had been reproachful, "Why don't you write? Why don't you call?," and she had angrily yelled at her mother over the phone. I pointed out that her mother sounded as though she felt very alone and was turning to her daughter for responsiveness. Mrs. Apple's fury suddenly abated. She returned the next hour with, "A light is going on. My mother is depressed! She gets like this every year in March and April. March is when my father died and April is when both of her parents died. [cf. p. 171 — Tommy's depressions in March.] I've always been looking for someone to lean on. I've been the strong one. The roles between mother and child are reversed. She's always seeking praise, support, all the things she needs. That's why I'm so bitter about getting money from her I don't need. Psychologically I never got anything from her. What do I do now?" I said we would go on and understand the effects on her personality of the reversal of roles she was describing and of her father's role in her development. "My father was enamored of his mother, and my mother was jealous. My mother said his mother wouldn't let him live. My mother was the domestic, and I was never competitive in her realm. I sat in the living room with my father and talked. My father did praise and support me; he was very critical of my brother, and my mother sided with Jack." To my comment that girls not only compete with their mothers, they want to grow up to be like them in certain ways, she objected, saying she never wanted to be like her mother, but like her grandmother who accepted her. Her mother had to show her how well she baked cookies; her grandmother let her bake them. "With my mother she did everything right and I did it wrong. It wasn't that way with my father. My grandmother lived with us for a time. My father liked her. He'd say to my mother, 'I don't know why you're not more like your mother.' But my mother was sweet compared to my father's mother. She was piss and vinegar—impossible! I don't enjoy baking, except for my kids and the pleasure it gives them. And I let them cut out cookies if they want to, and I'm not always telling them the *perfect* way to do it! That's what my grandmother did for me!" I said, "Mother always emphasized *her cookies* and not the pleasure for *you*." She went on, "She was fanatical about everything—she flipped beds and vacuumed the mattresses every week. And I had to help! It was her house, exemplified by how she did my room! [The patient used the correct word when she felt more understood.] It was the way *she* liked it! She never fixed up the room that was for our family. It wasn't for show like her living room! My father, on the other hand, was very positive. At ten, eleven, and even twelve, I still remember playing tickling games with him. I don't remember any physical handling from my mother! My father seemed to know how I felt without my even telling him. My mother and I were in different worlds." [When the transference experience was undisrupted, the patient always assumed that the analyst was with her, on her side, and understood what she was feeling. This aspect of the mirror transference can be traced directly to the empathic relationship with the father who "saved" her from the desolation she associated with her mother's "housewife mania."] "There was nothing I could do wrong in my father's eyes. My mother comes here to fortify herself! My father came because he enjoyed us! My father went about his own life—he loved his practice, his preventive work. My mother was a mother figure to him. She drove him to work, picked him up, fussed about his rubbers and all. Face it! He depended on her and her nagging him. His mother laid out his clothes every day of his life until he got married! My father was an only child. His mother lost twelve pregnancies. He was the only surviving child, so he was like a diamond to her. His father was the nicest, dearest man — nothing like his mother!"

The Beginning of Working Through

Mrs. Apple returned to the question of whether she felt guilty toward her mother, first denying her guilt, then qualifying it, and finally conceding its existence, but justifying it. She continued with a lengthy description of her longing to be responded to positively and her inability to accept positive responses when they came her way.

At this point in the treatment the move to the new house took place. "I went to bed exhausted and drained, and Shelly appeared with a bottle of champagne — that's typical of Shelly — and we made love. Afterward, I dreamed I was at a dance with Shelly. We were dancing, but I was very pregnant. I said to Shelly, 'You should go dance with Laura.' Then someone else I knew came to me and said, 'I don't know how to tell you this, but Shelly and Laura are carrying on a flirtation on the dance floor.' I didn't feel threatened. I just regarded it as an episode because I was pregnant and Shelly was deprived sexually. I wasn't worried about losing my husband." She associated to Laura, "She's a friend of mine whose husband died suddenly of a pulmonary hemorrhage. She was left with two young children. I had to break the news to her. She's never remarried."

Mrs. Apple was astonished when I pointed out that her friend's husband died suddenly, like her father, from a pulmonary hemorrhage. I also pointed out that as she moved into the house she wanted so much and shared the experience with her husband, she was attempting to deal with persistent feelings of guilt toward her mother. She reponded to further efforts to elucidate unconscious superego demands to make restitution to her mother by an intensification of her demands for positive recognition for herself. Dreams reflected her need for recognition from the analyst as the mirroring self-object, and the ongoing frustrations of the uninterpreted need. "I was at like a resort. Marge and a beautician were there, and some other people sitting around a table. I went to the bathroom to tease my hair and took a long time at it, unlike what I usually do with my hair. Finally I emerged in a nice pantsuit with my hair all teased and feeling very attractive and very pleased with my appearance. Apparently I'd taken so long everyone else had made his bed and was ready to depart for the day's activities. My bed was the only one that wasn't made." She associated to the importance of her long hair to her, her mother's objections because it made her nose look too big, to a time when her mother took her to the beauty parlor to have curls made when she was going to be a flower girl in a wedding and mother wanted to show her off, and to times when she was gratified by others finding her "cute." Then she recalled "how angry and frustrated I feel with you. You do not understand that my anger at my mother is because my mother didn't like me; I feel guilty that I'm angry at my mother, yes—but my not liking her is because she depreciated me!" When I commented that her mother must have thought she was cute, just as others had, "No! The curls and dress were only for her, so people would say her daughter was cute!"

The patient's protests against interpretations were calmer, and she was no longer furiously accusing the analyst of "insulting the whole analytic purpose." She was nevertheless insistent on her point of view—that her guilt toward her mother, although undeniable, had to be understood in the larger context of the latter's self-absorption. Thus she persisted in presenting herself for an admiring echo to her own display, and she persisted in her feeling that her needs went unrecognized.

The Traumatic Disruption of the Mirror Transference

For a time after the complaint "You don't understand
. . . " the patient continued to make progress—probably because I did not insist on the correctness of my interpretations,
but waited and listened. She said, "It's really sad if I get what
I want and can't enjoy it [the house]." She reported a dream,
"My mother was looking at my hair and saying, 'When are
you going to cut your long hair?' I said, 'I'm not going to.
I'm going to let it grow until it doesn't grow anymore.'" She
associated the dream with the house: "I want it to be perfect,
but to another part of me it doesn't matter that much that
it's not perfect. The only person I feel will criticize is my
mother. I am aware there are three door knobs in the kitchen. Two things function: Does it make any difference? If it
doesn't make any difference, why am I so exacting? I'm not
going to kill myself because the door knobs don't match; but
simultaneously I'm aware they don't match. That's a direct
reflection of my mother saying, 'Long hair makes your nose
look bigger.'" [These clinical data illustrate the metapsy-
chological concept of the vertical split and its developmental
origins. The grandiose self continues to insist on its own perfection, and continues to insist that the mirroring self-object
should enthusiastically echo, "You look nice. Your house is
terrific." Equally strong, the rational adult insists, "You
don't have to be so exacting and compulsive. Nothing is perfect, and to be enjoyable and good it doesn't have to be perfect." The failure of the grandiose self to undergo sufficient
modifications to infuse the personality with a firm residue of
certainty, confidence, and glow originally occurred as the
mother consistently failed to respond affirmatively to the
child who was different from her; and as, from the child's
point of view, the mother sadistically undermined her by insisting that all of the glory resided in her physical attributes,
her absolute tastes, convictions, and prejudices.]

As the treatment entered the second half of the second year, the patient's distress with Tommy intensified, and she continued the vicious cycle of trying to coerce him into health. His disorder worsened, and his fairly even, amiable father entered into the battle. He accused his wife of being too permissive and infantilizing; *he* was going to take over! Tommy began to sound "paranoid"; "Daddy hates me; he wants to kill me. Something happens inside of me that creeps into my neck, and I can't even talk, and daddy wants to kill me." He began coming to her with terrible nightmares—he and the rest of the family were starving to death; or they were being poisoned or destroyed by various means. [This paranoidlike thinking accompanied the child's traumatic states and fragmentation, and expressed concretely the attack on his inner cohesiveness, which he was trying to tell his mother about.] Mrs. Apple began to feel that she and her husband were growing apart. She desperately tried to obtain what she needed in an erotized form. She complained bitterly about her husband, "He never does what I want, the way I want it, when I want it." Her orgastic capacity frequently failed, and then she became more desperate—another imperfection, another "inadequacy" as she saw it. Her colon began to bother her again. Nevertheless, she felt she was making progress, "The kitchen cabinets aren't perfect and I can enjoy it! It's helped to realize my mother gets depressed. Knowing she's in a foul mood shifts the whole thing. Then I can see what she's saying isn't a personal attack. Then I don't have to fight with her as I did in March. I wonder if she was like that when I was younger?"

While continuing to wonder about what her mother was like when she was younger, she dreamed that one of her sons was hospitalized with severe respiratory distress. It appeared to her that he was almost not breathing, and she experienced severe anxiety; then she was enormously relieved because he began to get better. I wondered about the possibility of a childhood illness in which she experienced respiratory distress. "I was never sick like that, but did I ever tell you about the time Jack locked me in a spare refrigerator in the basement? I don't think it was out of malicious intent. We'd been playing. He tried to get in the refrigerator and couldn't fit. Then he told me to get in and locked the door. I couldn't get out and began to yell and cry. Ultimately my mother heard me and got me out." Then she wondered if she had told me about the digestive disturbance she had as an infant. I recalled that she had mentioned her mother's account of the disturbance and asked her to tell me about it again. "It's unbelievable, but my mother says when I was two or three if I had to eat foods I didn't like I'd hold them in my stomach for days and regurgitate them later. Especially carrots. Finally a doctor told her to eliminate the foods I didn't like and not to feed me carrots. Then there was no problem."

In retrospect, it appears to me that these memories telescope important failures in the mother-child unit. The recall of the episode of being locked in the refrigerator telescopes the feeling that her mother was unable to adequately protect her from the traumatic states brought about by her brother's behavior toward her. Later, when he "manhandled" her more than she could endure without feeling helpless, her mother was unaware of her state and did not intervene. She herself tried to deal with him by being "above it" (morally superior) until her humiliation at not being able to get out of his iron hold made her desperate with rage.

The recollection of her mother's account of the digestive disorder was a groping attempt to characterize her mother's unempathic feeding. Unlike her brother, who became obese and retained his stools, she resisted the overfeeding which was unattuned to her needs. Evidently her mother was completely unable to understand that although she thought certain foods were good for a growing child her baby did not like them. [Earlier in the treatment the patient made the same point when she said that her mother insisted on her drinking coffee with milk and sugar because that was how she liked to drink it.] Outside intervention from a reasonably informed physician resolved the feeding disorder per se, but this disturbance was merely the most overt manifestation of chronic interferences in the internalization process that eventuates in reliable self-regulation. Eventually, the patient substituted erotized self-soothing mechanisms for the tension-relieving psychological structure ordinarily provided by the mother in early stages (the thumb-sucking and rubbing which irritated her mother, and the more covert tongue-sucking which escaped her notice). Later in the treatment when the analyst noticed the traumatic tension states and responded with appropriate explanations, the patient began to acquire the capacity to calm herself and to avert feeling "swamped." For example, during a transitional stage when the analyst was still experienced as the one who calmed her, the patient dreamed that she was at the helm of a sailboat and water started to pour into the boat; the captain called out a warning. She was not swamped and even managed to stay on course. During the termination, internalization of the calming structure provided by the "captain" led to significant changes in her over-all functioning and perception of herself.

The hours continued to be filled with extensive elaborations on the theme of her mother's inability to give her what she wanted. "She could only think about what she wanted little girls to wear. I've been able to change my image with Tommy and accommodate to him and his liking jeans." She contrasted her mother with her friend Marge: "Marge is different from me and we have different tastes, but we appreciate each other." She dreamed, "I was changing bed linens with Marge. The sheets didn't fit. No sooner did we get them

on than I'd rip them off. It went on and on." Her associations included the idea that she was struggling: sometimes
the bed was made and it looked pretty good, but then she
wasn't satisfied with how it looked, so she was doing it again.

Mrs. Apple was working on a science project she had
originated for her children's school. While she was practicing
a song she planned to sing in connection with her presentation to the children, Shelly, who had perfect pitch, laughed
about her voice. She sang a few bars of the song to illustrate
to me. "I became so incensed and upset I thought I wouldn't
do the presentation at all." I said that her voice sounded off
to him because he had perfect pitch; however, it sounded
adequate for the purposes of the presentation. The gist of her
response to this indicated that the patient recognized that her
sense of injury at her husband's hands was out of all propor-
tion to his intent. "Shelly said, 'I didn't mean to pick on you.
I think you're fun, you're cute.' That made me realize I
wasn't reacting to him, but to all the years I was told I
couldn't sing, but that Jack had a nice voice. I had twelve
years of music. Ultimately I rebelled and quit. My parents
were very disappointed. They wanted me to continue. I said I
had no talent for music. Just as they were unrealistic about
Jack they were unrealistic about me." I commented that she
seemed to be in the process of developing more realistic attitudes about her actual capacities and her ability to use these
capacities, instead of always comparing herself to her "oohed
and ahhed-over" childhood brother and feeling the same dissatisfaction with herself now that she felt as a child.

This intervention had two effects. First, she said that
now she can understand her mother and both of her parents
better. She thinks her mother had such a problem with Jack,
she wanted not to repeat the same mistakes with her; and
both of her parents underplayed her achievements and successes because Jack was so jealous of her. They were trying to

protect him. [This somewhat precocious empathy for her parents emerged before her longings for recognition were worked through. Self-acceptance and the capacity to empathize with herself and her own needs were not yet sufficiently developed to be "nourishing" to her personality. I believe that the emergence of understanding of her parents at this point in the treatment repeated the early development of the patient's empathic capacity in a strained matrix in which the parents' needs took precedence over hers.] The second effect of the intervention was that she was steered in the direction of further consideration of the genetics of her disorder. "My mother boasted that she toilet-trained me at nine months. She said I wanted to. The other difference between Jack and me is the circumstances in which we were born. My mother was pregnant before Jack was born. She had a nine-month pregnancy—a boy was stillborn. So Jack was alive after they'd lost a boy. The first boy, the first grandchild. He was it for three years, and he was terribly indulged. And my mother thought he was so beautiful. She judged people by what they looked like. She judged people by the outside, not by what they were like on the inside "

In the next hours she elaborated on the basic feeling that she was not valued enough. It was in this context that she returned to her inability to feel really excited about the house. When her in-laws are cool when they come to see the house she feels picked apart. "You must be right. I can't get what I want because of what's in me. But, why can't they come and just say, 'It's nice'?" [A psychologically more accurate way to rephrase the patient's statement would be: Because she was missing the warm glow of satisfaction in herself, she was still looking for the glow from her in-laws.]

In spite of the attacks of rage which further disrupted her feelings about herself, she began to talk about a "minute shift" in her idea of herself as "antifeminine" and as the "boy-girl." "I don't attack Shelly if he gives me a lacy night-gown with, 'You should know that's not me!' I wore this boyish severe hairdo long enough. [The hairdo was neither boyish nor severe — it was chic and casual and well suited to *her*.] As you see, I still don't have curls and ringlets, but my hair is long! I always identified with my father. I patterned myself and my tastes opposite my mother. I didn't want to compete with her because I realized I wouldn't be successful in her realm. There was no room for me in her realm. I couldn't needlepoint as well as my mother! (She laughed, still strained.) I was going to be my father's daughter, the doctor. And my father said, 'The only thing I want from you is that you are happily married and have children.'" I wondered why she associated her tastes and ambitions so inexorably with being a boy. Had her father minimized her ambitions and disappointed her too? Why did she feel that wanting to be a doctor necessarily meant she wanted to be a boy? "I think the truth is I was trying to be a boy. I know my father would have been in ecstasy if my brother wanted to be a doc-tor. It was clear I didn't want to be like my mother. I don't have a feminine attitude about myself. I'm thrilled now if Shelly gives me something tailored, even though I gulp and wear the lace gown. My mother didn't like my father's gifts either. She never wore anything pretty to bed, and I told you how she looked when she cleaned house. She also looked like a zombie when she want to bed — with cream on her face. I couldn't stand the way she smelled!" She dreamed she was trying to find the right bed to sleep in, had intercourse with Shelly, and felt rushed because she had to get the children to school. She associated to her mother always telling her she needed to get more sleep. "*She* needed me to sleep. When I made the children nap when they were little, I knew *I* wanted them out of the way because I needed time for myself for a while." To my comment that she must have felt her mother wanted her out of the way, she responded. "I was always afraid to go into my parents' room. It wasn't that I was told I couldn't. When I had bad dreams, I didn't go to them. I'd lie in bed thinking of ways not to be so frightened."

The following associations place the manifest theme of exclusion from the "primal scene" in the broader emotional context in which it belongs. "I don't remember my mother taking care of me in the first house we lived in, though she said these fabulous maids cleaned and she took care of us. Jack was so obese she wouldn't let anyone else pick him up. She was always talking about how tiny and slim she was. This tiny woman with the big baby! I always felt big next to her. She was always making these comparisons." This material concerning what she regarded as a conflict over and rejection of femininity led directly to her father and her longing for him as an alternative to her mother. In a dream, she said to her mother, "Let's dig up daddy." She was enraged when her mother said, "We can't do that; he'll catch cold." "I'm angry, and I say, 'Don't you realize he's dead, he can't catch cold; you have to face reality! He's dead.'" Her associations first involved typical ideas about parental sexuality: mother was always mothering father and worrying about his health. She couldn't imagine them in bed, nor could she imagine her mother interested in intercourse. Then her thoughts took another tack, "My father was constantly saying, 'I'll die young and you'll remarry.' He was insecure about my mother. This idea of his death permeated our lives." Immediately afterward, she became terribly upset about Tommy "falling apart into a million pieces" (again) and his terrible nightmares of destruction, starvation, and poisoning. She feels she's failed as a parent. I suggested that Tommy's nightmares were concrete expressions of the psychological state which she described as fragmentation. She began to try again to "put him back together." Following another experience of feeling fragmented by her mother-in-law's coolness, she concluded, "The truth is I wasn't so rejected. I was overlooked. What I did should have brought gratification, and it was overlooked. 'That's just how Jeanie is.' It was no longer an act that deserved praise or recognition. I've realized another thing about my mother. Either she's all negative, or she calls and is pleasant as though nothing's happened. Then I get all set to go on with the positive relationship, and then she comes with her leftover gifts. It occurs to me: if Tommy is in a good mood, I have a good day; if he's desperate, I'm desperate and I have a desperate day." I wondered if her mother was on and off in the same way during her childhood. The question led to more material concerning her mother's reactions to her positive overtures. "I asked my mother for a bread recipe she makes. She wouldn't give it to me. She said, 'I'll bake it when I come.'" Bitterly, she added, "It wouldn't reflect off of her if I made it; I'd think she would be pleased I asked for her recipe! This leads me to new feelings about my mother. As I was growing up I never thought, 'She wants all the attention and won't give it to me!' But I'm saying that now. When I did anything, she took it over for herself. She wears what *I* wear now. What strikes me is my unawareness of my mother until my father died. She didn't bug me until then. Now I say, 'Why didn't she teach me how to bake?' From her point of view, she did. But she never allowed me to participate. She demonstrated. My mother never showed me her magic tricks of how to sew. I do domestic things now without any pleasure. I diminished the domestic role — 'Anyone can do that.'"

In the next weeks she oscillated between feelings that she was depressed because Shelly was abandoning her and feelings that he was the same, but she could not respond. Genuine discoveries about her past and the intrusion of the past into the present continued.

She "admits" her colon is bothering her. She laughs when I continue to point out that, in spite of her complaint that she has to be so independent, she insists on managing it herself. She dreams she has on a dress she liked very much in high school. In the same dream she sees a new house being e-rected on the foundation of her grandmother's house, but it is cheaply built and ugly. She concludes she is dreaming about the old and the new. The dress was one of the few that was her taste and not bought on sale. I said that she saw her-self more as she liked to, what was she objecting to about the building? She answered immediately, "The colon business." She recalls, "At the beginning of treatment you did not rec-ommend analysis *because* of colitis, but I think what goes on in me takes itself out on my colon. Somehow, my feeling about this illness is that it's self-inflicted and I therefore go through all my methodical steps to control it." I said that we should continue to try to understand her feelings that she herself brought it about and that she herself would control it.

In the meantime, her mother arrived for a visit. She is managing with her mother better, but she is "disappointed and disillusioned because I'm not going to be able to have the relationship with her I want." She called her doctor and she is relieved, "I can see I really need help, I was glad I went to see him." The next hour she reported the following dream, "I'm in the kitchen with my mother having just finished baking. There's an explosion. My kitchen is an ap-pendage to the rest of the house, and the explosion is where the kitchen attaches to the house. There's a fire. I'm crying hysterically, 'We have a new house—why does this physical mess and damage happen to me? Why do you have fires in your house?' My mother is angry I didn't rescue her. I said, 'I got everyone else out of the house. You can take care of your-self.' Then she tells me a plumber came to fix the toilet where the explosion occurred. He was crushed flat, but then Shelly lifts the plywood off that fell on him and he's alive again." Her associations included, "The wild idea that the plumber is trying to fix my colon. The toilet is my colon with its malfunctioning. I do not accept my colitis as existing. Psychologically it's like an explosion, 'What happened, why can't it be fixed? Why does this happen? Why can't I control it?' Dr. Y's saying, 'You're causing it yourself' is an attack on me. The attack is having the colitis—not a physical attack, but in a psychological sense." The "plumber-analyst" expressed the notion that indeed she had felt attacked from within by her malfunctioning colon, and that she had also felt attacked from without by the internist whose "gentle implication" she actually took to mean that the disease was her own fault. She had attempted to solve the psychological assault on her image of herself by denying the existence of the faulty organ rather than accepting it as a part of her "house," which she had to care for. Mrs. Apple said she would think about that, and prepared to face a one-week routine spring vacation interruption without the analyst while her mother remained for a few more days.

She returned to report that after her mother's departure Shelly bought her a "putting up with plaque." She was beginning to be reconciled to her disappointment and anger. "She carries home presents for everyone—I could hit my head against the wall and she won't bring presents for the boys. She brought me a twenty-year-old bedspread of hers and she immediately went and bought Jack's wife a beautiful gift from a terrific store here. She gave me that check for the house, but the things that are meaningful for me she's unable to do. She doesn't understand my long hair turns into a reflection of her long hair. She's forgotten what she said about mine and asked, 'How do you like my long hair?' Ultimately I won't be so critical of her. I can see a progression. But I am slowly convinced that the relationship I want can't be established. But inside myself I want a relationship. I have to understand that." She became tearful when I said that she sounded very sad now, instead of so angry that her mother could not give her what was meaningful to her. The next hour began with, "I can't remember ever being so frightened in a dream: Shelly and I were wandering around through churches and villages dismantling explosives that other people had assembled to destroy something. Then we were climbing small stairs to a steeple in a church, I think. We were dismantling more explosives and shoving them under a bed. We hear someone coming, and we run. We hear a woman's voice. We meet on the stairs, but we duck behind a door. I woke up trembling." She associated, "It was like I was really being chased. Something like life and death about it. I had dreams of being chased as a child. Then I always fell down. In this one I was definitely going up. I would never go into my mother's room when I was so afraid. That was another self-inflicted thing maybe. I was never told, 'no,' but my mother was very finicky. She was always dressed. [The patient was trying to find a way to express the feeling that she could not approach the "finicky" mother who was physically and emotionally unapproachable when she needed comforting.] The emotional intensity was so great in this dream it woke me up. The fact that we were climbing up makes it different, because as a little child I was always being chased and I was falling down. In this dream there was an act on my part. I was taking something apart to break up something destructive. I don't feel anything in me exploding. I don't see what needs dismantling. The most significant thing is, what causes me to be so frightened?"

It seems to me now that the patient was engaged in a frightening struggle to separate herself from a destructive merger with a mother who continued to treat her as an extension of herself rather than as a separate person. At the time, I recognized that she was sad as she contemplated the reality that her wishes for emotional responsiveness from her mother were met with continuous disappointment. However, I was unable to tell her that she felt as frightened as when she was a child alone with her feelings of being emotionally dropped and unsupported, and that now, as she was undertaking to define herself as separate from her mother, she looked to the analyst for the psychological supports which would allay her fears that she was coming apart.

I had learned from long experience that the patient felt nothing but irritation and anger when I focused on such explanations as her childhood wishes to separate her parents, her fears of such wishes, and the like. Consequently, I told her that she often felt that some of my explanations were artificial, and I suggested that we go on with the task of trying to understand her fears in a way that was meaningful to her. Her first association was: "I was very shocked yesterday to learn that a very competent person I know had to be hospitalized. Why did she get herself in such a state? I thought about her all day. I'd like to write her a letter. I don't understand how she can have such a severe problem it necessitates hospitalization. This is related to the dream—I think this dream involves something inside me that is not rational at all." [It was clear that these associations referred to her fear that although she was "a very competent person" she was in danger of a "crack-up." Nevertheless, I did not consider this to be a real possibility in spite of the fact that I was concerned about the level of anxiety she was experiencing. Although I formulate the psychological situation differently now, at that time it did not occur to me that there was an ominous underlying disorder, nor did I question the ultimate analyzability of her present state. The correctness of this clinical judgment is of particular interest, inasmuch as severe tension states and reversible threats of fragmentation are the rule rather than the exception in the narcissistic disorders. It is reasonable to think, however, that the tension state and accompanying fears of fragmentation were exacerbated and protracted because they were not recognized as the very center of the analytic task.]

Mrs. Apple started the next hour with, "Last week while you were on vacation and I was dealing with my mother I began thinking about terminating. Not realistically! But I'm on a different plane with my mother and with Tommy. He's a different child. He can play a game and not break down if he loses. But I still have problems I've avoided. It's interesting that trouble in my sex life always occurs after my mother leaves. I complained that she was the cause. I can't say this now. I feel sexually inadequate more times than I feel adequate. Your knowing me makes you know that it makes me feel really inadequate if I don't have an orgasm. I blame myself, then I blame Shelly. Something's wrong—he's dull and unimaginative and does the same thing all the time. I want him to take over. He says, 'I try this and that, and you are unhappy anyway.'" [The patient reacted to her occasional lack of orgasm very much as she reacted to her bowel disorder. She considered both to be evidence that the "image" she maintained about herself and her functioning was false.]

The characteristic oscillations in her mood and feelings about herself continued. During one of the depressive oscillations she dreamed, "I was riding a bicycle with exhilaration. The bicycle was taken away or stolen. I said to Shelly in the dream, 'I'm so angry I'll never talk to you again.'" She talked endlessly of Shelly's growing preoccupation with his work and of the fact that everyone gravitated to him. She insisted that she could not tell him what she wanted. She wanted him to know what she wanted without her having to ask or tell him.

It seemed as though the patient was living out the rage at the depriving mother with her husband as well as her analyst. She reacted negatively to attempts to explore the reactivated childhood conflicts from which it appeared she was regressing to a preoedipal position, with all of the demands for an omnipotent parent made by the preoedipal child. In response to her negativism and the frustrating impasse, I pointed out that it was difficult for her to accept explanations regarding her present dilemma as a repetition of childhood conflicts and their original solution. This appeal to the intact ego to reinstitute a working relationship inadvertently was the match set to an explosive.

Mrs. Apple returned to this intervention the next hour, "You've said I become hostile when someone makes suggestions unless I come up with it on my own. I decided you were defensive. Then I pondered what you said. I decided I've done with you what I've done with everyone else in the world. I've insisted I'm self-sufficient, that I have all the resources I need. But what astonished me is you accepted that. Really what I've been trying to show is I need help. I automatically respond, 'No.' Even if I reject what you say, I contemplate it. I have been trying to break down this defense mechanism. (Mrs. Apple was familiar with this concept from her reading.) What do I have to do to get through to people to make them willing to lend a hand? Whomever I try to lean on won't allow it. I can't understand why I'm not able to do that with you." I told the patient that I was trying to understand what she needed. "I have a built-in mechanism. I react to you as I react when my mother is criticizing me. Something else: Why do I totally not want to be like her? She's pretty, gregarious, a 'fun person' to others — not a totally bad person — just 98 per cent." She laughed. "If I was a good girl, it proved she was a good mother, and it was a reflection on her. My grandmother sat with me when I had the chicken pox. I never remember physical contact or affectionate games with my mother. There are tons I remember with my father and grandmother. I feel I was never allowed to be comforted by her. Everything she did for me was a reflection of her, and I hated it. Here I am 35, and in order for me to be me I have to be not like my mother. There's a terrible void in my background. She couldn't even talk to me when I asked her about menstruation when I was eleven." [This memory did not screen a sexual prohibition as I thought at first. It functioned as another telescoped memory concerning the mother's self-absorption and faulty empathy.] "My love affair with my father was on an intellectual level. The sexual area didn't exist for me because it didn't exist for her. When she didn't answer my question I thought of her as the Virgin Mary, and as an adult I find out she doesn't know anything about anything. I know you've said I tried to get close to my mother to cover over and get rid of my guilt. *I didn't*! I cut her off as far as my father and I were concerned. She goes out and buys Shelly a birthday card, 'You're top soap, bar none' and on my birthday she sends me a Friendship card out of the box of cards she's got at home. She's never been able to say to me, 'I think you're great.' It's taking something from her to say that to me."

The summer interruption drew nearer. I did not understand the "terrible void" as a hunger for the psychological structure that would enable her to maintain her own enthusiasm for herself, and the amplitude of the depressed oscillation increased, nor did she rebound from it. She dreamed, "I had an appointment for one of my children at the pediatrician's. I waited and waited while everybody else was taken. Finally I was told he'd gone for the day and I'd have to come back. I was enraged." She was further enraged at my interpretation of her feeling again, with the coming interruption, that I was leaving her as her mother left her when she was so absorbed, e.g., with her brother; and that I was leaving as her father had left her when he was involved with her mother. She persisted that she couldn't enjoy any aspect of femininity because, "I couldn't do anything without my mother saying, 'I can do it better.' So every aspect of being a girl ended up with my feeling belittled, frustrated; and every aspect of my being a boy was satisfying; intellectualizing with my father was satisfying. I can't grow a penis and become a man. I want sexual satisfaction, and I want to work that out."

I told the patient she was depreciating and demeaning herself because she depreciated and demeaned her mother in the hausfrau role and eliminated her mother as a person who had a relationship with her father. Much to my surprise, this interpretation did not elicit the usual "No." Instead, she agreed vigorously and said she realized now she could not diminish her mother without diminishing herself; that is why she wants to find some way of getting along with her even if it's on a different level. She concluded, "What she represents I've totally diminished so that I can't function as a woman until I work that out. I am really angry at my mother for being the kind of person she is. I came and said I hate my mother, which I'd never been able to say. I didn't establish a feminine identity." Her voice became shrill, and she wailed, "She was so destructive. Why should a mother be so destructive to a child? I never realized how much I hated her. I know my brother has worse problems. It isn't fair."

The next hour she reported another dream in which she was overwhelmed by the most terrible rage she had ever felt. "I was shopping with my mother. She wanted me to try on some clothes. I didn't want to, but I did to please her. Just as I got them on she said, 'Oh! My parking meter is up. I have to put some money in the meter. I'll be back.' I started screaming at her at the top of my lungs." Then the patient turned and screamed at me. "I finally know what you're talking about! That's not my mother in the dream. It's you I'm so angry at!"

She angrily rejected further interpretations concerning the effects of the coming interruption — namely, that she had to wait and wait only to discover that the doctor was gone (in the earlier dream) or that the mother-analyst was casually announcing, "I'm leaving but I'll be back" (in the present dream). And she angrily rejected the attempts to reconstruct the childhood situations she was reliving. It was as though the "working alliance" had been engulfed by an all-encompassing regressive demand for direct healing. As we parted for the summer, the serious questions about the further course of the treatment that were raised in the Introduction demanded answers.

During the interruption I reviewed the patient's clinical course. Kohut's (1968) schematic description of narcissistic transferences had been published a short time before, and I had attended his seminar at the Chicago Institute for Psychoanalysis. His contributions led me to consider three possibilities: (1) That the patient's insistence on a direct cure was not a resistance to the re-exposure to her childhood rage toward the oedipal and preoedipal mother; (2) that she was reacting to my uncertainty about the nature of the original disorder and the transference as though I were the self-absorbed mother who spitefully refused to respond to her; and (3) that, in fact, the bombardment by the patient's narcissistic rage had evoked an emotional withdrawal on my part which further exacerbated her rage in a vicious cycle. A brief informal discussion with Kohut about the patient's disrupted state and the last dream confirmed my growing conviction that the return of childhood structural conflicts was not in the center of the disorder. Instead, it seemed likely that the patient's insistent demands that her display should be re-

sponded to with, "You're terrific, I like you as you," belonged to an intelligible mirror transference. I realized that I
had been experiencing, first hand, the narcissistic rage of her
childhood, and the greatly augmented rage evoked by
another chronic exposure to an apparently unavailable and
unwilling self-object.

*Reinstatement of the Mirror Transference and
Resumption of Working Through*

When treatment resumed, Mrs. Apple was bitter and reproachful, and she threatened to discontinue the analysis.
She said she had barely managed to go through the motions
with her children and husband. She was vehement. "You
should never have allowed this to happen to me; it's your
fault; I shouldn't have even come back; I'm here and
I'll finish, but I'll never expose myself to you emotionally
again."

My insights were tentative, and my interpretations and
reconstructions were incomplete in this first attempt to clini-
cally apply Kohut's ideas regarding the analysis of narcissistic
disorders. Perhaps their most significant effect was that it
made it possible to be more directly in touch with the patient's emotional state and, at the same time, to interpret this
state to her. In effect, I told her that I thought I now understood more about her feelings of desperation: that I had been
slow to sufficiently grasp what she had tried so hard to get
across, and that she had become more and more hopeless
and depressed as she felt that I, like her mother, was emotionally out of touch with her. Her protests that the vacation
per se did not bring about her sense of "The doctor is gone
and can't see you" were essentially correct. Instead, this past
dream expressed how she felt when she was not being heard
and responded to psychologically in spite of the fact that she

continued to try so hard. The last dream in which she became so enraged was also not a reaction to the interruption
per se. Although it pictured the interruption (mother leaving
to put money in the meter, saying that she would return) it
was a manifestation of her deeper feeling about the chronic
frustration she had experienced, first in the relationship to
her mother who could withdraw and leave her without what
she was yearning for, and now again with the analyst from
whom she *still* expected understanding. At this point she became more vigorous and forthright in renewed demands instead of sounding shrill and accusing. She asked me not to
shilly-shally and to tell her more about what my understanding was of what had happened.

I explained further, then, the "correctness" of her accusations against me. "You shouldn't have done this to me,
you shouldn't have let this happen" could now be understood
as a repetition with me of her cry, "How can a mother be so
destructive to a child?" During the analysis when she felt she
couldn't get through to me, as during her childhood, her
sense of well-being, her ability to enjoy herself, to value herself, to feel sufficiently firm about the validity of her own
ideas, was frequently and severely disrupted. She began to
cry tears of relief and asked me to go on. I continued: These
disruptions of her feeling about herself and her own attractiveness as a girl, and now as a woman, came about as she
continued to feel exposed to her mother's overemphasis on
herself—her tiny body, her huge beautiful baby boy, her
hair, her clothes, her furnishings and antiques. Mrs. Apple
added eagerly, "Now I understand my feelings about my
mother's diamond ring and why I don't want it. She's always
said she's never seen another one like it. When she says, 'I'll
leave it to you,' I've always felt the same way I did about
getting checks from her: 'I have a diamond ring, I don't need
hers, I don't want it.'" I agreed that the way her mother

spoke about the uniqueness of her ring made her hear her mother saying, "I'm unique, look at me and what I have; admire me." I also pointed out that she had reacted to the way her mother insisted her things were unique by trying to define her own tastes and values as "diabolically opposed" to her mother's, as she was wont to say. She laughed appreciatively.

With this preliminary reconstruction of the genesis of her negativism, oppositional tendencies, tension states, rage, and depression, and their repetition in the transference, the patient's mood and state underwent a dramatic alteration. Her original enthusiasm for herself and the analytic work returned, and she was once again lively, vigorous, and ready to persevere. The next step in the work of reconstruction followed: I told her that evidently she had heard many of my interpretations as though I were always emphasizing my own importance and what I thought, when she needed to feel since childhood that the accent was on her and what she thought. She nevertheless kept turning to me, as to her mother, in the hopes that she would ultimately elicit the response she considered her due. The last dream before the interruption dramatized the way she felt "set up" for a disappointment. She was trying on clothes to please her mother (analyst) and was expecting, still, to be admired, appreciated and enjoyed as the whole girl who was of value in and of herself, not in comparison to Jack or to her mother. Just as she turned to display herself "in all of her glory," she was met with a casually administered rebuff and withdrawal. It was precisely this situation of feeling "set up" and then dropped that led, first to her insistence that she was right and to her insistent demands, and then to the rage and hopelessness of her depression. Mrs. Apple wept again as she confirmed the interpretation by recalling the numerous experiences with her mother that made her feel so devastated and "fragmented."

Provided with the emotionally convincing reconstruction of the origins of her bossy insistence that she was right and of her coercive and domineering demands, Mrs. Apple herself took the next step in the analytic work. She recognized now that her insistence that she could not "identify as a woman" and that she wanted to be a boy fit into the context of the chronically frustrated longings for approval we were discussing. It was not that she was "totally disinterested in feminine activities" as she had always proclaimed. These activities were always "contaminated" by the feelings engendered in her as her mother "demonstrated" how she needlepointed, baked, cleaned, and decorated, without an emotional investment in her childhood needs.

The working through of the demands of the grandiose self want on as of their own accord: Mrs. Apple contemplated mistakes without reacting as though she were a "stupid idiot." She was less preoccupied with Shelly's family and less irate about their excluding her. While she made positive overtures to them, she began to think about spending holidays with close friends who shared her feelings. She felt apprehensive before a visit to the West Coast to see her mother. On arrival there, she was appalled to find that her mother's home was full of a lifetime accumulation of "things" from which her mother could not part. She thus discovered the origin of the "leftovers"—the old bedspreads, dishes, knickknacks—her mother brought to her and expected her to want. She had to throw these things away because her mother was incapable of doing so. She dreamed of a dangerous, explosive visit to the Israeli war zone (a representation of her fear of what would happen on the visit). She felt in the dream that it was a serious matter, but a very nice man recognized she was in danger, and then she did not feel apprehensive and scared. She associated the man with the analytic sessions. She dreamed she was in a hospital. Other people were moving to rooms in a new section. "I'm content to stay where I am. I'm getting the right care." She said, without her previous feelings of "fabricating a story" when she tried to explain her own dreams, "I interpret that to mean I'm here in the analysis. I don't have to be instantly moved anymore; I felt things are going right, and they went right on the visit to my mother. It's completely different from last summer." There were two other parts to the dream: "I'm climbing up a hill like one I played on when I was little, around ten. Everyone was having difficulty climbing up it. I thought, 'How are my legs so strong?' My interpretation is I'm doing the 'leg work' in the analysis. I'm able to get up there, to take the steps. In the last part of the dream, my father and I were having a serious discussion about two problems: One problem had to do with a girl who had an upset stomach and cramps associated with going to school. Everyone agreed it was a common problem which could be handled. The other problem was about a boy. It was much more serious. I don't know what it was. My father and I were discussing it." [It now seems clear that the patient's childhood relation with her father compensated for her disappointment in her mother. She was repeating these positive steps with the analyst-father who now had an understanding that enabled her to take steps in self-understanding.] She immediately associated to her own bowel problem, her brother's serious problems, and her "boy-girl" problem with herself. She dreamed she was progressing along on a trip. There were slow-ups that could take place, but she was not afraid—she had gone through it before. "I thought of traveling the road as a child. Now it's not so difficult. It's you who know the way to get through it. I'm starting again after there was a separation. Even though my mother did what she always does and Jack was picking me apart when I was home, I didn't feel so picked apart." She returned to the girl with the stomach problems: "I had stomach problems when I was two, but I looked chubby. I couldn't have been undernourished. My mother had to be overfeeding me! It was too much. What should have been pleasurable with my mother was painful!" I said that Jack had complied with the overfeeding and she had not. She then went on to the realization that later her mother wanted him to control his overeating, and then he could not control himself. She could not control her thumb-sucking and fiddling with a piece of her blouse—which mother could not stand. [The patient's compulsive "orality" can be understood as sexualization of the deficit in the self-object relationship. She turned to her own body as a substitute for the cohesion-promoting experiences her mother could not provide.]

   She went on to recognize that her compulsive cleaning and overdoing when she is preparing to entertain is a driven means of being perfect and clean as compared to Jack.

   Mrs. Apple became extremely overburdened again as she began to anticipate her departure by plane for another hiking trip in the mountains. "I feel so disrupted, I don't know what to do." I pointed out that once again she was feeling that there was "too much" to master on her own. She dreamed, "My lonely little car is at the bottom of a hill. It's creepy. My car is infested with creepy, tiny beetle-sized orange bugs. I can't convey the feeling. I have to go through these swarming bugs to get to my car. I grab a handful to throw them out, and as I open the door to throw them out, more come in! I can't even express the feeling!! As I woke up I was grabbing with my right hand. Isn't that interesting? I don't just use my left hand. I am ambidextrous." I explained the dream as a concrete representation of a tension state she could hardly express in words. The intensity of her feelings came swarming in on her like the insects in the dream when she was once again feeling alone and on her own. [It seems likely that the patient's phobic reaction to airplanes and mountain hiking was related to the childhood anxiety expressed in her dreams of falling. Her emotional reactions to feeling set up and then dropped, without having adequate control over what she was exposed to, found expression in the current phobias. Kohut (1971) discussed an early version of the same psychological situation when he described the relation between feeling unempathically held and tossed about and motion sickness. The patient recounted numerous telescoped memories that dealt with abrupt changes in equilibrium that were not under her control. For example, Jack frequently overwhelmed her by folding her up in a mattress or by unexpectedly picking her up and swinging her over his shoulders. Although she was not hurt physically, she felt enraged and humiliated because she was helpless to stop him. Her parents were either unaware of what he was doing to her, or they too stood by helplessly because they were unable to exert any control over him.] Although the explanation given to the patient was incomplete, she went on to examine the diverse manifest psychological disruptions that were associated with her disruptive tension states. "Friday night I mispronounced two words, one I made up out of my head, and once I said 'erotic,' instead of 'erratic.' I was upset—everyone laughed. I was bad at foreign languages. I'm afraid I'll speak incorrectly and be laughed at.[4] In high school, I laughed with my friends. But I didn't laugh Friday night—it's not funny to me anymore." I said that it had never been funny to her. She laughed with her friends to cover up her embarrassment when she was trying so hard and suddenly felt she did not have perfect control over herself and their reactions to her.

[4] "A Knack for Languages," a *New Yorker* short story (Tyler, 1975), presents an artistic rendition of a young girl's traumatic fixation on the grandiose self and the severe inhibitions in the use of language which is one of the consequences of the fixation.

Then she described another manifestation of the disruption of her feeling of firmness.

Once again she is unresponsive sexually, cannot stand to be touched, and is withdrawn from affectionate physical contact with her children. "I can see that I want affection and that I turn it off. I can see that the thing I can't deal with is wanting it." [Some of the subtleties of the patient's psychology were not clear at that time. I did not realize, for example, that the very thing for which she longed could be "too much." Furthermore, it seems that, when the patient was so overburdened, she needed first and foremost to calm down. Sexual stimulation at such times added to a generalized psychological overstimulation from which she withdrew. My interpretations did not address these issues explicitly, although they dealt with her need to re-establish an equilibrium.] I pointed out to her that she was very critical of her own useful protective mechanisms—i.e., she reacted as though she were imperfect because she needed to protect herself from the feeling of being attacked by a swarm of insects. She mentioned that she was sort of looking forward to the hiking trip. "Just remember that when I'm hysterical in two weeks," she said humorously.

As she had predicted, she was "hysterical" again when the basement of the new house flooded just before her departure. Tommy was also out of hand. I pointed out that she was again feeling flooded, and I gained further insight into Tommy's state, which I was able to explain to her; he experienced his tension states and times of falling apart as an "attack," hence, the paranoid thinking. Anything other than firm support made him feel attacked by her or by his father. (Tommy's integration steadily improved as her feelings of helplessness in understanding him were mitigated.) She dreamed of crossing suspension bridges. "I made it to the other side. I went around obstructions. I knew I had to go back, and I knew I'd make it." She added, "Yesterday I began having this anxiety again that I had to do everything for myself." I said that these were the times that she needed soothing, just as she had needed soothing when she was a child — e.g., being able to crawl onto her mother's lap. First she vehemently resisted the comment. "Now I have to do everything for myself." Then she added, "I've been transferring my anger to Shelly again, the way I did last summer when I said he never did what I wanted, the way I wanted it, when I wanted it." She laughed as she mimicked her former peremptory tone of voice. Then she sobered, "I do turn to him for comfort, and he's not attuned to doing that." She dreamed, "I bled all over the bed. I was going to say flooded, but it wasn't overwhelming. I woke up and felt as I did when water was coming into the boat. I thought, 'I'm overwhelmed, but I'm not drowning. It's a slow leak! It's like the obstructions on the bridge.'" I agreed that there was an inner change, and she continued, "What's happening is there's a revival of feeling abandoned — that's stimulated by *your* going on vacation. What gets me is it's so strong! I do need to crawl onto someone's lap!"

When we resumed in the fall, Mrs. Apple told me about a serious car accident on their summer trip. Shelly had to swerve to avoid a head-on collision. They went off an embankment and stopped an eyelash away from electrical wires. The car was badly damaged, but no one was injured. The accident reminded her of the guilt she always felt over an accident when mother was driving and mother kept saying, "If you hadn't left your purse and gone back for it we wouldn't have been there." "My colon began bothering me. I analyzed it. It was ridiculous for my mother to put the blame on me! I didn't say to Shelly, 'If you hadn't stopped for a hamburger we wouldn't have had the accident.' My mother couldn't take the blame herself! I've been unburdened of the guilt I've felt all these years. My colon stopped bothering me. I unwound. My mother is here now, incidentally. *She's* the same. She brought something in a box. I thought, 'Let's see; it's got to be an old thing of *hers.*' It's my grandmother's cake platter. We adored her, so we'll keep it. And I can't believe it! She brought poems I wrote in high school, to 'this wonderful mother.' [She read the poems to me.] I wanted to do the right thing, I wanted to be pleasing to her. To my dad I wrote light poems. I couldn't express what I felt toward *him.*" Then she laughed, "I invited my mother to come! She had no one to spend the holidays with. It's my luck she came! I don't really want it, but she needed it. She says, 'It's so nice to know I'm wanted.' Remember three years ago when I was hysterical about the holidays, when the Apples didn't want to get together? Now I know the only way the family gets together is if I have them. My mother comes and sits and watches me and copies my recipes and tells me that she double grinds the fish!" She laughed again. "She's learning the 'modern way' to knit. She's learning the way *I* knit! I think I said, 'You're a wonderful mother,' when I was in high school so that I could be the perfect daughter."

As the visit continued she described her mother's intrusiveness [cf. the opening phase where she tried to articulate the disrupting effects her mother had on her sense of intactness]. "She's always making suggestions of how *she'd* do it. It's never, 'It's fine the way it is.' She watched me fold laundry! Why would she want to watch me fold clothes? I know — she's longing for contact! Her values and what she talks about don't interest me — small noses, blonde hair, 'They don't look Jewish,' and on and on. She did this all the time when I was a little girl. And her obsession about clothes. Her closets full of clothes, her preoccupation with outer appearance." I said that she felt rage all over again as she was exposed to her mother's preoccupation with things instead of being able to respond to her. She continued, "She makes negative remarks about my friends. She's unconcerned about the children's feelings. It depresses and fatigues me. She bugs me to sadness she's so self-centered. That's why she's saving everything. But sadness is tolerable."

The next hour she said sadly, "Before I left for my hour my mother said [regarding the analysis], 'Maybe you would be better off if you just played bridge.' I said to her spontaneously, 'If someone had carcinoma, and cobalt treatment was recommended, would you recommend bridge?' That's a severe statement. Obviously I regard this as a matter of life and death! I'm still defensive with her. If I weren't I'd say, 'You don't understand.' How can you answer that? *Bridge! That's what's between my mother and me—a vast bridge that spans our personalities and provides no meeting.* But it's sad, it's disappointing." Shortly afterward she was in another tension state over her mother's criticisms. I said that she was feeling overwhelmed again by her mother's lack of response to her insect bites. She laughed. I wondered if her mother had ever been able to respond to her tension states. "My mother said I was totally independent—like a miniature adult!" Once again she returned to the theme of her father: his loss, her trying to give him up through mourning, her terrible fears of having no one to comfort her when she's angry at Shelly, her fears last year he would die and be lost to her. I now realized that, when it came to some of her psychological burdens, her father had not been up to helping her sufficiently—as he had been unable to see what was necessary for Jack. A marked shift occurred when I communicated this insight. She said that until now she had been adamant that she would control the colitis, she would make it go away. Now she sees she's going to have to control it with medical management. "I should take care of myself physically—I've never done that." The meaning of the colitis seemed clear: "The colon is a defect in me. It's the same thing as my inability to find pleasure and satisfaction in the things I'm doing." Shortly afterward she continued, "Something has changed — the colon is part of me; until now my attitude was I'm going to get rid of it; the parallel is my nose: you don't cut off your nose — you learn to live with it; *it's part of your whole self.*"

The process of learning to live with herself was still incomplete and she began to complain again. She isn't getting what she needs from her projects, her husband. . . . *She* spends time helping everyone. She listens to Shelly's ideas, but he is not interested in her projects at school. "In saying I want to go back to work I'm saying I want a response. I'm not God. I can't say like God, '. . . and it's good.' [She was studying Genesis.] I've spent my whole life like God, saying, 'It's good,' and then being very critical of myself. I need someone to support me. I said three years ago, 'I can't do it myself.' Do you remember? To be meaningful, I have to have someone share it with me." I told the patient that indeed I remembered and that she had always needed a response to herself as the whole girl who was "good" and who had done something "good." Because she experienced her accomplishments and achievements as being casually taken for granted and not eliciting the enthusiasm for her and pleasure in her she expected, she had turned to trying, like God, to look on herself and what she created and to say, "It's good." Unlike God, however, she was not sufficiently pleased, and she could not rest. She added, "It's obvious I didn't get the responses I wanted from my mother. To a great extent, now I do provide my own response." A dream followed: "A little girl about ten comes into my house. She's sick. I put her to bed in the attic because I don't want her giving what she has to the boys. It's a regular bedroom in the attic. I settle her into bed. I come back to see how she's doing. She's miserable. She wants me to stay and entertain her. You know how kids are? My response is, 'What an obnoxious little girl. I've given her all this care and she wants my undivided attention! She's obnoxious—she can't lie quietly in bed and entertain herself.' When I woke up I thought, 'She wants *me*.' The little girl is *me*. The mother is my mother. The 'obnoxious' is my feeling about myself for wanting more attention. Then I thought, 'That's ridiculous,' and then I thought, 'You thought it, Jeanie.' I think of myself as an obnoxious person. I didn't have a *bad* room, but I wasn't satisfied with what I had."

When her colon responded dramatically to belladonna, and colon X rays showed no evidence of structural changes in the bowel, the patient's internist concluded that she was not suffering from ulcerative colitis, but from mucous colitis. And as she continued to examine the significance to her of the "defective" bowel, she concluded that the bowel "symbolized" or "stood for" all of her feelings of defect and all of the negative aspects of her "self-image," over which she had had no feeling of control. The she dreamed, "Shelly and I are pushing a baby carriage through a bad neighborhood. There's a baby girl in the carriage. That's *me*! We are suddenly surrounded by two people who are going to delay us and do something bad. I am afraid." She associated to her mother's slum property, to which she has always objected vehemently, and to her mother's dislike and depreciation of Mexicans. "Then the carriage and child are gone. We're in the second story of a two-flat home. [She associated to her grandmother's two-flat building.] Shelly and I are trying to escape from the upstairs of the house. We are running down the street. We pass a big automobile junk pile which has whole windshields and other car parts. We pick up a windshield and zap it on our car. The car is stripped down, but it has what we need to drive." Mrs. Apple commented, "I no longer feel alone and abandoned. That's real progress! From the pile of junk, we select a whole, useful functioning piece. I am getting away from the pile of the fragmented pieces of myself. The windshield symbolized a whole part. The car isn't incomplete. I leave the fragmented pieces in the junk pile. I was escaping from being a fragmented pile of junk into being whole. The most interesting thing is that I'm having a hard time with Tommy, and I still can't always just say to Shelly, 'I need your help. Stop screaming at him and support him.' But I don't feel so fragmented." Once again I contrasted her self-experience of wholeness when she was taken into consideration with her feelings about being the fragmented pile of junk when she was not. "My mother was always demonstrating her skill. I knit for the boys, but I'm not tied up in the knitting. I'm sure my mother didn't think, 'What would Jeanie hate?' But she sent me to camp when I was seven with peculiar clothes—culotte dresses. So in addition to being traumatized by being at camp for a month when I was seven [cf. the dream of hurling rocks at mother at camp], I had to wear these peculiar clothes." I told her that her feeling about her mother's insensitivity to her tastes reminded me of the way her mother fed her. She responded, "If I'd been a child like Tommy, I would have battled. I didn't. I held the carrots in my stomach and then threw them up. She never knew about the clothes. I've altered to fit Tommy—e.g., his wanting to wear jeans. I consider myself strong-willed, but next to my mother I'm mashed potatoes! Her way is the right way, and if you want to get along with her you have to say she's right. My brother ate and ate and ate and *I* said, 'I can't eat anymore.' She left me home alone with Jack when I was nine—he did all kinds of horrendous things and said, 'I'll break your arm if you tell,' and he could! So in essence she left me alone." I commented on her inability to go to her parents for help. "They never listened.

My father's attitude about what I wore, how my room was decorated, was, 'Discuss it with your mother.' I was terribly inhibited, terribly unable to express how I felt, what I wanted. Johnny is too compliant and always wants to please, but he's acquiring the capacity to ask. I never did. They would have gone to Jack with an accusation if I'd told. They were always accusing him. My parents were helpless. They didn't know how to protect me or themselves from him. He was always sorry after his furies, and for breaking things, but there was no one to help him! Somehow I saw that and began taking his side. It occurs to me now that I wanted to be like him in a way. I wanted to be like my grandmother—she was an ideal for me. I wanted to be like a multiple number of people I knew—a little here, a little there."

Beginning of the Termination

The next hour she reported a dream, "I'm on a trip high up on a mountain peak—like in California where I'm always afraid everyone will fall off a cliff! I'm in a restroom and then I start down a very steep path. I'm afraid I'll fall. I try another—it's still too steep and difficult; I try a third path—it's still steep, but I can maneuver my way down and get to the bottom. I know I can get down, and I'm not frightened like with the other paths. Then I dreamed the same dream again." She associated, "Now I'm climbing down, from the cliffs. I'm not falling. I'm going to come down in a reasonable way that's not frightening. I dreamed it a third time. Up at the top there were a man and a woman waiting in line to get to the bathroom. The plumbing wasn't working properly. The man said, 'Why don't you go in with me?' The man and the woman were together, and I didn't want to participate in that with them. I wanted to wait till I could go alone, and then I went to the paths again. I understand my plumbing [intestines] now—the difficulty with my colon." The next hour she continued her associations, "The height I'm at now is a plateau, not a peak." I commented that she was feeling more secure about herself. "My feeling is it's the end of the ascent. There are still things to be resolved up there—the bowel, the man and the woman urinating together, but that's all that's left. There isn't a higher mountain to climb up, but it's not all serene and green yet. I have to talk about you and me. Up until now I've had moments when I thought I should stop treatment, that I've gone far enough, and I'd feel overwhelmed with the idea the end's not in sight. Now I feel the end *is* in sight and instead of feeling jubilant I'm apprehensive. Something is altered. I always thought I had to make major decisions for myself, rather than that I could get direction. What's altered is I don't have to do it all myself and I don't lose something! It is now apparent to me that my mother-in-law, my mother, the children, they need to be told, 'I like you.' *I* also need, as I needed when I was a child, for someone to say, 'I like you.' Getting back to my relationship with you: I wanted my mother to say, 'I like you.' I still want her to say that. She won't. The way I'm working it out is with you. Then I can get along with my mother. My relationship with you is peculiar. It happens only in an analytic relationship. I need to have you as a friend, like I've said I've needed my mother as a friend. In a realistic sense, I can't have you as a friend. What I need from you, not literally, is for you to say, 'I like you; I like what you like; I want to be your friend.' But you're the doctor. Now what do I do?" I pointed out that after she felt that I had been able to listen to her and to understand her more, that she had, in fact, developed just these feelings in the relationship with me and had gotten over the fear that she would not be responded to. Now she was feeling differently about herself, as she felt that she was responded to, in a way she had always hoped her mother would respond to her. "My mother still tells her mah jong ladies, 'Jeanie does this and this and this.' But she'll never say anything positive to me. I know my father liked me. I'm not like her, I don't like what she likes." I pointed out again that the old insistence on herself as separate from her mother came about as she felt herself drained away by her mother's emotional demands on her. Her mother demanded from her what she, as a child, needed from her mother. Her rage at her mother was so inexpressible because she had not been able to understand how her mother could continually say, "Look how I do it," when she felt, correctly, it was her right as a child to be told, "You are learning to do it too. I like the way you do it, and I like you."

The next hour she said she was trying to analyze a fight she had with Tommy because he refuses to wear clothes warm enough for subzero weather. "It's his body. I don't know whether to make a to-do about it or not." I commented that this issue with her children and their clothes involved her in feelings about who controlled her body when she was a child. "I remember being in layers of clothes. I couldn't move. I can still feel the weight on my shoulders! Tommy said he didn't want to wear the scarf I made because it was too warm. I wanted him to have the privilege of not wearing the scarf!" I commented that she did not feel she had that privilege. "I had to wear the red sweater. My mother insisted that I wasn't dressed warmly. There has never been a time when I could manipulate my children like a puppet." I said she had felt manipulated like a puppet because there had not been some essential emotional contact with her feelings. That is what she was trying to express when she described her mother's stories about the carrots, and when she recalled the weight on her shoulders of the heavy, ill-fitting winter coats. [In essence, the patient's mother dressed her unempathically, *not warmly*, as she had fed her unempathically.]

In a series of dreams over the next months she endlessly tried on clothes. Frequently she was with a childhood friend with whom she still maintained close ties, the one girl she had really confided in during her childhood. With the re-establishment of a growth-promoting twinship transference rather than the "destructive" version she was trying to separate herself from with her mother, Mrs. Apple dealt one by one with her feelings of bodily imperfections, and one by one she integrated the "fragmented parts" (first focused on by her mother and then by herself) into a whole self that was pleasing to her even though it was not perfect. Evidently, the close relationship with her childhood friend (and with current friends with whom she became much closer as the analysis progressed) protected her when she was also disappointed in her father. In connection with her revived adolescent preoccupation with the fact that her left breast was bigger than her right she remembered asking the family doctor, whom she loved, if she could make the right one grow. He genially said, "No, but you could try vanishing cream on the left one!" She laughed appreciatively at the humor she appreciated so much from a person who really liked her and whom she liked. With the hypercathexis of each imperfect body part and the decathexis of the archaic insistence on perfection, she dealt again with her mother's "death syndrome" and her mother's increased self-absorption, increased demands for praise and admiration (every March). "I got a letter from her with so many 'greats' it's *grating*! Now I'm a great daughter because I'm thinking about her more. She's so depressed, she's so alone. She can praise when I'm responding to her and then she feels 'great'!" Mrs. Apple expressed irritation at having to attend a University ball and insistently proclaimed she would not buy a gown for such an occasion. I commented that she was uncomfortable about getting dressed up for an occasion where comparisons were made because she felt re-exposed to the childhood situation of comparisons — between her and her brother, between her mother and her. "In any comparisons with Jack that my mother made I got the short end of the stick! You can take that symbolically if you like!" [We both laughed.]I pointed out that once again she felt, "You're not asked to come as you are, but to wear the dress mother would focus on." She assented vigorously and added, "I didn't want to have to display myself for my mother, I wanted her to love me as I was. If Jack and I were standing and urinating, mother would have picked him with the cute body. My mother had a constant fear of anyone showing their body. My body is my body. That's it! It contains me." In this connection she re-examined all her driven behavior, which she resented but had never been able to flexibly limit: her "perfect" housekeeping; her insistence on what the children look like, wear, behave like; her drivenness to go off and be able to read; her drivenness to have to work instead of taking time to find what her organizational and creative skills fit into which will be fun for her. And she re-examined the feeling that everything in her was a mess and chaotic, or that her house was a chaotic mess, in the light of Jack's uncontrolled behavior, which was not reacted to appropriately. "My father said, 'People come to me for counseling,' and he was consulted on legislation for children's welfare, but he couldn't go to anyone for help. My fantasies of being a doctor involved me in the same fantasy, 'I'll counsel and help others,' but I had all this weight on my shoulders and I couldn't like medicine when I started studying it." I said that we were still involved in discussing the psychological burdens for which *she* had needed help.

A series of dreams and associations led her to discover that her father was not "perfect" and that she had been angry that it had taken the analyst so long to understand her and help her clean her mental house — i.e., her father was not perfect nor was the analyst. She recalls that she did not want her mother's diamond ring "because my mother was always saying, 'Mine is better.'" She thinks now she can have it reset for herself, and she dealt with the significance of the "diamond," including the fact that father was also mother's — and his own mother's — "diamond," and she never acknowledged that her father could have had the kind of feelings for her mother that Shelly has for her. She confronted me with a question, "Do you believe what Freud said in "Totem and Taboo?" Am I discussing the taboo against sleeping with the father and killing the mother because I'm there or because Freud said it?"

I interpreted both the current transference and the genetic significance of her question: I told her I thought she was asking me, "Do you insist on seeing me in your image, as you feel your mother insisted, or can you see me and what I am?" Mrs. Apple felt that with this response, "the door was unlocked" to resolve her feelings about herself. "I guess I always felt short-changed by my mother. I found a unique relationship with my father which I concluded was better than hers, with him." I said, "Your diamond ring is better?" She laughed and said, "Even though it's smaller! Granted, mine is precious to me." I commented again, "*Yours* is better!" She said, "That was a form of survival for me with my mother — that made it more complex for me." I agreed. As a consequence of her need for the positive relationship with her father, she turned to him and depreciated her mother, including her role as father's wife. Then she felt she had the unique gem in the meeting of the minds between her and her father. "It was my father's death which really brought up the problem with my mother. I felt sorry for her. That's interesting because I never thought of her having a relationship with him as I have with Shelly. I thought of what it would be like if Shelly died. It's interesting that my perception of my mother changed before I knew why. I began feeling sorry for her being alone."

With this developing capacity to empathize with her

mother, a deepening working-through process dealt again with all of the themes of the analysis of the fixation on the perfect self as a consequence of the mother's traumatic failures in empathy, and the father's lesser but nonetheless serious failures to assist her by understanding what was wrong with the mother, himself, and their relationship with their two children. Accompanying this minute process of working through the narcissistic disorder and its oedipal overtones, the patient's periods of depression, anxiety, feeling overburdened and alone recurred in a modulated form. She said, "I said I'd never expose myself to this again, and I am; but it's not like last July." She dreamed that she was all alone and very high up in a building whose exterior was bombed out. The inner structure of the building was intact, including an enclosed interior room where she could go without anyone seeing her. Then, while still dreaming, she had the feeling that she awoke and was looking out over a view that looked like a painting of golden church tops. In the first part of the dream she worried about being so high up, and she thought, "What would I do if I had to go to the bathroom on the ground floor and couldn't wait till I get there?" She associated this thought to her childhood masturbation when she was alone in bed with her fears. She also associated the thought to her current anxiety when her bowel is irritated and she worries, "What will I do if I have to go to the bathroom and can't get there?" I mentioned that I was reminded of the fact that her greatest fear concerning intercourse had been, "What if I have to have an orgasm and can't get there?" She laughed in a relaxed way and said that her whole image of herself no longer depended on having an orgasm every time she had intercourse. Following this discussion she dreamed, "I was in a store looking at a boy's shrink (a sweater currently in fashion). I tried it on, but I didn't want it. I bought a girl's." She associated to the fact that she thinks she has resolved her "boy problem."

Mrs. Apple began to talk about the possibility of termi-

nating the analysis. She wondered about going back to work or
to school next fall, about how that would effect the analysis,
and whether she would continue. First, I told her that I
thought she was naturally thinking about termination as she
reviewed the different ways in which she felt she had resolved
some of her major problems. Then I added that linking the
idea of termination to going to work or school perhaps repeated a move she had made during childhood when she prematurely turned to herself for verification that she was a
"competent person." As a consequence of that solution, her
feelings of competence were always being invaded by the tension states and feelings of failure that reached their height and
flooded her after her father's death.

This interpretation implied the need for a period of consolidation and firming of the self-approving structure which
was being acquired in the analysis. Although a date for termination was not set at this time, it was explicitly understood
that the work of termination was underway. Given this understanding, Mrs. Apple began to analyze the difference between
her fantasy of always being perfect, nice, giving, and understanding, and what she now began to see in herself as a spontaneous capacity to give and to refuse, to get angry without
getting so enraged and "hysterical," and even to ask for what
she wanted. "My greatest disappointment when my father
died was he was the one who enjoyed my children. That was a
source of vicarious admiration for me!" She analyzed her
"craziness" about clothes. "You had to look right—the way
my mother thought was right—because you were an extension
of her. She did the same thing with my father. She told him he
didn't dress right—to change his tie. They argued, but my
father did it. He was insecure, and he looked to her in matters
of knowing how to dress, I told you last week that I wanted
him to stand up for me and he couldn't! His death was a tremendous let down for me, and then I couldn't cope with my

mother. I was furious at you at the beginning of treatment when you said you didn't believe I knew that my brother needed psychiatric help! One of my father's greatest contributions was in preventive work with children, and he was unable to see the problems with his own family!" (In effect, the patient was telling me again that, early in the analysis, it sounded to her as though I were depreciating her only method of solution: to precociously take over functions her parents should have been performing for her. The rage she experienced was part of the deep childhood rage at the father who had "forced" her into this position by virtue of his passivity vis-à-vis her mother.) She continued, "My disappointment in my father was unconscious! My rational mind didn't accept that I was disappointed in him. Remember after the interruption last summer when I thought I was cracking up and I said I'd never go through that again? I am going through it again, but I can cope with a disappointment differently. I fantasized that the relationship with my father was perfect — I eliminated my mother, and I wanted to do boys' things in order not to be anything like her." The next hour she talked about the alterations in Tommy now that she can support him: he came to her last week and said his problems had been going like this (arms stretched wide apart) and now they are like this (two fingers apart). "That's what support can do for a person! I feel like I can get along now. I needed emotional support. I think my mother was so insecure about herself she couldn't give support. This is a progress report: I can do it. The terrible anxiety I felt is going away. I've been sleeping better, I have more energy. I was really depressed!"

The progress reports continued: "My house doesn't seem to get as dirty. That means I don't see it the way I used to. I've accepted the fact that there's going to be dirt, that I have an irritated bowel. I've accepted cleaning the house without driving myself to craziness. That's what I do with the bowel

now. If it's irritated, I eat milder food instead of testing myself
with garlic! I have accepted a physical weakness of my colon
and that I don't have control over why it gets irritated, but I
do have control over its management! Instead of resenting and
fighting the diet I can use it. I am very relieved someone has
taken over and shared the burden of cleaning the house with
me. What a wonderful gift! I know what the relationship between you and me is. It's sharing the burden, assisting me the
way I wanted my mother to assist me, instead of feeling, 'Ye
gods! I have that whole house to clean!' All the pieces are put
together instead of my feeling panicked about my hair, my
clothes, etc. About my feelings about being a woman: my
mother bled all over the floor her menstrual periods were so
heavy. There was something gross about the female role. I resolved I wasn't going to serve the man the way I imagined my
mother did. It's difficult to say you enjoy sexual relations when
you don't have an orgasm. It's against my whole fantasy of
being perfect and being the wife I was going to be. In all ways
I had this fantasy of being perfect—Tommy has to have his
fantasy of being perfect altered little by little so he doesn't fall
apart when he doesn't win all the time."

Mrs. Apple's mother arrived for a visit. Mrs. Apple gave a
detailed description of her ability to observe with more
detachment and some humor her mother's bringing the "leftovers" again, as though they were of value because they were
hers. A brief trip with her husband also went smoothly, while
her mother remained with the boys.

She forgot an appointment. "I didn't realize I didn't show
up Tuesday till I turned the corner today." She dreamed she
was trying to escape from someone. I wondered if she was still
trying to escape from the latest "indigestible dose" she was exposed to—her mother continued to call attention to minute
faults in the house; and to ask every day as she got ready to
leave for her analytic hour, "Where are you going?"

I said that her mother's peculiar blankness toward her is what made her feel she was coming apart. She responded, "I look divine in green. I came down in a green outfit, and my mother turns to my cleaning woman and says, 'Look at that cute outfit.' I'm the third party! They are having a conversation about me." [Cf. Kohut's discussion of talking *about* the child instead of to the child.]

Mrs. Apple prepared to leave for a three-week trip to Europe. "I want to talk about my leaving. All my thoughts are emotionally packed. When I leave and you say, 'Goodby, have a wonderful trip, I'll see you when you come back,' I'll feel I'm leaving a friend behind. That's what I wanted from my mother. A relationship exists between you and me. There'll be a void in not coming here even though going to Europe will be more interesting! The longing I have is to feel that kind of *feeling* to my mother, to feel that emotional response to her that doesn't exist! My reaction to the things she brings symbolized neglect. She doesn't understand what I want from her. While driving here today, I thought, 'Saturday I'll be in Athens!' I won't believe it till I arrive. [Compare the working through of the relationship with her father, which follows, to Freud's (1936) analysis of his disturbance of memory on the Acropolis.] I'll get to Europe, and my father didn't! Tied in with my fantasy of going is my relationship with my father. He had his whole retirement planned. Europe, Israel—and he dropped dead. Shelly and I aren't going to wait. My mother travels. She's been in Athens, and she has no recollection of anything!" She returned full of enthusiasm for the trip and the enjoyment she felt traveling with her husband.

Feeling "clutched" about having to take a driver's test, she recalled, "I always went into exams with a memorized outline in my mind. Then, after the exam, I forgot it. Now I have a background in history which I've accumulated. What I accumulated on this trip will become part of my working knowledge. A year from now I won't remember what I learned from the driver's test. But if I go back to school now, knowledge will become part of myself. There's an alteration in my whole personality. The outlines I made in school were like the lists I made. I still make lists sometimes—but five years ago I would have been making lists and checking everything off! I'm not anymore. I've started reading novels again since reading nothing except about the trip. I'm not reading to escape and soothe myself anymore. It's my pleasure. I've gotten everything I want this year—it's easy to give when you get some of what you want." She continued, "Somehow the trip to Europe is like cutting the umbilical cord between me and my father. I am not my father either! I don't wait all my life to get there. Religious rituals are not a value for me. They were for him, and I always wanted to please him. It's not necessary for me to have his values. There are certain values within me. I'm an adult. Now I want to please you! My feeling is I'm ready to terminate and I'm looking for you to say, 'Yes, you're ready.' There are some things still to be worked out. I'm like this teenager, 'What am I going to do when I grow up?'" I said there were differences now. "Yes, it's not as the boy, not to prove something. I made an association between you and my mother! I hunted for something for you in Greece for your glass collection. I looked at 20 million throughout Europe! I came close to buying one. I didn't buy it because it was not authentic." I thanked her for thinking about me.

Termination Proper—
The Consolidation of a Separate, Cohesive Self

The next day she said, "The relationship between you and me, and me and my mother, is alike in this respect: I wished and hoped we could be friends. We can't be friends in the usual sense, but the difference with you is that I can work that out rationally!" She dreamed that she was graduating and moving out of the college dormitory, saying fond and sad goodbys to close friends. "I'm coming to the end, and all I have is the realization that I'm not going to be able to have the relationship I wanted with my mother and that the same things that disappointed me then I can tolerate now! It's sad. I even feel sorry for her. I'm looking at all the problems I started with and seeing where they're at four years later. What has altered is me; not like a light switch; it's an evolution. There is my mother still drawing the curtains, and I don't feel so angry about it." She examined her attempts at perfection again and concluded that her adolescent religious rituals came out of her need to control all the things over which she had no feeling of control. I always thought of Jack's yelling as a total loss of control. I yelled at Tommy today, and he pulled himself together. I didn't lose face with myself for yelling. I realize it's an emotional outlet, not total loss of control. That's a big step for me, and it helped Tommy because I wasn't out of control and neither was he! I began to feel all of my old things because Shelly is so busy—abandoned, alone, I didn't know what to do. I let it be, and it altered. I have to think about what I'm going to do in the fall. I had an idea for another interesting project at school."

In the context of assessing her gains, she said, "We've been saying goodby, but we haven't set a time." We agreed that six weeks hence would be a good time. I told her that I saw her progress reports as her feeling in touch with herself and her feelings, feeling firmer about herself—disappointments, pleasures, and all. The next hour she responded to actually setting a date to terminate, "I have mixed emotions. I'm sad and glad. There's a sadness about leaving—something else has to work itself out. I wonder where you're going on your vacation this year; not like when I used to ask and you'd tell me, but noncommittal, and I felt like when I asked my mother about babies and menstruation. First, I expected my mother to tell me without my asking; then when I got brave enough to ask, I felt rejected; it was traumatic. I value your opinions, but I've decided my opinions are OK too. I don't have to reject an idea because it comes from my sister-in-law or mother. Now I can take what's applicable to me. The neon sign that my mother is trespassing can come down. It's mine, so it doesn't matter if she closes the drapes. [Note the further working through of this issue from several weeks earlier.] I think I'm over the hump of rejecting her leftovers. The other thing that's good! I'm not *driven* to start something next year. If I don't decide now, it's all right. Every time before, I felt if one thing ends, the other starts. I won't stay home, but I don't feel compelled, that's what's different. There isn't a master plan I'm going to follow, but I'll work toward what's valuable. I'm dependent on Shelly, but not desperately, as I was. Our relationship survived that! I can't say I'd die if he died. I realize eventually something will happen to him, to me. The business about Shelly and doing everything right sexually: I said he had to do what I wanted, the way I wanted it, when I wanted it. [She laughed benignly as she imitated her previous manner.] Somehow I accept people without their doing every-thing just right, perfectly. Everything my mother did I took as a personal affront. With Shelly and Donna the relationship is confirmed on both sides. With my mother it's not con-firmed. The only way she can accept me is if I'm like her. I do realize my mother does accept me. Shelly wasn't able to do it my way! Donna wasn't able to do it my way! My mother isn't me anymore than I am her! My mother wanted me to be her and I wanted her to be me. It would be nice if there were mutual ground, for example, pleasure and admiration for the kids. That's what's disappointing to me that I can't have that. I realize that I can't convince her to be me anymore than she can convince me to be her! My father's death brought about my mother becoming such a beast to me! I'd never resolved feeling, 'She doesn't like it, I can't ask her opinion because she only wants to impose herself on me, she can't look and admire, she can't let me have it my way, I didn't get what I wanted.' I've said I wasn't Cinderella. There was some immaturity on my part. I never sat down and told you all I got. Refusing is not rejection. She didn't want me to have it because she has to be beautiful." The next hour she continued, "I am aware of getting involved in this relationship, and it's not so simple getting uninvolved. I can't make a list of what I've gotten out of this analysis. It's an inner alteration. I started with, 'Do you want to give yourself up to be accepted by your mother, or do you want to be your own person and be rejected?' Now I don't feel that. I've accepted that the analytic situation is unique. It will come and go. Is it really going to end? At least now there's the relationship with you with all its compromises and conditions. It's a matter of accepting that little by little the relationship will be gone even with all its conditions. I'm still hung up with the desire of what I came for. There's a fantasy that our relation will alter, that we'd become friends. I started talking about that last week when I said I was aware that wouldn't happen. It suddenly came to me that wasn't the deal. If someone said, what did you want? I would have said I want to be friends with you, and with my mother."

The next hour she reported a dream that she, Shelly, and two close friends were traveling together in Paris. "We were going to Sacre Coeur, but I called it Ste. Chapelle. Only when I was coming here I realized it wasn't Ste. Chapelle. I say in the dream, 'I've never been inside.' We did get into both when Shelly and I were there. The interior in the dream is not like either though. There were lots of colors — yellows, blues, reds. Like the sun coming in through colored tubes. I comment in the dream, 'How lovely! I'm so glad I get inside.' Sacre Coeur is way up high — we were very disappointed in it. Ste. Chapelle was beautiful. In the dream it's way up on a hill, and it's very beautiful. It's not like the dreams of being way up and falling or coming down some scary way. Looking back now, it was my father's face in the dream. He didn't get to go to Europe, that's the difference between the two of us. I'm glad I went inside this church. It was very beautiful, worthwhile. I'm glad I took this trip into analysis. It was like I'd been there before but I hadn't gone inside. I'm glad I'd taken the time to go back and see the inside, not just the exterior. That has a parallel. I had tried to do the analysis myself. Realistically I wouldn't say the analytic situation was all beautiful! That's another difference between my father and me. He wasn't able to accept the psychological way. He did think he had shortcomings, but he was very unpsychological." I said, "You feel your interior is changed: you've talked about the analytic work, the differentiation of yourself from your mother, your father, and from me. It's now your interior." She answered, "I really enjoyed the analysis. I always found it intriguing—the ideas, dream interpretation, free association. There were trying times! The beautiful interior. There's a change in my image. I am walking into an inner being which is lovely." I said that since we would not be working together much longer it was worthwhile to put as much of this as we could into words, as she was trying to do: I reviewed her disappointments in the analysis, the trying times, and their leading ultimately to her feeling that her interior got better. "There are reds in the church in the dream. You know I didn't like red. The analysis wasn't perfect, you aren't perfect, and I'm not." She continued her review, "It's nice to be your own self. I don't want everyone to have the same tastes as I have. I've had to learn that I can't convert my mother. She will go on knowing she's right. It's ironic. Mothers and daughters are supposed to be so close. I feel I should be summing up, working out the relationship between you and me." I said I thought she was doing just that.

Mrs. Apple became very busy setting up a science exhibit at school. She thought again about the changes in Tommy. He can say to her now, "Maybe I didn't understand you," instead of always feeling accused and attacking. "It seems to me I had an unconscious fantasy of perfection. There's hope in our family, there really is!" With one week of the analysis left, she said, "I'm thinking about disappointments too, but I'm no longer driven. I'll probably go back to school."

I mentioned that I had attended a conference at her children's school and had seen the science exhibit there. She was enthusiastic. "You didn't notice that the boxes I had the exhibit on needed painting?" I said, "No, I didn't notice the cracks in the ceiling." We both laughed. "It's nice to feel that this unconscious resentment isn't going on anymore. I'm planning the science project for next year. I have it all in my mind; every day a new idea occurs to me. I've written my mother about a birthday present for Johnny which I'll buy here for her. It's the end of my 'Why can't you go out and pick something for him?' If I don't, the child won't get what he wants. I'm disappointed that my mother isn't a different person. She's not like me, I'm not like her. I don't want her to change me, and I don't have the right to try to change her. I guess the thing I wanted most was for her to accept me. There's this leftover fantasy, 'Wouldn't it be nice if we were close?' I struggled with it for so long because it meant my yielding to her way. I think I'm coming to the resolution for the right reason."

Mrs. Apple arrived fifteen minutes late for the final hour, explaining the "comedy of errors" that delayed her. "I don't know how I feel. I don't feel like it's really the last session. It's not traumatic like when you went away on vacation last year. How *do* I feel? As if I have a lot of freedom, it's strange, fun. I'm not getting married, having children, going to college—so that's new! I was always happy to go on to the next thing. I said

to you I only felt sad when I was leaving high school." I said I
thought she was feeling sad and glad at the same time. "I'll
miss the sessions. It's fun to discover; things got put together
here. There'll never be that designated hour. I sort of have
a feeling of accomplishment, like passing through something.
Terminating is the culmination of saying I can do it by myself.
I understand it won't be all a bed of roses. Roses have thorny
stems!" I told her I thought the change she was talking about
was represented in one of the many dreams in which she tried
on clothes. She was always struggling to get a dress to fit perfectly and then finally decided that wasn't possible. Now she
can say goodby with the idea that the dress doesn't fit perfectly
and there are still alterations to be made. She rejoined,
"There were other Julys when I felt I didn't have to come back,
and you said we should go on. There are still things to be
worked out. My self image is much more complete. I am able
to take the ups and downs more. It was crucial when I realized
I couldn't let my mother be her. I had always complained she
wouldn't let me be me. Accepting that I have to let her be her
released me! It was really that I was trying to make her be like
me. Since I don't have control over her I have control over myself! Once it dawned on me, everything fit into place! I
struggled to control her for 35 years! I have to control my own
responses. The struggle was I couldn't be me because I had to
be her. If I let her be herself I can be myself. My father said
bluntly, 'You can't be like me, go have babies.' What I wanted
from her was approval of mine. I don't have the resentment
now. Now I feel I can say, 'No, I can't do that,' if she makes an
unrealistic demand, without feeling guilty and all torn apart."
At this point she turned to me and said with a smile,
"I think you should have the last word!" We both laughed at
this final summing up of her acknowledgment of my role in
her genuine sense of accomplishment—the consolidation of
herself.

Several years after termination, Mrs. Apple called for an appointment to discuss the best means of helping her sons to reconcile themselves to the fact that they were going to move to another country. Her husband and she had agreed that an appointment to a foreign university provided him with unusual opportunities for his research and should be accepted. She looked exceptionally well and spoke with animation of the gratifications associated with her ongoing development and that of her sons and her husband. Her conclusion that the boys' anger about the move was understandable and could be tempered by adequate support proved correct. Follow-up holiday greetings from abroad continued to indicate that she and her family were thriving.

5

ANALYSIS OF A
MIRROR TRANSFERENCE
IN A CASE OF
ARRESTED DEVELOPMENT

This is a case of a young man in his twenties who was in psychotherapy for six months and then completed a five-year analysis. He originally came for help because of difficulties in finishing work assignments as well as persistent unhappiness in his marriage. It became apparent that the disorder that seemed to underlie the immediate complaints was a pervasive feeling of boredom. A striking symptom of lifelong voyeurism was revealed as well, once the patient changed from therapy to psychoanalysis.

The case is presented in an effort to demonstrate the emerging of the narcissistic pathology in tandem with the unfolding of the transference. As a self-object transference relationship was formed, it was noted that the patient needed to test the reliability of this newly discovered temporary structure repeatedly. His need for empathic understanding was paramount, and many of the analyst's remarks were directed to interpreting that very need. During the working through of the transference the patient was able to recall previously repressed memories, which led to genetic reconstructions. In a sense, the "meaning" of the voyeuristic behavior was explained.

Rather than go further with my deliberations at this point, I shall report the case, interspersing comments where I think they will be helpful, and concluding with a retrospective view of the treatment process and its implications for theory and technique.

Case Presentation

Mr. E. was referred to me because of general and vague marital problems. Upon first seeing him, I was immediately struck by his manner of dress. It wasn't so much the casualness of the attire — checked, colored, open shirt, striped pants, gym shoes — for that wasn't necessarily unexpected in a university graduate student, but the fact that nothing matched anything else. This pattern of dress, I later learned, had put off many people, but his warm, friendly, generally engaging manner quickly overshadowed this, and I shortly found myself positively inclined toward him.

Mr. E.'s initial complaint was that he was very unhappy in his marriage. About a year before coming to see me he had married a very outgoing, vivacious woman of about his own age. He had been misled, he said, by her liveliness, which he felt was a response to him. After they were married, he found that the wellspring of her extroverted demeanor was an emotional volatility bordering on the hysterical and, as we both later learned, probably had a depressive core. He said that she seemed to have a need to assume a position contrary to his no matter how trivial the matter might be; recently, they literally could not discuss the weather without having an argument. He felt that he had made a mistake in marrying her. She had been the first girl with whom he had been emotionally and physically intimate, and perhaps the intoxication of his first love had blinded him to the true state of affairs, probably causing him to overlook signs that should have warned him that his future wife was not capable of bringing to the union the sort of understanding he required. Rather ruefully, he elaborated that he was the last person who could tolerate the kind of self-centered, opinionated stance that his wife took, for he was extremely sensitive to even trivial slights, real or imaginary. For example, a friend once had to cancel a dinner date with him because his father fell seriously ill and had to be taken to the hospital. Mr. E. found himself humiliated and infuriated by this, and, even though he understood the situation perfectly well intellectually, emotionally he was so enraged by this "insult" that he was unable to talk to his friend for a week.

When, during the course of the first interview, I asked him to tell me something of his family background, he delivered a lengthy and rather dreary recitation about his mother to the almost complete exclusion of other aspects of his history. She had been ill with a progressive illness from "shortly after the time I was born" and always seemed to him to be distant, preoccupied with her illness, exhausted, and depressed. He felt that this depression pervaded the entire environment. She died when he was fifteen, and though he said he remembers clearly having had a strong reaction to her death, he could not recall what it was and therefore, of course, could not describe it to me. He had been told he was a premature baby, raised apart from his mother in an incubator for several months. When he was brought home he was seldom touched, picked up, or fondled because of a fear that he was still fragile and prone to contracting infections through contact. He described his father only as a businessman who was always going to make a million in a new business, but was literally bankrupt more times than not. He also mentioned, in passing, that he had a brother two years younger and a brother four years younger.

Although I liked Mr. E. and was aware of a wish to do what I could for him, it was not immediately clear to me how I could best be of help to him. I suggested that we meet again to explore his situation, to which he readily agreed.

During our second meeting he spoke very little about his marriage, but began to emphasize what he had only mentioned in passing in the first interview: his serious problems at work. Though he had been successful as an undergraduate and had been chosen to do advanced work in his field, he was now in difficulties. He was unable to finish assignments, papers which, had he written them, would have opened the door to professional advancement. He, correctly as it turned out, felt that his advisor, who thought highly of him and gave him every opportunity to use his potential, was becoming increasingly disappointed with his "procrastination."

In the second interview, when he again had occasion to mention his mother, he said simply that she had died when he was fifteen of a serious, chronic illness; he said this almost as if he had not told it to me before and as if the previous depression-laden detailed description had never taken place, suggesting to me that there was something unreal to him about his relation to her and that his attempts to mourn for her had been unsuccessful.

Mr. E. was at first reluctant to see me more often than once a week, and we continued on that basis for six months.

The ostensible problem which first brought him to me was the first to be "resolved." Although he never talked much about it, a few weeks after beginning therapy he told me that he had made up his mind to get a divorce. Actually he had already decided to do that before he came to me. His wife agreed, and the couple separated with no particular overt significant emotional reaction other than relief. Both seemed to feel that their situation was impossible and that their needs for one another had dissipated in the incessant quarrels that seemed to be the only activity they now shared.

Most of his sessions were spent in recounting his difficulties with his work. While he was with me, he felt that he wanted to do well and could do so now that he was in treatment. But his thoughts were not translated into action. He was to report repeatedly that though he always left me with the best of intentions and highest hopes, his actual performance was little better than before; his papers were not written and his research not advanced.

During those first six months of treatment while he was still in psychotherapy, though he continued to complain about his work inhibition, a significant underlying difficulty emerged. He described himself as devoid of any sustained interest, fated to be depressed, condemned to ennui. He often said how bored he was with life, and sometimes felt that if he were only stimulated he could become productive. He could not elaborate specifically what he meant by this.

Clearly, I was not dealing with an acute situational maladjustment; Mr. E. was suffering from a character problem, and the sartorial disarray I had noticed at his first interview probably reflected an inner disorganization. Equally clear was the fact that psychotherapy on a once or even twice weekly basis was not optimal to promote the necessary insight and working through. It would be necessary to explore this pathology in depth and have the opportunity to work through its origins in a transference situation. I therefore suggested analysis to him, explaining my reasoning. At first he was not sure that he wanted to commit himself to the "lengthy and time-consuming procedure," but a few days later he called me on the phone and said rather breezily, "OK, let's shoot the works." At our next meeting we agreed to proceed with analy-

sis and arranged for four sessions a week. It was then a few
weeks before Christmas.

Upon entering my office for his first analytic hour, Mr. E.
removed his glasses and placed them on an end table near my
chair, in spite of the availability of both a table and desk closer
to the couch. I took this as a sign that he was favorably dis-
posed to the decision to proceed with analysis.

He said he will probably be neglected by the chairman of
his department now that he is not producing work. This reminded him of the feeling that his father preferred a younger
brother, whose interests seemed to be closer to father's. Everybody else had somebody in his family, but he had no one to
pay attention to him. He reported a dream from the previous
night: "My brother, father, A. [his former wife], and I bought
a restaurant. This would give A. a chance to be the hostess,
my father would have a business, my brother would be the
manager, and I had nothing to do." He complained of
wanting to escape to a place where he would feel less pressured
by the contingencies of his life. He spoke of a party he had attended several nights ago and how he felt "out of it." He
doubted whether his professional interests were genuine,
maybe they were only an attempt to attain credentials? He
then announced that he was exhausted from this introspection.
In the next hour he discussed his fear of going to a masked
ball because "I have a special difficulty seeing what's behind
the mask, and where others may be amused or even excited by
this, I feel a sense of uneasiness." He stated without much
affect, "Maybe I'm a homosexual underneath it all" and wondered how he had gone from a masked ball to homosexuality.
He reported that on one occasion as a teenager he had some
mutual masturbation with a cousin.

At his next session Mr. E. handed me a Christmas card
and I thanked him. Shortly after getting on the couch he said,
"I am glad you didn't immediately try to interpret the

meaning of the card, thereby reducing the genuineness of my behavior." He said that, because of the fear that "it would just be interpreted," he had had some mixed feelings about giving it to me, but "decided to take a chance." In the next hour he confided to me for the first time: "For over fifteen years I have been spending a lot of time in public bathrooms to peep at men's penises." He added that he was doing this a great deal at the time that he first began treatment with me and had continued to do so through the months of our therapeutic work together.

One might consider whether Mr. E.'s "holding back" this significant information from the analyst might indicate an excessive lack of trust and therefore constitute a poor prognostic sign for the analysis. It was more my impression at the time, and the analysis bears this out, that, knowing himself to be extremely vulnerable to my responses, he contained himself and gradually opened up to me as he became confident that this would not bring on the dread of being misunderstood. He could not really let himself go until the treatment had progressed to the point symbolized by the interchange around the greeting card, i.e., I was able to accept the fact that he genuinely wished me well and was glad he was working with me, rather than distancing myself from his need for closeness by insisting, for example, that we find and interpret the underlying genetic significance of his act. This is not to deny that there were additional important meanings involved in his behavior. Attempts at transference interpretation here, however, would have been premature and would have increased the patient's resistance. I listened quietly and made no comment other than "M-hm," to let him know I was listening and had heard him.

After a long weekend because of the Christmas holiday he complained of being "out of it" and reported a dream: "It was in this room, except the couch was in the center of the room and I was elevated on the couch. On the way here today I thought, 'What is the meaning of my coming here and opening myself up to your reaction?' This thought must have been related to my thought of wanting to call you yesterday to see if we could set up an extra appointment. I felt quite down." He believed his need had been precipitated because an inebriated stranger had insulted and humiliated him. Shortly after that incident he had a series of voyeuristic fantasies which lasted most of the weekend, reinforcing his feeling of being "completely alone." This led to his thought of wanting to call me. As he left, he said, "Boy, it's good to be here."

That week he noted that the depression was going away and attributed it to some favorable remarks made to him by his supervisor. He noted that there is a sense of embarrassment when he gets up from the couch and expects that I might look at him directly as he leaves. (We were to reconstruct later that, on one level, the shame he felt when I looked at him related to his exhibitionistic wishes and also to his fear of disappointment that I might not notice or admire him.) In addition he wished to look at me and possess me through his eyes. His lack of physical contact with a sick, depleted mother who could not play actively with him led him to try to engage her through eye contact. He had become guilty and afraid that his demanding gaze was somehow destructive, and that he overburdened the fragile mother with his wish for visual incorporation. When he wanted desperately to look at me, he was unconsciously fearful that he would destroy and lose me as he had lost his mother. In regard to the role of vision in his development generally, throughout the analysis he was to recall a host of memories around staring and/or being looked at — for example, when in grade school students were gathered around the teacher, he shifted continuously so as to arrange to be in the direct focus of the teacher's vision. He recalled a "fragment of a dream." He was in a building at a long table with people standing at or near the table. Someone called him over and asked if he knew the name of a lyricist for some musical. He did not recognize the person who had called him over, but he seemed to be a nice person. He associated to a composer and lyricist who made a good team. His analytic hours ran from Monday through Thursday, and he reported that on Fridays and Saturdays he felt depressed and depleted, feelings that would gradually begin to lift on Sundays. He was not aware of the transference implications of this cycle, and I did not at first bring it up.

One Monday Mr. E. told me that he had spent a considerable portion of Friday and Saturday frequenting men's rooms. He reported a sense of feeling bizarre. In a desolate voice, he reported having spent the times he was not in men's rooms painting empty chairs in his apartment. Suddenly he shouted, "I demand to know what you are thinking. You think I'm a psychotic, don't you?" I replied, "I think you must have been very lonely." There was a pause, and then he burst out crying. When he was able to speak again, he said in a choked voice, "That was the first time anyone ever realized that." He paused again and added, "And I think that includes me." This brought home to me the dreadful anxiety with which this man had lived since childhood. Just as a little boy would be terrified to find himself suddenly abandoned in a strange city, so Mr. E. felt abandoned on the unfamiliar streets of his affective reactions. His loneliness, as he later emphasized for me, was not necessarily a need for companionship at object-libidinal levels, but a need to be echoed empathically. Only in being responded to by being understood could he believe himself to be acceptable, valid in his person, and not beyond the pale of humanity. He couldn't tell me about his perversion at first because it meant to him that he was crazy, beyond redemption, until I gave evidence that he could believe that I saw him as a human being and not a curious specimen whose "material of each hour" should be studied.

One weekend toward the end of the first year in analysis he contained his anxiety by painting a picture of me. But where my eyes, nose, and mouth should have been, he painted miniatures of himself. He associated to a picture of his mother and then to imaginary conversations he would hold with me when he felt anxious and in danger of acting out. About this time he himself became somewhat more conscious of his need for me, the longing for me that he felt on days he did not see me, and, although he associated indirectly to how his voyeuristic activity had served to soothe him at these times by uniting him with the "power" of men stronger than himself, he was not yet consciously really aware of any connection.

Contemplating an upcoming weekend, he commented, "I feel a sense of deadness just thinking of it." He said that the days on which he had analytic hours flew by. And then the weekends with their "dread." He reported a series of disappointing events in his life. When he stated with a sense of shame that "I might even be disappointed to have to go three days without coming here," I pointed out the relationship between his feeling closer to me and his fear of disappointment. The following Monday he reported that the weekend had gone somewhat better than expected. He spoke of some of the events of the weekend and then said he had felt very cold when he came to the analytic hour today, but now was feeling much better. He said he was more able to see the helpfulness of analysis. After his hour I happened to meet him on the street. During our brief conversation, he told me a joke. Suffice it to say the punch line dealt essentially with a miracle of a man suspending the forces of gravity and thus being able to fly. We both laughed together. The next day he got on the couch and began to speak in a quite furious manner. Just prior to his hour he realized that I was "trying to destroy him." He removed a small object from his pocket and said he was going to throw it right through the window pane. He accused me of being vicious, a brain experimenter, and said I was trying to hypnotize him. He demanded that I admit that I had recorded every phone conversation we had ever had. As abruptly as he had started, he stopped and asked, "Why am I acting crazy?" I interpreted to him that he recently had a strong yearning to be close to me (to be appreciated and admired), that yesterday when we had laughed together, though he got what he wanted, he also became overstimulated and saw me, the occasion of his danger, as a malevolent force. There was a pause, and then he reported a sense of relief. He said, although it seemed as if he was trying to scare me, in fact, it was he who was afraid, but couldn't even admit it to himself at the time. He also felt that the fact that I not only did not "get scared," but was able to show him the sense of his behavior and do it without humiliating him, was of tremendous help. The next day he reported that he had been feeling better and that he could now see what happens both here and in his life generally: a conflict between a need for closeness and a kind of vague explosion, sometimes because the need is not met, but also sometimes when it is. He said, "In analysis the experience is the treatment."

It was in the very next hour that Mr. E. volunteered the details of the onset of his peeping. At age eleven, he and his mother were at a county fair. He ate his lunch and dinner meal almost immediately "because there was nothing to do." The day was dragging by, and he wanted his mother to come with him and watch him on the high swings. She, by then very ill and too depleted to be interested, told him to go by himself. He, "as if driven," went instead to the men's room and stared at the men's penises.

One Monday, he stated in a haughty fashion, "As a kid I sometimes had fantasies of being Superman." After a pause, he added, " and possibly on occasion I sometimes still do." Indeed, he had done so recently. He mentioned that yesterday was his birthday. Then, in a cold, haughty tone he asked if it was my technique or my personal feelings that precluded my talking to a patient when I saw him in public. A request for further elaboration revealed that he had erroneously thought he had seen me and a woman, "I guess your wife," at a football game and that I had looked right at him but had given no sign of recognition. As he talked to me about it, he was less sure that I was the one he had seen. I told him that I thought he had wanted to share his birthday with me and that this had led to fantasies of seeing me. Then came the ever-present fear that he was not recognized, i.e., that I would not be responsive to his need. This then led to Superman fantasies.

On another Monday he reported that he had gone to a party over the weekend mainly because he didn't have anything else to do. At first the hostess paid attention to him, but later she became occupied with her other guests. He felt extremely bored, left the party, and went to a men's room. However, for the first time he left almost immediately. He recalled how as a child, the time of the day he hated most was between when school let out and dinner time. "Nothing to do." He associated to several events where he apparently lacked stimulation. A further elaboration of this led to his recognizing that when there is not enough stimulation he is tempted to turn to peeping. Then he began to perk up a bit, as he often did as we resumed our work after a weekend, and mentioned that he guessed not everything was as dark as he thought it was, that just prior to his analytic hour he had shown some of his paintings to a friend who was a professional artist and who had seemed genuinely impressed with his talent. He was glad to get this recognition and pleased that his friend was apparently quite sincere and not just flattering him.

One day he told me that a girl he dated was first being friendly with him, then dropping him, then getting friendly again; he felt frustrated by her inconsistency. He talked about a waitress who was rude to him after serving him a poor meal. After a pause, he said he was embarrassed to tell me two homosexual dreams. In one he was on a couch and his leg was pushing against mine. In the other he was in the underground garage with his father and they went into a men's room to urinate; a man bent down and tried to wipe his (patient's) penis. He was not sure if he wanted him to do so, and then suddenly decided he wanted the man to suck him. He tried to get the man to put his legs around him so that he could penetrate the man anally. Then he recalled another part of the first dream — I was caressing his chin. He spoke of his mother's illness. He now felt that she had loved him before her illness became so serious. He went into some details of her poor health, her symptoms, and the slow, but inexorable, deterioration of her functioning. He recalled sitting on the front porch with his mother; she had fallen asleep "in that tired exhausted way of hers." He, the little boy, was terribly bored, and he could clearly recall his wish, while waiting for what seemed an interminable time, that his father would come home.

He returned to his dream, saying, once again embarrassed, that the most humuliating part of it was the physical contact with me. I drew a parallel between his disappointment with his girl friend and the rude waitress and then turning to me in a dream, and his looking to the father for what his mother could no longer give him. I implied thereby that his "homosexual preoccupations" had understandable roots in the vicissitudes of his childhood development. [This exchange demonstrates that the genetic aspect of interpretation was not by any means neglected. It was now possible to link the past with the present without fending off the patient's wishes toward me (and thereby the development of transference). It should be noted that unlike the interpretation in cases where an oedipal conflict is predominant, the interpretations here deal with gaps in the development of psychic structure rather than with the origin of intrapsychic conflict in an otherwise cohesive self.]

The next day Mr. E. reported a dream that his chairman looked at several reports he had done and said, "I'll take it down to the bindery." He felt good that his chairman thought they were worth making into a book. He associated to psycho-analysis and how it had helped him — that he now understood the "authority" of his experiences. He was not sure what he meant by that, but thought of a leader holding the diverse elements of a country together. "Here [referring to the analysis] both fact and fantasy are treated with respect. That is a comfort to me — you accept what I said about my sexual behavior." He felt that this had made him less of a stranger to himself and that he felt less lonely as he saw that "there is understanding to be had. You are helpful because you are not threatened by my needs."

Mr. E. had been talking about the satisfaction he got from painting, and it was becoming increasingly apparent to both of us that he was truly talented in this area. He found himself investing more time in this work. He described his social life as going well. He mused that it was July already and associated to the upcoming summer vacation, the first long interruption of the analysis. This led to thoughts of dry bones. He reported feeling decrepit, complained he was lacking compared to others. He thought of lizards, rats, and a guillotine. He could actually see heads rolling and hear the squish of dead bugs on the pavement. I pointed out the shift that followed his thought about the summer vacation. He was embarrassed to admit how much he wished that I were not going on vacation. "But I do admit it." He said he was dis-covering that it is better to deal with these feelings than to hide them.

A couple of days prior to the vacation, he asked if I had

been in the office at noon that day because he had such good news that he almost called me: he had landed an important job as an illustrator. "It's a funny thing. In the waiting room I couldn't remember if you wore glasses or not." He associated to his mother wearing glasses. Then, "I wonder what I look like in your eyes. It's a great truth that when I lack a certain type of stimulation I get terrified." Ever since he could remember he had been preoccupied with a terror of what he would do when his mother died. He tried to push it out of his mind. He said that even though she had been dead more than fourteen years, "I think it's still on my mind." The hour before the vacation, he reflected on the details of his mother's funeral. Toward the end of the hour, he said that all his life he felt something was missing. He realized now, for the first time, that it was his mother. He thanked me for not interfering with his contemplations about his mother and in general, throughout the analysis, for not buttering him up, or expressing phony sympathies, and for helping him in the understanding of certain things in a way that was genuine and not deceitful and which thus allowed him to feel more genuine and less deceitful about himself.

When I saw Mr. E. for the first hour after the vacation I could see immediately that all had not gone well. While his manner of dress had become more organized over the months of treatment, now he appeared shabbily dressed and unkempt. He immediately launched into a sort of philosophical dissertation. He wondered whether there was any way of devising a formula that would establish where the center of infinity could be found. He spoke of dead, macerated animals and disconnected human limbs. I recognized the underlying theme of all this as a feeling that he had lost connection.

My essential stance here was to try to get across to him that I understood the difficulty he was having in getting started again after the interruption. In the third hour after vacation he reported that he could sometimes relieve his depression during the vacation either by peeping or by imagining conversations with me.

During the next session he became increasingly integrated. His sense of depression seemed to lift somewhat as he told me with some sense of "pride" that in actuality he had only peeped a few times during the vacation, and compared this to the beginning of the analysis when he did it "several times just over a three-day break." The next day he was dressed in a suit and tie. He said it was hard for him to say how much he had missed me over the vacation and that he was not even sure that he had realized it at the time. He soon associated to childhood when he had some foreign stamps and took great pride in them. One day his mother threw them out, not realizing "I was the only kid in the neighborhood who had stamps like that and all the other kids always wanted to come over and see them." Once, he had a part in a school play and asked his father to come to see it, but his father, giving a "flimsy excuse," did not come. He said, "So what, who cares if they understood me or not." He said he felt like an insect and then immediately, "I guess that's so what." It was clear to both of us that he was increasingly understanding the relation between absence of understanding and how he felt about himself. Mr. E. talked about how he aspired to be like me, that this very thought strengthened him. Sometime later, he expressed tender feelings toward me directly and reported a fantasy of wanting to carry my picture in his pocket, especially on the weekends, in order to retain some continuity.

Once, when he associated to surgical procedures and to being separated from parts of one's body, I interpreted that he experienced the oncoming weekend as an intrusion—as if a part of his self was being taken away. He responded by telling of his mother being rushed to the hospital, and of how afraid he was, partly from overhearing some fragmentary conversation by his aunt, that she would die. He was the only one left in the house. He dressed up in his mother's clothing and make-up. He supposed that made him sound like a transvestite and a clown. His father, upon returning home and seeing how he was dressed, "beat me up, and maybe he was right to do so." Pause. I suggested that he was trying to avoid panic by reuniting with his mother through putting on her clothes, keeping her and himself alive, so to speak, by becoming her. It was his attempt at reintegration as he felt his life crumbling under the impact of the terror that he might lose her.

During that weekend, Mr. E. told me the next Monday, he had an urge to go to a hotel washroom well known as a homosexual hangout. However, he noticed he was not as driven as he usually was when the urge to peep was upon him, and because of this he was able to delay. He began thinking and reviewing conversations he had had with me about his voyeurism and its meaning. By the time he got downtown he felt even less need to go to the men's room and was able to avoid doing so. The remainder of the weekend went well, and he got a lot of work done. He had been thinking, he said, that some of the incidents he had felt to be depreciating at times in his life were not truly intended rejections, adding: "Rejectors also have their needs."

The next day he reported a fantasy that I would be running for president. My campaign poster shows me holding a mirror in which the observer would be reflected; this was meant to inspire people in some way. He recalled a picture of his mother that stood on their piano. Then he remembered how he used to play for her and how she enjoyed listening to him. But one day she had to leave him in the middle of his performance in order to attend his younger brother who had hurt himself. When she returned, he asked to continue to play for her, but she said, "Don't bother me now." Mr. E.: "Out of sight, out of mind." He reported a fantasy of wanting to call me over the weekend. He had the feeling that when I disappear, he disappears.

[It is worth noting that only after considerable resistance to the deepening of the transference, manifested by a seeming indifference to me, had been worked through by calling his attention to the circumstances under which it occurred, and only after I had repeatedly seen how some minor change in my demeanor, voice, or schedule caused him to retreat into a cold, bitter and fatalistic attitude, and had interpreted his disappointment at my not understanding and/or not meeting his needs as he wanted them met at that moment, did the true nature of his relationship to his mother begin to emerge. Premature genetic interpretation would have probably closed off important memories. I mention this in order to clarify that my analytic activity should not be confused with promoting a so-called corrective emotional experience in its narrow and pejorative sense. The analytic stance necessary to permit a narcissistically vulnerable patient to uncover unconscious content and risk the attendant anxiety should not be confused with role-playing. At no time did I attempt to be a substitute parent to him. I retained an essential analytic stance so that bit by bit, and time and time again, he could look at his transference longings. The therapeutic value lay, not in becoming his mother, but in understanding his wish and not moralistically rejecting the immature and often socially unacceptable forms through which it was expressed.]

Mr. E. began to recall in more detail that when his mother was well, the family functioned as a family. He remembered how he tried to keep those times alive. Often, he used to fall asleep and fantasize how things had been when the mother was healthy, and contrast that with how they were going now that she was sick and dying, particularly his own sense of deterioration. He complained about the upcoming weekend. He was scared that he might slip again and revert to peeping—the weekend could be so long. I pointed out that when he was with me he felt a continuity about himself as he did with the helpful mother, but on a weekend it was like being with the sick or absent mother, and that in order to feel whole and to avoid the feeling of deadness he so dreaded he would revert to peeping. He replied that at times he sees the unity of his behavior—that even "the crazy behavior can be helpful" if it gives him a certain sense of unity. That it is better to be something, even a peeper, a sufferer, a person who is crazy, as long as he avoids being nothing.

On another occasion he mentioned that, for a period of time as a child, "We had a European housekeeper, she was one of the most giving women I knew. She liked me a lot, and I sensed it." He noted that some of the things he had thought about in his lifetime "were a little Messianic." He had been thinking recently about my style of interpretation. He felt I was warm and empathic. It reminded him of the European housekeeper "in the finest sense." He stated that his ambitions in life were potentially OK, but "I used to go at them like a combination Julius Caesar, Jesus Christ, and Superman." He implied that he was now getting some distance from this. I pointed out that it was interesting that, on the day he recalls a warm, empathic woman and associates to me, he also feels able to get some distance from his Julius Caesar, Jesus Christ, Superman fantasy. This suggested that these fantasies emerged when the warmth and empathy he wanted from other persons was not available. I then went on to reconstruct for him that his mother's unavailability made him cling to these ideas in their primitive state so they did not get a chance to be integrated with the rest of his personality and retained a life of their own.

In another hour he was philosophizing about the center of infinity. He stopped himself suddenly, saying, "What kind of crap is this?" He noted that yesterday he had felt closer to me than he had ever felt to anyone in his adult life. He felt that it was an important step that he could be so aware of this, adding "Then, today, I am a philosopher." I pointed out that perhaps when he felt he made an important step and also felt closest to me was the time that he also felt most vulnerable.

Once, at the end of the last analytic hour of the week, he was discussing something that was proving especially resistant to analysis. His sense of frustration was obviously mounting, and I suggested that we could continue on Monday where we had to leave off now. This was one of the rare times that I was directly attempting to provide a bridge for him (or me?) over a weekend by means other than interpretation. I was particularly aware that my "scientific" tone was a departure from my usual style. On the following Monday he reported a dream: He had been waiting for me to be finished with another patient; it seemed like an endless amount of time. Then he turned and shot more times than he needed to at someone who was behind him. He meant, he said, that the person was already dead, and yet he continued to shoot him. He complained of the lonely weekend, but felt he was essentially able to handle it. He associated to wishing that his mother would die just before she did, in fact, die. He thought of my involvement with other people and referred back to the dream where he seemed to be waiting and waiting and waiting. Perhaps the shot might also have something to do with the fact that his mother took shots in the last days "in order to keep going?" I recalled the Thursday hour for him. I stated that, when I mentioned to him that we could continue on Monday, my tone may well have conveyed to him that I didn't realize how long the weekend was for him and what it meant to him to be separated from me. Therefore, as with mother, he felt the tension of having me alive to arouse his longing to be understood, while simultaneously frustrating that need. In the dream, he wished me dead to put an end to that unrequited longing, to get the issue settled once and for all. Better to have me dead than to fear being repeatedly disappointed by my inappropriate response.

At another time he spoke of the beautiful face of an actress. He remembered that, as a child, he always studied his mother's face. He could not tolerate its inscrutability. Her face was like a mask. No matter what her underlying mood, she showed one face. "As I think of it now, it gives me the creeps." At another time, after a long holiday weekend, he mentioned hearing me swallow. He recalled studying mother's swallowing and respiratory rate in order to gauge the degree of her health or deterioration. He recalled rubbing his lips on pieces of rock. He felt he was just going through the motions, today, trying to recover from the holiday weekend. He was aware of listening more to the sound of my swallowing and breathing. So many times he had wanted to reassure himself that his mother was still alive. He referred back to the incident at the carnival where he was extremely bored and his mother could not participate with him, leading him to his first voyeuristic experience. He said he recognized something we had touched on before, but now seems "to know it better." He had previously thought that he was seeking to see me as mother, that is, a particular person like his mother, but what he is really seeking is someone who will give him the primary tenderness and concern of a mother. (He was making some distinction in his own mind between the mother as a person and the mothering functions.) "What I needed was a mother's interest, which is different from mother as a specific person."

On his way to his hour he recalled as a child having given his mother some pottery he had made. She said she liked it very much, but then gave it away. He then recalled his father testing him on his spelling assignments. He had difficulties in spelling, and his father used to tease him about it. Mr. E. felt that his father teased him because he actually didn't have patience with him. He associated going to a gymnasium where he used to jump on the trampoline and play Tarzan and Superman. He would get so carried away that the gym teacher often had to come and insist that he stop. He remembered that on at least one occasion the gym teacher said to someone, "That kid is out of it." I pointed out to him the sequence of associations from feeling rebuked by his mother to turning to his father for relief and, when this failed, involving himself in Superman and Tarzan fantasies to the point where the gym teacher thought he was "out of it." He agreed, but without much enthusiasm. I mentioned this to him, and he said that in a sense he had already felt rejected by me before coming today, "Although it has noting to do with anything you did or didn't do." He had felt especially close to me during the analytic hour yesterday and, after the hour, went into a store nearby, hoping to meet me there. He thought that if he began to think of it real hard, I might come in. "Mind power—a way to make up for a painful disappointment; however, relying on it often leads to more disappointment."

He had felt good recently when his father was enthusiastic about something Mr. E. told him and then later felt de-molished when a friend of his was not attentive. He recovered from this sense of annihilation by thinking about me. After he felt better, he recognized that he seemed to want people to an-ticipate his needs before he made them known. He had some feeling that perhaps his mother could do this to a significant degree before she got so sick. Later in the hour he said he had been thinking about the concept of betrayal. He felt he was coming to see the difference between a person's actually in-tending to betray him and only being capable of producing up to a particular point.

At the first analytic hour following the third summer vacation he was dressed nicely in a suit, top coat, and dress hat. He was very glad to see me. He shook hands and said,

"What do you say," in a very affectionate tone. He told about a camping trip he had taken during the summer. While boating, an oar broke, and it took quite a while for him to get back to shore, "But I did,"—slight pause—"obviously," he added, laughing, with a newly found sense of humor. He had been thinking about his mother. "Not extended or complete thoughts, but fragments of thoughts. My closeness with my mother was so deep that it was both gratifying and terrifying." He used to get totally humiliated and demeaned so easily. Now it's much better, but "I still need some work on this." "As a child I needed constant reassurance. My mother would get puzzled by how frequently I would ask her if she loved me." He burst out crying. When he stopped, he said, "I know it's close to the end of the hour, but I have to tell you how you being back gives me a feeling that things are going to be OK."

In the fourth year of analysis he began dating a woman, B. He noted that she was not depressed, "which is novel for me because I always seem to select depressed girlfriends." He felt the analysis had helped him to have more freedom in his choice of women. He felt that he would not be destroyed if he failed and would not be Superman if he succeeded with any particular woman. He felt active in this new relationship, "not the usual passive bystander." "Usually I have no awareness of a woman's needs, I just use them to mirror my own gratifications. I am not even always sure that we're two separate people. This experience with B. is quite different." Later in the hour he expressed compassion for his father—how difficult it must have been to have a wife who was depressed and/or ill most of the time. He showed optimism about the future. He anticipated a "good year." "The length, persistence, and continuity of the analysis are important to me and helpful to me in seeing that something is a continuous whole." He said that maybe a break in our meeting, for instance, a vacation, might not need to destroy the sense of continuity.

He was increasingly earning his living as an illustrator. He began to date B. on a regular basis and, because of "my lessened readiness to be humiliated, and her understanding of me," they got along well. "Maybe there was nothing seriously wrong with my first wife either, but I was impossible to live with, always alert to make sure no situation or attitude on her part would cause me to disintegrate. Not realizing at the time that often I was too sensitive, I always rationalized that all misunderstandings were her fault."

Mr. E. gained further insight into his voyeuristic behavior. He had taken for granted that the anxiety he experienced when he peered at men's genitals was the fear of getting caught, humiliated, or punished. He became aware that in fact the most serious fear, the feeling of dread, as he called it, preceded and precipitated his voyeuristic activities. He was able to accept and confirm my interpretation that his voyeurism was generated by a fear of dissolution, experienced as an awful feeling of meaninglessness that had to be reversed at any cost (actually an anticipation of fragmentation of the self). He was now able to get additional insight into his wish to merge with the powerful "father substitute" whenever he felt misunderstood, i.e., inadequately mirrored. At this time, during the third year of his analysis, he no longer engaged in perverse behavior, though he was sometimes aware of the urge to do so. He described the difference: "Now, when I think of peeping, I am able to delay action long enough to allow myself to try to figure out what's going on and to calm myself instead of being immediately overrun and finding myself in men's rooms."

During one hour he described with great intensity, fear, and conviction an experience he had reported on a previous occasion as having occurred outside the analytic hour, namely, that his face was his mother's face. (Any interpretation at this point was treated by him as an intrusion and, if anything, tended to reinforce the conviction of his fusion fantasies.) Slowly and with my attentive listening, he calmed down, recognized that it was a fantasy, and said that what he experienced was somehow connected to his exhausted mother's inability to respond to him. He elaborated that for long periods of time his mother was not completely withdrawn and tried to meet his needs and participate in activities with him, but she reacted in keeping with her own exhausted state and limited energies and not in accordance with the timetable he needed. He suggested that this was one of the origins of why he was sometimes impulsive and unable to soothe himself. In the next several days he began to contemplate the fantasy of his face being his mother's face without being terrified by it. He expressed his gratitude to me for helping him, and he was gratified that he himself was able to overcome a frightening symptom by self-analysis "in your presence." "I guess when I'm able to work this way or at least approach it outside your presence we can talk about finishing the analysis."

At another time Mr. E. remembered that he often carried a picture of his mother in his wallet, although he never looked at it. He began to consider what his mother looked like prior to her "exhausted mask face." He realized that he had rarely looked people directly in the face until he began painting portraits.

He became increasingly happy and secure that he could now provide for himself through analytic and self-analytic work functions he recognized he had not previosuly developed because "My mother was not available to help me in the right way." He appreciated that he had learned to do self-analysis from me and said, "I'm taking on some of your functions without fusing with you," and he laughed as if in relief.

The next several months were characterized by an essential additional working through of the themes mentioned above. He married B. From his reports, she was generally quite willing to try to understand him, which, of course, was helpful to him. He did suffer from partial impotence for a brief period after the marriage and at one time had an isolated thought of peeping, but it no longer "had any steam behind it." As best we could determine, this short period of relative impotence was related to fears of orgasm, loss of control, and merger. During this period he gained the insight that a compulsive masturbatory habit during part of his adolescence was "to keep me from dissolving into the world." His potency returned, and he never reported any further problems in this area. The over-all relationship with B. seemed to be good. He and his wife seemed able to communicate their feelings to each other in helpful ways and apparently without overburdening one another.

Mr. E. was disappointed in himself because a lecture he gave and felt well prepared for had fallen flat, and he described how he began to lose heart as he saw his audience's interest slipping away and how he had to struggle to force himself to work up some enthusiasm for completing the talk in an appropriate fashion. His associations led to instances of turning from his depleted mother to his father, who, however, was only inconsistently available. He recalled a dreadful day when he was home all day alone with his mother "watching her energies failing hour by hour." He traced some magazine pictures, which he anticipated sharing with his father later, "to bring myself to life." These were mainly of automobiles, "but one might have been of a man stripped to the waist." He recalled his excitement upon hearing the father approaching the house. He ran to show his father the tracings. The father's only comment was that he was old enough to draw free hand. He was devastated.

At another time he recalled that while he was at home with his mother and an aunt, they learned that the mother would need surgery, which was especially dangerous in her condition. He, frightened by the possibility of his mother's death, again eagerly waited for father "to make things better." Instead, father, upon hearing the news, was overcome and spent the night at the home of a relative. The patient spent that evening "studying pictures of naked men." He now wondered if this "studying pictures of naked men" was his attempt to draw strength from anonymous powerful males when father proved unable to help him cope with his fears of losing his mother.

As the vacation in the fifth year of analysis approached, he was walking down the street, apparently preoccupied. An acquaintance greeted him, and he, startled, realized that he had been holding an imaginary conversation with his mother in which he had been telling her the day's events. He likened it to the analysis, and felt that with the impending separation there probably was an intensified yearning for an earlier relationship with his mother. For the remainder of the week he alternated between memories of disappointments at the hands of his parents and an increasing number of positive memories. He now recalled how his parents taught him various things; for example, he recalled with pride how his mother taught him to ice skate, his father how to drive a car.

He apparently had a productive summer, but vaguely felt something was missing. A few days into the analysis after this interruption he reported falling asleep thinking of a Christmas carol. Then he reminisced that as a child one Christmas he had a part in a school play and his mother made a special costume for him. He recalled with great enjoyment his happiness and pride in performing before the audience in this beautiful costume. He came to feel that my return served a function similar to that of wearing the special costume that mother made for him.

Succeeding months were characterized by increasing self-analytic work interspersed with increasing tender yearnings in relation to each of his parents and to the family as a whole.

This period began at a time when Mr. E. was especially aware of missing me over an interruption of several days in the analysis. He gave an extremely detailed, but at first somewhat intellectualized and unemotional, description of the few days between his mother's death and her burial. Gradually the affect increased, and he seemed to be working through a traumatic state of mourning, culminating in the recollection of tender moments between himself and his mother. Later on, he thanked me for "not interfering" during this period.

Shortly thereafter he was especially happy to recall an incident when he felt particularly well understood by his mother. Another day he spoke of the warmth and understanding of the maid who was working in the house at a time when he was terrified that his mother was dying, contrasting this with his aunt's abrupt dismissal of him when he pleaded, after his mother died, to choose the dress in which she would be buried. At one time he wondered if his interest in studying a particular European language had anything to do with the fact that it was this maid's native tongue. As he recalled it, the maid had worked for the family for several years; however, when he discussed this with his father, his father said that she had only worked for them for several months.

He was becoming more reconciled with his father, although he wasn't "completely ready to forgive him" for disappointing him so many times. "I recognize that he had to be both mother and father, and who knows what I would do if I were called upon to do the same thing. The damn trouble was that he always was preoccupied with miracle schemes for making a fortune." He then laughed and said, "I guess of all people I should know something about the fact that megalomanic ideas are not always easily given up." In a "friendly conversation" with his father, which was a relatively new and surprising experience for him, he learned that his mother, before her illness, had considerable musical talent and that her brother had been an artist of considerable local reputation. It also turned out that, according to the father, Mr. E. had shown significant artistic skills as an adolescent.

He was enjoying his capacity for self-observation with insight and felt good "doing this in your presence but without your interference; most likely some day I'll be able to do it on my own."

In reporting a dream in which he and an older teacher were carrying a large container, he associated to the trips the family made to his grandparents' farm, fondly recalling his grandfather's teaching him to ride a horse. He fantasied what might have been if his mother had stayed well, and began quietly to cry.

One day he referred to the dreaded and boring feeling of being stranded with his mother, who could no longer meaningfully interact with him, leaving him "with nothing to do." "It was like always just waiting for her to die." He repeated an earlier reported memory of her telling him to go out and play with some toys in the driveway; he described the extreme loneliness of playing with these toys from morning to dark — every minute seeming forever. "I thought I'd go to pieces. Just thinking of it again makes my skin tingle and my spirit go blah." Sometimes when he felt that way, he'd rub his face on the pavement until it was quite sore. He thought of his bicycle and then in mid-speech was silent and seemed to wince. He recalled something he had not thought about in his adult life. "As a child I would ride my bicycle and contemplate redoing the entire architecture of the city." He was temporarily stunned by "the taste of the depth of my loneliness, and the megalomanic thoughts I would entertain to keep from going to pieces. A person can think crazy things and even do crazy things to avoid going crazy." These remarks were meant to soothe himself and also to engage me. I responded by verifying the accuracy of his insight. (Actually the fantasy of redoing the entire architecture of the city related to Mr. E.'s projected attempts to redo the structure of his mind.)

The next day he was cautiously happy. He was still "slightly frightened over the depth of my feeling and memories yesterday," but was more calm, as if feeling some sense of mastery. He felt that, "In a sense my deep craziness is out on the table, and it turns out I'm not crazy!" He laughed, not in mirth, but from a sense of relief. He understood the fantasy as a way to modify "literally unbearable tensions." Now that it made some sense to him, it didn't seem "so crazy."

The analysis continued with Mr. E.'s integrating and working through his various insights. His marriage and career were going well; there were increasing references to future plans, made with confidence and with enjoyment of his achievements. An appealing artistic opportunity was offered to him in another city, one that would provide new challenges, enhance his reputation, open new doors, and allow for a substantial increase in income. He was wanted in about 30 days on a series of assignments that would take him away "for up to a year." Feeling he could not conclude his analysis within 30 days and ruling out an interruption of this length, he refused, saying he was not available at this time. He felt he could reasonably conclude his analysis in about six months and set that as a tentative date for termination. He was happy feeling that he had arrived at a good solution to a complex problem instead of "freezing and getting preoccupied with devious malevolent forces."

In the next few months he alternated between feeling confident about the future and feeling a sense of relative depletion ("relative to the last two years but nothing like five years ago"). One week when termination issues were very much in focus, he had a temporary thought of peeping, but had no desire to act on it. He doubted whether he would ever need to peep again, but was startled to have even had the thought. I pointed out that the functions developed during analysis which reduced the need to peep were now under stress because of the termination (our actual separation from each other), and, understandably, old patterns of coping with stress would come to mind. He felt relieved, and soon his associations were to the future and with a sense of confidence.

One day he opened with a fantasy of stopping the analysis that day. He was surprised, since "I rather like it [the analysis]." Later he associated it to the times when he wished his mother would die. Feeling a tremendous mental strain in the presence of his emotionally unavailable dying mother, he had sometimes wished her "gone already to get it over with." As he recognized the relation of the opening fantasy and me during the termination, he stated, "One can never do too much work on integrating both past and current realities, or at least I can't."

In the last week of the analysis he reported that, while falling asleep, he had the image of the two of us walking with my arm around his shoulders. He spoke of his future plans. He felt that I helped him greatly. He said he would think of me and no doubt miss me. He had a feeling that I genuinely liked him. I confirmed this. I told him I would think of him in the future and that working with him had been gratifying. At the end of the last hour, he gave me a firm handshake, looked me in the eyes, paused for a second or two, and said, "You're a good person." I was visibly moved, thanked him for his sentiments, and wished him the best.

Conclusion

Mr. E.'s perversion was an attempt to reintegrate a crumbling sense of self. The genetic reconstruction indicated that when he was overwhelmingly disappointed in his mother's unavailability he turned to father, hoping to compensate his potentially fragmenting self by still relatively sublimated participation with the powerful father. When this was not available, the behavior became increasingly instinctualized as the wish for union was, for example, enacted in the area of studying pictures of naked men and, ultimately, in voyeuristic behavior in men's rooms.

One must speculate about why voyeurism rather than some other symptom expressed this need, for the analysis did not specifically answer the question of "symptom choice." Perhaps it was the fact that the patient had inherited a far greater than average endowment of the visual modality, a faculty that was in any case apparently hypercathected when he was not given body contact during infancy, and began to increasingly participate with his environment through visual modes. Certainly, there were many significant and often moving associations during the analysis around the lifelong burdened and "overburdening" use of vision. These cannot all be detailed here, but include the following kinds of examples: at the start of analysis, he was self-conscious mainly around looking at me or my looking at him at the end of any hour; following his mother's funeral he was eating a meal of fish and felt the fish's head was staring at him; as a child, before his overt voyeurism, when goldfish died from the heat of a nearby radiator, he at first felt his "persistent gaze had destroyed them"; as a grade school student he felt "good" when he could make "direct eye contact with my teacher" and always tried to do so, "in retrospect, like an addiction."

This presentation is not intended as a model of treatment for voyeurism or other perversion. No analytic treatment can be based on the presenting symptomatology, and there is no guarantee that voyeurism is in every instance an attempt to compensate for the kinds of deficits experienced by my patient, indeed, it need not necessarily originate primarily from pathology of the self. This having been said, I do think the case illustrates a technical aproach to patients who have in the past sometimes been considered unanalyzable or in whom attempts at analysis have failed. Most important, of course, in this case was the patient's transference around the need to be mirrored, his devastating disappointment when he felt not understood in this need, and the very clear way in which one could see psychic structure being built as the mirror transference was worked through. The need to be mirrored is part and parcel of development and will appear in one form or another in every analysis of narcissistic personality disorder, perhaps in every analysis.

The patient's feeling that "in analysis the experience is the treatment" merits further elaboration. Although some would suggest that this is a general principle of any analysis, while others might be inclined to subsume it under the heading of a "corrective emotional experience," the specific point of this analysis is that in this instance the proper working through of the analytic transference allowed him to realize the authenticity of his experiences (his self), a factor which developmentally was sorely missing.

The analysis also provides an additional example of a child's attempts toward restoration of the self following threat to its integrity in relation to the mother. Mr. E. turned, often in desperation, to the father to supply frustrated mirroring and/or idealizing needs, which, if available, might provide the necessary stability to his fragile and highly vulnerable self. At best, the father was only inconsistently available to the son's needs. This because of the father's apparent reduced capacity for the useful empathic response to him and, at times, also because the child, frustrated in relation to the mother and therefore in the context of a deteriorating self, turned to the father with greatly intensified and regressed drive forms which proved to be even more of a burden to this father. As a result, the potential for restoration of the self through mirroring and/or idealizing vis-à-vis the father also failed, and the potential for developing internalized stable structures gave way to a reinforcement of the emergency needs to sexualization.

Perhaps the most important criterion for analyzability was not known until the analysis was very far along. The patient eventually recaptured significant positive memories of the initially depreciated mother. This suggests that she had been able to foster the development of some sense of cohesive self in her baby. In other words, we were dealing here with an increasingly exhausted, terribly ill mother, not with one who was essentially overwhelmed by motherhood and thereby undermined the development of the sense of self right from the start. This explains, at least in part, why Mr. E. was able to respond to the analyst's empathy and to accept interpretations when these were reasonably correct, unlike other, nonanalyzable, patients in whom the matrix for a cohesive self development is missing and for whom a symbolically meaningful relationship with another human being is too threatening.

6

COMMENTARY
ON THE ANALYSIS OF A
HYSTERICAL PERSONALITY

The presentation of this case has a twofold purpose: to demonstrate how a patient with a manifestly hysterical personality disorder can be understood and analyzed using the organizational framework of the psychology of the self, and to show how a change in an organizing theoretical position necessitates an alteration of clinical technique.

Though entitled the analysis of a hysterical personality, the designation is meant here to be only descriptive of a broad spectrum of disturbances. At one end these are organized along classical structural lines, and at the other along the lines of self-object pathology, or as a combination of both (see Kohut, 1972, 1977). The case presented here would perhaps be more accurately designated a hysterical-like personality, the suffix "like" denoting a special organizational variant of the usual, manifest, transference neurotic hysteria. It was my impression from the evolving transference that in this case the patient's central disturbance was essentially that of a narcissistic personality disorder, and the transference was thus understood and, for the most part, so analyzed.

Treatment of this patient was begun shortly after Kohut's work on narcissistic personality disorders and the organization of the self was published. The case was one of the first in my practice to which the insights of the psychology of the self seemed applicable and were systematically employed. The difficulty of feeling at home with the technical departures implicitly required by an alteration of theoretical guidelines will become apparent in this report.

I have not presented this case in process form. I have focused, instead, on several significant problem areas I consider crucial to and most illustrative of the patient's pathology. I have indicated how I dealt with these problems during the analysis and have at times digressed from the case itself to discuss some clinical theoretical issues raised by the material. And, finally, I have also indicated how, with increased knowledge and greater empathy for narcissistic disturbances, and with the wisdom of hindsight, such problems might have been better responded to.

Background

Mrs. R., 33 years old, was married to a moderately successful businessman one year her junior. She had previously been in analysis for about a year, but the analysis was interrupted when her husband was unexpectedly transferred to another city. She had been led to understand that the move was only temporary, so she suspended treatment for several years, planning to resume her analysis when her husband was transferred back to his home office. He was not. Mrs. R. was deeply disappointed to find herself in still a third city, but decided to begin analysis again and at that time was referred to me.

At the time she came to me the patient's difficulties were the same as those for which she had initially sought analysis: a chronic depressive mood, a profound and pervasive sense of dissatisfaction with herself both physically—"I hate how I look"—and intellectually—"I can never think clearly or say what I'd like to say"—and a mild agoraphobia. She felt inadequate as a mother to her six-year-old daughter, inferior to most other women, and helplessly timid. When alone at home or when shopping in the central business section of the city, she was anxious or uncomfortably tense. Usually she felt too inhibited to enjoy sexual relations as fully as she would have liked to, and that added to her sense of inadequacy. As I later came to understand, she lacked a firm sense of a reliably cohesive self or of reliable inner firmness despite a superficially nonpathological, and even quite appealing, social façade.

Mrs. R. was a gently pretty, shy-mannered woman who appeared younger than her actual age. She had difficulty looking directly at me when she was first interviewed sitting up, and she spoke in a voice so soft that at times it was almost inaudible, a trait that continued through the first several years of her analysis. She dressed attractively in a distinctive, low-keyed way, her taste running to the "natural" look, which was nevertheless the result of considerable thought and careful selection of fabrics, colors, and patterns. She often wore distinctive costume jewelry that gave an unexpectedly elegant touch to her appearance.

From the first time she was seen, and for quite some time after that, Mrs. R. entered and left the office almost soundlessly. At the end of her hour, she would get up from the couch and quickly look away from me toward the door. Then, crossing the room, she would glance at me briefly over her shoulder, look to the floor and then straight ahead again until she was out of the office. We later learned that this bespoke a devouring desire to look and to be looked at, to be replenished—a desire transformed by timidity and inhibition into a kind of nod.

Mrs. R. was the middle child of a sibship of three, including a brother seven years older and a sister three years younger. She was born to an upper middle-class family in a moderate-sized community in a Western state where she was raised and where she developed an abiding love of the beauties of nature. This feeling for nature was an important factor in her choice of her husband, who shared these feelings, and it played a role in the creative work she later undertook. One important source of her emotional investment in the beauty of nature was that it served as a refuge from what was for her an inadequately and uncertainly responsive human environment. As a child, she had felt emotionally isolated, and she had found solace for her loneliness in the reliably present natural world. (She was particularly fond of the Emily Dickinson poem that begins: "The mountains grow unnoticed.") The determinants for Mr. R.'s love for the outdoors, as the patient reported it, seemed quite different, so that what she had initially hoped for from him, a kind of bolstering alikeness in part based on this common interest, was unfulfilled and became a source of deep disappointment to her. It increased her sense of insecurity, which she had hoped his responsive participation in her most precious world would help to diminish.

Her father, a mining engineer for a large firm with a branch office in her home town, was a respected member of the community, but he never achieved the recognition he sought and felt he deserved from his firm. She felt this failure of his as a great let-down for her, and it served as a paradigm for her other disappointments in him. Her reactive hostility toward her father's "failures" was sometimes unjustly revived with her husband. From what the patient said, her father was quite attached to her and she was by all odds his favorite and, to an extent, his confidante from her later teens to the time of her marriage. She felt that he was always emotionally closer to her, and she to him, than was her sister. The patient's seven-year-older brother apparently played only a minimal role in her emotional difficulties and in her analysis. It may be that some features of her relation to him were condensed into feelings about her father, but her brother was apparently sufficiently older and sufficiently uninvolved with her during her formative years to have had relatively little effect on her. However, as will be seen, her relation with her three-year-younger sister was of considerable importance.

Her father's fondness and concern for the patient as an individual was crucial in the maintenance of her sense of well-being. He did expect, however, or at least strongly hope that she would some day marry a socially prominent, well-to-do, attractive man and continue to live nearby as a contented housewife and dutiful daughter. Though he was somewhat (unjustly) disappointed in her eventual choice of a mate, he could not seriously complain insofar as the patient's husband seemed to fulfill his prescribed requirements. In the years before her marriage, her father had vehemently objected to some of the men she dated, and there were numerous scenes. Nevertheless, she felt more loved and esteemed and more responded to and understood by her father than by her mother and, indeed, created an idealized version of him as the model for her "ideal" man.

From all I could tell, the patient's mother was a decidedly idiosyncratic, self-centered woman. At times her described behavior had a strongly compulsive-hypochondriacal quality. Her personality disorder may have been partly covered over by the fortuitous circumstances of her marriage, her general social milieu, and an endowment that protected her and obscured from others the peculiarities, emotional insensitivity, and inappropriateness of many aspects of her personality.

These were more blatant, however, in her relations with her family. Her peculiarities were further covered over by the apparent appropriateness of her role in community affairs where her needs for recognition and uniqueness in relation to others were impersonally organized in the form of adulation from a distance. She was able to achieve this through her organizational abilities and her activities in socially approved, good works. Aside from that, as the years passed, it became clear to the patient that the mother preferred her sister. The two girls developed a cool dislike for each other which continued into their adult years. From late adolescence on the patient became the rebellious child. Her sister continued to conform to the mother's perfectionistic demands for currently fashionable dress, deportment, and social conformity; for making friends with only the "best" people, maintaining a good figure, eating proper health foods, and behaving in a genteel manner; and above all, accepting without question her mother's opinions. The patient thought that the ever-increasing distance from her mother began at the time of the birth of her sister. From what she recalled she did seem to have suffered an emotional wound that was compounded by her mother's increasing dissatisfaction with her, which never healed and which separated them more and more as the years went by. However, Kohut (1977, p. 187) states that "gross events—such as the births, illnesses, and deaths of siblings . . . can play an important role in the web of genetic factors that lead to later psychological illness. But . . . it is the specific pathogenic personality of the parent[s] . . . that account[s] for the . . . inner conflicts characterizing the adult personality . . . the gross events of childhood . . . often turn out to be no more than crystallization points for intermediate memory systems, which . . . lead to truly basic insights about the genesis of the disturbance." The birth of this patient's sister must be seen, then, in the light of a further shattering of an already disturbed, fragile relationship between her and her mother, her self-object. Certainly, other children survive the birth of siblings without any major difficulties, and, in fact, such an event in the context of an over-all satisfying relationship to one or both parents may act as a healthy stimulator of further normal growth and independence (Kohut, 1971).

Mrs. R. was bright and so had little difficulty in school, but she became increasingly shy and anxious. She did not get along well with other children, who easily intimidated her. She was afraid to learn to ride a bicycle when everyone else did, and she often came home crying to mother because the other children ignored her or had hurt her feelings in some way. The patient's mother was decidedly unhelpful to her with these everyday crises, and the patient's tension states had to be resolved by psychological methods, e.g., restitutive daydreams, which she learned to effect within herself without the aid of a helpfully responding mitigator. Her mother, occupied with her activities in various women's groups and concerned with social climbing or with the needed acknowledgment of her value by others, was often away from home. Her ability to respond to her daughter's unhappiness, loneliness, and distress was clearly limited. Mrs. R. later concluded that her mother could not understand her or help her with her anxieties, since she herself was chronically anxious, preoccupied with her own affairs, critical of any emotional sensitiveness and of the "crudeness" of other children. The patient, left to her own devices for solace — reading, daydreaming, being interested in nature — lived more and more in an encapsulating, soothing fantasy world that protected her from the unappreciative, hostile real world. But she also became more isolated, lonely, and depressed.

The loneliness persisted, though to a lesser degree, during the patient's high school years, and she continued to spend much time alone, reading and daydreaming. As early as

her latency years she developed a number of complex exhibitionistic-masochistic fantasies, which at first had no overt sexual content but became sexualized during adolescence. These
persisted till about the time of her first period of treatment
and recurred occasionally during her treatment with me.

When she was in her preteens and throughout her adolescence, there was a running battle between Mrs. R. and her
mother over the patient's figure and her weight. Her stocky
mother had a tendency to obesity, but controlled it to some
extent by eating "healthy" foods which were "just as good as
fattening foods. If I'm hungry, I just munch on delicious
celery sticks, carrot sticks." The patient, on the other hand,
took after her father and was small-boned and rather thin.
She had a fashion model's angularity and flat-chestedness.
These were anathema to her mother who was constantly trying
to fatten the patient up, ostensibly for her own good. In her
mother's mind such a degree of slimness could only lead to
ill-health. It seemed to challenge her self-conception as a good
mother and a bountiful provider. It did not at all fit her
standards of attractiveness, which were governed by the
fashions of another time. The mother relied on the reassuring
solidity of her own physique to give her the sense of solidity
she lacked and for which fullness of body had become the
reliable representative. The patient's slenderness seemed to
the patient's mother a symbol of her own inner insufficiency
and inability—qualities she could not abide in her child.
(This reconstruction was, of course, made on the basis of
information reported by the patient through her increased
understanding of her mother.) The battle against under-
nourishment continued throughout the patient's childhood,
adolescence, and adult life, and was an ongoing issue even
during the analysis. This battle was one among several that
marked Mrs. R.'s relation to her mother. A current example
of the continuing assaults on her sense of worthwhileness and

capability occurred during the time Mrs. R. was refurnishing her apartment. She had very distinct ideas about what good architecture and interior decorating were and communicated these enthusiastically to her mother. Though her mother seemed to be listening and to understand her, the patient would find that her mother had somehow changed the conversation to a subject that had to do with herself, her activities, or her own life, or she would enthusiastically begin to talk about or show the patient pictures of the interiors of traditional homes, which, she indicated, were really in the very best taste. On the other hand, she anxiously worried and, as the patient experienced it, infantilized her by repeatedly warning her about germs, cold weather, dampness, overdoing any physical activities, the dangers of being molested by strangers, etc.

Apparently, beyond these special ways of relating, Mrs. R.'s mother was a rather detached, emotionally uninvolved person, and the patient often experienced her mother's interactions with her as having a vapid, eccentric, ritualistic quality that sometimes gave her a "creepy" feeling. Although Mrs. R.'s father wanted her to remain his "little girl," he was openly affectionate with her and could be directly concerned about her emotional problems and her career. He tried to be as understanding of her as his psychological make-up would permit, but he was not really able to go along with her emerging ideas of greater emotional independence. Yet, compared to the patient's often suddenly irritated, hypercritical mother, he came across as a genuinely affectionate if misguided parent. Thus, the emotional gap between her and an admiring, accepting, and loving "other" was to a significant degree filled by her father, who in his own way made up for her mother's limited responsiveness.

Following her graduation from college, Mrs. R. worked for about a year in a large Western city where she had several "love affairs." These did not include sexual intercourse because she felt too inhibited or ashamed, or felt that it would somehow be too dangerous for her "to go that far." Her boy friends ranged in type from men-about-town whose interest in her was limited to sex, to at least one man who seemed to be more genuinely serious about her. She enjoyed the emotional and physical intimacy up to a point, but she persisted in avoiding sexual intercourse with him for the conscious reasons already described as well as a newly developed fear that she would lose control of herself and become so in love with sex that she would become erotically depraved. Given these difficulties, particularly her fear of losing psychological control of herself, she left her job and returned home. Within a year she married a man who was reasonably acceptable to her parents. However, with the birth of her first child, she became increasingly concerned about her adequacy as a mother. There was a recurrence of a chronic, low level of depression, and of irritation with her husband for not being sufficiently responsive to her. She experienced a sense of nameless, empty dread and dissatisfaction with herself, with life, and an increasingly pervasive feeling of uncertainty and fearfulness about almost everything she did, from changing her child's diapers—had she done it well enough or not—to a moderate agoraphobia. All of these became increasingly taxing and disturbing and led to her first analysis.

This analysis was characterized by moderate symptomatic relief and the mobilization of an intensely idealizing, sexualized transference which, as the patient thought in retrospect, had the quality of an adolescent, erotized infatuation with a sophisticated, sagacious, protective older man who would "fulfill" her and always be available to her. Intervals between sessions were filled with daydreams about the analyst, his home life and professional activities, hoped-for chance encounters, and a languishing sense of painful waiting and painful loss. During the two-year period when she and her husband lived away from the city where she had been in analysis, she wrote several letters about herself to her former analyst. She was deeply disappointed with the relatively curt, businesslike tone of his replies. She was nonetheless puzzled by her reaction, since she felt quite sure that she could not really expect any more than that; still, she felt shaken.

The reasons for the ending of her first analysis have already been given. In her initial sessions with me, Mrs. R. had a desire to tell all "the facts" of her life as she saw them because she felt that was the "proper" thing to do and because, as it was later understood, she had a need to stick to the facts to distance herself from the other nascent, affective issues which she sensed would be too disturbing to her. This was already an indication of a character formation that was defensively constructed to ward off what might in a general way be called instinctual anxiety. She feared her own emotional depths.

The working formulation arrived at over the first few months of analysis was that the patient was suffering from a narcissistic personality disorder, that her narcissistic transformations had inadequately progressed along the line of the development of the ego ideal, that is, that she required a self-object relationship with an idealized man to maintain a feeling of inner stability and self-value. Beyond her initial or concurrent defensive attitudes and her disappointment in not being able to resume treatment with her still idealized previous analyst, the transference established itself along lines similar to those which had developed before: She hoped to repeat an intensely idealizing transference with me, and initially this did occur. However, this time there was a decided, early shift to a mirror transference in the comprehensive sense (Kohut, 1971). It was this transference then, in its more narrow, archaic form, a merger transference, that dominated the analysis and most of the analytic work. Regarding this, it ap-

peared that Mrs. R.'s development had been severely disturbed by her mother's concealed pathology and by her sister's
birth. The latter, however, seemed to be important initially
because it shifted an already relatively unempathic though not
uninvolved mother's attentions further away from her and accented her mother's physical caretaking responsibilities at the
sacrifice of an over-all feeling for the patient's budding personality development. The patient then turned to her father
for broader, more sensitive attention, adding a further burden
to that relationship and leading to a complex, emotional mixture of feeling toward him, feelings that combined mirroring
wishes with idealizing needs. The emotional relation to her
father was thus intensified and burdened by the coming together of both major narcissistic developmental lines (Kohut,
1977, Ch. 4). The erotization of her transference to the analyst
and extra-analytically to other men was in part a consequence
of the earlier inadequate modification of both these narcissistic lines. These transferences had become admixed with early
drive impulses manifested as transference sexualizations
(Kohut, 1971, 1972, 1977). It was these erotizations that most
clearly gave the patient's pathology some of the manifest
characteristics of a hysterical personality disorder.

The differentiation of Mrs. R.'s pathology from those
dominated by oedipal conflicts and regressions to preoedipal
fixation points was an important issue in the understanding of
her pathology. A triadic, structural neurosis did not appear to
me, either initially or later in the course of treatment, to be a
sufficiently encompassing formulation to explain adequately
the patient's personality formation or her symptoms. The
patient's difficulties did not at any time appear to stem simply
from a three-way oedipal struggle or from the relatively
circumscribed problems and dangers that the conflicts of such
a neurosis would be expected to manifest. Rather, they
seemed to arise from a chronic sense of deep injury and depri-

vation, a consequent sense of deficiency of normal self-regard and self-value, and of the inadequate setting up of a reasonable set of internalized goals. Lacking both stronger goals and self-regard, she relied on fantasies of magical supplies (responses) from idealized and mirroring others and on conscious and unconscious grandiose conceptions of herself which were highly vulnerable and easily shattered. The relatively easy collapse of the latter left her with a re-exposed, chronic, underlying sense of deficiency and an even more deeply buried and inhibited feeling of rage. An external self-object seemed to be her primary source of gratification. I hope the analytic material that follows will lend credence to this formulation. Early in treatment the formulation was certainly more tentative and vague. I have stated it more precisely here to make clearer to the reader the ideas and conclusions that evolved in the analytic work and guided it with increasing consistency.

Let me suggest a general orientation to this case which arises from the point of view of the psychology of the self. There is a shift in emphasis from one central assumption that has been considered crucial to the classical formulations of psychoneurotic pathology. This assumption is based on the axiomatic concept of the centrality of the Oedipus complex in normal development as well as in pathological formations (see Kohut, 1977, pp. xv, 77-78 for a discussion of the principle of complementarity and the place of classical theory in psychoanalysis). Despite the notable and persuasive emphasis in many recent theoretical discussions and in observational descriptions of the importance of early stages of development on the organization of the healthy and pathological development of the mind, and despite the long-standing implications of epigenetic development where later stages of development are dependent on earlier ones for their experiential meaning (see Gedo and Goldberg, 1973), these ideas have not seemed to exert as much influence on psychopathological formulations as they might have been expected to. It is as if the Oedipus complex and castration anxiety have been unquestioningly maintained as the fulcrum on which healthy and disturbed personality organization is balanced, despite considerable evidence to the contrary (see Greenacre, 1960, p. 173). In formulations about self-object development there is, instead, a greater tendency to understand normal and pathological development from earliest infancy on up rather than as regressions from the oedipal stage back. There is also a shift in emphasis from the drives to a more holistic approach—to the developing personality as the child experiences his body, his mind, and to the larger more complex and more complexly nuanced emotional environment into which he is born and in which he is raised. The shift in emphasis is both a clear-cut, radical one and a quiet, subtle one, and the latter is probably the more meaningful. The change is less in the nature of the noisy change of the history of a nation following the loss of a significant war that suddenly and radically alters the course of that country's destiny, than it is a change in the over-all spirit of the times brought about by an alteration of values and a new way of experiencing and understanding the world, a change that exerts an unavoidable influence on the meaning of the activities of the everyday life of the nation's citizens. So it is not that the drives have lost a war, but that the drives (except under special circumstances) have lost their unique and pivotal position as *the* central force to be reckoned with, and that, instead, they have become repositioned as a part of the whole. They are still an imposing feature rising from the plain, but they are not the Great Divide.

Analysis and Commentary

As indicated, Mrs. R's analysis began in the shadow of the disappointment that she could not return to her previous analyst because she had moved to another city. She complained initially that I lacked her former analyst's charismatic qualities which previously had so vitalized her. However, this "vitalization" was soon revived in the form of an increased feeling of well-being which she attributed to various superior qualities she began to discover in me. Concurrently, she began to dream of a search for an exciting gem which could be secured only through the help of another, unknown person of either gender. This charm could be discovered in some out-of-the-way, often dangerous section of the city. It had the manifest form of an antique jewel, brooch, necklace or some other kind of unusual jewelry, the possession of which would endow her with the sense of profound security and well-being for which she had always desperately longed.

One early dream of particular vividness and intensity stands out among the others. In this dream she was in a foreign country, probably Mexico, crawling on all fours on the ground. The hard earth was strewn with glittering emeralds or other precious stones. As she eagerly gathered them up, a reverberating godlike voice boomed down on her from above. There were no words, but the meaning of the voice was clear: She was not to take the gems, they could not be hers, they were not allowed her. This dream was interpreted to her as her wish to acquire something precious in the analysis, something precious that she could make part of herself. I was the transference god who had the power to permit her or prohibit her from achieving this goal. The patient listened to the interpretation, made some effort to connect it and the dream with what she was feeling at the time, but in general she let it pass. I did not press her about it and did not go futher with it myself. I sensed that it was a dream of considerable significance, the precise meaning of which I did not fully understand. I made note of it and kept in mind that its meaning should be further explored at such time in the future when both the patient and I would (I hoped) have more information available to us about the broad personality organization from which it arose and what wish or description of an attitude about herself it was meant to express. (See p. 350 for a later interpretation of the meaning of the dream.)

I believe this luminous dream was one of those marvelously compacted images that sometimes occur early in analysis and express a repressed central wish, a feeling state, or sense of self which, if it (or they) could be understood to its fullest, would permit the analyst, if not yet the patient, a glimpse into a deep, still walled-off infantile core of the self. At the moment of its first revelation we can, like Carter at Tutankhamen's tomb, say only that we see "wonderful things."

To some extent the patient had recognized the transference nature of her desire for a repetition of the experience with her previous analyst and her disappointment with the present one (with the implicit preconception of what I was to be); but gradually she was able to find solace in my attempts to understand and to convey to her the states of mind that lay behind the untransformed wishes, injuries, and the sense of emptiness and despair she had not recognized or understood and had not been accustomed to translating into secondary-process language. For a time this function was idealized in somewhat the same way as the previous analyst had been.

In her first hours of analysis she complained of my coldness toward her, especially of my not smiling enough, although at the same time she felt that I was reliable and trustworthy, a no-nonsense kind of analyst. She began to feel less irritated with her husband and less distant from him than she had been. Several times she found herself shivering inexplicably as she lay on the couch—"Perhaps it's fear or excitement"—and one day, without ruminating about it first as she "always" did, she removed her glasses (which she placed in her purse) in an off-hand, absent-minded way. In response to my comment about this action, she said, "You know I'm always on guard, and taking off my glasses without thinking about it is an enormous event." I said that I believed it was. (In addition, the development of the patient's self-observing and analytic working abilities are in evidence here.)

Though not recognized at the time for what it may have been and so not presented to her as something to consider, the shivering may have been the somatic expression of what she was not yet able to be in touch with psychologically, but which later was understood and interpreted to her as her relative lack of recognition of the intense psychological reaction that being listened to, responded to, and understood, etc., stimulated in her. Also suggested in this reaction is her relative lack of regulatory mechanisms for the absorption or control of such preaffective states.

The next several hours were spent talking about her mother, how irritating she is, how afraid Mrs. R. is "to explode" at her. She cried. "It's so embarrassing, so humiliating to have such feelings about her, and it makes me uneasy." I said that she must feel unhappy that that is what the relationship between the two of them has been or has come to be. She agreed and cried a little. She said she recognized that her smiling at me at the end of the session was not just a defense or apology, but a desire to be smiled at in return. "It would mean approval, acceptance, or that I've not said anything too terrible." She said, "Perhaps treatment will help me to be more giving, because how I'm treated here somehow gives me a better feeling about myself."

It is important to note here the salutary effect of the beginning mobilization of the transference very early in the analysis. This may not be the case for other kinds of patients who for various reasons react initially with anxiety and defensive withdrawal from the analytic situation, e.g., the patient who fears that his poorly differentiated self is endangered by the intimacy of a procedure that too massively reawakens repressed or walled-off longings and feelings of deprivation and rage too intense for him to deal with. Mrs. R.'s response of "fear and excitement" may be an indication of some degree of that experience in her. However, she began to feel more at ease, less inhibited, more pleased with herself, less irritated with her husband, etc. In short, she began to experience a sense of satisfaction with herself through the establishment of a still diffusely experienced transference which in retrospect I would understand as having elements of both an idealizing father transference and a gratifying transference to a mirroring self-object. The patient experienced me as trustworthy and responsive, a no-nonsense analyst who perhaps would not disappoint her.

[I think it would be useful to interrupt the treatment narrative here in order to expand on a transference issue that has been dealt with considerably in discussions of transference in structural pathology, but which I believe can be understood in a different way in terms of the clinical implications of the psychology of the self. One should differentiate the diffuse, nonspecifically experienced (or understood) effects of the psychoanalytic situation from the understanding and systematic working through of specific pathogenic childhood experiences in the transference. If treatment were to overlook the specific origins and meaning of Mrs. R.'s early pleasurable excitement (albeit tinged with fear) and of her increased sense of well-being by relegating them to the clinical theoretical position of a therapeutic alliance or some related concept such as basic transference, the patient might or might not be satisfactorily analyzed (Kohut, 1971). If the patient's core problems are essentially oedipal and if self-object, narcissistic issues are of minimal importance in the patient's pathology, then perhaps little will be lost if the narcissistic aspects of the personality organization are simply kept in mind as a general characteristic of psychopathology; inasmuch as they are not central in a particular pathological constellation, they need not be dealt with explicitly. (See Kohut 1977, pp. xv-xvi, 207n for a discussion of self pathology in the narrow sense and self pathology in the larger sense.) If, however, the patient's pathogenic problems are predominantly a pathology of the self, consignment of the relevant self-object transference experiences to the affective-ideational role of the therapeutic alliance or the "basic transference"—only, that is, to a merely adjunctive, diffusely supporting emotional position (like Freud's positive transference which one doesn't analyze until it fails or interferes with treatment)—then a significant sector of the patient's narcissistic pathology which is embedded in the therapeutic alliance or the basic transference will be bypassed and left unanalyzed, though oedipal issues will be adequately dealt with. The analysis of the oedipal disorder may, of course, be of considerable value to a patient and will, along with the unrecognized and unanalyzed "supportive" responses of the analyst, enable the patient to conclude treatment with symptomatic relief and a general enhancement of his personality. Such an outcome will be all the more likely if the patient is able to use the analyst silently for his own (merger) needs without either the former or the latter ever consciously being aware of the specifics of that use. A somewhat less nonspecific effect may follow from the partial or incorrectly understood and incorrectly emphasized role of one or another of the narcissistic transferences as well, e.g., the analysis of a mirroring mother transference when the central pathology resides in the pathological vicissitudes of an idealizing father transference, or some other variation of the preceding. In either case, the results of the analysis will be less than optimal, and the partially helped patient will leave treatment to find his way through life as best as he can.]

To return to the patient, in a later hour she said that she was "afraid of losing control" in treatment. She's afraid of lots of things like that; if she has an orgasm, she is afraid "my arms and legs will fly off. Oh, I hadn't meant to say that!" On the other hand, she has always been fascinated with "powerful, handsome" charismatic men, and has woven elaborate erotic fantasies about them. In her daydreams she would say to some such attractive, unknown person, "Do you love me?" and he would begin to respond, "Yes." Her wish for a clearly positive reaction to her was not limited to men or to daydreams. When she told her mother she was pregnant, she added, "So be nice to me and like me." "It was to have her appreciate me for accomplishing something really good." The frightening idea "that [her] arms and legs would fly off" surfaced again at the time of termination. Such fears of feeling overstimulated, of losing control of herself, and of feeling disorganized intellectually and emotionally became a recurrent theme throughout her analysis, though I shall not report it in detail. For example, there were a series of dreams having as their manifest content Mrs. R. driving her car along a highway, then down a steep hill; then she would have the sudden panicky realization that the steering mechanism of the car was breaking down or that the brakes had given out and she was about to crash. These dreams could be understood in the context of the failure of the sufficient development of a steadying regulatory ability of her ego and in the current sense of the transient fragmentation of her vulnerable cohesive self. As I later understood it, these feelings arose when her mother had failed her, ignored her, lost interest in her. Then the regulatory function that her mother's involved, responsive presence provided began to fail because it had not yet become an autonomous, internalized function. So it was with the fantasies of sexually aroused men. Their powerful response would sometimes fortify her. At other times, however, when her needs were more intense, the now overcharged erotic feelings were also dangerous because of the basic inadequacy of this regulatory capacity. Further, the intensities of stimulation stirred up by sexual thoughts or activity reawakened warded-off, repressed feelings of overwhelming needs in relation to an early self-object. Such needs had not been adequately responded to (before they became pathologically distorted), and because they had been unanswered by the self-object, their emergence aroused massive disappointment and massive attacks of disintegrating rage when they were stimulated again (Kohut, 1972).

In a later hour Mrs. R. said that she was still concerned about my not smiling at her and that she couldn't feel comfortable with me without that. She reported a dream from the preceding night: "I was picking blueberries, there were several paths to take. Someone's telling me which one to take to find the blueberry patch. I get there and pick berries with a stick. It's hard to get them." I agreed that it was difficult to get there, and I added that there seemed to be something within her that interfered with her getting to the berries. "And you use a stick, rather than your hand." She thought that was true, something within her stops her. Once, her mother didn't call for ten days after the patient had told her off. At other times mother floods her with little gifts and advice. Analyst: "I think that what's important is the effect on you when you feel she's dissatisfied or disinterested in you. My not smiling is an indication to you that I'm disinterested in you, too."

[To take this line of thought further, I now would say: "As in the dream of the blueberries you would like to be helped to get to what you want, something that would make you feel good about yourself, a relationship with someone that would give you the feeling that you're liked and responded to—as you said, 'be nice to me'—then if I smiled at you, you would feel able to get to the berry patch, to an inner feeling in yourself that would make you feel good. But at the same time you're afraid of experiencing such an intense wish, and you try to get to it and keep yourself away from it at the same time by using a stick rather than your hands. A stick keeps you more at a distance but at least it lets you get to the berries. It's difficult for you to feel secure about letting yourself go because you feel you haven't been or won't be understood or adequately responded to, here. It's scary for you to go that far, to be that direct about your feelings."

A symbolic masturbatory wish and fear might be considered the correct line of thought here, and perhaps that is partially correct, but I believe the essential meaning would be the same as that just described: it would be the simplified, sexualized expression of a more complex self-object wish or an auto-erotic substitute for it and not the expression of an oedipally organized wish. (See Kohut, 1977, pp. 120-121 for a discussion of sexualization as a disintegration product.)

Within the context of a broader understanding of the patient's core pathology, this dream can be used to demonstrate a way of understanding dreams that uses metaphorical imagery and forms rather than discrete, manifest symbols and associations to them to indicate underlying issues about the self and objects which the patient as yet only dimly grasps. In this instance, this patient could not as yet openly expose such feelings to herself or to the analyst. However, she experienced the analytic situation and the analyst as mobilizing such feelings, feelings that were still too ambiguous or that are too firmly repressed or split off from her, and which she still has considerable conflict about recognizing in herself.

Freud himself used both a symbolic topographic method and a metaphorical one in his interpretation of dreams when, on the one hand, or at one extreme, he emphasized the universality of certain symbols and, on the other hand, recognized a certain story line or concealed narrative.]

The patient said she was "afraid to free associate because it means freedom of something, like picking the blueberries by hand. Being so close, like having an orgasm with my husband, it means I'd be too open and too close, and that terrifies me." A few days later she recalled childhood memories of sitting on her father's lap as he read her the funnies. "Later he didn't like to do it, yet I felt so good with him then. When he was away on a trip, the day was incomplete." Then she cried. She thought that she had never been able to imagine that men could be attracted to her, and yet she wanted that so desperately. And it would have to be in a physical way, then she'd feel more satisfied with herself. It was hard to believe that "mother could be so critical of me, it was easier to believe something was really wrong with me and that she was just honestly pointing it out." She thought that her investing her father with so much importance and idolizing him so much was because something was so missing in her relationship with her mother or some feeling about herself was missing. She thought things were better between mother and her before her sister was born, but she couldn't really remember that.

The following weekend she had a terrible headache and finally took codeine to get relief. The headache recurred on Sunday. She wondered if it had to do with the long Thanksgiving weekend from Wednesday to Monday. "I feel I'm losing control, and you're not there and you don't really care." I said that her headache could be related to the long interval between appointments here and that she's afraid that if she feels too much about being here, about talking and being responded to, that she'll be let down, hurt by my being away too long or my not caring. But that instead of feeling that, or because the feeling is so strong, she has to defend herself against it, and then in its place she gets a headache. The next day her headache was gone and she said: "I'm furious with you for being as you are, you're not human, you have no feelings. You shouldn't take so much time off. Besides, what you're saying implies I'll have to work to understand myself in treatment. I've never had to do that, it's been bestowed upon me or offered to me. I'd rather have Dr. A. [her former analyst]. I was brought up to expect that I'd be taken care of and I still want it, just to sit back and nurse." [Mrs. R. had heard my "interpretation" quite well. Instead of a headache, which derails her feelings through somatization and which is then unavailable to her, she is able to become aware of and to make use of the psychological issues that have given rise to her headache, e.g., her feeling of abandonment by me, whom she had begun to rely on and to trust, and the feeling of rage this abandonment leads to. But it is still too intense and disorganizing, and overflows in all directions.]

In the following days, her feelings began to change: "I want to feel you're awful, then I don't have to feel I need you. Yet I feel you're really not awful at the same time." Then: "Yesterday I had feelings about you and I couldn't tell you . . . very positive feelings . . . that I wanted you to take care of me forever. It's frightening to have such feelings." I said, "Yes, I think such intense feelings do scare you, like when you were shivering on the couch a while back. You try to do away with those feelings, or you feel you rightfully deserve to have them responded to. And in a way, or at one time, they should have been, you should have expected that. But to have those feelings repeated now, here, is disturbing to you, it's puzzling, and scary."

Patient: "Yes, I want to feel I'm special here, too, as I did with Dr. A. Like when I wanted a Raggedy Ann doll. I never got it, but I never asked for it either. I don't know if I was afraid to ask for it or if I felt I should get it without asking.

And I'm afraid to tell you how much I want something or how I do feel about things because you won't like me then."

After a weekend she confessed that she sat home all day thinking about me. She just wanted to be here, just to cry all the time, she felt so depressed. Then she began to feel better after she'd been here a while and I began to talk to her. The next day she told several long dreams about women being stripped naked by some men in a concentration camp; the women were going to be used for sexual purposes. Though she was only an observer of the event, she thought she'd want to be the sexiest of them all. She associated to adolescent fantasies of living in a nudist camp or of posing nude for a painter. She thought of the movie, "The Pawnbroker," how his wife was used as a whore. She recalled her breasts. "I wanted to be exposed like that." Around age ten to twelve, she had a repeated fantasy of being tied naked on a table, or of being beaten or of walking a gangplank nude. She thought she must be depraved. She was surprised that she was able to tell me all this.

[This sequence of weekend separations from analysis, depression, and dreams or fantasies of a sexual exhibitionistic-masochistic nature was recurrent in the beginning of the analysis. The dreams and fantasies were understood to be the manifestation of partial disintegration products, of a distorted and partially dehumanized, stylized, and sexualized wish to regain contact with the lost self-object analyst in order to restore the sense of well-being that had been disrupted by the absence of his responsive presence in the intensifying merger (mirror) transference (Kohut, 1971, pp. 114-115). They grew out of the revival of her childhood feelings of desperate loneliness, which, with their continuation in adolescence, she had assuaged with the creation of various pathological grandiose exhibitionistic fantasies of barbaric imagery in which remote, sadistic, virile men paid fascinated attention to her. Although this sequence and its meaning was not interpreted to her at this time, it *was,* later in the analysis. And while an interpretation of her attempts to restore herself by this method did not in itself have a salutary effect, the recognition of her vulnerability to the loss of the analyst's responsive presence, which he was able to understand and interpret with increased sensitivity, did eventually have a modulating effect. It helped her to re-integrate the deteriorated sexualization into the broader self-object experiences from which they came.]

These confessional themes, which embarrassed her because of the increasing exposure of deeper, more intense feelings to herself and to me, continued. They alternated with the feeling that I was disgusted with her or that she was angry with me for not responding enough or in the right way; yet, at the same time, she felt more secure with, more understood by, and more trustful of me. She recognized that when she felt that way about me she usually cried. They were tears of relief and of reunion with a responsive "other" who refueled her with feelings of aliveness that she was beginning to lose. Weekends and brief holiday interruptions continued to be very difficult for her because at those times she felt utterly abandoned "like that baby animal left without food" or a desperately crying child lost in the park without his mother (from some current dream imagery). She thought her intense wish for ever-present responsiveness and reassurance was somehow related to her mother's self-absorbed chronic anxiety (often concealed), and her constant concern about the dangers in the world. On the one hand, she didn't believe that most of mother's warnings should have been taken seriously, on the other hand, she thought she'd been deeply affected by them. Perhaps what she didn't get was a reasonable, available, and soothing presence "to hold in there" with her when she felt upset or angry. Instead, her mother made her more anxious by her flash-irritability or her self-absorbed unavailability. Yet, in some ways she always did get most of, or something of, what she wanted from mother—clothes, etc.—but that was an easy and superficial way out. But she's beginning to think that mother was getting things for her that she, mother, couldn't get or hadn't gotten for herself, that mother was doing it for herself and not in response to her (the patient's) needs. My comment was that all that can be hard on a child, and without a store of such comforting early experiences, frustration is more difficult to bear later on.[1] And further, that somehow she also was not encouraged to, or was interfered with getting to things on her own, and that was complicated by her chronic low-level of energy—a kind of depressive lethargy.

The patient felt that was a really new idea, a revelation—that one has to feel good about oneself in order to feel able to work or that one has to work to get what one wants. Instead of doing that (working), she had just had fantasies when she felt deprived in some way. They got her out of her depression, but she didn't have to work to get results. She hadn't felt energetic enough to work, only to daydream. The fantasies she recalled best were the later ones having to do with men being in love with her. Yet, at the same time they weren't really sexual; in fact, she somehow didn't believe that penises existed. Once when she was ten she saw a baby boy in the nude, but she didn't look at his genital area. Anyway, what was important to her was the feeling of closeness to a man, of

---

[1] This idea could have been expanded on in a way that would have begun to open up an area of fuller understanding which eventually would have been more useful to her. I could have explained that aside from mother's empathic deprivations, her emphasis on the gratification of childhood wishes in the particular self-centered and often infantilizing way she did gratify them was also frustrating to other, more maturing progressive developmental tendencies that the patient might have been helped into had her mother been responsive to her in those areas (Kohut, 1977).

feeling like a little girl with either mother or father. All her complaining aside, she felt that that emotional position was being both intensified in treatment and taken from her at the same time. It was exciting and yet disturbing. Still, at times of stress Mrs. R. tended to dream about a blatantly sexual relationship with an analyst or some man in a high social position, like the minister of a church she had once attended who had excited her, and who in the dream was swept away by his overwhelming lust for her.

[Had it been recognized at this time, it might have been helpful to the patient to point out the perhaps double nature of her erotized fantasies: when she felt deprived by her unresponsive mother, she gratified and soothed herself by various kinds of stimulating pleasurable fantasies—of finding blueberries, of being sexually aroused—and she turned from the hoped-for response from mother to her own body or to a fantasied response from idealized men like father who would appreciate her and whose vigorous strength she could feel invigorated and filled up by—no diet foods they—and on whom she could always rely. These fantasies and dreams were only part way along the road to the expression of a still less defended, less guarded expression of the profound intensity of her need for emotional nourishment from the self-object other.]

In the fourth month of treatment Mrs. R. began to recognize more deeply and was able to talk about how I meant something important to her in a new way, not just in the sexual mode around which she had tended to organize a heightened sense of self-experience. She felt deeply stirred by the idea. That night she dreamed:

I was driving along a street and passed a rambling old New England-looking house, like my house but much taller, like a skyscraper somehow. Later, I was in the house. A woman had just died, I think, a woman from another era, Victorian but in a Jane Austen heroine way—thin, petite, not tall. She was in an open coffin and I didn't want to look at her, but somehow I did and she began to come to life. I think her hands began to move, or her head. I got scared and went to find the maid. The woman and the maid were plain-looking, but tastefully plain. Yet, there was something phony about the woman as she was, the Victorian thing, she couldn't have been a real person that way. I don't know what she was like in her mind—maybe nothing.

Mrs. R. associated that she had had intercourse the night before in a different position; it was embarrassing because she'd been married so long and had never tried it before. "I can accept my body from the waist up but not below, and I could even watch and enjoy my breasts being touched; it was exciting; I've never done that either."

We returned to the interpretation of this dream a number of times in the course of the next several weeks. I am here paraphrasing and condensing what I said at the time and later about her "awakening" from the dead, defended life she had organized to protect herself by. I suggested that the dream combined several related ideas into one story image. The new feeling she had spoken about in the previous hour and in hours before that in relation to me—the main element of which was a sense of greater confidence and trust in me as a reliable, responsive person who understood her—had led to a good feeling about herself, and a greater positive acceptance of herself both in a general way and in a more specific, sexual way. These new feelings had led to an increased freedom to experience sex with less shame and greater openness. The old house, then, was herself, as was the dead woman coming to life. And those feelings were emerging here in the skyscraper (office) building. She was still afraid of that developing aspect of herself, so she depreciated herself or distanced herself from herself or diluted the experience by including the maid in the dream image. She experienced all this as intriguing, and yet she still repudiated it and returned to her safe but partly disdained "phony" self, her Victorianness. Nevertheless, contrary to the dream's partial negation, she was also beginning to feel that she could let herself start to come to life. She could try something new sexually, just as she had been feeling something new in herself, greater self-confidence and trust. In a broader emotional sense, one expressed the other. I said all this simply, stressing the newness of her feelings and the excitement and danger she must have experienced in the dream, during intercourse, and in the relationship here which had led up to the dream. She spoke about these ideas in several succeeding hours, and in one of them she said the ideas and feelings were so encouraging that she just "drank them in."

Much of the analysis was epitomized by that hour. She vacillated between various emotional positions of feeling dead, unloved and unloving, or responded to, understood, and accepted in a profound way for what she was psychologically, for how she felt about herself, and why and how without consciously knowing it she had experienced herself and the world. She learned to recognize how the present reflected the past (at least, as much as it actually did), how her parents, particularly her mother, had inadvertently injured her or interfered with or failed to support her growth in certain crucial areas; and why then her father, who, whatever else his pathology, was sincerely interested in her, and later other men became so critically important for her (and with an even higher valence than might be ordinarily expected in a girl or young woman) as promoters and substantiators of her as a valued person and as the essential invigorators of her "dead," depressed self.

She recognized that she experienced her sister partly as a representative of her mother's attitude toward her, that is, as an unsatisfactory, unacceptable person, and, even worse, as a usurper. And she recognized how in order to try to recapture the old needed response from her mother she had tried and still continued to try to submerge and merge herself in her mother's protecting but stultifying embrace in which she could once again find some minimal solace and prettified, if hollow, attention and security.

These experiences were worked through over and over again in analysis over a seven-year period. During this time she reacted to unempathic injuries with varying degrees of helplessness, empty depression, haughty rage, feelings of exhaustion and psychic disorganization, and a return to some of her old ways of restoring herself, e.g., by a search in thought-fantasy (and to a lesser extent through experiences in her life) for various kinds of magical cures. Each repeated greater or smaller emotional loss of me was with increasingly reasonable consistency followed by the re-experiencing of me as an emotionally solid, responsive presence on whom she could rely despite her reactive rage. And she experienced me as someone who would vigorously persist in an emotional involvement with her despite her tendency to detachment and retreat to quiet, defensive grandiosity or affective isolation. And as someone who would honestly recognize and respond to her growing sense of important inner value. All this effected a firming of her sense of well-being. Her intense reactions to emotional deprivation-loss and her difficulty in recovering from them were partly reflected in the length of time in treatment. The latter could be accounted for both by her enormous, partly covered-over, partly "deadened," vulnerability, which required considerable responsive stimulation, analytic empathy, interpretation and reconstruction, as well as by concurrent, developmental support and a "filling in" of previous deficiencies of development—more so than a relatively well-structured transference neurosis and the pregenital regressions found therein might require. In addition, the length of treatment probably resulted from my relative unfamiliarity with and lack of awareness about the new theoretical concepts and methods of treatment I was applying as well as some countertransference problems that I will describe later.

A few more vignettes will delineate some as yet undescribed psychic constellations and their place in Mrs. R.'s personality organization.

The patient's isolated belief in her specialness, despite her also consciously experienced sense of worthlessness, was complexly derived. It had its more diffuse origins in her earliest presibling relation with her mother or in her later relation to her father, and was compounded and given an additional dimension by her distorted later relation with her mother. These essentially negative affective experiences were maintained partly as a consequence of failures of more positive affective stabilizing experiences in her development which might have reduced her sense of deprivation and chronic subliminal anger. The antidote to her needfulness was given form in a number of dreams. It was a staggering blow when she began to recognize that the method was not tenable, at least not in the distorted way it had evolved—as an extension of her grandiosely unique mother or as the darling of her idealized father.

These particular aspects of her grandiosity were understood theoretically as a split-off sector of her personality (Kohut, 1971), which expressed an identificatory tie to her mother (and to a lesser extent the more pathological aspects of her relation to her father) in the form of her mother's grandiose sense of uniqueness and the legacy of the grandiose modes—now made her own—that her mother habitually used for sustaining her own sense of self-value. For example, Mrs. R.'s subdued style of dress, the "natural look" punctuated with a touch of elegant jewelry, was gradually recognized by her and by me not just as a woman's everyday desire for an attractive appearance, but as the expression as well of a covert, isolated sense of superiority, which, while it manifestly opposed her mother's ideals of fashion, was in its own way the equivalent of her mother's membership in an elite world and was for the patient a union with her in that exclusive, rarefied atmosphere.

Another manifestation of this split-off or isolated grandiosity came to light in her description of what seemed to be pedestrian shopping trips. During one session a tone of excitement and urgency in her voice as well as some stated sense of shame about her "binges" seemed to indicate that there was more to it for her than an interesting outing. Some of her shopping binges had a "secret," addictive quality to them. She just had to do it. It then became clear that without consciously thinking about it, she had made herself the supplier of hard-to-find household items of a specific kind, which she had acquired over the course of several years. Anyone in need of these items would either ask her for them, or, if she heard about a friend's need for one, she would supply her with it. This particular specialness became so crucial to her that she became furious if someone in her circle of friends was able to supply the necessary item before she could come up with it. The importance of this to her and her dependence on it had a desperate quality which she later began to recognize for what it was—a vehicle for maintaining an experience of uniqueness of her self.

Put more theoretically, beneath the horizontal split resided "repressed, unfulfilled, archaic narcissistic demands [which were] related to [her] mother's rejection of [her] independent narcissism" (Kohut, 1971, p. 185). Her low self-esteem and shame propensity were partially made up for by a (vertically) split-off grandiose fantasy of herself. And while I have mentioned its secretness, it also had attenuated, clearly conscious elements. Further, this uniqueness had an empty, impersonal tone. It was also a clue to the quality of her relation to her mother and to a fear of directness in personal experiences.

Her relation to her mother was characterized by a dream in her second year of analysis. It followed an interpretation the day before to the effect that she would like to be able to let herself experience feelings of various kinds because she recognized that if she remained encased in a protective barrier of distant superiority she would lose touch with others, and that was frightening — perhaps more so than being exposed to the real dangers of loss and death she had been talking about. These latter might be painful, but the understandable, protective bond set up in her relation to her mother also interfered with her ability to get in touch with her deeper feelings, among which was a feeling of vigor and independent self-aliveness. The next day she started the hour by confessing that she had been crying a little while listening to me talk about her shut-off feelings, though she had deliberately avoided letting me know she was doing it. She hadn't really been able to let go as much as she wanted to. Yet, if she had been alone in the room she wouldn't have cried at all. She had a dream that night which seemed to have to do with anger at her husband. She thought, however, it was in response to what had been said about her letting herself feel more, but in addition, she thought it might have been an expression of anger — and that was feeling more, too. In the dream she was in a fit about being shut out of her house. I asked if she felt shut out in some way here, or shut out from herself. She said, "I feel I've no right to be angry ever. In the dream I was even angry after I could get in, but it wasn't in the right way, not in the way I want to get in." The next day she had the following dream:

> My parents came to visit, and I was going to surprise them with a birthday party for mother. There'd be lots of people there. I was very organized beforehand. It meant a lot to me to show them how capable I was. I had a combination of shrimp and blueberries that I'd fixed the week before and put on a shelf in the pantry. Also several cakes. But I never looked at them after I made them. Then it was the day of the party, and they (the shrimp and blueberries) had dried up to tiny specks. I felt awful, stupid, incompetent. I served them anyway with some other stuff. Then I thought they might be poisonous.

Mrs. R. thought that the dream had a "built-in failure" in it or an angry feeling toward her mother concealed by or mixed with a desire to please her, which was nevertheless doomed to failure.

It seemed clear that the discussion of her recently more easily expressed concealed feelings, specifically feelings of anger, had stimulated just that tendency and those feelings and that in the dream this was paired with her equally important wish to please her mother and to get a feeling of approval and interest from her. When I suggested that she was trying out her angry feelings, she laughed nervously, but there was also some clear, though slightly smothered relief that a thought about poisoning her mother could be considered at all. In retrospect, another way of thinking about it would be that the dream could be understood as an expression of the poisonous relationship and dried-up feelings that had developed between the patient and her mother over the years, despite the patient's need to merge with and a wish for nourishing, responsive approval from mother. She was attempting in the dream to get that again—but the attempt failed. The

blueberry imagery might again suggest her desire to reach or
to revive some pleasurable feelings that had been stored away
in herself (in the pantry) but mother-analyst had not done
enough to keep them hydrated in the past or in the transference present, and that enraged her, just as not getting into her
house enraged her.

A dream the following day about an unwanted and
possibly dangerous train ride through Nazi Germany was interpreted both as the danger she experienced at having her
angry feelings brought up and a desire to escape from that
danger by getting off the train (another part of the dream),
that is, by getting away from the interpretation — from the
analysis that brought such ideas to light — and from the newly
mobilized, angry feelings in herself. However, in succeeding
hours she began to feel that she was seeing all kinds of realities
she had never seen before, or knew about but hadn't really
"known" with the same immediacy, e.g., that people really do
lie, are selfish, are not really as interested in others as they
make-believe they are, but that if she ever really needed the
analyst he would be available to her, even if it was in an adult
way that would "force me or, I should say, help me to be
realistic." Clearly, she was not escaping into herself so much.

In the fourth year of treatment Mrs. R. and her husband
by chance sat in the row ahead of the one in which my wife
and I were seated at a public performance. I had not noticed
the patient seated directly in front of me until the first inter-
mission. I then leaned over and greeted her, addressing her by
her last name. She was disconcerted by my presence, but
responded in kind, and there was a brief exchange of intro-
ductions and a few polite comments about the performance.
In her next hour on Monday the patient immediately brought
up the chance encounter and commented about the performance, which she had liked and which, she correctly surmised, I hadn't. But what was most annoying to her was that

she had been addressed in a formal way as "Mrs. R." This small dark cloud presaged a series of storms that were to recur for several years. Why hadn't I called her by her first name? Clearly, I was excessively formal, cold, unfeeling, insensitive. No, she wouldn't dream of calling me by my first name except in fantasied conversations, or even of using my first name in conversations with others, but there was absolutely no conceivable reason why I should not use her first name whenever there was reason to use her name at all. Using nontechnical language, I explained my then sincerely believed rationale for not doing so. In essence, I said that it altered the analytic relationship and the unfolding of the transference in a counterproductive way. (I should have recognized that the elaborateness of my explanations and a particular tone of absolute certainty—which I knew and understood quite well from other situations—hinted at some countertransference problems, despite the fact that my technical stance might be considered classically unassailable.) She countered by offering numerous arguments for her point of view. I suggested that we try to understand what it might mean to her to be called by her first name. She said it would make her feel better, she needed it, it would make me more human, it would allow her to feel closer to me. While we both felt these ideas were reasonably correct, they did not hit the mark, and, indeed, this issue was never as clearly resolved and worked through as it might have been.

[From my subsequent understanding of the patient, when the problem was no longer the central one it had been, it seemed apparent that it would have meant to her that the analyst in the transference was an idealized adult in relation to a child who had to have someone to look up to, and who indeed did have an ungrudging interest in her which the very essence of her being required to sustain itself with. It was something that had never become a reliable self-sustaining part of her. (After all, her blueberries, her developing self, *had* ripened in an emotional drought.) Further, the use of her given name would have meant being recognized as a total individual in her own right, not as her husband's wife, as an extension of him as she had been of her mother, but as her full childhood and adult self. The use of her first name might have had an integrating effect on her anxiety-prone, fragmentation-prone psychic structure. And further still, the analyst would have been different from her cold, formalistic mother who was so concerned with surfaces and appearances; he would have been the sensitive, responsive, understanding, self-object parent she had always longed for (and who indeed she had had a right to have at a phase-appropriate age). It seems to me now that the analytic process would not have been undermined by such a response. Rather, the patient would have been able to bolster herself with the response and in time she would have been able to understand the transference meaning of it. It would, along with other interactions, have helped to provide for this patient the optimal analytic atmosphere essential for the therapeutic work. This should not be considered nonanalytic behavior leading to a corrective emotional experience, but, on the contrary, a correct empathic response which would have created an atmosphere of comfortable professional intimacy and encouraged the mobilization of a deeper transference which in time would allow her to touch the blueberries *directly* with her hands, and which would help the desiccated "poisonous" relationship and her reactive frozen defensiveness to be overcome. Instead, my ignoring or misunderstanding of this led to storms of helpless disappointment and anger which finally wore themselves out. The patient was eventually exhausted by an unyielding stance and the first-name issue for the most part was washed away in the tears of other storms or blown away by my lack of understanding of its significance.

I do not believe that it would be correct to consider the use of the patient's first name a parameter in Eissler's (1953) sense of the term. That term was designated for use in relation to conflict pathology at a time when a strict formal therapeutic atmosphere was considered necessary and optimal for the revival of an uncontaminated transference neurosis (see Kohut, 1977, Chapter 6 for a discussion of this issue in general and its historical context). It was an ingenious solution to increasingly frequent clinical problems that required a clinical approach that was (at least temporarily) different from that dictated by the rule of "abstinence." I believe that, at worst, one would consider calling the patient by her first name "reluctant compliance" (Kohut, 1971) and, at best, as part of an expectable and acceptable analytic atmosphere that may develop between two people who are long-time collaborators in a unique and deeply personal therapeutic endeavor.

As Kohut has stated in other words, neutrality in the analytic situation is not comparable to the necessarily minimal, personal involvement of a hard science experiment or even to the necessary personal detachment of the operating surgeon — or, to be more in tune with the realities of the stance of most analysts, an attitude toward the patient that, though coupled with genuine clinical concern, has been bred in an atmosphere of required scientific distance, a distance presumably required to effect a useful therapeutic tilt or "barrier" (Tarachow, 1962). But neutrality in the analytic situation is optimally, at least, ordinary expectable psychological responsiveness, the responsiveness of an individual who has spent a lifetime understanding the emotional life of others (and himself), and who can verbally respond under necessary circumstances as the expectable self-other (parent) of infancy and childhood.

I believe that my (countertransference) reaction to the patient's demand resulted from a reactivation of my own archaic needs for responses that had not been dealt with in my analysis or on my own, and that I was not prepared to let surface in myself, or, consequently, to allow the full unfolding and comfortable empathic understanding of in my patient. Instead, I responded with classicism used as a defensive rationalization. This whole issue of the analyst's defensive reaction to unrecognized and unanalyzed wishes in himself stirred up by his patients — particularly when he is dealing with relatively new clinical conceptualizations — deserves further study and amplification. My compliance in this instance would initially have provided the patient with an analytic atmosphere comfortable enough to allow her limited or distorted growth to be remobilized or modulated or both. It would have later been made explicit and interpreted (see Kohut, 1977, p. 92, the two-step procedure in analytic work). The "issue of the first name" was perhaps not a specific one at all, but became a final common pathway for various other failures of understanding. Yet, the patient improved because of an over-all sufficiently correct therapeutic atmosphere and understanding of her. The "first name issue" became part of her adaptation to me and her "compliance" to my rules.]

Another issue more critical and more complex than the preceding one, and treated with an even greater sense of self-justification, occurred in connection with the birth of Mrs. R.'s second child. By this time she was in her fifth year of analysis and had experienced the various vacation interruptions, occurring during the course of treatment, with increasing tolerance and inner stability. The birth of this child[2] was to occur sometime in late August (her due date was uncertain) around the time of my summer vacation, and she ex-

---

[2] Actually, Mrs. R. gave birth to twins, but the diagnosis was not made till late in her pregnancy and so had no specific influence on her needs and fears. When a multiple pregnancy was discovered, it simply intensified those affective states and made her demands seem even more justifiable to her.

perienced a resurgence of doubts about her ability to be an adequate mother to an infant whose "enormous needs" she felt panicky about being able to gratify—particularly since she had only recently begun to experience her own needs as capable of fulfillment. However, the reliability of that fulfillment was as yet still shaky and still far too dependent on the positive responses to her by others, which she overendowed with meaning, or on the magic of a fantasy world in which idealized men responded to her sexually and thereby enhanced her sense of value, or on more regressed, pathologically distorted merger feelings that were dependent on the analyst's physical and empathically correct emotional presence. Further, her anxiety about the necessary gratification of a newborn's needs may have been particularly great because of the deprivations that she at least thought she had experienced at the time of her sister's birth.

In effect, she was talking about her own "enormous needs." To be denied the gratifications of these was to repeat what she felt had been her lot in life. This repetition was one of those moments in time which, intensely telescoped and magnified, brought together a complex of her emotional life that meant everything to her. Unfortunately, because of a number of disparate reasons, it, too, led to a sense of terrible betrayal by (in her mind) an insensitive and self-occupied parent.

The delivery was expected to occur during the time I would be away, or possibly in September, by which time analysis would have been resumed. As early as the end of June the patient began to have dreams indicating a revival of her old sense of inadequacy and inferiority, which now centered around the feeling that her genitals were unattractive or disgusting. She said, in association to a dream about female genitals, "I try to like or accept it [her perineal area], but I have to cover it or myself with jewelry or clothing to make it more acceptable. But I really dislike it." My understanding of this problem was incomplete, although I did interpret to her that her specific feelings about her genitals were a focus for feelings about her over-all sense of deficiency.

I now realize I should have dealt with this issue in a fuller way and tied in this "deficiency" with her pervasive sense of inadequacy, an inadequacy that had developed out of her mother's disregard for her core grandiose self, the unfolding of which had been passed over in favor of the split-off pathological grandiose self that mother favored.

[I believe the basic issue for her at this time centered around psychological issues which had been important to her for so much of her life. Was she a valued person who had a right to be given solace, was she a gem who had a right to be admired, could she expect me to behave like a magically idealized parent who would know about her activities and about her desperate need for reassurance, and could she experience me as a self-object in the multileveled mirror transference which she still required? The distinction between these various needs, while spelled out here for expository purposes, was not at the time of her intense stress so clearly differentiated in my mind or in the patient's.]

Once again, the analyst would fail her. My justification this time was even sounder than it had been before: I would be out of the country during the possible period of her delivery and therefore would not readily be able to get in touch with her during that time—though an attempt to reach her by phone might have been possible. Instead, I asked if she would let me know by mail if she were to deliver during the time I was away. We made plans for my getting in touch with her on my return, and for the continuation of the analysis at that time or as soon afterward as her obstetrician would allow.

The patient accepted this arrangement without any indication of dissatisfaction, but — and the connection at the time was not made except as an indication of her general sense of abandonment at a time of need — she revived the issue, presumably settled long ago, of my still addressing her by her last name. She ruminated about being called at the hospital or of her calling me on my return and being addressed as Mrs. R. She said, "And if I have to think of you as someone saying Mrs. R. to me during the entire time you're away, I don't think I'd be able to stand it. So I'm yelling at you in advance. I'm encouraged to do that by your having been so helpful and understanding last time [regarding an unrelated problem we had successfully worked on]." On the last day before vacation she had a long dream in which a man called her by her first name in a tone of voice so sweet that it made her feel like crying, as indeed she had once done when I had correctly explained something to her in a voice she had experienced as particularly touching and gentle. She associated to the dream that she was worried about my not being here for a month or perhaps more. "I'm upset and angry that you're going away. You won't be here to pay attention to me. I won't have any emotional support when you're gone." My various statements, intended to convey to her that I understood how difficult it was for her that I was to be away at a time when she felt all her old fears of being ignored and abandoned by a preoccupied self-object whom she desperately needed to be always unquestionably available, had little effect. She cried through much of the session, repeating that she would just have no one to rely on, but by the end of the hour she put on a bold front and, with a brave but tight smile, wished me a good vacation, and I wished her well.

As it turned out, I *was* on vacation at the time she delivered and I did not learn about her delivery till I returned and found a birth announcement addressed to my office.

The patient was still in the hospital at the time. I called her and congratulated her on the birth of her twin boys about which she was very excited and somewhat anxious regarding their care and development. I spoke with her about the relatively uncomplicated delivery, etc., and we made tentative arrangements for her return to treatment after a few weeks at home. She sounded rather neutral about the birth of the twins and about the call, and there seemed to be nothing unusual in the conversation to arouse my concern.

Upon her return to treatment, she complained a great deal about the rigors of again being the mother of not just one but two infants after an interval of several years, but felt far more sure of herself and found to her delight that she did not panic each time the babies were fretful, cried, seemed ill, or were ill. What did emerge, however, was unexpected. Despite her clear awareness that I could have had no way of knowing precisely when she would deliver, she was convinced that I would, of course, call her when she did deliver, particularly since she was going to have twins. Somehow I would know, and would attempt to reach her by phone from overseas during my absence. Somehow I would make a special effort to get in touch with her. What she emphasized was her need for what seemed like a magical kind of knowing about her. (But again, I see in retrospect, the emphasis should be less on the magical as such and more on the idea of magical as an indication of the intensity of her need, which led to unreasonable or magically-tinged ideas about realistic possibilities.) Despite the verbalized conscious recognition of the improbability of such an eventuation, despite its importance to her, it developed that my not having called her on or near the day of her delivery had been a terrible blow to her. I had been too concerned with myself to be concerned with her. She felt that it was a blow from which she could never recover, and the more she thought about it the more enraged she became. After numerous swings between outrage and rational understanding of the difficulty of the fulfillment of her unresponded-to wish, she began to recognize that, whatever the reality situation might have been, she would have felt injured. Her needed transference image was that of an idealized, omnipotent, and mirroring parent who would know about and be deeply concerned with her desperate need for a positive admiring response and for soothing reassurance. Anything less than that was inadequate for her. She also recognized more clearly the failure of her assumed power within the context of an archaic merger transference, power that was massively disrupted by my lack of (a phone call) response to her. Further, she realized after my vacation began that she had been terribly angry before it had begun at all.

The inherent, realistic difficulties and the transference irrationalities of all this notwithstanding, I believe that *in principle* the patient was correct. Her psychological make-up was such that a special effort at this time was probably in order. Such an effort would have acted not simply as a compliance to regressively distorted demands, but as a concrete, needed acknowledgment of and the providing of, an appropriate analytic atmosphere for her massively intensified needs. The next several sessions made this clear enough to me to enable me to say to the patient, in effect, that she felt that when she needed me most to respond to her, to understand and recognize her anxieties, to help her feel calmer, I went off on my own and ignored her. That left her feeling as she did as a child when she should have been helped with her feelings of intolerable tension, but wasn't in a way that would have been right for her. Instead, she was left to find solace through her own devices. Of course, this statement alone did not remedy the injury—the damage had been done—but other similar statements in response to like injuries did have an ameliorative and modulating effect on her clearly recognized rage, and the issue growing out of the birth of the twins faded out of the analytic picture in time.

[The basic issue that arose in conjunction with this problem had not been tackled. My thinking about this now would follow along lines similar to those already mentioned in the "first name issue." The patient had already linked them together by her revival of that problem just before the vacation: she was stating in the only way she knew how, that she required a concrete indication of understanding and concern to help her maintain an only recently arrived-at sense of trust and confidence, which might disintegrate again into a feeling of valuelessness, despair, and disorganizing rage at her unempathic parent. On the other hand, it is a possibility that again, as with her name, the crisis was an artifact created by an analytic situation characterized by an at least partial misunderstanding of various crucial aspects of the patient's requirements. The crisis, therefore, would not have taken this particular form (though the intensity might have been present in a different form) had the analysis been more adequately conducted. Yet, it is nonetheless possible that, no matter how skillfully the analytic work had been (or even because it had been optimally skillful), the patient would have responded in just the way she did because the analytic work had led her to a position where this complex of specific vulnerabilities had been mobilized. These vulnerabilities would have come to the surface in treatment sooner or later, in one form or another, though possibly not with the same degree of (traumatic) intensity as had been evoked by the unfortunate confluence of various emotional streams and external events, which, all together, were too much for the patient to handle. Under other circumstances, they might have been mobilized and worked through bit by bit with less pain and with less frequent episodes of disorganization.

We can further ask whether, if the meaning and importance of the request had been recognized, it might not have been analytically indicated to comply with the patient's needs and to have phoned her near the presumed time of her delivery. Again, the reasoning for this would be the same as that adduced for the "first name issue." The question of actual clinical conduct probably cannot be definitively decided on for either of these particular clinical problems, since there are a number of variables that would have to be taken into consideration. And one in particular might tip the scales in one or another direction: the analyst's comfort with either therapeutic stance. The clinical-theoretical issues of what has been called reluctant compliance, of optimal therapeutic atmosphere, and of the analyst's countertransference are more crucial (see Kohut, 1971, p. 291).]

Beginning in the sixth year of her analysis, a short time after the birth of the twins, Mrs. R. began to feel sure enough of herself to start a small plant and home gardening accessories shop. (Her love of the outdoors had been brought indoors?) This enterprise acted in part as an organizing framework for her inherent abilities, her ambitiousness and her wish to be "a person in my own right." Despite many realistic obstacles to this venture, it proved to be a reasonable success. This woman, who earlier in her analysis had been so unsure of herself that she seemed to be afraid of her own shadow, and whose genuinely genteel manner and pleasant, softly modulated voice had at times become eerily wraith-like (see the woman-in-the-casket dream), found that she was able to cope with burly, cursing craftsmen, unscrupulous landlords, stubborn and conceited artisans, roving street-gang types, and so on. She found that she could bargain with the best and that she, who had never had to deal seriously with the real world of money (father would take care of that for her), could even learn to balance her books! Though her enterprise was an artistic success, and to a reasonable extent a financial one, it did not suffice. At first she was genuinely happy, even euphoric; then worries about the possible incorrectness of her commercial and aesthetic judgments, which at their deepest level were a reflection of her old sense of inadequacy and emptiness, once again emerged under the stimulus of occasional realistic setbacks, and led to her characteristic doldrum emotionality.

However, the patient was in a transitional period. Her sense of inner security was threatened when her very success meant a further loosening of the enmeshment with her regression-inducing, narcissistic mother (the mother of the vertically split-off sector of her personality, and of her pathological infantile grandiosity), a mother who remained as indifferent in the present to her newly found healthy assertiveness and to the newly found strength apparent in many aspects of her emerging, nuclear self as she had been in the past when the patient had strayed away from the circumscribed realm of her values. (This sense of insecurity was experienced in a still persisting transference to her mother as well as to me.) The threat of losing a needed bond with the analyst-mother alternated with her growing, healthy, independent behavior and a feeling of growing energies emerging from beneath the repression barrier, from beneath the horizontal split of her personality organization. Negative transference reactions and a return to the merger grandiosity with the analyst-mother alternated with increasingly firm steps to healthy grandiose development. When the unconscious reasons for her retreats (arising from the expectation of indifference and "found" in the analyst's indifference) were understandingly pointed out to her, and when she recognized what she chronically expected and feared—nonrecognition—and what she retreated to—the archaic narcissistic mother transference—she once again was able to permit herself to expose her nuclear grandiose self to me for my confirming, facilitating recognition. This back and forth went on for a long period of time. It was a core therapeutic experience, a major focus of the essential analytic working through (see Kohut, 1977, pp. 210-211 on analytic work with vertically and horizontally split-off and repressed sectors of the personality).

Mrs. R. then began to talk about the possibility of termination. This seemed to be a genuinely motivated move. Her essential difficulties had been brought to the surface (and the surface linked to the depths); they had been recognized, understood and, it was thought, modified to whatever degree they could be at this time. Major transference issues had been mobilized, worked through, and resolved, and the patient had developed some appreciation for and dominance over her major difficulties.

She thought back over the past year in analysis, particularly the struggles with the establishment of her business (in essence, the concrete expression of the establishment of a relatively secure, independent, competent self) and all that that had meant to her. She said: "It feels so good that you've been through all this with me." She wept openly. I connected this remark with her feelings at the time the twins were born—that she wanted me to be available, aware of her fears, appreciative of her anxieties and her ambitions, of her longings and feelings about herself, and that indeed I had been through it with her. With a burst of her newly developed candor and freedom of expressing her feelings (in contrast to her old self of the downcast looks), Mrs. R. replied, "When I said a while ago that I'd like you to see it [her place of business], but was afraid to ask you or was afraid of being there if you should come to see it, and you said that you thought it best that you not come at present, but that you recognized how important it was for me to be able to *think* of your seeing it and appreciating it and perhaps even telling me that it was really beautiful—hearing you say that was as

important to me as your actually going to see it. It meant you
knew how much it meant to me, how proud I am of it. And
your phrase, that I made it sound as if it were filled with
'nameless wonders,' did something for me again, something
that never was done for me before — you appreciated the
importance of my spark of creativity, and that reverberates all
through me in many ways. It's very important to me."

A tentative termination date was set for about four
months in the future. However, because of the disturbingly
massive return of some of her most severe anxiety symptoms
and her old feelings of insecurity and inadequacy, and a revival in her dreams of the idea of escaping to the safety of, by
now, well-known and understood sexualized mergers with
idealized, powerful men, the termination was postponed.
The rigidity that had marked some previous decisions about
her treatment was not repeated. Another date was set for six
months beyond the initial one — her choice of timing.

The delay had several psychologically significant effects.
An over-all nonspecific effect was probably related to a
general psychological principle. That is, given the multipli-
city of experiences, attitudes, and emotions that had been
dealt with in Mrs. R.'s analysis, termination required first a
further strengthening and integration of not yet sufficiently
autonomous modes of functioning.

For Mrs. R., an important nonanalytic, indirect contribution arose from the increasing maturation and healthy
development of the twins, whose infantile needs were no
longer so demanding. They had begun to respond to her in a
way that was less reminiscent of her own difficulties of infancy and childhood. Their needs became less "primitive" for
her when they could respond to her in a more organized way.
Another factor was the recognition that neither of the second
children was a reincarnation of her usurping sister. This issue
had been understood on the basis of interpretation and re-

construction, but seemed to require the additional reality of the clear-cut character differences between the two (the children and her childhood baby sister) and the gradual development of the patient's deep pride in, rather than deep jealousy of, her children's accomplishments. We recognized that when her own self felt reliably sturdy, she did not feel deprived by or jealous of her own children, who were getting what she had wanted for herself. Still another significant point, which was most important from an economic point of view, was the working through again, on a more fully cathected, this-is-it basis, of crucial issues previously dealt with in the analysis of her developmental problems. These were now re-experienced in a relatively rapid and integratively summarizing, and, therefore, in an affectively and conceptually clearer way than they had been before when they had been understood in a more piecemeal, compartmentalized fashion.

A fourth point, perhaps implicit in several of the others, and yet the most important of all, was that she was better able to feel that she had not been seduced into a renewed, self-object dependence, which she had always been searching for, and then deserted while she was still not strong enough to maintain the positive feelings mobilized by that relationship on her own as an integral part of herself. Nor did it end before she was able to differentiate her present rage at losses from archaic rage at losses in the past, a differentiation the empathic analytic atmosphere and the analyst's persistence had helped her to achieve. Though I had recognized the old desertions revived in the transference and had attempted to respond to them with empathic understanding specific to the disruptive experience, my responses may have been far less than optimally effective and the unaffected injuries may have, indeed, as was conjectured earlier, gone underground. The analysis of the remnants of their remaining observable psychic forms was still insufficient to effect a lasting modification of the once again covered-over basic injuries. The delay of termination, then, permitted the patient to have a further chance to allow her injured and enraged self to re-emerge and to be further analyzed. She required more time to consolidate the modifying, neutralizing experiences which would remain as permanent structures and would thus strengthen her previously fragile self.

I shall review some of the highlights of this true termination period. She was still recovering from the premature decision to terminate and was dealing with feelings aroused by the new termination date. She dreamed: "I've gone somewhere where you had to be black and I wasn't, so I hid in an underground place. It was important that I shouldn't be seen." She associated: "I'm in a alien land. I've alienated myself from some pleasurable things, like time to spend with my family." This led to thoughts about doing things for herself, which meant that she'd lose the old, supportive, accepting responses of her husband and her friends. "They'll get angry and that's a danger." Analyst: "Is it dangerous for you to feel and act in an independent way — as in the dreams of several months ago of being deserted in the bad neighborhood, when we were first considering termination or, as you said then, like giving up a kind of dependent tie to your mother or to me? And then you go underground again, you retreat into yourself as you did as a child?"

Over the following months the patient had a number of such dreams about being in an alien culture or land or in a bad neighborhood. These did not seem stimulated by specific failures in the analysis. The alien land was a land without the analyst or the analytic situation, like home without mother when she came home from school, or like mother without the appropriate response to her that she needed. But at the same time, she began to detach herself from that feeling of need for the self-object. She recognized that she was different from mother and that she needn't be subservient to her or be like her in order to maintain the covert bond with her that she had previously required. This was a tie she had either tried to deny by being blatantly different, or, earlier in her life, had attempted to maintain by suppressing her developing, independent self by slavishly conforming to her mother's standards of deportment, taste, and attitudes toward the world — by a loyalty to her which in effect meant that she remain a harmonious extension of her. In exchange for that loyalty she could expect a modicum of her mother's soothing, responsive, or, at times, even sensitive presence. She thought now, "I can really like people and that's so different from mother who really can't; she can like people only in terms of what they add to her — but that's how she is, and I can't change her."

Further analytic work in which the patient sensed a reliable response by the analyst to the continued emergence of her nuclear grandiose self led to increasing self-maintenance of her self-esteem without the outside support-responses on which she had always relied. Her dreams reflected the gradual modification of her dependence on these outside resources for the maintenance of a stable self. Once again she was with her mother or sometimes with her husband, searching the market places of the far corners of the world for some remarkable or rare item, often antique jewelry, the acquisition of which would bestow on her a feeling of inner uniqueness and profound security. In these dreams she would sometimes find the desired object, but her mother would ignore it and suggest another, which the patient found not to *her* liking or which lacked an essential something — a certain quality of beauty that would do the trick. Or her mother would lose interest in the search, and the dream would end with a sense of helpless disappointment, frustration, or even disorganizing panic, as strange-looking natives, rowdies, began to move in, too close. These dreams were repeated with some variation in their manifest content as her inner self-organization continued to be reshaped. Sometimes her husband or the analyst took the place of her mother. He, then (the idealized father, husband, analyst) became her strength, her protector against a dangerous childhood world of indifference to her, and the rowdies who threatened her—a world of inner chaos and rage. At times, though, she again began to feel as she had in one of her first dreams at the beginning of the analysis. You will recall that in one intensely focused dream (see p. 311) she was in Mexico, crawling on the hardened earth strewn with emeralds which she had started to gather up; a godlike voice declared that she could not have them. The dream expressed a feeling state that had not been adequately understood or interpreted at the time. In light of the intervening analytic work the old dream could now be better understood, and in conjunction with the market-place dream it was interpreted to her as follows (paraphase): The gems were a representation of her brilliant, infantile self that had remained unavailable (repressed) to her everyday self-experience. The god had disapproved of her gathering up these emeralds of her self.[3] But without those (nuclear self) gems she was (later) the dead Victorian woman in a casket. Her unconsciously experienced self was left enfeebled, dried out, and dominated by shame and low self-esteem. She had not been given enough of a sense of being loved, or of affirmation of the value of her self in her developing years by her self-absorbed mother or, later, by her

---

[3] She experienced her mother (the nurturing breast) as hardened foreign soil, and she experienced the access to her gemstone self as prohibited by what began as indifference to her core self. This indifference later became transformed into a superego-like no, the callous god's "No," that was now her own cruel peremptory warning to herself to stay away from, not to touch, not to try to reach the depths of herself lest she be once more subjected to the pain of an archaic wish that would have no hearing. The interdiction had begun as disregard of the essential independent uniqueness of her core nuclear grandiosity (cf. Kohut, 1977, p. 100) and instead urged a pathological narcissistic merger (and identification) with her mother.

more responsive but infantilizing and ultimately disappointing father. And, already vulnerable and prone to a depressive sense of loss, she lost the gems her experiences with him had given her, the gems which in her dream for a moment at least she imagined to be hers. While she had them, they had given her a stimulating inner sense of self-appreciation that formed a core of her vitality. In treatment the analytic soil was more suitable to healthy growth, and a sense of more solid self-value began to take firmer hold.

The later variations of her gem-search dream graphically document the gradual developments and realignments of her emotional organization. The most apparent changes consisted of an increased emphasis on her husband's rather than her mother's accompanying her on these trips, and then, more and more frequently, a search through the market stalls for the desired object on her own. In the last several of these dreams, unaccompanied by anyone and feeling quite comfortable, she carefully checked over the contents of the various booths and several times found various articles, not necessarily unique antique brooches or other kinds of jewelry, but art objects that were aesthetically attractive and that she purchased—sometimes still with the help of the sudden appearance of her husband who supplied her with sufficient amounts of money. However, what changed more subtly was not the kind of articles found or who was with her, but the *feeling that the work of selection itself was exciting* and that *she was capable of doing it*. She had both in her dreams and in reality become something of an expert and a connoisseur rather than a searcher, out of desperation, a searcher who had to conceal her own sense of deficiency through the glitter of a talisman. Now, she was more capable of finding what she required to gratify and stabilize herself through her own efforts.

In the end, then, she did acquire some of what she had initially craved but which had been denied by the god's voice. However, the emeralds whose beauty she had sought to bestow upon herself, which she had searched for to enliven herself with their glittering intensity, had become instead the emotional quality of more secure inner development of a more stable self. This was a development that endowed her with a sense of worthwhileness that she experienced in conjunction with her inherent and now more fully realized abilities. Together they formed an enlarged available sector of her nuclear self (above the repression barrier). (See Kohut, 1977, pp. 3-5 for a discussion of the value of strengthening a particular sector of the personality, even though other early self-object problems are not dealt with or resolved as such.) She had to a greater extent been able to give up her split-off narcissistic merger with her conditionally approving but limiting and unreliable mother and her idealized sexualized relation to her more reliable father and to father substitutes. In the analysis she had re-exposed her deepest longings to herself (and to the analyst), and with the help of the analyst's more reliable responsiveness, and verbalized acknowledgment and conceptualization of these needs and wishes, she had been helped to strengthen her deprived and shaky self and to re-mobilize her previously inadequately responded-to or ignored (repressed) primary self. Her basic injuries, of course, remained. However, the complex mixture of defenses and pathological personality distortions which she had developed in order to survive had been rolled back to a fair extent. She acquired a relatively stable sense of core value by way of consistent, overall positive, unshrinking, unretaliative responses to her longings, her depression, and her rage. The total response was not the love she had always hoped for, but it was close enough to such a depth involvement with her to enable her to develop and maintain that essential ingredient of a resilient vital psychic life: self-love, in its best sense, reliably within her self.

Further Comments

While some attempt has been made to convey why an analysis of a hysterical personality with its expectable triadic structural and conflict pathology is included in a casebook on narcissistic personality disorders, a more focused effort to deal with this issue is in order at this time. The question that asserts itself is: How can one reconcile the nosological entity of hysteria with the disorders and the pathology of the self?

The pathology of this case may remind some of Zetzel's (1968) paper on hysteria and the "so-called good hysteric." That is, the patient's personality organization might be understood theoretically in several ways: as a structural, transference neurosis—an oedipal-phase, hysterical personality disorder; or as a case of hysteria with a more than usually severe degree of regression from a phallic level of development; or as a case of a primarily preoedipally fixated personality whose manifest symptoms superficially mimic those of a true oedipal hysteric. I would again suggest that the material of the case can be more correctly understood from the point of view of self psychology and the vicissitudes of self-object relations. Using classical structural psychology, one could understand the patient's pathology in the following (admittedly oversimplified, schematic) way.

The patient arrived at the oedipal phase of development with whatever particular coloration her preoedipal, libidinal development had suffused it with and, having been devastatingly confronted with the fact of her lack of a penis, angrily turned away from her depriving mother, who also lacked a male genital, and fixed on her father, the possessor of that organ, who could supply her with it or its possible, equivalent, a baby. This hope also being unfulfilled by her father, she then in time turned to other men who could supply her with those valued possessions. In the meantime

she denigrated the depriving, deficient mother and idealized her father and other men. Her sadomasochistic fantasies could be conceived of as her infantile concept of the
sexual act derived in part from primal-scene experiences or
fantasies and her own inherent feminine masochism. Her
search for the gems (of the god) or their variants was a search
for her own missing phallus or for the symbolic equivalent of
it, or for a man who could provide her with it. Finally, her
agoraphobia was a fear of her desire to be sexually
stimulated or attacked by male strangers, who were sign-re-
versed symbolic substitutes for her father, and led to a defensive retreat back to the security of the preoedipal mother.

My summary presentation of the case in terms of the
psychology of the self cannot, of course, be considered an entirely accurate one; it is a working hypothesis. Mrs. R. was
raised by a mother who either earlier or later in her life was
or became idiosyncratically responsive and selectively unresponsive to some of her daughter's essential infantile and childhood developmental needs. To state this most succinctly,
the patient was "seduced" into an intense self-object experience and then "abandoned" when her sister was born. The
patient's description of her childhood loneliness, her shyness
with other children, her easy intimidation, her constricted-
ness in play, and her sense of inadequacy vis-à-vis her peers
are assumed to be her apprehension of her inner, fragile
psychological state manifested as a cognitive experience of
the fragility of a large sector of her self and its executive
capacities. This relatively feeble self-cohesiveness was compounded by her mother's continued selective emotional
abandonment of her after the birth of her sister by her self-
absorbed, self-centered, and hypercritical attitudes toward
the patient. These continued into her adult life. How much
of this might have been offset and absorbed by the patient's
psyche had she been able to develop a firmer self and a

greater fullness of spirit in her earlier years prior to her sister's birth is not possible to answer. However, it seems clear that she was unable to manage either her proneness to feel depleted or the depressive moods that arose out of the recurrent sense of the loss of a needed, responsive self-object. Without that responding self-object, the core of her self began to feel empty and to lose its vitality, and, along with an increasing urgency to restore a sense of well-being, it began to disintegrate. At such times, an early emotional equivalent, a precursor of the dangerous rowdies—the attackers of the minimal stability of her emotional equilibrium—must have begun to move in threateningly. And at such times, archaic methods of self-healing through pleasurable sensorimotor feelings and simple positive affects and fantasies (and later of conceptually more sophisticated and complex, pleasurable grandiosities) must have taken over. The more pathological of these grandiosities were apparently not sufficiently altered by accepting and modulating parental responses, or they were channeled to coincide with the parents' (particularly the mother's) own grandiosities. And they must have reasserted themselves in various pathologically intense, archaic forms. The precise affective-ideational nature of these early forms is, of course, unknown, but some of their later, repetitive, standardized manifestations, like the grandiose-exhibitionistic and, later, masochistic-exhibitionistic fantasies, were known to her and reported in her treatment. They became the available, now habitualized functional pathways that, through dreams and daydreams, she could use to dispatch the dangerously fierce hungers of isolation, loneliness, and disorganizing narcissistic rage.

Finally, another developmental step arrived, which, while present earlier, gradually took on an increased role in the amelioration of her unstable self. This emerging variant of the earlier more dominant, mirroring relationship offered renewed possibilities for the sense of gratified coherence of her still shaky self-organization and of pleasure in her uncertainly satisfactory self. That step emerged in relation to her self-object father, who, by his generally more constant and positive relation to her, provided an affirmative atmosphere for her development at various levels of her grandiose self (but probably more so on the level of a narrow mirroring response) and was also available for her psychological use as an ego ideal. These idealized qualities were constructed of a melding of her own narcissistic self and his actual virtues (Kohut, 1971, pp. 40-41). The loving inclusion of her in his powerful world (or her including herself in that valued self-object system) gave her yet another chance for the stabilization and further development of a cohesive self. The particulars of this interaction were, of course, also overlaid and intermingled with the important coloring influence of a little girl's response to her father, the embodiment of that special class of people, men, who possess special endowments and powers and who have, as an aspect of both, a tantalizing sexual role which can be normally intriguing or pathologically erotized. For this patient, whose needs for gratification and stabilization of her self were so intense, her father's unique quality of maleness must have played a particularly important, at least double role: of being a male with the special value of maleness for a female, and of being a self-object person whose mirroring of her and whose availability for narcissistic idealization could help to solidify her own positive sense of her self. Together, these several qualities must have had more than a simple additive effect. They reinforced each other so that the whole became more than a sum of its parts. Sexuality became fused with self-integration (Kohut, 1971, p. 69); put another way, sexuality could be and was used in the service of self-integration, and, at times, in her real life—or at least in fantasy—it could do away with disorganization and depressive despair. But now there also developed a fear of an addictivelike response to her intensified and over-determined reaction to the attractiveness of men when she was on her own in a strange city without the usual supportive responses of a family, a family whose at least minimally responsive and structuring presence could help to stabilize her easily disrupted self and could help to reduce her reactive disabling rage. Yet, she had also outgrown them and therefore could no longer depend on or feel that committed to them, despite her continued need for their stabilizing functions.

In relation to the problem of her dependency on the response of self-objects to maintain her sense of well-being, a specific mode by which she had effected this (a mode related to the traditionally conceived dynamics of the hysterical personality and the oedipal phase of development) should be made more explicit in terms of the psychology of the self. That mode is of course called penis envy in classical formulations of hysterical oedipal pathology.

As I followed the clinical material, keeping in mind the expanded orientation of self-object theory, it seemed to me that what has been called penis envy could be more convincingly understood as the fused representation of a complex of wishes arising from an insufficiently developed and sustained satisfaction with her core self. It seemed to me that the patient's sexual fantasies arose at those times of deprivation when her self-cohesion was threatened and her shaken self required emergency shoring up. The fantasies were invaluable organizers and reorganizers of her cohesiveness by virtue of the focused, primal intensity of their eroticism. Through the perfervid sexual tone with which her mind and body were suffused, by the very pervasiveness of such an affect, her fragmenting or enfeebled self was reconsolidated. The sexualized experience became, if only tran-

siently, a force that unified her self. Though the idea of
sexual men or of the phallus may have at times symbolized
and called-up this affect in her, the unifier she was searching
for had a broader and deeper emotional source. She was
searching through the market places of the world for something she hoped did exist somewhere, but which she had
never been able to find or to feel she had reliably obtained
for herself before. She searched for the gem that had been
and was to be herself, the precious core self of a dimly remembered and almost lost childhood memory. (For a related
formulation, see Grossman and Stewart, 1976. For a discussion of the role of the Oedipus complex in disorders of the
self and a discussion of the concept of the complementarity
of structural and self psychology see Kohut, 1977.) For this
patient "penis envy" had become one specific form among
others that served to restore (temporarily) the equilibrium
and solidity of her core self. (See Kohut, 1977, for a discussion of sexualization in self pathology.)

The gems lying on (sprouting from?) the hardened soil,
the blueberries she might reach (or which she had in hand
but which had dried out), and the jewelry for which she
searched were all pictorializations or ideational expressions of
the *essential affective substance* she hoped to make her own
and to maintain viably in her nuclear self. Her later dreams
of pleasure in her creative work were evidence that to some
extent this had occurred. Whether that essential affective
substance was experienced as a quality of her mother (a
breast-feeding experience), her father (his penis), or her own
sensually gratifying genital is not at issue since, in principle
(though, of course, not terms of experienced levels of development, or in the unquestionably necessary practical steps of
content analysis), they were each of them the equivalent of
the other. They would, if transformed into an abiding, positive sense of self, enable the patient, to a far greater extent

than she had ever been able to before, to survive on her own, fueled by her own inner sense of well-being.

The major therapeutic efforts of the analysis clearly did not follow the classical model of interpretation of oedipal and preoedipal configurations and of making conscious the unconscious conflicts arising from these. Considerable therapeutic work did focus on raising to consciousness affects about which the patient had previously been unaware, for example, her intense rage with her mother for her indifference, with her father for his having "failed" her by not living up to her idealization of him. But making conscious such affects not previously fully experienced is not unique to the analysis of patients with disorders of the self; it is part and parcel of every well-conducted analysis. The crucial work lay in a different arena. It centered around (1) the establishment of the optimal therapeutic atmosphere (including the analyst's emotional engagement with the patient) which would permit the patient to overcome the self-consciousness and embarrassment of the revelation of early self-object childhood needs for a responsive and acknowledging, mirroring and idealizing experience with the analyst; and (2) the verbalized acknowledgment and explanation of the meaning of those self-object wishes in depth in the transference (see Kohut, 1977, pp. 257-258, for a discussion of these two aspects of the therapeutic task).

Putting aside the specifics of the case, what the patient experienced with the analyst was consistent understanding responsiveness and understanding recognition of the nuances of her self-experiences—these stated in words as close to what the patient felt or said, or could not yet say, as empathy with her childhood states of loneliness, rage, and of her passion for love in all its forms would allow. Specifically, the patient's old farmhouse dream, with the coming to life of the woman in the casket, was an indication that her previously deadened (ignored) nuclear self was stirred to life by the analyst's responsive presence and the overall encouragement of the analytic atmosphere.

What the patient experienced that enabled her to allow the dead woman to come to life was that the analyst did not withdraw and, as had her self-objects in her childhood past, again leave her to effect her own pathological reorganization of a cohesive self, a self still dominated by archaic wishes, fears, and rage. Instead, he helped her to mobilize and recognize those primary affective states and her injured core self by persisting in the face of the outrage of her narcissistically wounded self-esteem. As this was done in a sustained and reasonably competent fashion, the remobilized transference wishes — not necessarily an exact reproduction of early childhood states (cf. Kohut, 1971, pp. 123-125) — could be worked through and modulated by the process of transmuting internalization (Kohut, 1971). She could then become a self-satisfying connoisseur who could more surely gratify herself, and she could be satisfied with her more securely functioning self without having to rely to such an inordinate degree on the mirroring by or merger with idealized "others," or without having to retreat from the inevitable failure in those relationships into isolation and pathologically frozen self-absorption. And the strengthened enlargement of those newly developed sectors of her self-object and self-experience could then be more consistently relied on to maintain a sense of essential self-esteem and self-worth.

I have attempted to make clear how an appreciation of the insights of self-object psychology offers a valuable approach to the understanding of hysterical character disorders. I suggest that some psychopathological constellations that have previously been formulated as structural hysterical disorders are, like this case, in fact a variety of a narcissistic personality disorder with certain variables that give them an overtly hysterical stamp. The treatment of such patients in terms of oedipal and preoedipal pathology may lead to adventitious improvements or therapeutic failures. More far-reaching and more valid analyses of such patients may be effected using the insights of self-object psychology and the necessarily altered therapeutic attitude that arises from those insights.

7

A CASE OF CHRONIC NARCISSISTIC VULNERABILITY

The following case report and commentary consist of a summary of a detailed set of process notes covering two and a half years of an analysis that lasted somewhat over three years. The material was made available to the casebook group by a colleague from another community. Although only sketchy notes were kept of the last eight months of the analysis and there was a paucity of material describing the analyst's subjective thoughts and feelings at many points in the analysis, we decided to include the case nonetheless. Although hardly an exemplary analysis, it raises a number of basic provocative questions, some of which still cannot be answered with any degree of certainty. The case possessed two important attributes in that it was considered uniquely appropriate for analysis and was understood and managed by the analyst in a way that led to dramatic results in a short period of time.

Our group saw two sets of issues arising from the case: one having to do with the patient's dramatic therapeutic transformation, the other with the patient's pathology and its

determining influence upon his experience in the transference. Unresolved is the question of whether this truly was an
analysis, even within the limits of the circumstances and parameters one may have to accept with certain pathological
personalities, regardless of whether the pathology is along narcissistic or object-libidinal lines. We were particularly concerned with the manner in which certain transference configurations seemed to be well elaborated, yet others, although
clearly present, barely came into focus. In addition, there was
a good deal of discussion among members of the casebook
group regarding a striking feature of the transference experience: the vivid and dramatic manner in which the analyst
appeared to tune into the most severe and disabling level of
the patient's pathology and managed to respond, almost
from the very beginning, to his needs in a way that was extremely effective.

The second set of issues, on a more theoretical level, has
to do with the nature of the patient's pathology, its origin
and its influence upon the transference as well as on his life.
We have coined the empirically derived term *chronic narcissistic vulnerability* to describe an individual who suffers a
lifelong and at times acutely disabling deficiency in his (ego)
capacity to manage internally generated, nonspecific narcissistic tensions and who is at the same time unusually vulnerable to unpredictable and unexpected stimulation from the reality world. The patient about to be described seemed to suffer
from an imbalance between chronic internal tensions, unpredictable stimuli from his object world, and his ego's regulatory
capacity. These tensions were diffuse, primitive, and not
organized around any particular fantasy; they lacked the
qualities of ideational configurations or specific object direction that would suggest they were either predominantly
aggressive or libidinal in nature. This is not to gainsay that
such tensions do not hint at a specific genetic origin through

their resemblance to developmental fixations. One of the intriguing questions illustrated and partially answered by this case is the relation between three elements: clearly defined psychosexual phases and their normative conflicts; chronic but periodically intense failures of function by the empathic parental self-objects; and the failure of integration of phase-appropriate, self-management structures and ego defenses.

From the point of view of developmental pathology, this case raises the issue of the relation between two kinds of trauma: (1) small, but persistent failures of empathy experienced by the developing child and resultant lifelong difficulty with proper integration and management of tensions; (2) the massive, "once-only" failures of a narcissistic self-object through such things as death, abandonment, or psychosis, which lead to a chronic vulnerability to unexpected events like rejections, separations, and losses. This patient experienced both kinds of trauma.

The major technical issue raised by this man's pathology, which colored the entire analysis, was the tendency for his ego to feel impaired from two directions simultaneously. From within he was in danger of being chronically flooded by nonspecific, primitive, narcissistic tensions that could be related to the burden of his always "out of tune" mother. From without, his analyst's unfortunately long absence due to severe illness stirred an acute traumatic disintegration in him that resembled his reaction to his mother's probable depressive psychosis. Thus, within the analysis he experienced an inevitable re-enactment of early developmental experiences in which he was subject to inappropriate overstimulation and disruption, and also to gross abandonment.

Several of these issues will have light shed upon them through the data presented in this case report. However, even by the end of the discussion and the conclusions, some of them will have to be left open and uncertain. Nonetheless, even the effort to struggle toward incomplete understanding will have served a constructive purpose for the curious psychoanalytic scholar.

A summary of the analyst's process notes is interspersed with commentary and is followed by a discussion that elaborates on the issues just presented.

The Patient's Background

Mr. B. was a 26-year-old graduate student in the process of getting a divorce at the time he came, self-referred, for analysis. He suffered a combination of vague subjective complaints together with a clear sense that "there was something wrong inside." In his social relationships he felt unable to get himself or his life together; his chronic sleep difficulties were now significantly worse; he was having trouble completing his Ph.D. in sociology at the university where he taught. He felt his relations with his wife typified his problems with women. Initially, he tended to be enthusiastically carried away by the subjective pleasures of a new experience, especially the relief of his chronic tension, but within a few weeks of a new affair, he would become profoundly upset and depressed, reactions he ascribed as much to something within himself as to the failures of the woman.

A six-month psychotherapy experience had been undertaken the preceding year at his former university — ostensibly to save his troubled marriage. For reasons unclear, it had ended in a stalemate. The patient stopped it while roundly blaming himself for its failure. He seemed to have good contact with his own feelings and was particularly intent on understanding himself. Although my initial understanding was somewhat tentative, I felt he was a suitable candidate for analysis. I was particularly impressed by his ability to organize his life so as to provide situations of respite in isolation in order to recover his own inner balance and to restore his energies. As nearly as I could tell from his descriptions, he was considered a very competent teacher, and, despite a checkered academic history—he had made several major changes in his choice of career—he seemed to be deeply invested in his current work. Although he was relatively attractive and youthful looking, his over-all appearance had a disheveled, disorganized, adolescent quality.

By way of background: He was the older of two boys born to a troubled Southern family. Father was a hard-working but not very effective lawyer, preoccupied with running his wife's family business. Mother, the offspring of a genteel important local family, sounded as if she were chronically preoccupied with herself and her own somatic discomforts. After the death of her twins in childbirth when the patient was about two and a half years old, mother's troubles had become much more florid. Mr. B. was taken care of by a succession of maids for the following two years.

Mr. B. had been a rather vigorously outgoing, outdoorsy sort of youngster, intellectually bright but physically inept. By his mid-adolescence, he felt the atmosphere of home to be unbearably oppressive, although in the initial interviews, the reason was not clear. There was a sense of father's preoccupation with his own business and his ultimate subservience to mother's manipulative self-concerned needs, together with some evidence that the mother was endlessly focused on the patient, but in some painful (for him) way. Being a good student, the patient elected to go to school as soon as possible, but he flunked out of college after a promising start. Essentially at the family's insistence, he shifted to pre-law in another university and eventually graduated. After two years of law school he again became upset, quit, got married, and shifted fields of study again. Despite the family's objections, he transferred to a graduate program in sociology. Because the family then withdrew financial support, he has been fully self-supporting since.

Case Report

Mr. B. had several preliminary interviews during which analysis was discussed as the method of choice for his long-standing, diffuse, self-focused complaints, especially in the light of his previous treatment failure. At what was planned to be the first couch hour, he appeared obviously uncomfortable and disorganized and indicated his wish to sit up, and, of course, I accepted that. He spoke mainly about his current life: the decision regarding the divorce is now final, his teaching is flat and empty, and yet his role as teacher is the only one in which he feels truly comfortable. He asked if I had seen a particular movie, and before I had time to answer, he burst into an emotional statement about the uniqueness and value of each individual's life in society; he then broke into tears. After recovering, he indicated that he is attempting to solve some of the economic problems in his life, to settle his coming teaching contract, and to get on with his Ph.D. problems. I said it sounded as if he had been making plans for the analysis. He is convinced that the essential thing in his life is to know really better what he thinks and feels, but he fears his feelings are almost too chaotic to be described even when he can recognize them. He spoke glowingly of his younger brother and then about his unsuccessful efforts to make contact with his father and share some of the pleasure of fishing with him. He talked bitterly about his mother's complicated combination of controlling him and rejecting him. His feelings in this area are terribly chaotic; he is afraid he is going to weep again because there is so much he has to get out. When I suggested that we had a good deal of time and that he could take things as slowly as he needed to, he was visibly relieved.

The next hour—the first couch hour—he began by informing me that his penis is sore and that he is worried about it. He is angry at the way his mother always made him color his feelings about everything. He is equally angry at Betty, the wife he has just divorced, in part because he was unable to have intercourse with her for the last year or so of their marriage. Now my ceiling appears to be filled with images of vaginas and breasts. He has always been afraid of women and very inhibited in his relations with them before marriage. Now, as he feels calmer, the patterns in the ceiling appear less frightening and more geometric. He wonders why the marriage never really felt safe to him, and he thinks of his mother's endless warnings to him about the dangers of the world—flying, driving, diseases, and the like. He wonders if he is afraid of silence. When I intervened and asked him if my silence was bothering him, he responded irritably that his mother always used to intervene in similar silences and insist on an answer to her question, "What's the matter, what's the matter? Why aren't you talking to me?" He thinks analysis was his choice in contradistinction to having more psychotherapy, which he felt forced to enter in graduate school because of his wife's pressure and the impending disintegration of his marriage. He used to be uncontrollably furious at her because of her inability to be completely predictable and completely available. He once broke the shift lever on his car by slamming it with his hand when she was late returning from shopping. He wonders why I am seeing him at such a modest fee, and decides it must be because I am especially concerned about him, and then asks me for detailed confimation of this. I agree in general with his concern, but suggest that if I were to answer, it would stop his associations and he would feel intruded upon. He laughed delightedly. How lucky he feels to have somebody who is this understanding of him. He again broke into tears.

He began the next hour by informing me that he had been to the doctor who assured him that his penis is all right, and then he told me of a collection of miscellaneous psychosomatic symptoms, which he suspects are the result of his current anxiety. He is pleased to be able to tell me about his chronic impulsive anger, and wonders why it is such a terribly upsetting thing. I said it must be especially upsetting when the anger catches him by surprise. In response, he rolled over, half sitting up, looked at me in amazement, and asked how I could be so fully understanding so quickly. He sometimes beats his pedigree cat. Even as a child of three he used to lose his temper uncontrollably. He and his father started throwing punches at each other when he was thirteen, as a result of which he was sent to a psychiatrist for several interviews. One of the things he likes about living in the woods in the country by himself is how peaceful he feels as he watches birds and small animals feed in his various feeders. How difficult it is at times for him to sleep when he is so angry and chaotic. He recalled similar difficulties sleeping when he was sent at age two and a half to his grandfather's house when his mother lost the twins. He thinks this is because they left his teddy bear at home. As he left, he remarked on how worked up he gets in these hours, and yet how he manages to calm down by the end.

He came in for the next hour dressed in a somewhat more organized manner and immediately told me that he has decided to inform me about his masturbation. He confessed that he only began doing it since he entered graduate school, although his mother accused him of masturbating in high school when he was confined to bed in a long leg cast for several months at the age of fourteen. Almost casually, he added that part of the problem between himself and his wife was his premature ejaculation, and he immediately went back to the problem of his anger. Despite the fact that he and his brother are good friends now, until he left home in adolescence, he and his brother fought all the time and fairly violently. Nevertheless, he envied his brother's ability to have stayed out of the parents' fights, whereas he was endlessly brought in, especially through his mother's enticements via her hypochondriacal complaints. She made him feel helpless, guilty, and inadequate that he was not able to do more for her; he immediately associated to a torrent of sadistic fantasies for this manipulation. He noted that he often comes to a pause in his associations in the latter part of the hour, and, as he begins to feel more alive, the designs in the ceilings and walls and doors come alive, sometimes pleasantly, sometimes unpleasantly. At the moment, he sees vaginas and penises and dismembered parts of bodies floating around. Despite all of this, he feels that he is gradually lifting a vast weight off his chest.

As a three-year-old, he was so clumsy that he constantly bumped into things. As a result, he was required to wear glasses and has worn them ever since. He nonetheless remained relatively uncoordinated until the middle of his adolescence. He complained that I am not structuring things and connecting them up very well for him. I told him I hoped to do it gradually, but I did not think it was time yet. He thinks I am right to be taking things so slowly. In the ninth hour he felt under terrible pressure, and he wondered if I would prescribe sleeping pills for him because it was undoubtedly the lack of sleep that was wrecking him.

He confessed to kicking his cat after thinking about his rotten marriage. This was a Monday hour, and he told me of two dreams, one from Thursday and one from Friday. In the first one, he was with Betty and trying to keep from ejaculating, but very disgusted with himself because he couldn't. In the second dream, he was lying on the floor with a woman student of his, but her father was there so he had to be very discreet; he was pleased with how comfortable he was, just lying there quietly with her. He talked more about his problems with sleeping and his endless ups and downs with sleeping pills. At the end of the hour he asked me directly if I would prescribe sleeping pills for him. I demurred, indicating that I thought the issues needed analyzing, and he accepted this disappointment quite readily.

He was struck by how well he felt after the last hour and how, for the first time in many months, he was able to get some creative scholarly writing done the night before. He wondered if the upset weekends are related to missing the analysis. At the end of the hour, he remarked that I have a nice warm smile. When he said that things seemed dull because nothing very much is going on in his outside life, I responded that perhaps more is going on inside him now. In the following hour he expressed annoyance at my previous remark and then talked about his mother's endless ritualization of the relationship. For instance, he had to kiss her good-night when she went to bed. He had a dream in which he was living at home in a small town and had gone to the post office to mail a package, but the woman clerk deliberately overweighed the package, and, even though the patient accused the clerk of cheating him, he paid what he was asked because some other woman came in and convinced him that he had been wrong to argue. For most of his childhood and adolescence, mother dressed him in clothes that felt "peculiar." Since going to college he had discovered that everything he owned was actually too long for him. He now realizes that Monday hours are terribly tense, and it is only after Tuesday that he finally begins to calm down; he suspects that this is similar to his inability to calm down after separations from his wife. Can I help him understand why at times he feels so empty and so needy of his exwife and at other times so unmanageably outraged? Sometimes he feels he needs her so much that he actually couldn't bear to see her; it is just too disorganizing. He is immensely pleased with the fact that I listen and remember. The analysis is like a very special gift, and he hopes he will be able to trust me even more.

[Almost from the very beginning of his first diagnostic interview the patient demonstrated vividly how he will experience the analysis. He was able to verbalize remarkably clearly the sense of chronical inability to manage states of tension. He was able to describe his endless fear of surprise and disappointment by the unexpectedness of people's reactions to him. His response to this is regression to archaic states of disorganization, irritability, and helplessness — that is, to a kind of partial fragmentation. He responds to the analyst as if he were pretuned to her minimal expressions of appropriate empathy. Most important of all is her apparent readiness to respond in his terms, at his level of need, whatever that may be. Initially, she seems to have to do so very little, almost simply to "be there" in the background in order to diminish his chronic readiness to fragment. Naturally, he is hyperalert to changes in his own tension states, and this becomes the basis for his capacity to know and to describe what he needs in contrast to what he has missed in his background. And he hints at the expectation of finding what he needs from the analyst — finding it automatically available and not having to ask. Granted that this man had several months of preparatory psychotherapy, it is still striking that he required no "education" in the process of introspection. He seemed to "know" what to do with himself, as if he were both open to his own inner experiences and capable of verbalizing them constructively.

Of some importance is how clearly he set forth at this early point in the analysis the pattern for the use he is going to make of the analyst's interpretations: He will submit her specific interpretations (especially their quantitative features) to his own searching scrutiny. This may be explained in part as an "alertness," protective of his chronic, lifelong state of internal uneasiness — a useful defense suggestive of some basic weakness in the [external?] stimulus barrier. It also suggests the probability of persistent early experience with a mother who, while she might have been responsive, was always intrusive or always out of tune with his needs. The analyst should therefore expect him to be perpetually hypersensitive to any interpretive error in the nature of a failure to be tuned into his more precise psychoeconomic need state.]

I canceled the following hour because of a minor illness, and when he came in, he remarked on how surprised he was to hear me call him by his last name; he feels really as if he should be called Ronald, or Ronnie, like a kid. He is afraid he is holding something back and wonders if he should open his chest and bare his soul. The night following the canceled hour he had a dream of being at the camp where he had been very unhappy in his preadolescent and early adolescent years. A real war was going on, kids were hurt, bleeding. There was terrible shelling and bombing, destroying everything; a Marine officer had come and attempted to rescue the patient by leading all to safety. He saved his camera and binoculars, even though a bad soldier had attempted to steal them. When I asked him what had happened to precipitate the dream last night, he snapped at me that the dream had come early that morning and not last night. In the next hour he was angry, blaming it on a stupid lecture he had attended and during which he had almost fallen asleep. The hour ended with him alternating this with a description of how peaceful he feels lying on my couch—even when I don't understand him. Sometimes the patterns and lines in the ceiling and walls remind him of his mother's scarred abdomen (from a Caesarean section). Despite his panicky feelings at the idea that the divorce might have annihilated him, he is pleased to discover that it hasn't.

Seeing me every day is a kind of "anchoring" experience, yet he is disturbed by the peaceful tranquillity he experiences here because of the periodic intrusion of these extraordinarily vivid, abstract geometric patterns on the ceilings and the walls. It is almost as if the patterns come alive and have some existence independent of his creating them. Usually, they become transformed into dismembered naked women—arms, faces, breasts, vaginas, and then back again to patterns. Could this kind of discomfort be related to my being a woman, or is it a holdover effect from the crazy tennis-match, "competitive challenge" character of his previous psychotherapy?

Mr. B. reported, after a brief vacation break, how pleased he was with the trip he took with his new girl friend, but then he became very upset. He is afraid I will restrict or inhibit his sexual relationship with this girl, and he wants to reassure me how important it is. Once, however, she showed up early for a date with him at a time when he was planning one of his new classes, and he became so disorganized that he couldn't eat with her and had to send her away. He is equally chaotic in his verbalizations with me, and I finally suggested that he had probably been disorganized by his rage at the young woman who he felt was demanding something of him when he was preoccupied with something else. Immensely relieved at this interpretation, he described how the situation with the girl reminds him somehow of his mother who hooked up a loud buzzer (like a fire alarm) in his room so that she could call him down whenever she required his presence. Inevitably this led to a temper tantrum, although sooner or later he did go downstairs. His tension gradually subsided, and he dozed for a few minutes. He woke up and wondered if the real problem was that he could not seem to pay some attention to his own needs. And this led into wondering about me and my life, but, after all, it is his feelings and his ideas that count and, for the first time, he confessed laughingly to the wish to hug me and kiss me and hold me or even invite me to a dinner of freshly caught bass.

He is convinced that I really know just what he is going to say almost before he says it, in contrast to his mother's inept responsiveness, her utter inability to tolerate anyone's anger or discomfort or estrangement. He worries about this increasing need for me to keep him "plugged in and tuned up" (that is, to himself) so that he can use his own energies constructively, to work on his thesis and continue with a new course he is developing. He is dramatically aware of his increasing vulnerability to separations from me, as well as from the girl friend. One childhood solution consisted of his looking for "excitement" when his parents left him alone in the house by rummaging through his mother's drawers and then feeling her underclothing—especially against his cheek! By age five he learned to read, and he quit head-banging and head-rolling. Maybe that has something to do with the driven quality of his academic activities; starting in grammar school he felt he never could learn enough, and he seethed with a constant, driven sense of having to push himself further, intellectually.

He had a nightmare in which enemy agents (guerillas?) have taken as hostage a close friend of his, a good-natured man. They threaten to shoot him despite the patient's desperate efforts to intervene, politically and monetarily. He sees the dream as involving the two parts of himself, one of which he described as treasonable and destructive, that is, enraged, anti-establishment and disorganizing. His rage is directed alternately between his exwife and his girl friend; this led to memories of his mother's failures, for instance, the palliative, "pretend" quality of her solutions: mother immediately jumped in when somebody was frustrated or hurt to offer an inadequate, poorly timed, or just plain wrong solution, but one with which everyone had to agree. In his home, happiness was rather like an embalming fluid, a state to be maintained even if it drowned everything else. A rage episode at his girl friend, precipitated by her unreliability, reminds him of his childhood rages; after one disappointment in his mother, he clenched his teeth so hard that he actually destroyed his orthodontic retainer and wound up with a mouthful of broken plastic. He is particularly pleased with my ability to listen and to wait, and to let him do his own learning here. My presence is invaluable, but not always my words—even my best words! He becomes distrustful of my seeing him at such a low fee, and wonders if I will turn out to be just like his mother, or perhaps I am the superwoman that somebody with his craziness really needs. In response to an unempathic comment I made, he had a dream about playing a game of handball in which he couldn't seem to hit the ball correctly, feeling that he must attempt desperately to place each shot perfectly. In the course of this dream, he became exhausted. In associating to the dream, he said I was failing to keep him plugged in and he feels he has lost me, like the little teddy bear that was lost on the trip to his grandparents. As the spring separation neared, he became calmer and more active in his hours, discussing his intellectual work at considerable extent and with much pleasure.

In the first hour after my return from spring vacation, Mr. B. appeared disheveled again and complained about a number of psychosomatic symptoms and a general disorganization in his working life. His mother is pressuring him to

come home next summer, and he confessed to his erratic
anger at me, overtly because I had just left him. He had quit
his earlier treatment in the first hour after his previous psy-
chotherapist returned from a lengthy six-week vacation. He
had a frightening dream — animals getting killed in a forest
fire, his woods being destroyed, etc. His rage continued, and
he talked about all the people who had left him and the inevitable disruption that ensued. I suggested that the un-
manageability of the tension, no matter what its type,
seemed to be the thing that wrecked his ability to organize
himself and to think competently. He expressed relief. In
adolescence he discovered that other households did not work
like his; in his household, dinner was any time between five
and ten in the evening, whenever his mother apparently had
enough to drink, and he wonders about his terrible difficulties with time, which so far have not interfered with the
analysis. He is curious about the suddenness with which he
had fallen into a relationship with a young woman student of
his, a relationship which was now beginning to break up because of her increasing unreliability and demands. Did he
begin the relationship with her in order to protect
himself from turning his feelings in a totally intense way on
the analyst? He played with his pipe during this hour, for the
first time, and then smoked it. He asked me then about my
summer vacation plans. He wondered if it wouldn't be better
for him not to miss any more analysis than was absolutely necessary, but then confessed that maybe he would like to take
a week off on his own after my vacation. He had a pleasant
fantasy of his father's visit and a kind of real closeness
developing between himself and his father. He cried momentarily, became thoughtful, and said: "You know, I really
know nothing of listening to myself; this is my first experience with it." He continued to be puzzled by his rage reactions to me. Sometimes when I am silent, he is perfectly

content; at other times the tension mounts unbearably. Sometimes he can't wait for my first intervention, and at other times he feels like leaving as soon as I open my mouth. He recalled that one always had to respond to mother after she said something about herself. She incessantly and intrusively kept after you until you'd make some confirming response to her description of her current emotional state. It is never really dialogue. I suggested that perhaps he has felt he existed only for his mother when she needed him or he her, and his response was, "Oh, my God, you're so right!" That is why he raises cats. At least they need him all the time, and he feels that he "exists" when they lick his hand and come up to him and nuzzle him.

Last weekend he visited some friends who had a five-year-old girl, and impulsively Mr. B. had decided to take her for a walk. The child was so delighted with the way he was able to encourage her to talk that she looked up, told him he was a very nice man, and spontaneously hugged him; Mr. B. nearly cried. He indicated that he'd like to end the hour at this point and wondered if I would be angry at him, and then was pleased to discover that it was virtually the end of the hour.

Suddenly he is angry with everybody, me, his mother, his exwife Betty, his current girl friend. He is annoyed by the diplomas on the wall of my new office—nothing is familiar. His parents have rented his room to a young college student and they seem, in his words, "very cheerful about having replaced me." Sometimes he feels annihilated by not really knowing whether or not I'm interested, or understand him even if I am interested. He notes how pleased he is when I remember what he had said six months ago, or when I don't seem particularly perturbed when he dozes off during hours. He doesn't really want to know where I am going on vacation because he might not be able to manage the enormous curiosity and overstimulation he will experience if I discuss any personal details of my life with him. Humorously, he wonders if there is any point in his having sexual fantasies about me since I am obviously not going to have an affair with him!

He had a dream about taking a trip, and it reminds him of how he used to comfort himself when his parents left him alone by endlessly searching through their empty suitcases, but without any specific goal in mind. Then he dreamed about an excellent college teacher of his who inspired his interest in sociology. He thinks he went into teaching because the finest, most responsive people he knew in his grade-school years were teachers. As the time for vacation arrived, he became increasingly anxious and finally asked me where I was going. I told him. He toyed with the idea of seeing another therapist on an emergency basis during my absence, and then wondered whether he might secretly date my secretary as a substitute, but decided that he is still endlessly searching for the mother that must have existed before all those interruptions or whatever it was that went wrong. When I leave him, he fears that part of himself will get lost. As we approached our last two hours, he had a dream about an empty lake resort town and how upset he is to discover his parents there. Their own cottage is different and unusual in that it has a special room for his older brother, and he is surprised at this. Moreover, something seems to have happened to his little fishing launch: it has become an ordinary-looking, underpowered row boat which he can't make work. People still tease his mother on several occasions for having pinned his skin to his diapers without knowing it when he was an infant. He expects me to make everything right, since I am as powerful now as she was then. Putting me out of his mind for a month, as his mother would advise, is a rotten solution. In the final hour before summer vacation he was depressed and silent and said straightforwardly that he doesn't want to get into anything that would have to be interrupted because it would simply be too disturbing. Slowly he drifted off into telling me how choked up he is with his feelings of gratitude for how much better he feels in the mere eight months we have been working. Ten minutes before the end of the hour, he sat up and indicated that he'd like to go. I said I understood; he shook my hand and wished me a good vacation.

[These several months have seen several striking developments. He noted increasingly the calming effect of talking in analysis, and tried to sort out both the meaning and the reliability of this experience. Frequently, however, he seemed burdened by the analyst's attempts at interpretive intervention and also by her silence. Similarly, he became aware of his distress at separations from and reunions with the analyst. His uneasiness in situations of extreme gratification from her were in a sense equivalent in quantitative terms to his anger and hopelessness when her properly empathic responsiveness was unavailable to him. The inference is that an incomplete primitive merger with her seemed crucial to his well-being at this time. Frequently her responses never seemed to be exactly right, presumably because his internally based cohesiveness and stability were so fragile.

Mr. B. introduced several content themes rather casually (another "safety" characteristic of his), and the analyst may not have fully recognized their significance. (1) There were a number of dramatic examples of the mother's appallingly aggressive, intrusive, primitive controlling behavior with him, especially her use of bizarre measures to prevent the development of what was ultimately to become his salvation: a capacity to achieve at least partial, temporary "respite" separations from her. (2) He formed impulsive attachments to girl students of his, relationships that started out very

enthusiastically and somehow came apart at the seams within
a month or two. (3) There were occasions during hours when
he became quite drowsy, stopped talking, and once even
dozed off. When this came up, he associated to his adult-ac-
quired masturbation as producing an essentially similar,
drowsy, soothing state, and reminded the analyst that he was
a head-roller and head-banger as a child. The patient
seems to have become comfortable enough in his regression
to elaborate clearly but incompletely the major traumatic
developmental experiences of his childhood. From the dream
material, from his tendency in times of crisis to soothe himself
with fantasy images of distorted female body parts and,
finally, even to resort to dozing in the hour as a comforting
experience, it may be surmised that the single crucial trauma
of the patient's life was the effect on their relationship of the
mother's pregnancy when he was two and a half. He seems to
have experienced this pregnancy not only as a traumatic
stimulus, but also as a dramatic abandonment of the grossest
sort. On top of that, it initiated a profound deterioration
process in her. However faulty her mothering might have
been before, it appeared to have become significantly worse
after this pregnancy. The typical psychosexual developmental processes for that phase, i.e., early phallic, seem to have
given a specific coloring and content to Mr. B.'s adaptive,
compromise solutions: a regression to a kind of oral soothing,
by himself; a kind of biting, tearing rage at the bad female
procreative parts; self-soothing, physiologically based acts
leading to a pattern of primitive efforts to do defiantly and
stubbornly for himself what mother failed to do. Unfortunately his adaptations remained poorly integrated and
readily fell apart, leading to a further regressive externalization, substitution, and, ultimately, danger of fragmentation. He anticipates the analyst's leaving by attempting
to substitute other women and other (part) objects because

his own recently acquired functions are still so terribly weak. In that sense he seems to be repeating what might have been his own primitive ineffective self-management efforts at the time of the mother's withdrawal.]

Typically, when we resumed he was initially quite uncomfortable and disheveled. He had had few crises except for the chronic, running battle with his exwife. He literally does not have enough money to pay her settlement and to do his Ph.D. at the same time. Although analysis does help him in a very genuine way, he cannot manage the flood of anger he feels upon my return. I interpreted his anger in relation to making the readjustment to my function in his life and thereby getting into a new balanced state, involving me. This seemed to overstimulate rather than calm him. Within about four or five hours he calmed down and told me humorously how irrationally angry he had been with me. Nevertheless, it was good to be himself here as he never could be with his mother.

Mr. B. wonders how much I really am like his mother; will I grill him about his behavior, will I insist on knowing what he does every weekend? Will I insist that he make every appointment on time and never ask for a schedule change? He suspects that some of his intense concern over how angry he is with me, even now, is in terms of not being able to manage the fear that his own separate independence may damage me somehow — but he doesn't follow this up. He had a dream in which he was off with his brother in a nature park filled with animals, especially bears. There was a great open place, all in technicolor and everything was beautiful except that he kept getting his feet stuck in the mud flats and had great trouble walking. It had areas that looked ghostly, like a moonscape. He was there with all sorts of people from various times in his life, and then, strangely enough, the bears turned into people and he kept trying to take pictures of them. He associated to this his desire to learn to be a decent photographer. He wondered about his desire to take a week off and visit the Isle Royale with his new girl. He feels like the little toddler who is just learning to walk and, while he is uncertain of his feet, is really terribly eager to try it on his own. Did he ever tell me that as a little toddler he had been locked out of many of the rooms of his parents' house because he was so clumsy and uncoordinated he was constantly blundering into things and breaking them?

He informed his exwife that he really doesn't intend to continue paying her at the rate he was doing, that his needs are important too. But this decision made him feel terribly anxious, as if something vital was continuously being lost. He has found a new girl, much more reliable than the one that he had been going with for the first few months of the analysis. I announced that I would have to cancel two hours at the end of September, and he accepted this without much question. He had a dream about having trouble getting admitted to a hospital because of something being wrong with his stomach, but he isn't particulary afraid of dying. He associated with pleasure to childhood experiences with hospitals because they had always been delightful places where he was the center of a good deal of attentive interest, so much so that on two different occasions as a child he cried when it came time to leave the hospital to go back home.

Although his life seems to be going along better at the moment, he fears that sooner or later he is going to do something that will disrupt the reliability of my effectiveness with him. Once again he fears the world coming apart, and he is becoming unplugged from me. Did he ever mention to me that he was severely punished by his parents when he was seven for coming to the aid of a small friend of his who was being attacked by a bigger boy? He hit the bigger boy on the head with a baseball bat, causing a concussion. He gets so upset when he is not able to understand why his relations with people go so wrong, especially when they take the form of their unpredictable disapproval of him.

He suspects he might be upset at the two hours I am planning to take off, not because he will miss me so, but because it disrupts his expectations. Matters become more complicated because I was sick the hour following the two canceled hours. Mr. B. then called to cancel the next or fourth hour in a row.

The significance of these separation experiences was revealed immediately, when I informed him that in about a week's time I was scheduled for completely unexpected gastro-intestinal surgery which would keep me out for four to eight weeks. He was terribly upset, but recovered enough to assure me he could manage himself alone, and to hope I would be OK. The reason he canceled the Friday hour was because he was frightened by his own behavior concerning a particular incident. He had forgotten his boat keys in school and in order to get into his boat he had had to force the hatch open. This had precipitated a series of "assault" fantasies which culminated in his preparing to initiate a fraudulent insurance claim: i.e., his boat had been broken into by robbers and valuable items had been stolen from the cabin. He stimulated the rather imaginative son (of the marina manager) to support his story about having seen some evil-looking fellows sneaking around the dock and actually wrote a letter to the insurance company, but he came to his senses before he mailed it. He confessed that he doesn't understand how he could think of doing such a bizarre thing. He recalled that the week before this episode, he had the overwhelming urge to buy some expensive boating and fishing gear. That *must* have been his reaction to my cancellation of the previous hours. There doesn't seem to be much point in talking further, though, since I am going to be away. He dreamed of

some unknown woman who was leaving him, and he was
feeling pain and frustrated while waiting for a phone call
from her. The dream expresses his reaction to the coming
separation. Recently he has been watching me very carefully, and he wonders if at the age of two or three he could
have watched his mother's pregnancy that alertly. Will I
think about him while I am in the hospital? Will he be able
to manage without my giving him a prescription for sleeping
pills? Noting his recently more erratic behavior with his
friends, he decided that my chief function to him seems to be
to stabilize his life, especially in his nonanalytic relationships,
and he wonders how well he is going to be able to take over
that function during my absence. At the end he sat up,
smiled, and said he will keep an eye on himself for me and he
hopes I will do OK in surgery. I called him in about a week
to tell him the surgery had gone well, but that I would be re-
cuperating for another six weeks. He was clearly deeply appreciative.

When the treatment resumed, he indicated that things
seemed to be better. He had become aware that he is now
able to be with people for the sake of the experience and the
activity, rather than just to fulfill his need to have someone —
anyone — present. He has been increasingly active with his
male friends in my absence, but the frantic uncertainty and
reactivity to his girl friend continues. He has transformed the
crazy fantasy of the thieves breaking into his boat into a plot
for a novel he is writing, but which winds up with the "hero"
becoming more and more paranoid and ending up in a
bullet-proof house, shooting it out with the enemy agents. He
is uneasy about having substituted for a friend as an un-
trained leader in a group process session with students, and
wondered if I can help him in this activity. I referred him to
some resources. He wondered if there is a relation between
his memory of his mother's endless, bizarre, ruminative
worrying about herself after the death of the twins and his

peculiar insensitivity in not sending me flowers when I was hospitalized. He had a dream in which he gets lost in the wilderness lakes because of his inadequate maps; and the maps change into admission forms for commitment to a mental hospital, and then he realizes that he is the one who had been committed, but that it wasn't irrevocable, and, besides, someone nice is there who seemed helpful. In the end it becomes a nightmare when some big shape looms up behind him; terrified, he awoke. I suggested that I was the threatening shape that had frightened him. He insisted I was wrong since I was the nice somebody who was going to make everything come out OK. He associated to a sadistic teasing babysitter who cared for him the year after his mother lost the twins.

As a result of an unavoidable cancellation on my part he became furious, saying, "When you're here, I can act sensibly in my own behalf. Without you I can't think of anything except the immediate, urgent situation of the moment." The next trauma was the cancellation of his scholarship funds for the coming two-month summer session, during which he had planned to be in residence at his former university completing work on his thesis. He came in, threw the letter from Washington in my lap, and confessed to enraged fantasies of "bombing the Capitol," while pacing back and forth. He became more frantic, finally pleading with me, "Doctor, please help me. I am going to explode." I talked to him about how reasonable his disappointment was over having the grant withdrawn after it had been promised, connecting this to previous experiences of disappointment with his mother, when she failed to maintain his self-esteem. As he calmed down enough to sit, he said that the real hell of feeling this way is that he knows he is childish, but he is unable to prevent it. At the end of the hour, he got up and asked me to come to the window to see his new (i.e., used) jeep. I admired it, and he was pleased.

He wonders about dating my secretary, but decides he is setting a trap for me in that he expects my permission, approval, and guidance. He would be outraged and enraged if I were to take over those functions, but disappointed if I didn't. One of things that decides him against it is that my secretary probably types up some of my material about him, and it would simply be too sticky! His curiosity about me focused initially along conventional lines: Why am I not married? What is my personal life like? I suggested he was attempting to sort out the difference between his fear of hurting me by being aggressively intrusive and even angry as against hurting me by simply *having* certain feelings or questions with my permission. He admitted that he really didn't want me to answer the question; still, it seemed so unfair that I should know everything about him and he should know nothing about me. This was followed by a striking dream of himself, his father, and his brother taking care of a very demanding, unmanageable baby elephant, which he associated to various aspects of his mother's impossible, uncontrollable demands. I commented on his possible desire to control me by opposition. He was struck with the idea of his defining himself by simply opposing his mother's wishes for him, and he recalled that once, in early adolescence, when his parents had gone away for a weekend, he had insisted on staying home. He became so disorganized that he ended up deciding in the middle of the night to cut down an old tree to calm down by working off some energy.

In the next hour he went back to the repetitive experience from earliest childhood and defining himself by opposition, saying: "I often feel as if I've just pushed off from shore in a rowboat, and I suddenly find myself alone in the middle of the lake and not knowing what to do. When you were in the hospital, I felt as if I'd become becalmed out there. In my small circumscribed world, I am really ill-equipped to deal with anything outside of the immediate boundaries that my mother has set for me." Finally, a month after the resumption of the analysis following my surgery, he was able to tell me that he really is curious about how I am feeling now and he is able to suspect that this month has been hell, as was the month of September, because of his anxiety about the unexpected separation and his inability to have prepared himself for it. Am I aware how closely he scrutinizes me all the time, particularly my face at the beginning and end of the hours? He wondered if the analysis is more upsetting now because he realizes he is afraid to turn around and look at my face. He wished I would row out afte him, but he knows that when he decides to, he can row back to shore. He is *not* going home to mother during this Christmas vacation, despite her manipulative entreaties. Can he count on my periodic, appropriate comments to help him be more reasonable about his new activities? He showed me a picture of himself. After he got home, he looked at the snapshot again and decided that I wasn't just patronizing him when I said it was a good likeness. He does appear enthusiastic and pleased in the picture—so different from the way he usually appears—even in adult photos.

His more comfortable state comes to an end rather abruptly, as I discover after I return from my brief absence. His cat requires expensive treatment for an illness; he is short of money; he calls home, and his mother suggests that he ought to have the cat put away since it wasn't worth the $100. Mr. B. weeps as he describes how the cat feels like a part of himself. His mounting rage at his mother's insensitive rebuff, at me, at his disappointment with the current girl friend, culminates in regression, fantasies of sadistic sexual activity with all the women in his life except me. I interpreted that he is asking indirectly for help with a problem he had been very reluctant to deal with: his profound uneasiness with the experience of a woman's body, essentially his mother's body—not only its unavailability but its harshness and coldness. He responded by describing passive, masochistic features in his sexual relations with his exwife and most of his girl friends. In childhood, mother used to recoil when he reached out to touch her, and she verbalized clearly her dislike for all human bodies; they were dirty, messy and "bad." In the last hour before Christmas he felt awkward and disorganized and reported having difficulty sleeping, as if something basic were missing from the analysis again.

[The crucial events in this period center around the continuing recapitulation of the patient's experiences of abandonment which had occurred around the mother's pregnancy and postpartum psychosis, together with his renewed efforts to face the issue of his resultant faulty development. Fortuitously, the analyst's unexpected surgery constituted for him a threatened massive abandonment, different from the smaller predictable weekend separation and vacations. His initial reaction at this point in the transference is in the form of a splitting of what had been previously a more or less stabilized merger transference. His inherent inability to manage first being abandoned, then being called back only to be "surprised" once again evokes even more intense oral-sadistic rage and near sociopathic acting out of a pseudologica fantastica sort. Only later does he attempt to convert (via his creativity) this acting out of a derivative of his emerging grandiosity into an initially unsuccessful novel. The analyst's soothing and stabilizing efforts to substitute for his missing structure, although partly effective, are no longer satisfactory to him. We see the beginning of his efforts to utilize a kind of aggressive rage turned into opposition, as a form of motivation (= signal?) for initiating internal management efforts of his own (see P. Tolpin, 1974). Obviously, the analyst's inability to monitor just right the quantitative variations between anticipatory soothing, on the one hand, and validation and admiration of his own performance efforts, on the other, leads to a further significant imbalance and hence an inevitable (?) breaking up of his formerly stable transference. His efforts at inner autonomy and protection from overstimulation, described by his image of rowing out into the lake, represent an awareness of the need for a clearer and better defended self, but one that, so far, does not give any clear evidence that it is built on reliably stabilized new structure. He must still row back from·the middle of the lake to be with her. Yet, the transition from disintegrative overstimulation to sadistic rage, partly acted out, to a kind of oppositional "I must separate myself from this equally imperfect, periodically abandoning mother" may represent the beginning of a very early effort at structure formation. His fantasies of dating the analyst's secretary appear to be motivated by more than simple displacement or revenge out of frustration or guilt; it may be evidence of the desire to demonstrate his ability to manage a better relationship by himself. Here is perhaps a hint of the incipient grandiose self: "I deserve your secretary: you should help me to obtain her!" Over the course of the next several months' work one might anticipate the further dissolution of the primitive merger transference, and the beginning of a more mature phase of grandiose self. He seems (in his more reliable moments) to be calling upon the analyst not to provide him with an ideal "across the board" perfectly responsive, perfectly effective experience, but to support, *behaviorally* and interpretively, his own "narrow" efforts to become "whole by himself."]

Mr. B. reported that things are going well with the new girl. She slept at his cabin over the weekend and he was able to work well. But he is worried. She is getting ready to

leave on the semester break, just as he is beginning to like
himself with her. All of a sudden, he hates his body at times
like this. Sleeping and thinking and orderly work are impossible. Now, nothing is working right and he feels awful
again. I interpreted to him that what was probably so especially upsetting was that he was just barely beginning to
experience himself—especially his body—as lovable, loving,
and touchable. His response was, "Crash, bang—that hit it!
You are absolutely right." His first wife and his mother both
regarded the body and the body functions as filthy and dirty.
Spitting was the very worst thing a person could do, his
mother said. For the next month he reacted to my interpretation: his appearance and dress became more erratic; he
missed hours; even his car wouldn't work right; he
complained that some hours are terrible hours; he has
become unplugged from me. I interpreted my role in his current psychic disequilibrium; i.e., the overstimulating effect of
my interpretation. But it took several weeks for him to calm
down. In the course of this, in the absence of his "good" girl
friend, he started a brief affair with a controlling, demanding woman and had a number of barely managed rage
episodes at both of them. In an effort to sort this out, I
suggested there must be aspects of his mother's influence we
still don't understand and, during the next few weeks, two
new data emerged: For the first time, in describing his
mother, he produced a picture of a woman whose mind
raced like a spinning top, who conversed "to the air" incessantly, and was after him all the time. He is sure that, as a
child, he felt overburdened and unmanageably angry at her.
As April approached and he pondered his continuing distressed state, it dawned on him that the twins were born in
April. Had he ever told me about the time in early latency
when he gulped a bunch of his mother's sleeping pills and
was secretly pleased to discover how upset she was, even

though he had to be rushed to the emergency room and have his stomach pumped?

By the middle of March, he was once again occasionally able to stop hours near the end, and, with a smile, indicate that he felt well enough to suspend the analysis until tomorrow. But what bothered him was that even though he feels I am understanding and helpful during the hours, as he leaves everything gets disorganized and chaotic again, and on weekends things become truly catastrophic. Somehow, just as he gets himself stabilized in one situation, or in one period of time, he has to change for another, and then everything disorganizes. He is pleased at times to make love to his new girl and rages at the sense that she is exploiting him, clawing at him, sucking him dry—the way his mother does. It reminds him of his latency experiences of unbearable tension states, produced by his mother's endlessly stimulating, holding him, and pawing at him, insisting that he talk to her, and literally not letting go of him physically for hours at a time. She'd ask him to plug up the holes in her life. Then it dawned on him that the time of his worst distress from her overstimulation occurred just before his seventh birthday. Within the next few months he had begun an activity to which he confessed with great reluctance: chronic stealing from stores. This practice has continued intermittently since and is restricted to specific items: books and sports and hobby equipment. Once, as a young teenager, he was caught stealing stamps from a professional dealer. Recently, when his cat became ill, he stole toys for her. He decided to tell me about it now because he initiated a fraudulent claim for a piece of boating equipment recently purchased. I focused on the probable state of inner disequilibrium this must have been designed to correct. He agreed, suggesting that it was due to his disappointment in the analysis to work continuously for him. But the true roots are deeper, he suspected. Stealing is like his fabrications of cleverness, designed to impress people. By being clever enough to get away with his stealing, he can feel admired. He can imagine in fantasy that I might admire his phenomenal cleverness, since he has probably stolen hundreds of things in his life, but has been caught only once. I suggested that stealing seems to come mainly as a desire to replace something in him that is missing, but that functions as if it were his nonetheless. He was both pleased at my response and resentful at having to tell me, and accused me once again of interrupting his equilibrium. Half in anger, half in humor, he suggested that telling me about his stealing is like telling me about his frequent bouts of compulsive masturbation; he feels now that "somehow" he should be able to control it. But this is not exactly the same way he would use the fear of telling his mother about certain things to attempt to control those things. I am totally nonjudgmental, whereas his mother wanted to know all about his behavior, not to help him manage it, but literally to become part of it, as if to possess him. Humorously, he suggested that maybe he should wear a Do Not Disturb sign with arrows pointing both to the inside and to the outside!

Gradually, through the spring, he began to feel better as his self-esteem rose a bit. He dressed better and shaved his beard. He became more selective with his friendships, and he began to feel that the hours once again were more helpful than painful. And he started work again on his thesis as he did in those precious two weeks in December. He compared himself to others in his department in terms of salary, teaching competence, and evaluation by the students and by the chairman. Since he has been so plugged into me in the past few weeks, he is talking less to other people and therefore has more energy for his own tasks. In anticipation of my coming spring vacation, he experienced in the hour before last some unusual dizziness and faintness, and he had to sit for a couple of extra minutes before he could leave.

When I returned from vacation, Mr. B. informed me that his idealized girl, Joan, the one who had visited her home during vacation, had elected to return home to be with her only brother who is rapidly dying of a fatal malignancy. For the first time he felt he had managed himself reasonably reliably during the week I was gone, essentially by protectively and selectively limiting his contacts with people. He had been out in the middle of the lake, but very dexterous with both oars and the bailing can. He is pleased that he can ask me about my vacation and that he can listen to my answers without feeling that he is drowning in details the way he would with his mother. He wondered at how unexpressive he was with his concern for me at the time of my surgery last fall. His mother endlessly interfered with his primitive coping efforts, and he surely is appreciative of my not doing that! For the first time he wondered whether his on-again off-again attitude toward his thesis related to its possible role as one of the few stabilizing factors in his chaotic life over the past several years. Now I have become a stable point like the thesis.

He began an affair with a new girl, who initially appeared warm and responsive, yet who caused him episodes of discomfort. But this time he wants to analyze his reactions to her before discussing it with me — as if to use me to "check" his own evaluations. He had a dream: "It was completely disgusting. I was in Italy, an onlooker at a horrible spectacle. People in public disgrace were put into a long narrow ditch like a cesspool which was filthy, and other people would walk by and spit on them if their heads were up. If their heads were down, then they were immersed in the filth." He thinks of his childhood punishments, how, when he was adjudged guilty of having hurt his mother or was caught in some forbidden act, he would be sent all day to an empty room.

A new anxiety began to intrude when he recalled that, without the special postgraduate scholarship, he really didn't have enough money to return to his home university to finish his thesis this coming summer. Might I let the bill ride for a few months so that he could use that money? I did not respond directly. He had an elaborate, complicated dream essentially involving a flood of sexual feelings, perverse and sadistic, about various girls he has known, condensed with anxiety about the rebuilding of his broken-down boat. This is occurring under the benevolent guidance of a reliable marine engineer—clearly me, he feels. He wondered if he might return to shoplifting to make up the deficiencies in his budget. I suggested that while he obviously wants me to dissuade him, the real issue is that it would be very hard to continue the analysis if he were jailed. He is pleased by this humorous rejoinder and indicates that he will be able to pay and go back to school this summer. Sometimes his childish gluttony is uncontrollable. Could this relate to the mechanical way he feels he was raised—i.e., every few months his parents would have a different solution for the perfect way to raise him and would apply it rigidly and unfeelingly, and when that did not seem to make any difference in his behavior, they would then switch to something else, abruptly and with no warning— leaving him "disconnected"? Is it crazy for him to believe that when people don't understand or don't respond properly, they really are trying to destroy him? I suggested that in the sense of his remnants of the young child's way of thinking, it really is a rational idea. He welcomed—at least partly—my telling him that his judgment isn't always reliable, even when he feels he is perfectly safe. But he does resent the inevitable implications of my attempting to control or influence him and, perhaps most of all, of implying that without my presence, his own judgment will never come through reliably. He wondered if one of the reasons for his recent ups and downs is his dawning recognition that the fantasy function of his stealing, even more than the act itself, is what my interpretations have begun to impair.

He continued his correspondence with Joan, trying to understand her motives for sacrificing a slice of her best years for a dying man. He is able to value her for it, despite his confusion. But why their precious two weeks together were so good he cannot explain. He is pleased that once again I have come through by not attempting to pry information out of him about his feelings in this matter, or presenting him with a conventional explanation. My letting it come out in his own good time is what he is so struck with, even when that involves a "shifting of gears," which he cannot yet manage comfortably.

[In this period the subtle transference evolution continues. The extensive material about his relations with women seems to suggest a partial recognition of the failure of development of a solid, reliable cohesive mind-body-self, so vital for gratifying sexual activity. Faced with any frustration or disappointment, not only does he not manage his regressively emerging oral and oral-sadistic tensions, but there seems to be no reliable background or baseline of a separate whole self through which he can both initiate sexual activity and experience achievement with pleasure, even when he is in "equilibrium." This presents itself most vividly in this period through his increasing recognition of his many-faceted failures with women, i.e., with the "seething" effect on him of contact with a woman's body, with his inability to be relaxed with a woman or even to sleep (after intercourse) and, although he only reveals this later, to be effectively potent with women in the sexual act itself. In mother's total lack of resonance with his developmental timetable, not only did she fail to comfort and soothe in advance as tension was mounting, but of equal importance she probably failed to facilitate and guide his childish body curiosity along acceptable construc- tive lines permitting him to initiate his own activity and then responding delightedly to his own efforts. In the course of validating his recognition of his mother's failures, he elabo- rates a detailed picture of a seriously disturbed, probably true manic-depressive mother who undoubtedly suffered an unrecognized postpartum psychosis. By the beginning of his latency, she had apparently stabilized around utilizing the patient to fill in, functionally, her own structural deficits. His latency solution to the mother's chronic overstimulating in- terest in him was to take from the world in a regressively sub- stitutive way what he apparently felt she had been unable to provide for him. His stealing was not merely the taking of part objects that were the goal of his thwarted libidinal de- sires, i.e., thwarted by mother; his stealing was an elaborated symbolic substitute for the needed affirmation of the normal exhibitionistic desires his mother had denied him. He was and is able to weave "special" fantasies about his ability to deceive the world and thereby to feel valuable through his cleverness. It is a kind of perverse pride he feels in accom- plishment, a pride about which he can now be faintly humor- ous, as he "shows off" to the analyst.]

He is making active plans for the summer; what do I think of his taking two and a half months off. His own de- partment chairman has made a reliable promise of some modest university funds available to finish his thesis, and he can make it with the help of a bit of extra money from his parents. But his parents refuse the money, acting as they have always done: assuring him that he is going to be able to manage "splendidly" without their help. He attempts two things in the service of coping. He begins an affair with another new girl, who is low key, responsive, relatively undemanding, but ominously, somewhat fragile. He is initially delighted with her because when she starts staying over at his house in the woods on weekends, he is able to work on his thesis very effectively, simply with her being present. He increased his social and recreational activities with his male friends. In the session, he worked over his feelings about his father, leading to a kind of mourning reaction when he imagined the relationship that might have been and never will be, and he wept. An unexpected temporary change in my offices occasioned by some needed repair work reinforced his tremendous curiosity about me, and once again he became preoccupied with women's body parts, especially breasts. His curiosity is now focused on the role of the part in relation to the whole, rather than simply on isolated (sadistically) dismembered parts. He wondered at his freedom of being able to talk to me about this curiosity in contrast to what he thinks must have been his mother's terrible unavailability of her body to his little-boy, tentative exploratory curiosity.

Suddenly, his complex financial plans, based on a part-time selling job, came to crisis, and in the middle of an hour he asked if he could borrow $10 from me for the weekend because he had not a dime for eating money. He was obviously very anxious about asking me, and, after hesitating a bit, I lent it to him. In response, he had a rather complicated dream about financial concerns, owning two cars at the same time. Then there is a vivid scene in which he goes to visit a friend who turns out to be living on a lovely coast on a South Seas Island. The man is out surfing, and he is left with the man's wife, and she will teach the patient how to surf, but the husband-friend snubs the patient when he returns and the patient feels acutely uncomfortable. He was very angry with me when I pressed him to associate to the dream in terms of yesterday's experience in the hour, and eventually he talked about his sense of "closing down the hatches" and wanting me to understand that and to respect it, rather than asking him "to keep analyzing." In the last week before the vacation he told me in great detail about the subject of his thesis, which had to do with an analysis of the writings (i.e., the influence of personality variables on the ideas, style, and professional behavior) of one of the ranking but least well-understood twentieth-century German sociologists. Mr. B. was convinced that this man, in both his personal life and his writings, attempted tediously to work over the consequences of unmastered abandonment traumas from his childhood, that is endless problems of uncertain identity, self esteem, anxiety, and the like. He was convinced that there must be a similar unmastered, traumatic element in his perpetual vulnerability to his own disappointment in people's responses to him. For instance, as a child, when he was out driving with his mother, she never stopped the car to let him go to the bathroom, but instead insisted that he was only pretending, or, if not, she was "sure" he could wait, "if only he'd try." In the last hour he was preoccupied with the idea that interrupting relationships is equivalent to some kind of destructive, nonexistence, as if he were losing a part of himself. My presence prevents this and stabilizes him; how will he manage without me? At the end, he told me he feels like crying once again, but calmed himself enough to shake my hand and to wish me a pleasant summer. He will drop me a note, and I indicated I will be pleased to hear from him.

Scarcely a month later I received a letter in which he indicated he is not doing well. Three things happened. First, he discovered that the university would not let him register for his thesis completion work because of a recently discovered "Incomplete" in an important graduate course. Second, the thesis committee chairman thought that the hundred pages of his thesis represented a promising start, that is, it had reasonably good content, but needed a lot of reorganizing and tightening up to make it "acceptable" even as a beginning. Most important, he discovered that he was "droopy," and while this term is rather vague, my sense of it is that he was unable to get himself organized and work effectively. He speculated that some of this had to do with unresolved feelings about the thesis itself and the idea of committing himself to completing it.

He called in August, indicating that he wanted another week to think about himself and would be in to see me early in September. When he came for his first hour, he appeared uncomfortable; he reported that he had taken a part-time job as a paid organizer for a conservation and outdoor club. Despite the distress in the summer, he had stayed on at school getting some work done on his thesis. With considerably mixed feelings, he had gone south for a brief visit to his parents. To his great pleasure he found that he and his father could talk to each other as they hadn't in years, and the father reminisced about his own youth and how he too had had to break with his family, i.e., leave home and stay away! The patient visited his brother's family in company with his parents and became involved in an irritating altercation with his mother over the sticky fuss she was making with her grandchild. He saw both his exwife and Joan, and confirmed for himself that both relationships were truly over. He is breaking up with his current girl friend; she had become pregnant (though not by him) just about the time he left, and had had an abortion. In a moment of weakness he had offered to marry her, but she had arrogantly rejected his offer, utilizing the occasion to lecture him on his failings, that is, his personal unreliability. The friend in whose care he had left his fishing boat had "holed" the hull — fortunately in shallow water. He is uncontrollably enraged at this man, one of his supposedly more mature friends. Erroneously, I first focused on his unmanageable anger and its historical roots. He rejected this, and I followed his lead to emphasize how appallingly unexpected and unpredicted so many of these events must have seemed to him. As he calmed down, he remarked on how easy it is getting back into analysis and yet how annoyed he is when I don't understand him initially. Still, there is something different about his new balance with me this time. Everything seems more intense—but the basic difference must be in himself. He has some difficulty in locating me, i.e., somehow I don't seem to be quite the same for him as I was before vacation. It reminds him of the way he would go to summer camp, get involved in new things, seem to feel that he was becoming a different sort of person, come back home, and then, all of a sudden, get caught up in the windmill again—the windmill being his mother. I suggested that he was sensing that I was having difficulty getting tuned in to him, since it also takes me time to accomplish that task. At the end of the hour he said that, realistic or not, he felt I was treating all this as if he were suffering from a plantar wart when actually he had a broken leg. At the beginning of the next hour, I suggested that what had not come through clearly in my understanding of him was how much he had accomplished this summer and even in the brief time he had been back this fall, and how clearly he is maintaining the separation between what belonged in the analysis from the other activities of his life. He asked me to read a scholarly article he had written over the summer, and for my comments. He was pleased with the awareness I had of his difficulty in standing at a distance from his own ideas in order to evaluate them with his full critical faculties.

He began to question much more actively his relation to me in terms of what I am like, what my interests are, and why I am not married. He might have sexual fantasies, but what good would they do? He concluded that the real importance of this intrusive concern about me is as part of an experience he never had with his mother, namely, that of participating with appropriate vigor and independence in a changing relationship. Either he remained the helpless, needy, passive infant, or else he didn't exist as far as she was concerned. He was more frequently late for hours and dealt with this in a matter of fact way. He looks for signs of my reaction to this. Am I aware that he is checking my interpretations when he feels they are ill-timed or incorrect?

He began fishing again, asked to borrow an heirloom rod and reel, originally his grandfather's, and is delighted that the father consents to send it. He attempted to involve me in discussions of fishing, together with wilderness-survival technique, animal behavior, and the like, and was humorously disappointed when I didn't seem to know much about these matters, "even though you've been to medical school." He is struck with how different things look in my office, but he is not upset. Could this sense of difference have anything to do with some kind of internal change he is undergoing? He began to spar with me over arrangements: scheduling of hours, fees, vacations. Am I aware that he is doing something that he could never do with his parents, i.e., struggle "comfortably" with me over the little problems of everyday living? The way his parents handled such problems was either to ignore them, or to take total control and solve his problems by themselves so that he never learned how to do such things for himself. His favorite cat is about to have kittens, and he wants my confirming opinions about his own ideas for the handling of the delivery, her feeding, and the like. He is pleased and impressed with his persistent enthusiasm, and I commented on how its presence seems to influence his judgment positively.

Suddenly his finances are in a state of disaster again, and can I lend him five dollars so that he can eat over the weekend? I hedge a little bit, and he is very annoyed with this, accusing me quite correctly, not of unwillingness, but of not understanding how humiliating it is for him to ask. I lend him the money, but ask him if he isn't perhaps once again not facing something, i.e., it is two weeks until his next pay check. The problem of this moment is this weekend, and he does have a long-range solution he hasn't told me about, i.e., some other money due him. He reflected on his sense that he was able to ask me, not in the context of an impoverished, chaotic kid, but with a simple awareness of how needy he is. I, too, really am different, yet dealing with me over the money request is like going through the whole crazy business with his mother again. I suggested that he fears doing with me what he has always done: angrily dissociate his better self from his needs, or collapse in the face of them and submit to my whims. Eventually, he became quite drowsy through several of these hours, and we finally recognized that some of these experiences with me are simply too intense for him.

He had an eminently successful wilderness fishing trip, although it required him to cancel several hours. On the trip, Mr. B. had a dream about being with his mother and aunt and his mother's father; his mother was offering him money to do something, and Mr. B. felt enraged and screamed at her for attempting to seduce him back with money. He wondered if this dream is a perception of how the intensity of his needs keeps forcing him back to his mother, though he resents it. He told me somewhat laughingly that in his preparation for the trip he actually was rather inappropriate. Because he was afraid of being bogged down by too much weight, he and his friend took inadequate amounts of food and water along and quickly realized that they were actually depriving themselves. He wondered whether he was playing out a distorted effort at mastery of his unmanageable needs.

A disturbance in his sleep on the trip reminded him that he has not been taking sleeping pills for many months. Had he ever told me that before he was three years old he knew what Seconal was? When he went to wake his mother up in the morning for breakfast, his mother would say, "I've had several Seconals because I couldn't sleep last night. You'll have to take it yourself." In his clumsy childish way, he would toddle off to the kitchen to fix his own breakfast. When things were a chaotic mess, father would then get up to sort them out and feed him. Often his mother never really became clear-headed before noon, because she had drunk so much the evening before. Although we had actually run overtime, he asked me if we could continue because he felt so pressed to finish describing these incidents.

In the following hour he remarked on how coming back into the analysis after such an intense and overwhelming hour is very difficult. Would he get isolated from me in the past as a kind of protective device, because it is dangerous to let anyone—even me—do anything for him at certain times? He would like to think that if I am not completely and perfectly "with" him, then I must be against him—but he knows better. He is struck with how like some of his angry, adolescent students he is sounding with me today. How can he be so annoyed and so oppositional when just six months ago he was so frightened of any such feelings with me? He is reminded of the primitive temper tantrums and rages his mother never "permitted." It is so important that he not feel he is knuckling under to me. How do I feel about working with him when he is so angry and oppositional and so resentful? Don't I get angry or pessimistic about all of his struggles? I said that sometimes the sense of frustration is a bit contagious, but that I don't get angry or pessimistic—and he laughed.

Once again he became more upset by our weekend separations and he thought of the current lack of a girl. Supplying himself with a constant stream of girl friends may be motivated by his desire to bridge the three-day weekend absences in the analysis. Yet coming back on Mondays does not seem quite like the total shift of gears it did formerly. It feels as if there is some kind of opposition between his maintaining a sense of autonomous integrity and his endless wish to have me comfort him. The experience of fishing with his male friends seems so different from all this. Is he the victim of some held-over-from-the-past idea of his about age and status — i.e., that he can only feel good and important and valued if he is looked up to and admired by students, by young friends, by young women? His parents constantly made him aware of his precise age and the mechanistic expectations and permissible limits that went along with that precise age. I suggested that the tough problem was that as a youngster he was a lot of ages simultaneously.

He wrote to his parents that, in the light of his realistic financial burdens, he really does not want them to send him the usual meaningless Christmas gift. "Would you believe it, Doctor, my mother called immediately, insisting that she be permitted to send one little, harmless gift, or else she'd feel deprived!" The feeling over the telephone was like sticky glue falling on him. He acquired a new girl friend who, in contrast to the last one, is low key and willing to let him lead, makes fewer demands than his previous girls, and he is delighted to discover that he can in turn be casual with her.

Following several weeks' interruption because both of us had flu, he was again filled with thoughts about separation and discontinuity in relationships. But his kittens are developing the ability to get along without their mother. She is now becoming uncomfortable with them, and he wonders if this detachment process from the mother is a normal thing. Will they know how to take care of themselves when she throws them out? He wondered if he has made the analysis into some kind of now burdensome superstructure (his term) that it really is not supposed to be, and wouldn't it be better if he continued a similar process of slow detachment such as his "outdoors" behavior seems to exemplify? He feels revitalized, comforted, and reintegrated by the closeness with his new girl, and yet he must separate himself regularly from her, too. Maybe he lacks the capacity for a continuing feeling of confidence in a changing relationship. At the same time, any threat of feelings that are too intense or unmanageable utterly destroys his sense that there is reliability in the situation. In his mind, people always seem to be in the process of departing or preparing to depart in a way that makes confidence and stability tenuous and unreliable. Maybe the ultimate problem in separations is not that one doesn't get back with the person, but, if the person is like his mother, she has no sense then of what went on in the relationship previously, i.e., who he is or what he is really like. His mother, like him, must suffer from the feeling that once the object is out of sight, it no longer exists. When one gets back together, it is an entirely new, fresh situation, and it has no history. He was literally thunderstruck for a moment. He immediately associated to his decision to have Judy, the new girl, have an exact map of where he will be on all his fishing trips so that she will know at any one moment on any one day where he is — so *he* will feel more comfortable.

As the pre-Christmas vacation interruption approached, he once again became more comfortable with himself, more in command of the hours, and talked thoughtfully about his sense of increasing stability and competence in his teaching, his hunting, his friendship, his "analyzing." But he is anxious about his new girl because of her pre-existing plans to go home and perhaps not return. At the very end of the hour he had an attack of dizziness and weakness and had to sit back down on the couch for two or three minutes in order to overcome it.

[The material that emerged in connection with his tentative plans for summer vacation illustrates the persistent tendency toward regressive concretization that can occur in his fragile efforts to manage himself in the face of his still significant vulnerability to the analyst's absence.

This was heralded by his subtle financial demands on the analyst, clearly related not only to his actual need resulting from mismanaged finances, but also to the beginning of a partial taming of his grandiose stealing. When he asked the analyst to let a bill ride and she did not respond quickly enough, once again his greedy, phallic-sadistic images recurred. And, finally, he begins to suggest in his associations the significance of the role of teaching and being taught as a model for his expectations of the new role for the analyst. In a subtle way, he wants her to hold up certain expectations of self-management for him and then let him struggle with them—but not to a traumatic level—to soothe and reassure if necessary, but most of all to confirm and admire his ability to manage himself along such lines. Thus his increasingly being late and asking for alterations of schedule is not simply an assertion of independence or premature autonomy, but a subtle way of expecting that the analyst will recognize the significance of his other life activities and his ability to value them by himself, and that she will in effect confirm this for him. This constellation of newly emerging attitudes begins to pave the way for an even more complex and subtle mirroring wish along the lines of his relation to an idealized father, which made its appearance in the next several months.

But now, however, it may be the unpredictability of the analyst in the new role suggestive of the tentatively idealized teaching, guiding, confirming self-object. In the "searching" dream, the man is ultimately unavailable, and when he returns he really does fail the patient. It is as if the patient, through his dream, is attempting to teach the analyst what needs to be done in the face of his fragility over the possible loss of her as a "facilitating center" for him. He can now differentiate, grossly, the nature of the improper structuralization and that it is *his conditional* fragility, rather than the lack of structure, that is now the source of his anxiety. In a sense, then, once more the problem is not that *she* sometimes doesn't function well enough *out there*, but one of *location*, i.e., the structure in *him* does not function well enough yet. Selective validation of his efforts seems to be the more sophisticated demand he places on her now. This failure of an integrative center of his own becomes clear in his own perception of himself through the summer when he realizes that he is unable to work as effectively as he thought he might, and yet, in the process of re-establishing his relation with the analyst in the fall, he nonetheless maintains a persistent area of inner autonomy. The visit home seems to have permitted him an elaboration of more autonomous and neutral understanding about several overwhelmingly charged relationships; mother, exwife, exgirl friend, and the reawakening of the alter ego father relationship of which he never had enough. This summer experience facilitated a new approach to his chronic conflicts with his aggressive energies and also gave him a usable, incremental taste of "constructive loss."]

When I returned from my vacation, Mr. B. greeted me by saying, "You know, there certainly are times when I wish I weren't put together the way I am. I haven't heard from Judy; I haven't been sleeping; I've had the angry fantasies of cut bodies again, and I'm just all out of contact with everything. Please say something to me. I know I'm angry, but I don't know what to do about it." I suggested to him that he is afraid that if he shows his anger to Judy she will be frightened and it will drive her away. He sighs with relief and says, "Exactly. Let's not have any more separations even though the damnable trouble is that they're probably useful." He raged at the reactionary, insensitive university administration, the bad president, his unreliable friends, and then smiled a bit and said that all we're doing this hour is getting him settled down and back into a working relationship with me.

He has been taking pictures much more extensively, and sending people holiday cards consisting of a photograph of himself. He is reminded of his mother's remark, "Out of sight, out of mind." New Year's Eve was spent in the darkroom he has fixed up, and he is preparing some portrait shots which are going to be publicly exhibited. Do I think that was an appropriate way to bridge the separation? I confirm his ideas about the way he handles himself, and he realizes he still needs me to do certain things for him. When he did bring in the portrait pictures and showed them to me, I was struck with how lovely they were and what an unsuspectedly high level of creative talent he had in this area.

Judy's unwillingness or inability to contact him leads to endless obsessing about the relationship: What does he feel? What should he do about it? But he went shopping for the first time in months, and didn't even feel tempted to shoplift this time. It sure helped to separate himself "really" from other people. Had he ever told me about the type of dreams he had when he separated from people like his mother and now Judy? There is a kind of whiteness or nothingness about the face of the person in the dream, as if it were blank and empty. Recently, when he looked at his picture of prep school graduation, he had the fantasy, for a moment, that a mistake had been made and somebody else's picture was substituted. In his darkroom work he will stare intensely at the portrait until it precipitates fully on the film from the developing solution — and then he is relieved.

Judy returned briefly, and he has the feeling that something is different. He is more sure of himself; he is not retributive; he goes more slowly; he finds himself in control of things, and he is pleased. He wonders about the difference between separations from men.

Then things are muddy again. Judy is dropping out of school for good. She is going back home to the South, possibly to marry someone else, and he is very, very upset. He fantasies offering to marry her immediately to prevent this. For the first time he is talking to himself, "Ronnie, you just have to see what happens. You just can't rush into things." She is immature in certain ways, but perhaps she does have the capacity to grow, just as he will have to learn how to sustain a changing relationship, something he never learned with his mother. He sure is going through a lot of girls during this analysis, but at least they are getting better as the analysis progresses. One thing he has learned in the analysis is the way experiencing things makes an awful lot of difference, but if you don't really experience what has happened to you, you never grow—all you do is just sink further into the swamp. In their final days together, he became very protective and tender with Judy, bought her a camera as a going-away present, and taught her how to use it the way his brother taught him. He reported a feeling of appropriate pleasure in many different ways with Judy, and he was annoyed that I did not seem to appreciate it quickly enough. He wondered if he may be doing this in order to leave her with memories of the kind that will guarantee that she will have to come back to him. Has he ever told me about a problem he finally solved? Formerly, he would ejaculate less than a minute after entry; now he has managed to make it last a long time, and Judy is the only girl with whom he has ever been able to do this.

His mother called him after he sent her a self-portrait which reflected his sense of pride and accomplishment. "Doctor, that woman is crazy! She said that the pictures prove something she has always known, that my orthodontia was more successful than my brother's!" The last hour before my absence in February, he noticed that no matter how crazy things are and how burdened he feels, he is handling it differently. Perhaps this means that some day maybe analysis really can end, something he never let himself think before now. He had an acute anxiety episode just before the last hour, and he indicated that he still thinks some of the little-boy painfulness about separation must be present, but it certainly has diminished in quantity.

On return, he reported some distress, but not nearly as much as previously. His teaching had been going furiously well, including his exciting new courses and he is deeply immersed in the defense of student demonstrators. He was afraid I might disapprove of what he is planning to do, just as his mother would. He can't stop thinking about the idea of marriage to Judy, and yet in a sober way he realizes that this would be inappropriate at this time. Finally, he proposed by letter; then qualified it in terms of waiting until he finished his thesis in the summer; then he wrote her that he really ought not to make their relationship hang on the thesis. He became annoyed with me for being so slow to realize that all the time he has been expecting me to approve of his increasingly sober and cautious, rather than impulsive, efforts to sort out his intentions with Judy.

He had a dream about walking in the country with his grandfather, and he is reminded of the early influence of this strong, pleasant man in his life. He wondered if there is any significance to the fact that his maternal grandmother died just about the same time that his mother lost the twins. In another dream he is back at his old college, but with no one that he knows and he is living in a modern dorm, a circular high-rise building. He looks out the window and sees a tornado coming. Everyone piles out of his room and down a cold, open, frightening staircase, and at the end of the dream he is hanging by his fingertips on to a ceiling beam across the

bottom of the staircase, waiting for the tornado to hit. He remarked that so many of his dreams these days seem to involve
having a structure of some sort in danger.

He grew increasingly upset, finally decided to send Judy a
one-way ticket to come back, and asked for my approval. I
suggested that he seemed to be undertaking an active effort
along a new track to master his separation difficulties. He con-
templates flying south to see her, and then, as he calms down,
begins to wonder whether he was concluding more from the
relationship than it actually had involved. He is starting to feel
better once again, as he did at the first of the year.

He canceled several hours in order to attend a conference
on black sociology, since he has created a course at the university that he has been teaching, a course he finds very exciting,
and he talked about his initial realization of the limitations of
many of the recognized authorities whose conventional concepts he used to teach. Judy is increasingly on his mind, but in
the interval since we talked about her last, she seems to be
more clearly a real person with whom he can communicate
and who has a real presence in his life, even though they are
800 miles apart. He writes her that the relationship will continue, albeit at a distance, and they will discuss marriage in
the future, though not as a concrete solution to his anxiety
about the loss. Following a pleading phone call from his
mother, the fantasies of women's bodies disemboweled and
chopped up began to haunt him again for the first time in a
long time. He was struck with how empty and lonely and dis-
integrated he feels when telling me about the situation. He
dreamed about being back in law school and hearing a lecture
which makes no sense at all. He turns to a friend sitting next to
him, and they agree it doesn't make any sense. When the
lecture finishes, he gets up and makes a two-sentence addition
which integrates the whole lecture and solves the legal problem with which the lecture was attempting to deal. He is

pleased, but feels a little bit uneasy with his behavior. He nodded off to sleep briefly and decided that he has to learn more effectively how to selectively isolate himself in order to live with the kind of tension that the situation with Judy represents, i.e., a reawakening of past anxieties. It is painful and frustrating, but it is worth struggling for. He really does exist for Judy, but suspects that he can't really feel certain yet because the past problems keep blurring her. But at least the ghosts are familiar and not so frightening.

Judy received the ticket, called him immediately, and he felt better. But afterward, he felt so overwhelmed by the change in the level of forces within him that it was almost as if it hadn't been worth it. How his needs blinded him to the realities of the women in his life: his exwife, his many controlling girl friends. Will he ever be free of being driven by his needs? I commented that his wish to be comfortable, even to take pleasure in himself does not blind his judgment and control his behavior the way it did formerly. He laughed and said that when he really begins to love himself a little bit, he immediately has to love everybody in the vicinity. His act of sending the ticket reminds him of those dramatic, unmanageable "togetherness" experiences with which he regularly ended his separations from his mother. Is the idea of getting married becoming transformed into another rigid institution, like the unresponsive university, or the "programs" by which his mother raised him? Am I aware that he proposed to Judy during one of the weeks when I was absent? And he asked, with much humor, how could I let him do that?

He asked me if I will let him live with his tension as unpleasant as it is, or like his mother, will I require him to solve his problems immediately? He suspects that he wants to skip all the intervening steps in learning how to deal with a relationship. Now that he knows that separation from Judy is the key, he wants to make the separation problem end immediately.

A dramatic hour began by his continuing to sort out his ideas regarding the place of teaching in his life. His tendency is to get buried in current experience, like teaching, the way he gets buried in his love relationships. He still must struggle to develop any degree of useful detachment, distance, and the capacity to postpone—so essential to the maintenance of his equilibrium. Then he asked me if I knew that he really was not going to be able to carry out his threat to fly south if Judy wouldn't come to see him, and I indicated that I suspected that. Angrily but quietly, he wondered if it could be that he had the notion that I was having trouble letting him go. He never could "comfortably" miss his mother—or she him. At bottom he always was afraid of what separation might have done to her, and now he could have a similar fear about me. After a quiet moment he started to laugh in an uncontrolled, giddy way, and it took several moments before he could stop himself. All of a sudden, everything was so speeded up that he was unable to catch up with the way he was thinking, in order to tell me about it. He must have been flooded by something terribly stimulating. What he realized, when he was "out of control" was that it was his mother who wanted him to return, but from his point of view it really was stupid for him to miss her so painfully because being with her was equally unbearably distressful. The only solution was to unplug himself from both states—being with her, being away from her—as if unplugging cancels out the capacity to remember the bad past, or project a better future. Until now there never was any capacity for him to sustain any relationship. He talked about several sociologists whose ideas seem to embody and support his explanation. Quietly, he remarked on how good it is, after a separation from me to get back to see

me because he genuinely feels pleased to be back in my presence. He ended the hour by remarking that he watched me
walk down the hall the other day, and I seem to walk with a
lumbering gait, "like a bear." He laughed a little because this
reminded him of that famous teddy bear that he slept with
when he was a little boy and then lost. He decided it is not a
terribly attractive walk for a woman, but it really is uniquely
mine.

[In this last period the significant hints of termination as a
desired end and the lines along which it will develop begin to
emerge more firmly. His separation experiences from the
analyst are becoming more tame. His complaints are bitter,
but he is beginning to recognize that they aren't simply directed toward her imperfections as much as toward the recognition of the complex difficulties in his finding a truly balanced internally based solution to his needs. He is more
appropriately straightforward and reasonable with his disappointment with her slowness in recognizing the (new) father-
brother alter-ego material. His skepticism about the ultimate
reliability of figures in the outside world for him vs. the desirability of reliable inner structure seems increasingly clear.
The episode toward the very end in which he experiences a
state of overstimulation in the hour and then manages himself, he understands along these lines. As a corollary, he begins
to realize the impossibility of ideal solutions—i.e., "nothing
would have worked" with his mother. He now seems to have
transformed the cruder grandiose exhibitionism together with
his anxiety about the location of vital functions into a more
creative sublimation having to do with photography and
cameras (see Kohut, 1977). The experience of the empty self,
as represented not merely by the "droopy" inner feelings, but
by the dramatic story of the "blank empty" face, seems to be
evidence of his increasing recognition of the failure to have

been sufficiently cathected through mother's having looked at him, and to have experienced himself, thereby, as sufficiently exciting to her in eye-to-eye contact (Kohut, 1971, pp. 115-117). Parenthetically, this dream experience of the blank face or "whiteness" does not seem to be a dream-screen phenomenon (Lewin, 1948) in that there is a clear lack of libidinization and no evidence of sleep as a satiating experience. His matter-of-fact description of his altered sexual experiences, the structuralization phenomena in his dreams, and his increasingly more neutral behavior in pursuit of his career goals all suggest a degree of inner change and firming up which seems to be occurring without extensive overt "working through" verbalization in the analysis itself. It is as if he is showing the analyst "bits and pieces" or derivatives of processes of internal change rather than overtly working through with these changes in her presence. His empathy with himself and with his women seems to be a noteworthy result of all this.

Perhaps the most significant transference evidence of approaching termination is his cautious awareness that he can tolerate disappointments in his expectations of the analyst and that his own capacity for selective self-management, although imperfect, is acceptable. He is beginning to bring into the analysis awareness of his own difficulty in helping the analyst let go of him, and attempting to influence the relationship actively, as he was not able to do with his mother. The very last material regarding her resemblance to his teddy bear suggests not only his ability to relinquish his idealized expectations of her, but also that he no longer *needs* the soothing that he attached so unrequitedly in the past to this transitional-like object which was clearly still outside of himself (M. Tolpin, 1971). It is as if he is saying that she may not have equipped him as fully as he wished to be, but at least he is significantly better equipped than he was when he started.]

Throughout the next ten months until termination the following winter, only very sketchy notes were made available. This occurred apparently because of a significant increase in the treating analyst's other professional responsibilities. The patient, according to the summaries, appeared to be vigorously pursuing his active course of management of his life and his hours, including the separation experiences. His distress with such experiences gradually diminished, and his expectations of the analyst seemed considerably tamer. At times his unique way of expressing this was by experiencing the analyst as an "exasperating" person. He continued occasionally to miss appointments, though more frequently indicating this to her in advance. He made major decisions regarding his life, including marriage in June, only casually informing her of these intentions. After his marriage he very gradually shifted his professional work from academic sociology to more "public advocacy" activity, working with one of the respectable special interest organizations in the sociology field. Finally, in January, following a comfortable period of vacation, he accepted an offer in another city, thus automatically making a decision to terminate the analysis, which he did completely by himself. The analyst suspected that the termination decision represented an (indirect) attempt to avoid experiencing more fully a variety of issues only minimally involved in the last phase of the analysis, especially organized around the fatherlike mirror transference that was beginning to emerge. Nevertheless, persistent evidence of his steadily developing qualities of maturity in interpersonal and work-role activities, his energetic self-reliability, all bode well for terminating this phase of analysis. In addition, the diminution of his need for archaic sources of gratification, and the presence of improved over-all capacities for better management of his inner equilibrium inclined the analyst to err on the side of incompleteness in the analysis and to "let him go his own way."

Discussion

A. Diagnosis

The easiest way to approach the many questions raised by this case may be to start with the patient's presenting pathology. From the material of the first interviews, Mr. B. appeared to be suffering from a recurrent and worsening narcissistic depression. He was emerging from a failed marriage with feelings of anger, humiliation and shameful responsibility. A recent experience in psychotherapy had stalemated, adding to his feeling of personal failure. He was unable to relate with any gratification to colleagues and friends. Aside from a limited ability to teach, all scholarly pursuits had been abandoned. He felt moody, unhappy; he had no energy and a serious and worsening sleep difficulty. Yet he seemed to be aware that in some of this behavior he was unwillingly repudiating aspects of himself, a process now clearly out of hand. Although overtly suicidal ideation was absent, the degree of isolation, the barely managed moody hopelessness, the fragility of his limited relationships and activities, together with the severe energy depletion, all pointed to the diagnosis of a narcissistic depression of moderate severity. Mr. B.'s life history suggests the current reaction represented a worsening of what had been present intermittently but with varying manifestations ever since the onset of latency. At his best, he seems to have been stabilized in some form of a chronically vulnerable character state. This vulnerability appears to have involved a predisposition to becoming traumatically overstimulated whenever disappointed by reality frustrations he could not anticipate or threatened by internal tension states he could not manage. The common paths of responses to avoid some state of gross overstimulation leading to fragmentation were either of angry depression and hopelessness, or of withdrawal into protective isolation.

The question of underlying structural diagnosis as it bears on analyzability is unclear, initially, in part because of the paucity of the diagnostic data. An understanding of the patient's striking response to the analyst in the first several interviews suggests, however, that some very limited cohesion of a nuclear self, however fragile it might be, had been achieved developmentally at a quite early childhood level. His intense manner of attaching himself immediately to the analyst and thereby feeling more orderly and comfortable, bears out the validity of Kohut's (1971) fundamental point regarding the establishment of the diagnosis: *the nature of the transference as it evolves in the initial period is the best diagnostic clue of all.*

Mr. B. appeared to have access to some of the innermost levels of his poorly integrated personality: his aspirations, his impulses, his needs, and his own unreliable management of them. Convincing evidence of his faulty tension-regulation equipment presented itself very early and directly.

Other aspects of analytic behavior also had crucial diagnostic significance. From the beginning, he felt no conventional constraint to be the good patient who would dutifully analyze his dreams to completion or regularly finish one subject before going on to another. This behavior contains strong diagnostic hints of the underlying fixation level, i.e., archaic grandiosity. Additional evidence may be inferred from his conviction from the very beginning that the analyst's empathy would provide an integrative atmosphere in which he would be able to verbalize what he needed, that she would understand, and he, feeling understood, would begin to feel better. At an unconscious level, he seemed to expect that somehow he would find a way to utilize this intangible process to transform the experience with her into structures permanently useful within himself. Thus, the vivid response to her "holding" behavior and the obvious evidence of his infantile grandiosity suggest a presumptive diagnosis of an analyzable narcissistic personality disorder.

B. The Fundamental Pathology

Mr. B. gives clear evidence that all his life he had felt uncertain of himself, fragilely integrated and vulnerable to excitement states, whether originating from internal tensions or external stress. His goals remained uncertain, his human relationships unstable, and his internal equilibrium oscillated from the threat of overstimulation and fragmentation to understimulation and empty hopeless despair. This pathology appears to have originated in an intense relationship to a disempathic (in the sense of being not so much unresponsive as always out of tune with the ebb and flow of his momentary emotional states) mother who, at her best, was probably an unstable, poorly integrated borderline personality given to the extensive use of alcohol and pills to manage her recurrent cyclic mood states. The father, less clearly pictured, was available to the patient only selectively and episodically. Mother's failures occurred around such issues as stimulation, soothing, distancing, timing and dosage of response. A consequence of this was a perpetual tendency on his part to be caught off balance whenever he attempted to reach out to her with his age-appropriate wishes and needs. He felt either overcontrolled and engulfed by her, or left to fend for himself in a state of emotional abandonment. To survive, he retreated into what he felt was painful, barely tolerable aloofness and isolation sustained by a series of secondary erotized part-object substitutes for the unavailable mothering functions — his intense episodes of searching through his mother's clothes and rubbing his face against them, of filling his mind with sadistic-erotic images of parts of women's bodies, and his chronic adolescent and adult stealing. Certainly his solutions suggest that he had severe difficulty, not merely in managing excessive tension, but in even maintaining an underlying balance of the different parts of his personality. In that sense, he sounds like an individual suffering from late preoedipal damage (see Kohut, 1971, p. 47), i.e., fundamental difficulty in handling drive tensions because his unintegrated infantile self provided a poor matrix for the reliable internalization (and use) of age-appropriate ego functions. However, there is evidence that he suffered an additional weakness: a deficiency in the cathexis of his superego. The history of his ready changes in love objects, his many shifts in life goals, his stealing, his pseudologica-fantastica episode would validate this latter supposition. The core problem may not have been the ultimate presence or absence of a series of structures for the reliable control of tensions and the monitoring of his performance activities, but more the question of the *value and predictive certainty* he felt in the use of those devices when they were under his own control. It was not an inability to deal with the world because of some fundamental absence or inadequecy of ego functions and superego elements, but rather an enormous *fragility* and unreliability coinciding with an uncertainty of the staying power of these regulatory structures — as if they lacked some crucial quality normally present. Because he seems so vulnerable to the ever-present threat of paralysis of his ego apparatus when excited by overstimulation or disappointment, his immediate solution seems to be that of giving up and running — i.e., removing himself from the (externalized) stimulus — to prevent a more severe regression or disintegration. Superficially he resembles a latency-age child who may attempt initially his own solution to managing his life and exploring his world, but who gives up at the first experience of anxious uncertainty, overexcitement or disappointment. (See the principle of the vulnerability of new structures, Kohut, 1971, p. 44.) In consequence, he appears to have been doomed to a life of endless repetition of frustrating, incomplete, and therefore unintegratable learning experiences. Because his coping efforts were so unsatisfactory, he never really could feel that his experiences belonged to him sufficiently so that he could work them over and then integrate them effectively. Consequently, every new experience felt like "the first time"; each new relationship with a human being, each new problem to be solved was viewed as if it were a totally new task with which he had had no prior experience (other than negative) and as if it would all turn out to be either hopelessly puzzling or disappointingly incomplete.

In terms of Kohut's (1971) notion of a common cause of late preoedipal pathology, there is impressive evidence for the etiological role of his mother's pregnancy with the twins who died in childbirth as the critical event decisively altering his mothering relationship. From the available data, it is not easy to determine the degree of this woman's primitive adequacy as a mother in the first two-plus years of the patient's life. One may speculate that, although she might have been a significantly troubled person, her competence as the mother of early physical care (M. Tolpin, 1971) probably was minimally adequate. During the first eighteen months of life, Mr. B.'s developmental needs were conceivably still relatively simple and only modestly organized by a still quite immature and flexible ego that was highly dependent in its functioning upon a primitive merger relationship with her. Even if she were unpredictable, it is conceivable that he experienced her responses to his needs as satisfactory, because his needs coincided with the ebb and flow of her own childlike oral tension states.

The mother's pregnancy and subsequent withdrawal after the birth of the twins, events that ordinarily might have served to initiate or intensify the dramatic changes that constitute the early phase of the oedipal experience, were in all probability too sudden, too overwhelming—and hence too traumatic—for him to master. Moreover, by the age of two and a half, his inner developmental timetable was too complex and no longer sufficiently flexible to match the fortuitous tension states of his (by then) quite sick mother. By the birth of the twins she might have become the source of and the object of a host of new phase-appropriate demands from him, such as "admire me," or "let me touch you," but she must have felt utterly unable to handle them, even if he were able to direct them to her. Afterward, she appears not only to have abandoned him in *his* terms, but to have transformed him into a more rigidly held, narcissistic object for *herself* to stabilize her own disequilibrium states (Kohut, 1971, p. 65). It is as if after the death of the twins, *his* response is what kept *her* stimulated and integrated or, at least, minimally functioning. In addition, there are hints of a more complexly erotized element in her relation to him, at times transforming him into a virtual fetish for herself. There is ample evidence that *her* complex primitive merger needs required that *he* always be available at her command, if not physically present to respond to her. The cost was a profound setting aside of the primacy of his developmental needs and the authority of his own expectations. His rage and despair can only be imagined! If he failed her, she might well fly off into a disintegrative episode or retreat into an empty, nebulous alcohol haze—two reactions whose similarity to his adult symptomatic states suggest some unconscious identification with her "solution." His description of the openly pathological disorganization of the rudimentary social fabric of family life—the activities of eating, sleeping, physical care, and the like—stand as witness to the severity of her underlying sickness and the fragility of her defenses. The several months immediately following her postpartum depression when Mr. B. was two and one half to three, may have been the time of origin of his sleeping and eating problems, his motor incoordination, his severe anxiety states, and his numerous body fears.

By the time he was seven and had some degree of experience with other adults (had his mother also begun to integrate?), he could break away, finding more effective integrity-maintaining substitutes for her unreliable responsiveness. Eventually, these experiences became partly "internalized," predominantly organized around a fixation of the grandiose self. His stealing money from her purse and then extending this to nonmaternal objects—implicitly, omnipotent behavior under his control—became not only a way of separating himself from her, but of substituting something more nearly his own for her absent responses. This wish for admiring confirmation of his own performance was directed by fantasies in his mind under his control, such as, "I am clever; I can deceive, and I can get away with it!" Not only is this evidence of his untransformed grandiosity as well as his superego problems, but, equally important, it illustrates the "perverse" way he went about winning his separation and managing his own autonomy.

The absence of certain historical data, as well as the mutual decision to terminate the analysis before the full elaboration of a higher level nascent mirror transference, limit our knowledge of the patient's adolescent development. The situation that began with his trading punches with his father and ended with being sent off prematurely to university in mid-adolescence all seemed to be steps along the line of his attempting to strike out even more decisively on his own. Nevertheless, this exaggeration of normal adolescent separation experience may also have served to reinforce a further hierarchical ordering of his own management devices.

Mr. B.'s childhood provides a unique "experiment in nature," which serves to illustrate the relationships between an objectively traumatic "real" event and its intrapsychic meaning for the child affected by it. At the same time, it offers an opportunity for considering two other things: (1) it provides

a basis for attempting to compare the chronic persistent low-
level trauma this man undoubtedly sustained for many years
after his mother's depression with the effect of the single massive trauma constituted by her gross and immediate postpartum withdrawal. (2) It also provides an opportunity to
examine a new thesis for understanding the possible relation between the development of self (i.e., narcissistic) structures of the personality and instinctual (i.e., libidinal and aggressive) development. This speculative explanation is built
around the fundamental observation that failure of the
parent's interpersonal *psychological* tension-regulating function may lead the child to attempt to substitute age-appropriate, *physiological* tension-management devices under his
own control. For example, when the mother rocks, soothes,
holds, strokes, "coos," or hold the child "just right," he calms
down and sleeps. Or when the analyst listens right and
responds "appropriately," he feels understood, and in some
nonspecific way, calms down and puts himself back together
and may even sleep. If the mother's function fails, he rolls
rhythmically, or bangs his head, or hits things. Similarly, as
an adult he strikes the couch or paces back and forth. When
the analyst's response is unavailable or out of tune with him,
he has "binges" of compulsive sexual activity or fills his mind
with seething erotic-sadistic fantasies before finally withdrawing into protective isolation. During early childhood
development, some degree of erotization of the physiological
substitutes for the missing psychological structure occurs, in
part because normal libidinal development makes such energies not merely available but overdetermined in their exciting
desirability. Unfortunately, such erotization has several disad-
vantages: it leads to fixations, that is, predisposes to regression
and blocks further development of major elements of sexual
and narcissistic energies; it is not capable of useful, "bridging"
psychological (i.e., fantasy) elaboration; it becomes a source

of secondary distressing conflicts. As the normal oedipal experience begins to loom, a two-and-a-half-year-old should have had successful earlier efforts at internalization of age-appropriate incremental, self-object experiences leading to a cohesive infantile self, together with elementary tension-regulating structures and to a conviction of object constancy. But this patient's major disastrous experience, his mother's abandonment at the very beginning of the oedipal phase, confronted him with a serious handicap hardly limited to a simple problem in "sibling rivalry." His beloved mother was unavailable, unresponsive, or grossly threatening; his need for his rivalrous father was too desperate. His solution for the resultant unmanageable tensions and fears consisted of such things as masturbatory self-stimulation and self-soothing; rummaging through his mother's drawers and rubbing his face with her undergarments; running away to escape her physical "pawing."

The process becomes even more complicated, when, in consequence of the utter unreliability of the parental self-object soothing function, the child disavows the parent as a significant (if not totally decathected) object and begins to rely predominantly, if not totally, on physiological mechanisms and their accompanying (libidinized) part objects. He then becomes dependent on such transactions to provide a constant reassurance of his aliveness and his intactness and for his normal stimulation or soothing needs. Precociously forced to rely on his own immature psychic mechanisms, to effect compromise solutions, he becomes perpetually threatened with the danger from both sources of stimulation, and the inevitable, dangerous ambivalences are impossible to resolve without treatment. From the theoretical point of view, it may be that infantile-incestuous fixations (and their secondary oedipal-like "physiological" symptoms) develop as a result of a failure to internalize the normal tension-regulating functions of the self-object relation with the parent, rather than the reverse, as is customarily assumed. Hence, an oedipal fixation may be the *result* of impaired structural development, not its *cause* (Kohut, 1977).

Was This an Analysis?

The majority of our Casebook Group felt that this case should be considered an analysis, but an incomplete one. A few members had major doubts that it was much more than a sensitively managed, elegantly effective, "corrective emotional experience" (Alexander, French et al., 1946, p. 66), which was leading into an analysis when it was prematurely terminated. Perhaps an essential definition of what constitutes an analysis is in order. Let us define analysis as a depth-psychological therapeutic procedure characterized by the development and elaboration of a transference neurosis (via regression of part of the psyche) and its subsequent resolution by interpretation. This follows from Freud's definition of transference (1900, p. 562): "We learn . . . that an unconscious idea is as such quite incapable of entering the preconscious and that it can only exercise any effect there by establishing a connection with an idea which already belongs to the preconscious, by transferring its intensity to it and getting itself 'covered' by it." There is an editor's footnote on the same page elaborating this definition for the clinical situation of analysis: ". . . Freud regularly used this same word 'transference' (*'Ubertragung'*) to describe a somewhat different, though not unrelated, psychological process . . . namely, the process of 'transferring' on to a contemporary object feelings which originally applied, and still unconsciously apply, to an infantile object." Kohut's application of this concept in the narcissistic personality disorders is (1971, p. 24): "Such [narcissistic] transferences (defined as the amalgamation of object-directed repressed

strivings with preconscious wishes and attitudes) are present. . .
(and become mobilized during therapy) in those sectors of the
personality which have not participated in the specific narcissistic regression." Two pertinent questions arise immediately: first, do narcissistic fixations themselves occur in a state
that is analogous to the state of repression in the transference
neurosis? And, if so, may they become amalgamated with preconscious structures of the personality and so develop into a
transference neurosis similarly to the circumstance existing in
the structural neuroses? Kohut answers both questions in the
affirmative (1971, pp. 24-28).

With regard to Mr. B., we must ask to what extent and in
what form archaic infantile structures became merged with
the preconscious representation of the analyst, became experienced as such by the patient, while yet being differentiated
from the original experience with the parents. We must also
ask to what extent such resulting transference constellations
came to be analyzed, worked through, and renounced, or else
tamed and transmuted into new meaningful structures.

It is apparent that Mr. B. emerged into adulthood with
an archaic fixation on infantile grandiosity that was the result
of a mixture of both repression and disavowal of aspects of his
"normal" self development, such that certain energies and po-
tentialities were prevented from participating in the normal
maturing activities of the central and preconscious part of his
personality. Several important clinical implications follow
from this generalization: Mr. B.'s ordinary ego functions were
burdened by the presence of a higher-than-normal chronic
state of tension—and probably unneutralized tension at that.
His immature tension-regulating systems, i.e., ego functions,
attached in turn to important developmental fixations, were
thereby robbed of an opportunity for normal developmental
transformations into more mature, flexible structures. Even
more pathological, as adult defenses they were energy-expen-

sive, inefficient, and productive of endless secondary (interpersonal) complications and conflicts. The unique quality of
his underlying defect was the sense of uncertainty and unreliability in effective function of his immature self-esteem regulating, self-cohesion maintaining and self-expressing structures—a defect, in turn, probably related to their inadequate
idealization. His maladaptive solution to his difficulty was intense reliance upon external self-objects to facilitate maintenance of the unreliable internal structures he had
developed, or to serve as desperately needed "real" substitutes
for these structures when his own internal functions overtly
failed. How such a basic definition of this man's nuclear pathology bears on the central issue of whether or not he was in
analysis can be organized along the line of several subsidiary
questions: first, the role of regression, repression, and disavowal, second, the adequacy of development of transference
structures; third, the degree of working through and effective
transmuting internalization of the transference. A crucial ad-
dendum is the meaning to be assigned to the phenomenon of
emergence of new transference constellations and the be-
havioral evidence of a hierarchical reorganizing of his own
(self) management mechanisms.

    With respect to the question of repression and disavowal
in the form of a vertical split (Kohut, 1971), this man's behavior in life and in the analysis suggests relatively little defensive depth, that is, a paucity of countercathectic structures
or alternative defensive pathways. He entered dramatically
and immediately into an intense feeling relationship with the
analyst in which she was experienced as "part of himself." She
was assigned an imperative role of serving to facilitate the
regulation of his tensions in order to keep him integrated and
working in an orderly way. At the early stages of the analysis,
her actual presence and verbal intervention were required for
this. When he was out of her presence, he functioned very

badly and was often partially fragmented or acutely depressed, especially on weekends and during vacations. He persisted *throughout the analysis* to need her actual presence in
order to work in a reasonably integrated, consistent, and
autonomous way, even when she was no longer assigned the
overt interpersonal function of soothing and calming. Part of
working through involved the achievement of a more stable
self framework as the matrix of more orderly use of ego
controls. Thus, he was able to learn to manage by himself the
regulation of lower order structures. Yet, until nearly the end
of his analysis he continued to require her regular presence to
maintain the stability and functional efficiency of progressively higher levels of his hierarchically organized personality
structure. Otherwise he would revert, temporarily at least, to a
cyclical "all or none" state (from buoyant to dejected) as if no
consistently reliable internalized and autonomous higher level
defenses existed.

In terms of the issue of the amalgamation of these archaic
fixations with the current person of the analyst at a preconscious level, there was no question about the repetitive, intense, current re-experiencing with the analyst of fresh ver-
sions of the many different, self-object relationships of the
past. He recapitulated endlessly the exaggeratedly distorted
failures he experienced at early childhood levels with his
actual parents, even when he clearly recognized such failures
as at least partly a function of his internally distorted perception rather than the analyst's actual behavior. She was experienced not only as an unempathic, out-of-tune, bad parent
whom he had to transform and make different in order to survive and grow, but also as a good parental object who from the
beginning would be there, automatically perfect in her response to him, the idealized mother he probably had never
had. A third transference configuration may be discerned: his
role as the sick individual selected by one or both parents to

keep mother in some semblance of order by gratifying her narcissistic needs through a primitively symbiotic merger with
her. The further cost of this self-object relation was the sacrifice of some of his own normal right to need gratification,
especially the right of responses arising from an internally
determined growth pattern of his own. In the termination
period he began to experience himself as having a parallel,
albeit distorted, version of this third transference role with the
analyst, i.e., he experienced her too-ready willingness to
soothe or reassure as corresponding to the mother's hanging
on to him for reasons of her own. Thus, all three transference
aspects were recreated: an early idealizing mother-transference along the lines of a responsive and satisfying merger; a
dreadfully disappointing and unresponsive one; and a grandiose "I'm-special-for-you-in-a-distorted-way" one. A speculative question arises: did he flee from the analysis when he
feared his analyst had, in countertransference terms, actually
recreated his most disabling transference, "I'm special for you
only because I exist solely for your needs"?

There was a fourth transference configuration, partially
mobilized, but one which the casebook group felt was not accorded sufficient elaboration: his wish for an experience of
new learning, integration, and then practice in the atmosphere of the analyst's quiet, reflective, distantly supportive
presence. He frequently seemed to desire from the analyst
some expression confirming his efforts—whether or not they
were fully effective, fully reliable, fully adaptive. By the last
phase of the analysis he seemed intent on securing her recognition and acceptance of the limitation of *her* ultimate ability
to make him work better from the outside. He wanted, instead, to experience her pleasure in letting go of him because
his own efforts were becoming worthy and valid: *he* wished to
be in charge, despite her greater competency. Such a transference configuration involves elements of true mirroring by the

analyst as a knowledgeable, teacherlike person—something he might well have felt cheated of by virtue of the truncated adolescent experience with his father. There is evidence of his making overtures to her to exhibit some of his sublimations as well as his compensatory solutions (Kohut, 1971), such as his nature-conservation-animal interests, his creative efforts at photography, his own mastery of analytic ideas. Thus, in addition to his desire to acquire elementary tension-regulating and protective functions from merger with the idealized good mother of early physical care, there was a second wish: the desire for confirmation and mirroring of his own new efforts by a relatively more distant, probably masculinelike teacher and guide. Several dreams, occurring toward the end of the second year of analysis, as well as his "paranoid" fantasy, all involving disappointment in men, confirm the developmental roots of this configuration. He left the analysis before much elaboration, let alone working through of this new, more integrated, and more autonomous transference (neurosis?) occurred. But even its incomplete emergence and development constitute evidence of a vital transformation. The old primitive merger with the grossly idealized "analyst-as-functions" had to have been partly given up, that is, transmuted into a more integrated, predictable set of ego functions operating in the framework of a more stable, reliable self system, *or else the new, more mature transference wishes and attitudes would never have made their appearance!* Thus, the very emergence of a new transference configuration constitutes evidence of the achievement of a significant gain in self-cohesion and self-management and self-expression. (See Kohut, 1977, p. 185 for a discussion of the developmental phenomenon of "The Second Chance.")

In many ways, the circumstances and the nature of the working through in this analysis are rather special. First of all, what was worked through? And how far? Partly given up or

transformed were the patient's wishes for the analyst's presence as a perpetually available, facilitating self-object — a
tension-regulating, understanding, managing presence in his
life. As for the acquisition of insight, he accomplished as
much with his own thinking outside the analysis when he was
away from her as he did by working in her presence. Especially
in the latter phase of the analysis, the interview notes suggest a
certain casual reluctance, shared by both patient and analyst,
to elaborate the connections between the past with his mother,
the present with the analyst, and his current experiences on
the outside with some other woman. One has a sense that
when he brought in reports of some new understandings he
had acquired while walking through his beloved woods by
himself, what he required of her was the she simply acknowledge and accept these selflessly and not insist on his exploring
them her way, or elaborate them by amalgamation with her
ideas. Increasing evidence of his disappointment in her reflective and confirming function combined with his reports of
more neutrally managed analytic efforts of his own may have
been significant factors in predisposing both of them to think
of termination after only a little more than two years of work.
Still unanswered by this description is the question, why the
casualness in the verbal working through? Did he still experience the analyst's expectations as too reminiscent of his mother's intrusive "talk to me" entreaties? Could this not have been
better analyzed instead of just "accepted" or was this simple
acceptance the best possible solution, in light of his history?

An immediate question involves the matter of the legitimate gratifications of the transference, i.e., what does any patient have the right to expect of any analyst along the lines of
empathic, devoted, reliable understanding and responsiveness? Mr. B. frequently expressed *his* version of legitimate
gratification wishes along very concrete and demanding lines.
The focal issue appeared to be his demand for instant recog-

nition, understanding, and an acknowledgement of their vital importance to him, rather than his insistence on absolute willingness to supply instant gratification. For instance, when he said at one point after she hesitated to lend him money, "You don't understand how humiliating it is for me to have to ask," he was telling her something of the unconscious meaning of his asking. It was not merely an expression of his still existent archaic grandiosity, but also of his tenuous efforts to handle the inevitable shame and humiliation attendant on exposing to her this vulnerable state of his attempts to manage his own life and his own finances. Both of them could clearly acknowledge how vital her understanding was in preventing this shame, and then he could work through at least part of his disappointment then and there. For him, an atmosphere of some selective, occasional gratification of the *manifest* request, as well as some selective frustration, appeared optimal. Ultimately, the nuclear transference expectation present in this instance was the wish that the analyst "prove and re-prove," endlessly and concretely, the perfection of her empathy, understanding, and devotion. The ordinary vicissitudes of everyday analytic work provide an endless supply of opportunities for experiencing the frustration of such a wish. Much of the working out of the transference involved mixtures of optimal selective gratification and inevitable disappointment of this imperative demandingness. If managed properly, his disappointment in the analyst's actual functions becomes the motivating force for elementary primitive efforts of his own learning and structuralization, i.e., "I want to be able to do for myself what, ultimately, you cannot do for me!" However, to resolve this transference in a way that leads to transformation of increments of experience into internalized structure required a great deal of time, patience, empathy, and endless repetitive efforts by the analyst.

Without doubt there is evidence for significant working

through of transference configurations leading to structural transformation, but the limitations are significant. First of all, within the analytic situation itself, by the end of his work, Mr. B. had developed an increased sense, though an imperfect one, of the wholeness of his personality and the stable continuity of his life relationships and life activities along some sort of self-guided developmental progression. He had evolved an increased inner capacity of self-monitoring and self-managing and even for self-analyzing. The frequent intensive disintegrations he suffered by the end of the analysis became briefer, less complete, and more quickly recoverable. By the middle of the analysis, he was watching himself for the analyst. By the end, he seemed to be watching himself for himself — *but still having to watch* to maintain his integration and equilibrium. ("I've been very dexterous with the oars and bailing can!")

There is other evidence. By the end of the analysis he had become able to initiate and carry through relationships with women that appeared to be based on mature, even aim-inhibited considerations, and his activity in these relationships appeared to rise from his more firmly integrated, consciously managed, valued self. He was able to make available in his loving, as well as his working, life a kind of staying power he seemed not to have had before. He had evolved some capacity for empathy with the analyst which he was able to recognize had not been available earlier, and certainly he had become empathic with the woman he eventually married. He had evolved a series of creative, productive "compensations" for the residual, unanalyzed, developmental defects (see Kohut, 1977). His forbidding superego appeared to be more dependably useful and his ideals more certain. He had become able to recognize that there were going to be serious limits to this analysis, some of them of his own conscious making, some of them intrinsic to the deepest layers of his personality. He conveyed an air of sad acceptance: further transformational changes and restructuring of forces would have to come from within him, rather than from some new life situation or new love object. Despite the limitation imposed by the patient's pathology, especially his need for concrete demonstration, he appeared to have worked through the core of the primitive, early "bad mother" transferences. In addition, he had a-chieved some constructive experience with both the gratifying and disappointing aspects of a positive, higher level, reliable merger transference. He was making headway toward the evolution of a reliable, competitively flavored, higher level mirroring transference. Perhaps anticipating the problems he would have in successfully experiencing this configuration, he *actively elected* to leave the analysis in order to "try it on his own," as he undoubtedly was *passively forced* to leave his mother in adolescence and perhaps even early in latency. It is as if he partly re-enacted and restored, though on a higher, more realistic, and actively ego-dominated level, the path of distorted development that had been forced on him prematurely in his earlier life. His solution to the tasks of managing his own developmental needs and influencing constructively his own world seemed to involve three things: (1) more critical selection of his love objects and implicit acceptance of less than perfection in their response; (2) trust in his own inner competencies—their now improved reliability and durability; and (3), if necessary as an ultimate defense against overstimulation and its still threatening consequences, utilization of temporary, more selectively controlled withdrawal into a state of temporary isolation, the most persistent of his lifelong adaptive solutions.

8

CONCLUSION

We have presented the reader with the histories of six psychoanalyses as they were conducted and reported by six different psychoanalysts. We admit that these partial expositions of our imperfect efforts do not wholly satisfy us. Our understanding is not complete, our explanations sometimes lack clarity, our theories are not yet all-encompassing, our techniques still grope for greater refinement. The residues of our own archaic narcissism make us yearn for the impossible perfection of the completely analyzed case. Though we have inevitably fallen short of our ideals, we nevertheless trust that we have demonstrated the application of a new way of looking at psychoanalytic data with resulting benefit to the theory and practice of psychoanalysis. In this chapter we shall attempt a summing up of our aims and conclusions.

Our aim was to engage the reader in an intellectual adventure of crucial importance to him as a psychoanalyst. Our intent was to share with the reader our experiences in looking at clinical material from the viewpoint of a psychology of the self. By so doing, we hope to have helped him trace diagnostic constellations and transference patterns that otherwise might have escaped his notice. We expect that our ambiguities will stimulate him to seek his own clarifications and that our failures will spur others to greater research efforts. Thus, we offer no hard and fast guides to diagnosis or facile directions for treatment. We do offer a body of theory and clinical experience that we have found to be very fruitful in expanding and deepening our psychoanalytic work. Thoughtful analysts who have chosen to participate vicariously in our efforts by immersing themselves in the clinical and theoretical challenges presented to us by these six analysands will, we hope, achieve insights that will help them face similar challenges in their daily work.

Let us try to anticipate some of the questions that might be raised by our colleagues. First the question of diagnosis: All of us agreed that all six analysands were properly diagnosed as suffering from narcissistic personality disorders. This unanimity stands in sharp contrast to the difficulty of spelling out in each case the precise criteria for arriving at this diagnosis during the early hours of the evaluative process. In some cases, a period of previous psychotherapy or psychoanalysis had resolved the major diagnostic dilemmas. The diagnostic exclusion of psychosis or borderline state (neither of these conditions is analyzable in our view) seemed based on such vague criteria as good job history, or unimpaired functioning. In fact, such assessments are based as much on the analyst's preconscious appraisal of the ease of empathic communication with his prospective analysand as on a carefully collected past history. In other words, the analyst uses the initial interviews as a test for transference readiness and for an evaluation of the type of relationship that will develop. He will be especially alert to evaluating ego strength from the patient's response to the diagnostic and psychoanalytic situation. How well can the analysand adapt to the demand to associate freely? Recognizing that the beginning analysand cannot possibly be in full compliance with the basic rule, what do his actions tell us about the cohesiveness of his self and his analyzability? Do the regressive swings toward fragmentation become wider, deeper, and less easily reversible or do they become increasingly shallow, manageable, and absorbed into an emerging, stable narcissistic transference, especially as a result of carefully dosed clarifying interpretations? The emphasis rests not so much on extra-analytic criteria, though these may be useful to alert the overly confident therapist, but on the dynamics of the developing analytic relationship. While assessment along these lines sounds difficult and potentially hazardous, in practice, no problems were reported either with these six cases or in the group's general analytic experience.

The recognition of psychotic potentials and of borderline precariousness are immediately urgent tasks to prevent a psychoanalytic debacle. Less pressing is the need to differentiate specific pathology organized around oedipal conflicts from that organized around the struggle of the self to maintain cohesion. It is well known that oedipal neurosis may hide behind a mask of broader narcissistic defenses and frequently becomes manifest in phallic-narcissistic organization. Similarly, narcissistic personality disturbances often present a gamut of flourishing sexual pathology, in particular some of the perversions, which have at times been misunderstood as an acting out of drive or defense components related to oedipal conflicts. It is possible to construct lists of symptoms that would be associated more frequently with one or the other of these types of disorders. Our analysts found that Kohut's repeatedly stressed admonition to avoid early diagnostic closure and to await the unfolding of the pathognomonic transference is the single most reliable way to arrive at a clear-cut diagnostic distinction. Such a "wait-and-see" attitude also avoids contamination of the transference by unwarranted intrusions, which, especially in sensitive narcissists, may evoke explosive reactions. These are easily mistaken for transferences when, in fact, they are reactions to actual or threatened narcissistic injury. All six of our analysands sooner or later revealed intense sexual preoccupations of quasi-perverse nature. Taken out of context, the associated fantasies sometimes had the contents of primitive sexual drives or defenses suggestive of triangular neurotic constellations and, respectively, penis envy or castration anxiety. Yet, invariably these erotic structures were precipitated by the vicissitudes of dyadic relationships and revealed themselves to be sexualizations of narcissistic strivings or defenses, whether extra-analytically or in the transference. True transference object love, where the analyst is perceived as a separate person with his own goals and desires and who is loved for who he is, was not seen as the central transference issue in any of these six cases. Intense need, however, for the analyst's benign presence, for his approbation, or for his being admirable in all respects was the ubiquitous sign of narcissistic transferences in these cases.

It is clear that the analysts had no difficulty discerning narcissistic transferences once these became cohesively established. The emergence of these transferences occurs despite resistances that have to do with protection against the vulnerability to rebuff and humiliation. Frequently, the resistance against the wish for a merger leads to desperate attempts to control the analysis and the analyst. Control becomes a central issue for the patient, not only because of his susceptibility to the consequences of possible disruption of a merger, but also because of his vulnerability to the hyperstimulation resulting from the wished-for closeness. The defensive maneuvers are subtle and numerous, but special mention should be made of the occasionally observed overt disdain for the analyst as a repetition of a defense against an emerging idealizing transference.

Perhaps the most common sign of a beginning narcissistic

transference is the analysand's report of experiencing disconcerting symptoms on weekends. These may consist of perverse or other sexual acting out, or hypochondriacal episodes, or irritably arrogant behavior, or painfully depressive moods, or a feeling of emptiness and depletion. In all our cases, these types of exacerbations of symptoms occurred during weekends or at times of other interruptions in the work of the analysis. This symptomatic picture is readily understood as a manifestation of partial fragmentation of the self subsequent to the disruption of the narcissistic transference. Discharges of tension by action are attempts to avoid the painful experience of enduring a state of fragmentation. The analysand alone usually cannot make the connection between his suffering and its precipitant in the disrupted transference. But the pattern is clear enough to allow the analyst a tactful demonstration of the relation of the current experience to its genetic precursors. Recognition and explanation of these gross disruptions increase the sensitivity with which lesser and increasingly subtle disruptions can be perceived by both analyst and analysand. In this way even minor breaks in empathy become the foci around which the working-through process transforms small increments of affective experience into the enduring configurations that in psychoanalysis are termed structure formation (transmuting internalization in Kohut's felicitous term). All our six cases clearly demonstrate the disruptive breaks in narcissistic transference brought about by gross events such as absence of the analyst, including an emotional "absence" brought about by a transient lack of empathy. These cases also abound in instances where the analyst's lack of empathic understanding leads to similar transference disturbances. In such instances the disruption was always followed by a flare-up of the symptoms of disturbed narcissistic balance that were characteristic for each analysand.

While there were no difficulties in recognizing the existence of narcissistic transferences, it was not always easy to classify these precisely according to Kohut's scheme. To differentiate the demand of the grandiose self for mirroring confirmation from the demand of an uncertain self for approbation from an admired idealized self-object may sometimes require an empathic sensitivity to the subtle back-and-forth of a psychoanalysis that can only be experienced but not clearly reproduced in written case reports. In general, the most primitive transferences, such as mergers with their unmitigated archaic demands on the analyst, could be more easily fitted into their proper category than the more developed mirror transference proper or the idealizing transference. Similarly, regressive swings to more archaic forms or even to fragmentation could more easily be perceived when they emerged suddenly than when they occurred more gradually as the patient shifted toward more mature forms of relationship.

A few comments should be made regarding certain errors evident in the conduct of these analyses. There was little evidence of gross distortions due to countertransference issues, and there is no need for an extensive discussion of that problem here. Perhaps because the cases were conducted under Kohut's supervision, potential countertransference attitudes could be clarified and resolved through self-analysis. It is often the analyst's own residual archaic narcissism that may become the instigator of countertransference reactions when analyzing people with narcissistic personality disorders. In addition, an analyst's untherapeutic reaction to a patient may stem from the fact that he has no way of organizing the material. It is this inability to order and understand what he hears that then becomes a narcissistic trauma for him which, in turn, may be based on unanalyzed grandiose fantasies of his own. One of the important contributions of Kohut's work is that now, having an enlarged schema for understanding what patients are saying, the analyst's potential for narcissistic injury is not stirred up nearly as readily. Consequently, even though no analyst is "perfectly" analyzed, he can now function more properly, just as Freud's delineation of the Oedipus complex permitted a previously poorly understood analysand's communication to become comprehensible *instead* of stirring up in the analyst his own residual conflicts in that area (cf. Gunther, 1976). The analyst may experience boredom and rage when the analysand's grandiosity diminishes the analyst into feeling utterly negligible. Contrastingly, when the analysand's idealization results in the analyst's experiencing an uncomfortable arousal of his own grandiosity, he may be provoked into sharp denial of his own importance. Neither of these very common countertransference reactions was reported, though they might have been present at times and probably were suitably managed. More subtle countertransferences manifested themselves as breaks in the continuity of the analyst's empathic understanding. Such loss of empathic contact was of course not always the result of countertransference. A useful clue to the countertransference nature of distortions is the analyst's recognition that his interpretations were tactlessly timed or phrased and felt to be particularly humiliating by the analysand. The alert reader will no doubt have discerned instances of these and other kinds of countertransferences in the text. No major interferences in the analytic processes, however, appear to have occurred.

The single most influential factor causing errors and delaying the analytic process was plain ignorance of the structure and treatment of narcissistic disorders. These cases were analyzed over a time span that began before Kohut published his first pivotal reformulations (1966), and that overlapped the period when all of the participating analysts had become familiar with the new psychology of the self. This struggle (against inner resistances as well, of course) to see, then learn, and then apply a new point of view was often dramatically present in the background as these analyses unfolded. One must credit the patience and sensitivity of the analysts with maintaining an effective analytic posture that kept the analytic process active in spite of periods of bewilderment. Sooner or later, Kohut's conceptualizations became the orienting grid for the clarification of understanding and led to interpretive interventions which moved the analyses forward.

The principles determining the use of the interpretive process in narcissistic personality disorders are no different from those involved in the oedipal neuroses. The analyst listens with even-hovering attention, which is his counterpart of the analysand's free associations. By virtue of his own analysis, training, and experience, the analyst is acutely sensitive to his inner experiences and thus becomes consciously aware of mental states evoked in him through empathic contact with the analysand. Such empathically derived data then become the raw material for processing into the hypotheses that are tested by interpretations. Of course, as the analysis progresses, the analysand also becomes increasingly aware of his inner states — becomes more empathic with himself — so that he begins to formulate and test his own hypotheses. The development of this self-analytic function becomes one of the criteria for readiness for termination, as will be discussed below. Some patients, as we have seen, for defensive reasons do not allow the analyst to exercise his interpretive function for a long time because the analyst's activity is experienced as an intrusion or humiliation. The rather shallow insights produced by these analysand's pseudo-self-analytic function are, however, usually quite easily distinguished from the genuine article and frequently tend to cluster in the early phases of analysis. In contrast, genuine self-analytic insights tend to occur most frequently in the middle and especially the last phases of analysis.

The case reports in this book make it evident that, for the

most part, the analyst's employed interpretations as their mode of communication. Parameters (Eissler, 1953) in the form of noninterpretive responses which could have been intended to gratify the analysand were not necessary once the narcissistic transferences were recognized and interpreted. Analysts continuously feel under pressure to gratify, whether analyzing narcissistic disorders or neurotic ones. In the former, the demand is for so-called narcissistic supplies, for the praise and admiration that will gratify a deficient self which is starved of self-esteem. In the neuroses, the demand is for sexual gratification, be it ever so subtle, to reduce the instinctual pressure. It seems a widespread belief in analytic circles that the patient's demands for sexual gratifications are easier to resist than the demands for narcissistic supplies and that analysts who treat patients with narcissistic personality disorders tend to gratify their patients with vitiating effects on these analyses. The case reports here show that, despite, in certain instances, some difficulty in maintaining a strict analytic posture of interpretation, by and large, the analysts gratified neither the demands for mirroring archaic grandiosities nor the demands for approval from archaic idealized self-objects. These demands were consistently interpreted, albeit in a tactful, nonhurtful, nonhumiliating manner. In fact, this is the essence of the analytic treatment: interpretation without gratification per se. The analysts' acknowledgment and understanding of archaic narcissistic strivings, without condemnation, allow open and empathic communication to flourish, analogous to the acceptance without condemnation of infantile sexuality. Such an analytic ambience gratifies neither narcissism nor sexuality, but is equivalent to the average expectable emotional environment that facilitates the analytic process (cf. Wolf, 1976). The analyst does not actively soothe; he interprets the analysand's yearning to be soothed. The analyst does not actively mirror; he interprets the need for confirming responses. The analyst does not actively admire or approve grandiose expectations; he explains their role in the psychic economy. The analyst does not fall into passive silence; he explains why his interventions are felt to be intrusive. Of course, the analyst's mere presence, or the fact that he talks, or, especially, the fact that he understands, all have soothing and self-confirming effects on the patient, *and they are so interpreted.* Thus, the analytic ambience that makes analytic work possible becomes itself an object for analytic interpretation. The whole analytic process in this way blocks exploitation for mere gratification.

Much preliminary work has to be done before transference demands become interpretable. Again, the principle is the same for neurotic as for narcissistic disorders. Interpretation starts from the surface before it reaches the depths. Recognition and explanation of defense precedes interpretation of the underlying structures striving for expressive action. Investigation of extra-analytic behavior may have to precede the clarification of intra-analytic transferences. Broadly speaking, no interpretation is complete without the reconstruction and inclusion of the genetic context which was precursor to the contemporaneous dynamic. This supports and buffers the transference interpretations.

The priority of defense over impulse interpretation has already been mentioned. In the narcissistic personality disorders, the defenses serve to protect a vulnerable self against regressions toward fragmentation. Splitting and disavowal are as prominent as repression. Phobic avoidance of situations of danger to the cohesiveness of the self is frequently observed, e.g., the avoidance of wished-for closeness to protect against the overstimulation which tends to fragment. The search of an exhibitionistic self for grandiose acclaim, coupled with the fear of a shattering experience of being rebuffed or ignored, may lead to a debilitating paralysis in the face of opportunities for proving oneself: severe work inhibitions may protect against the unbearable fragmentation anxiety attending situations of exposure.

In general, the analysand tends to experience all interpretations, even when most tactfully managed, as critical or demeaning. It usually diminishes one's self-esteem to learn about the limitations of one's self-knowledge or of one's self-control. To learn this from someone else who by virtue of his knowledge appears to be less subject to these limitations repeats a childhood trauma and often feels as if insult has been added to injury. The most effective way to ameliorate this is achieved not by the analyst's reassurance of his benevolent intent but by demonstrating the inevitability of the pathological distortion in the given genetic context.

Reconstruction of the salient points of psychic trauma during the analysand's early years of life is an essential part of the dynamic processes of the analysis. This results in more than fleeting relief; it results in enduring structural changes. It does not follow, of course, that every interpretation can be complete and can include the appropriate genetic reconstruction; nor is reconstruction altogether the analyst's task and responsibility. A careful reading of the case reports reveals the important participation of the analysand in rounding out incomplete interpretations. These complementing responses aid greatly in fleshing out the skeleton of the genetic reconstruction. Moreover, they are excellent evidence for the correctness of the interpretation (and its associated theoretical hypothesis) and can add to the conviction of both analyst and analysand that they are approaching closer to a fuller and more truthful understanding of the past (cf. Freud, 1937). More than anything else, such efforts at reconstruction deepen the analysand's empathy with himself. He starts to see his own past in a new light—the inevitable limitations of humanness, the tragic flaws of self and other—and he begins to accept himself more, as guilt and shame diminish. It seems futile to ask whether such analytic insights precede or follow the structural changes that make a psychoanalysis also curative. They appear together.

Much significant early developmental history was often revealed during the first few hours of these analyses, almost as if defenses and transferences had not yet succeeded in covering up the deeper structures which, during the subsequent months and years of the analysis, will have to be so slowly and painstakingly brought to light. Analysts do well to note carefully these early spontaneous revelations without disturbing them by too much questioning, which may alert defenses. The full significance of such freely given genetic material usually becomes apparent only much later during the analyses. In all of these six cases, the pathogenic context that framed the analysand's childhood was clearly related to the vulnerabilities of the emerging self. Each case differed in the particular dynamic structure of the genetic ambience: a grossly intrusive mother or one preoccupied with illness or a disdainfully neglecting mother, and so on. Fathers failed their children by their weakness, or through their lack of involvement, or by their inability to provide needed protection, etc. Unpredictability and unavailability of either or both parents is always traumatically disruptive to the healthy development of a cohesive self.

Different constellations of genetic traumas suffered by these analysands are well documented in these reports and need not be repeated here in detail. Some general comments, however, are in order. Genetic reconstructions sometimes have to transcend recollected memories and recreate the total atmosphere of the parent-child interaction independently of actually remembered incidents. Though these reconstructions may lack the objective certainty of documented history, they often describe the subjectively significant aspects of a past history with great plausibility. Such plausibility reaches a level of conviction when, at the end of the analysis, the various reconstructed and remembered pieces fall into a total pattern that makes sense and that explains the analysand's psychological history. Perhaps the analogy of a jigsaw puzzle is useful here. Outlines of the emerging pattern may appear early, but certainty of a correct reconstruction has to await the placement of the last completing piece. In an analysis, of course, there never is a last piece. An absolute certainty can only be approached, but not reached.

Transferences and countertransferences, recollections and reconstructions, all these evoke further empathic data which lead to deeper and more encompassing interpretations. But mere intellectual insight is not enough. A curative psychoanalysis requires structural changes, i.e., it requires enduring corrective changes among the distorted intrapsychic configurations that manifest themselves as psychopathology. According to Kohut, structural changes come about through transmuting internalizations, which make up the final steps in the working-through process. These analyses demonstrate that for a long time after achieving a particular insight—let us say, for example, into a persistent transference constellation such as an idealizing transference, nothing much changed. Again and again, the same demands were made, the same affects recurred, the same patterns were repeated even though they were fully understood. Only very gradually, sometimes imperceptibly, was there an amelioration of the affective severity and, perhaps, of the frequency, of the recurring patterns; working through is always slow and somewhat painful. Each tiny step occurred in response to a break in the analyst's empathy, usually a minor break with manageable affect that did not severely fragment a still vulnerable self and therefore did not totally disrupt the cohesive transference. Such "optimal failures" stimulated the ego to take on

functions which up to that time had been performed by the
self-object. As a result, the self was strengthened, became less
vulnerable and more cohesive; it had acquired some new
"structure." As mentioned before, this process is facilitated by
correct and complete interpretations that weave together
genetics and transferences.

Working through may seem to be an interminable process, but eventually all the six analyses discussed here ended.
The decision that a proper moment for termination has been
reached is often a difficult one.[1] Have the major defects been
repaired? Have the major conflicts been resolved? Has sufficient progress been made to entrust the remaining work to the
newly acquired self-analytic function? Questions like these
were raised during the discussions, and the answers were not
always unanimous.

There are many signs that major personality reorganiza-
tions had occurred. All the analysands had become increasingly empathic with their families, spouses, parents, children,
and, above all, with themselves. Rebuffs and separations that
at one time had been fragmenting to the self with attending
symptomatic turmoil were now taken in stride with only
fleeting regressions. Object relations, as they were no longer
subject to the vicissitudes of narcissistic sensitivities, had improved. Humor, always an indicator of the ability to achieve a
certain flexible detachment and distance from the self, sometimes made its first appearance as the analytic task progressed.
But the most dramatic witness to the changed personality
organization was the prominent emergence of important
creative talents in several of these analysands. For some, this
meant a new career in fields where they could exercise their
newly found creativity.

---

[1] An extensive exploration of the issues pertaining to termination is presented
in Kohut (1977).

Some readers may find the data, theories, and opinions presented here startlingly new. Some of the conclusions challenge some long-accepted psychoanalytic teachings. We hope the reader will agree that psychoanalysis is defined by its method and not by its evolving theories. But more than agreement, we hope to stimulate serious thought and discussion. More than 60 years ago, Freud wrote in response to some of his critics: "If one could only make it clearly intelligible to the best among them that all our assertions are taken from experience (so far as I am concerned, from experience which one may try to interpret still differently), but not cut out of whole cloth or conjured up at one's writing desk. . . ." (Freud and Pfister, 1963, letter of December 7, 1909, our translation).

Similarly, we hope that our readers will test our assertions against their experience.

REFERENCES

Alexander, F., French, T. et al. (1946), The principle of corrective emotional experience. In: *Psychoanalytic Therapy, Principles and Application.* New York: Ronald Press, pp. 66-70.

Eissler, K. R. (1953), The effect of the structure of the ego on psychoanalytic technique. *J. Amer. Psychoanal. Assn.*, 1:104-143.

Erikson, E. H. (1950), *Childhood and Society.* New York: Norton.

Fenichel, O. (1941), *Problems of Psychoanalytic Technique.* New York: Psychoanalytic Quarterly, Inc.

Freud, S. (1900), The interpretation of dreams. *Standard Edition*, 5. London: Hogarth Press, 1953.

———— (1915), Observations on transference love (Further recommendations on the technique of psychoanalysis, III). *Standard Edition*, 12:157-171. London: Hogarth Press, 1958.

———— (1936), A disturbance of memory on the Acropolis. *Standard Edition*, 22: 239-248. London: Hogarth Press, 1964.

———— (1937), Constructions in analysis. *Standard Edition*, 23:255-270. London: Hogarth Press, 1964.

———— & Pfister, O. (1963), *Psychoanalysis and Faith.* New York: Basic Books.

Gedo, J. E. & Goldberg, A. (1973), *Models of the Mind: A Psychoanalytic Theory.* Chicago: University of Chicago Press.

Glover, E. (1931), The therapeutic effect of inexact interpretation: A contribution to the theory of suggestion. In: *The Technique of Psychoanalysis.* New York: International Universities Press, 1955, pp. 353-366.

Greenacre, P. (1960), Regression and fixation: Considerations concerning the development of the ego. In: *Emotional Growth.* New York: International Universities Press, 1971, pp. 162-181.

Grossman, W. & Stewart, W. (1976), Penis envy: From childhood wish to developmental metaphor. *J. Amer. Psychoanal. Assn.*, 25/5 (Supplement on Female Psychology): 193-212.

Gunther, M. S. (1976), The endangered self: A contribution to the understanding of narcissistic phenomena of countertransference. *The Annual of Psychoanalysis*, 4: 201-224. New York: International Universities Press.

Kanner, L. (1937), *Child Psychiatry.* Springfield, Illinois: Charles C Thomas.

455

Kohut, H. (1966), Forms and transformations of narcissism. *J. Amer. Psychoanal. Assn.*, 14:243-272.

_____ (1968), The psychoanalytic treatment of narcissistic personality disorders: Outlines of a systematic approach. *The Psychoanalytic Study of the Child*, 23: 86-113. New York: International Universities Press.

_____ (1971), *The Analysis of the Self.* New York: International Universities Press.

_____ (1972), Thoughts on narcissism and narcissistic rage. *The Psychoanalytic Study of the Child*, 27:360-402. New York: Quadrangle Books. Also in: *The Search for the Self.* New York: International Universities Press, in press.

_____ (1977), *The Restoration of the Self.* New York: International Universities Press.

Lewin, B. D. (1948), Inferences from the dream screen. In: *Selected Writings.* New York: Psychoanalytic Quarterly, Inc., 1973, pp. 101-114.

Mahler, M., Pine, F., & Bergman, A. (1975), *The Psychological Birth of the Human Infant.* New York: Basic Books.

Nagera, H. (1975), *Female Sexuality and the Oedipus Complex.* New York: Jason Aronson.

Ornstein, A. & Ornstein, P. (1975), On the interpretive process in psychoanalysis. *Internat. J. Psychoanal. Psychother.*, 4:219-271.

Tarachow, S. (1962), Interpretation of reality in psychotherapy. *Internat. J. Psycho-Anal.*, 43:377-387.

Tolpin, M. (1971), On the beginnings of a cohesive self. *The Psychoanalytic Study of the Child*, 26:316-352. New Haven: Yale University Press.

_____ (1977), A clinical developmental distinction: Prestructural self-objects and oedpial (preoedipal) objects. Ms. presented at Panel on the Infantile Neurosis in Child and Adult Analysis, Meeting of the American Psychoanalytic Association, Quebec City, April 29, 1977.

Tolpin, P. (1974), On the regulation of anxiety. *The Annual of Psychoanalysis*, 2: 150-177. New York: International Universities Press.

Tyler, A. (1975), A knack for language. *The New Yorker*, Jan. 13, pp. 32-37.

Wolf, E. S. (1976), Ambience and abstinence. *The Annual of Psychoanalysis*, 4:101-116. New York: International Universities Press.

Zetzel, E. (1968), The so-called good hysteric. In: *The Capacity for Emotional Growth.* New York: International Universities Press, 1970, pp. 229-245.

INDEX

457